—FORGOTTEN—
BRUMMIES

-FORGOTTEN-
BRUMMIES

The men and women who shaped today's
Birmingham, who are now largely forgotten

LES WILLIAMS

BREWIN BOOKS

BREWIN BOOKS
19 Enfield Ind. Estate,
Redditch,
Worcestershire,
B97 6BY
www.brewinbooks.com

Published by Brewin Books 2021

Reprinted January 2023

© Leslie Neil Williams, 2021

A CIP catalogue record for this book is
available from the British Library.

ISBN: 978-1-85858-739-4

Printed and bound in Great Britain
by 4edge Ltd.

Contents

DEDICATION

This book is dedicated to three family members who are no longer with us, my late parents, Ellen and Dennis, and Uncle Tony Room. They were much loved, they are much missed, and their lives as proud and hard-working Brummies, helping their families thrive, are the inspiration for this book.

Acknowledgements

The starting point for this book came from my son, James, who first drew my attention to the blue plaques erected by Birmingham Civic Society to commemorate the influential sons and daughters of the great city we call home. Before this conversation, I had barely noticed these around the city, and certainly did not appreciate the wide range of people and institutions memorialised by them. James and I embarked on our own project of visiting all these and photographing them, and this led to my undertaking further research on these people and places, and has resulted in this book. James has been my constant companion in recording these, and similar memorials in many villages, towns and cities in England, and deserves recognition as the catalyst for this book. The location of Birmingham's blue plaques can be viewed on a very useful interactive map at https://www.birminghamcivicsociety.org.uk/map/.

In developing these narratives of twenty-nine people, I am of course grateful to all those historians and writers who have gone before and I have taken great care to ensure their work is acknowledged in the footnotes to each life.

I would like to thank in particular the late Roger Lea, formerly Chairman of the Sutton Coldfield Local History Research Group for his assistance in confirming the location of George Bodington's Driffold House Lunatic Asylum, and Tim Boddington for his encouragement and support. I also wanted to thank Celia Jones, Personal Assistant to the Chief Operating Officer and President of the British Orthopaedic Association, for kindly sourcing and sending the text of Peter M. Dunn's lecture on his father, Naughton Dunn.

My thanks also to those organisations and individuals giving permission for images to be used. They include Henrietta Lockhart, Collections Officer at the wonderful Winterbourne House and Garden, University of Birmingham, for permission to use the photograph of John Sutton Nettlefold.

Louisa Anne Ryland's photograph is reproduced by kind permission of Birmingham City Council, while use of the portrait of Neville Chamberlain, by William Orpen, was kindly approved by the Curator of the Parliamentary Art Collection at the Houses of Parliament in London. The portrait of Harry Gilbert Barling is by Lafayette Ltd and is part of the Wellcome Collection. I am grateful to Artware Fine Art for permission to reproduce the portrait of Major Dr John Hall-Edwards, by Arthur Trevethin Nowell, and to Princeton University Art Museum for the Midland Tyre advertisement image. Permission for the use of the photograph of Naughton Dunn was kindly provided by Simon Grainger-Lloyd at the Royal Orthopaedic Hospital and the Royal College of Obstetricians and Gynaecologists agreed to the reproduction of the portrait of Dame Hilda Lloyd by Anthony Devas.

I have tried to ensure that copyright has been acknowledged, and am grateful for the help and support of many people with whom I have discussed issues and subjects. Any errors in the book are, of course, my responsibility.

Finally, I would like to thank my wonderful wife Elaine, who has always supported me unconditionally in everything I do, with her love, patience and advice. She has lived with these twenty-nine people, as well as myself, for two years now, and my gratitude to and love of her is boundless.

Introduction

This is a book about the people who made modern Birmingham, now largely forgotten by almost everyone, including today's Brummies. Birmingham is well-known as the UK's second largest city, of more than a million people, credited for being the cradle of the Industrial Revolution, having more miles of canals than Venice, a concrete jungle with the Spaghetti Junction motorway interchange, and the youngest population of any European city. It is derided for its Brummie accent, and the lack of success of its football teams. Visitors to contemporary Birmingham, now the fourth most popular tourist destination in the UK, will today find a vibrant, busy, modern and modernising city that has been regenerated over the last twenty years. Modern Birmingham offers millions of tourists each year a European-style experience, in its conference, cultural, concert and sporting venues, and its extensive and highly rated restaurant and leisure facilities. Birmingham is a welcoming, forward-looking city, with ambition for its people, and a key contributor to British life.

However, this is not a travel brochure for Birmingham. As a native Brummie, I wanted to explore how the place was formed, developed, and became what it is today. I became fascinated by how individuals had made an impact on the life of the city and, sometimes, the wider country and world. Brummies, whether native or 'adopted' (living or working here), have shaped the modern world across all areas of human endeavour. Whilst this may not be completely unknown, what surprised me was the lack of consciousness about the contributions these individuals made, even though the evidence of it stands around us physically, and in the way we do things. If history is the summation of the stories of individuals, it is possible to see how today's Birmingham was shaped, influenced, or made by the individuals highlighted in this book. As John Thackray Bunce has written: 'Birmingham has reason to rejoice in the services rendered to her by those who are proud to have renounced their own birth-places to become her sons [and daughters] by adoption'.[1] This applies equally to those born here.

There are twenty-nine short lives included here, from the early sixteenth century to just after the Second World War, based on my view of the most important, interesting and, in many cases, least well-known people who have made a difference.

I have excluded James Watt, Matthew Boulton and William Murdock, but lesser known members of the Lunar Society, including William Withering and James Keir, are included. Readers will recognise two familiar names, Joseph and Neville Chamberlain, included in their own right for their contributions to Birmingham. They are also important as context for describing the life of Joe's eldest son, Austen, who is hardly remembered at all.

Others are more obscure, such as Louisa Anne Ryland and Sir Josiah Mason, quiet philanthropists with big hearts, and substantial wealth which they were keen to share. A number were famous in their own times, such as William Hutton, Birmingham's first historian, who gives us such a vivid picture of the then town; and Thomas Attwood, a remarkable political reformer, responsible for many of the freedoms we experience today. Some are virtually unknown, such as John Rogers, the first martyr of the persecution by Catholic Queen Mary; Joseph Sturge, ardent campaigner for votes for working people and the abolition of slavery; and Peter Stanford, born into slavery in America himself, who became Birmingham's first black minister.

Several were international pioneers in their areas of expertise, relieving the pain and suffering of millions of people throughout the world. These include George Bodington, who pioneered innovative treatment of tuberculosis; John Hall-Edwards, the first to use X-rays, to his own considerably painful physical cost; Joseph Sampson Gamgee, who developed aseptic techniques still used in health care worldwide, and set up the Birmingham Hospital Saturday Fund; Robert Lawson Tait, the father of modern gynaecology; and Dame Hilda Lloyd, an obstetrician who set up 'flying squads' to alleviate the pain of pregnant women in distress.

There are those who established institutions to help the most disadvantaged, which still provide care and support, including Dr John Ash, founder of Birmingham General Hospital; William Sands Cox, who established the Medical School, which would join with Josiah Mason's Science College to become the University

1   John Thackray Bunce, *History of the Corporation of Birmingham: with a Sketch of the Earlier Government of the Town, volume 1* (Birmingham: 1878), p.37

of Birmingham: and Sampson Lloyd, who made a fortune in ironworking and founded a bank in Dale End that became Lloyds Bank. Our way of life has been changed significantly by John Sutton Nettlefold, the first town planner, and James Brindley, who, although not Brummie by birth, brought canals to Birmingham, with a dramatic impact on trade and employment opportunities.

Other stories surprised and intrigued me, and I have included that of John Baskerville, printer and typeface inventor, whose journey continued many years after his death, and the remarkable story of days of riots in July 1791, called the 'Church and King riots', or the 'Priestley riots', after Dr Joseph Priestley, the discoverer of oxygen and dissenting minister who preached in Birmingham.

Not everyone included here was a saint, as they could be as flawed as the rest of us. Samuel Galton Junior can be justly accused of hypocrisy, William Sands Cox of disdainful arrogance directed at his critics, Joseph Chamberlain of rampant imperialism, his son Austen of misogyny towards supporters of Votes for Women, and many of an unerring and often selfish quest for wealth. It is also important that each individual's history is seen in the context of the times in which they lived, so while each short biography can be read on its own, they are set within a brief context of the relevant stage of Birmingham's development.

At the end of each biography is some detail of how these people are remembered in the city, through memorials, statues, buildings, institutions, and even street names.

I end these stories of Forgotten Brummies in the middle of the twentieth century, partly because the second half of the last century seems to have led to less distinct identities for cities and regions. This is perhaps a consequence of better communications, particularly through electronic means, which secures an instant world-wide audience for ideas, thoughts, opinions and debate. This makes local variation reflective of the characteristics of an area virtually impossible, and perhaps results in less numbers of interesting personalities appearing locally.

My intent is to bring some elements of Birmingham's past, if not to life, then at least into people's minds. In his role as historian and antiquarian, Hutton has a good description of this purpose:

'the antiquarian brings his treasures from remote ages, and presents them to this: he examines forgotten repositories, calls things back into existence, which are past; counteracts the efforts of time, and of death; possesses something like a re-creative power; collects the dust of departed matter, moulds it into its prestine [sic] state, exhibits the figure to view, and stamps it with a kind of immortality.'[2]

While not an antiquarian, I would hope that people find some value and interest in these important lives, as described by an amateur local historian.

---

2   William Hutton, *An History of Birmingham, 2nd edn.,* (Wakefield, West Yorkshire: 1783), pp.274-5

1.

Birmingham emerges from the Dark Ages

For any community, there is little historical material on which to base a record of development and growth until the Domesday Book of 1086. While there is evidence of settlements near local rivers from thousands of years BC, few definitive conclusions can be drawn. Implements have been found from the Old and Middle Stone Ages locally, and later from the New Stone Age in Handsworth, Stirchley and Deritend. Bronze Age artefacts from around 1400 to 1000 BC have been found in Sutton Park, and the Iron Age hill forts at Wychbury Hill in Hagley and Berry Mound in Shirley indicate substantial settlements. The Romans had a significant presence in Birmingham from around AD 48 until around AD 120, evidenced by the large Roman fort at Metchley, on the site of today's Queen Elizabeth Hospital and University of Birmingham Medical School, and in numerous Roman roads going north-west. The fort itself covered ten and a half acres, later extended by a further four, and accommodated 3,000 troops within its double ditch, and high earth ramparts, topped with a wooden stockade. Although this was apparently abandoned in AD 57, it was re-built in AD 80, on a smaller scale, covering six and a quarter acres, contained within the curtilage of the original camp. Roman coins and a major Roman villa or temple have been discovered at Coleshill, but apart from these, little suggests that the area around modern Birmingham was anything other than sparsely inhabited woodland.

The Anglo-Saxons settled in small communities in the eighth century, including Weoley Castle. The name may derive from Old English, meaning 'clearing in which there is a heathen temple'.[3] Settlements formed around water, of course,

---

3   Victor Skipp, *A History of Greater Birmingham – down to 1830, 2nd edn.*, (Studley, Warwickshire: 1997), p.13

and the Hwicce tribe may have come from the south, while the Anglian Mercians spread out from modern Tamworth, and settled in villages to the north, including the area around the confluence of the Rivers Rea and Tame. This became early Birmingham, the name deriving from this period, describing a hamlet (ham) of the followers (ingas) of Beorma, immortalised in the memorial at the bridge over the River Rea, at Gooch Street, Highgate. These settlements were formed in the seventh or eighth centuries, were relatively well developed, and in recent years, the Staffordshire Hoard has provided exciting evidence of the sophistication of precious metal working in the area.

On a sandstone ridge, the feudal Birmingham of the eleventh century was farmed, according to Domesday, although the land was not particularly fertile, and the area was neither densely populated nor prosperous. Its value, expressed as its rent yield annually, was just twenty shillings, one pound. This is far less than many surrounding, larger manors, such as Handsworth, Yardley, Northfield and Aston (five pounds each), Sutton (four pounds), or even Selly, incorporating Weoley and Bartley (seventy-five shillings), and Edgbaston (thirty shillings). Aston was the largest and most populated. Some had churches and priests, but that was not the case for early Birmingham, 'one of the poorest manors in one of the poorest parts of central England'.[4]

As England's population grew from around 1.5 million in 1086 to between 4 and 6 million by 1300, Birmingham grew as a population centre, most probably because of the granting of a charter between 1154 and 1166, to Peter de Bermingham, Lord of the Manor, to hold a weekly market every Thursday in his castle. This stimulated trade and may have prompted migration to Birmingham as a commercial centre, and from this point, the village grew so that by 1232, several trades, including merchants, tailors, weavers and smiths, were recorded. In 1250, the right to hold a four day fair at Ascensiontide (in May) had been purchased, and by then Birmingham was a manorial borough. This indicates that there were burgesses, freemen with a burgage tenement, usually a house plot in the town, or ownership of acreage in the fields around the town. By the early fourteenth century, some metalworking was undertaken in the town, and tax records (subsidy rolls) indicate that Birmingham had become the third largest town in Warwickshire by the 1320s and 1330s. It was by now 'the most populous and prosperous place in the whole of the Greater Birmingham area'.[5] This progress did not continue unabated, as population growth stagnated, as in many parts of England, in the fourteenth

4   Skipp, *A History of Greater Birmingham – down to 1830*, p.17
5   Ibid., p.22

century. The Black Death in 1348-49 and 1361-62 killed more than one third of the population following successive disasters of poor harvests and famine. Markets in smaller villages, such as Sutton Coldfield, disappeared or struggled, but Birmingham managed to survive relatively well. Based on activity around the marketplace, particularly in livestock, merchants attracted wealth, and demand for produce and products increased. By the middle of the fourteenth century, a goldsmith operated in the town. Some merchants spent some of their wealth on endowing charities and guilds to support the poorest in society.

There was little evidence of organisation, beyond paying due observance to the rights of the Lord of the Manor. In 1392, the Gild of the Holy Cross, an ostensibly religious order, was established to maintain a chantry and two priests in the parish church of St. Martin (now St. Martin's in the Bull Ring), to provide the sacraments to the living, and to say Mass for the souls of the deceased. This guild was not wholly religious, as it also hosted social events, feasts and meetings, and offered practical services through providing a bellman, midwife and organist. It offered charitable help and support to the poor, including almshouses, gifts to the poor in the parish, and took on the repair and maintenance of two stone bridges, one of which is thought to have crossed the River Rea, linking Birmingham to Deritend and Aston. Bunce has commented that the 'foundation of the Gild of the Holy Cross must be regarded as a most interesting and important endeavour to develop, by the union of all classes, a kind of local government' and that it was 'an association very characteristic of Birmingham...united in purpose, practical in object, taking from any source the arrangements thought to be most helpful, and putting aside customary observances and methods not manifestly suitable to the desires or needs of the town'.[6] This set of behaviours will recur throughout this book, on an individual and collective basis.

The Gild of the Holy Cross was located in a purpose-built Gild Hall, with gardens, in New Street. Dissolved by Henry VIII, whose commissioners in 1546 incorrectly classified it as a wholly religious and charitable order, King Edward VI re-established the Gild in January 1547, for educational purposes, as part of improving the provision of schools. A report to him describes Birmingham as 'one of the fayrest and moste profittubble towne[s] to the Kinges highness in all the Shyre [sic].'[7]

Another guild was created in 1380 in Deritend, in the manor of Aston. The Gild of St. John the Baptist became the location of a new parish church, with the

---

6   Bunce, *History of the Corporation of Birmingham*, pp.21-2
7   Ibid., p.30

right to appoint their own priest being granted in 1382. In the second half of the fifteenth century, this guild built a new guildhall including a home for the priest and a school for children of the guild members. Remarkably, this still stands and is the oldest complete medieval building in Birmingham, although most of it dates from the sixteenth century. The first school in the town, it was attended by John Rogers, who was burned at the stake as a heretic for refusing to renounce his faith, during the persecution of Protestants pursued ruthlessly and relentlessly by Queen Mary in the later 1550s.

JOHN ROGERS
'The first martyr of the Marian persecution'

John Rogers was born in Deritend, then a part of the parish of Aston, in 1500 to 1505 (there are conflicting dates recorded). William Hutton explains in his 'An History of Birmingham', that Deritend is derived from the fact there was a gate across the river at the edge of the lower town, separating Birmingham from Aston parish: *Derry-yate-end*, with 'derry' meaning 'low'; 'yate', 'gate'; and 'end', 'extremity of the parish'.[8]

Rogers' father John came from Aston and worked as a loriner (or lorimer), a maker of small iron objects, particularly parts for a horse's bit, spurs, stirrup and bridle. John Senior married Margaret Wyatt, a tanner's daughter, whose family came from Erdington and Sutton Coldfield. John was educated originally at the Gild School of St. John the Baptist in Deritend, associated with St. John's Church. The Gild was suppressed during the reign of Henry VIII, with all its property sold in 1549, but the Hall of the Gild of St. John remains, now the Old Crown Inn public house, on High Street, Deritend, the oldest surviving medieval building in Birmingham.

John attended Pembroke College, Cambridge University, graduating with a B.A. degree in 1526. In 1532, he became Rector of a church in the City of London, Holy Trinity-the-Less, in Knightrider Street, close to St. Paul's Cathedral. The church was destroyed in the Great Fire of London in 1666, and the site is now the Mansion House tube station.

Rogers moved to Antwerp in the Netherlands in 1534, to be the chaplain to the Company of the Merchant Adventurers, an English merchant traders' guild, involved mainly in the export of cloth. While in Antwerp, he met and became a friend of William Tyndale, a scholar and leading figure in the English

---

8   Hutton, *An History of Birmingham*, p.270

Protestant Reformation. Under Tyndale's influence and teachings, Rogers rejected Catholicism and pursued protestant doctrine, which placed him in jeopardy. This was a real and constant danger, as evidenced by Tyndale's arrest in 1535, and imprisonment for more than a year. Tyndale was accused of heresy, convicted and strangled, with his body then being burnt, on 6th October 1536.

In 1536 or 1537, Rogers married Adriana de Weyden, a Flemish woman, whose family had sponsored Miles Coverdale's 1535 bible. Adriana was perhaps tactfully described as 'more richly endowed with virtue and soberness of life, than with worldly treasures'.[9]

While Rogers was not arrested while in Antwerp, he sought to preserve the teachings of Tyndale, and rescued his work and papers, including a partial translation of the Bible into English. This in itself was perilous, given that many Roman Catholic bishops, such as the infamous Bishop Stephen Gardiner, and priests, considered any deviation from the original Latin to be an act of heresy in itself. Undaunted by this, Rogers began to compile a complete bible in English, using translations of the Old and New Testaments by Tyndale and Miles Coverdale. This bible could not be published openly without attracting prosecution, and it was therefore printed under a pseudonym as being the work of one 'Thomas Matthew'. This name may have been used as it combines the names of two disciples. Although there is some debate about the extent to which the resulting bible was Rogers' work, it is claimed that illustrated initials of 'IR' in the text and footnotes relate to him. In any event, the bible became known as the 'Matthew Bible', and its production is usually ascribed to Rogers. Further weight is perhaps given to this by the fact that it was printed in Paris and Antwerp by Adriana's uncle, Sir Jacob van Meteren. 1,500 were printed, destined for England and Rogers' 'scholarly and majestic tome' was praised by Archbishop Cranmer, who recommended to King Henry VIII that he license it. It therefore became the first officially authorised version of the bible in English. It would be further revised by Miles Coverdale in 1539 and formed the basis of the Great Bible, the Bishops' Bible in 1568, and eventually of the Authorised Version of the King James Bible in 1611, which remained the dominant version for the English Christian world for another three hundred and fifty years.

After six years in Antwerp, Rogers and his wife moved to Wittenberg in Saxony, Germany, and he matriculated from the university there on 25th November 1540. At this time, Rogers and his wife had two sons, Daniel born in 1538, who died in

9   Chester, 1861, p.14, cited in *John Rogers (Bible editor and martyr)*, no date

1591, and John, born in 1540, who died in 1603. These were the first two children of the eleven that would be born to them.

Rogers became a superintendent of a Lutheran church in Meldorf, in the district of Dithmarschen in Schleswig-Holstein, on the North Sea coast of Germany, and became a friend of Philipp Melanchthon, another leading figure in the Protestant Reformation. Life for a protestant reformer remained potentially dangerous in these times, as highlighted by the lynching of a preacher in Meldorf in 1524.

Rogers remained in Meldorf until 1548, and was praised by Melanchthon as 'a learned man … gifted with great ability, which he sets off with a noble character … he will be careful to live in concord with his colleagues … his integrity, trustworthiness and constancy in every duty make him worthy of the love and support of all good men'.[10] Being prepared to live 'in concord' did not mean that Rogers would not address issues about which he felt passionately. He was a co-author of three articles which sought to correct local errant behaviour about baptism and the publishing of banns, but also called for the authorities to enforce the legal penalty for murder, which was execution, instead of the local practice of allowing murderers to buy release from their sentence.

In January 1547, Henry VIII died and Edward VI came to the throne at the age of nine. The realm was ruled therefore by the Protector, his uncle, the Duke of Somerset, as regent. It is known that Rogers had returned to England by August 1548 when he wrote the preface to Melanchthon's 'Weighing of the Interim', or 'Consideration of the Augsberg Interim'. This was a decree of 15th May 1548 issued by Charles V, the Holy Roman Emperor, which ordered protestants to readopt catholic beliefs and practices, including the sacraments, but made some concessions, in that it allowed protestant clergymen to marry, and lay people to receive communion in both bread and wine.

Rogers became Rector of St Matthew's Church in Friday Street, close to St. Paul's in London, on 11th October 1548, and then was given the living of St. Margaret Moyses, on the same street, on 10th May 1550. He became vicar of St. Sepulchre, which still exists, as St. Sepulchre-without-Newgate, on Holborn Viaduct.

These were difficult and often brutal times, for anyone who dissented from the established religion of the state, based on the affiliations of the reigning monarch. Faith in one religion could be outlawed rapidly in the event of a change of king or queen.

---

10   Mozley, pp.122-3, cited in *John Rogers (Bible editor and martyr)*

Under a protestant King, Rogers' career in the church continued to flourish and on 27th August 1551, he was made prebendary of St. Pancras in St. Paul's Cathedral, thereby becoming a senior member of clergy, similar to a canon in modern times. Giving up the livings in Friday Street, he was made a lecturer in divinity. He continued to express himself forcibly on issues of importance to him, at one point denouncing the greed of courtiers profiting from the seizure of assets from monasteries. He declined to wear rich vestments, preferring to wear a small round cap.

In April 1552, his wife and the two sons born in Germany were naturalised, his wife adopting the English name of Pratt.

After the early death of Edward VI, and the ill-fated nine day reign of Lady Jane Grey in 1553, the accession of Queen Mary I presaged conflict and danger for protestants. A confirmed and aggressive Roman Catholic, Mary's attempt to impose catholicism on an often resistant populace resulted in violence, riots, suppression and executions, rightly earning her the sobriquet 'Bloody Mary'.

By August 1553, Rogers had been identified as 'a seditious preacher' and was investigated by catholic bishops. This was in light of his preaching at St. Paul's, setting out his support for the 'true doctrine taught in King Edward's days' and his attack on 'pestilent popery, idolatry and superstition'. He defended himself robustly and with great skill, and was not convicted of heresy, but he was ordered to remain in his home by the Privy Council. He did this for five months, without taking opportunities offered to him to escape to continental Europe. Part of his defence was that he was preaching the religion approved by Parliament, which was true, although it would soon be outlawed by the Queen's general proclamation against preaching on 18th August 1553. During this period, he was replaced as prebendary at St. Paul's on 10th October 1553, depriving him and his large family of income.

He was arrested again after a riot at St. Paul's in which Edmund Bonner, Bishop of London, was attacked. Although Rogers ensured he was not harmed, the Mayor of London had him arrested, it is said, to prove he could control the city. Bishop Bonner, who became known as 'Bloody Bonner' for his role in the Marian persecutions, sent Rogers to Newgate Gaol on 27th January 1554. After almost a year in gaol, in November or December 1554, Rogers and other protestant prisoners wrote to Queen Mary, protesting against the illegality of their imprisonment and seeking a trial in the near future. Rogers' request was met rapidly, as in December, Parliament passed legislation allowing the execution of heretics, and his trial began on 22nd January 1555. Bishop Stephen Gardiner presided over the trial and despite his forceful argument denying heresy, recorded in his journals, Rogers was convicted as a heretic on 29th January and condemned to death by Gardiner for 'denying the Christian character of the Church of Rome and the real presence [of Christ] in the sacrament'.[11]

On 4th February 1555, he was taken to Smithfield for execution. Bishop Bonner refused him permission to speak to his wife and children, who were in attendance, the latest born of whom he had never seen. Prior to being tied to the stake, Rogers was offered a pardon if he would recant. He steadfastly refused, behaving to the last with dignity, grace, and adherence to his beloved faith, as Foxe's 'Book of Martyrs' attests:

'Mr. Woodroofe, one of the sheriffs, first came to Mr. Rogers, and asked him if he would revoke his abominable doctrine, and the evil opinion of the Sacrament of the altar. Mr. Rogers answered, "That which I have preached I will seal with my blood." Then Mr. Woodroofe said, "Thou art an heretic." "That shall be known," quoth Mr. Rogers, "at the Day of Judgment [sic]." "Well," said Mr. Woodroofe, "I will never pray for thee." "But I will pray for you," said Mr. Rogers.'[12]

Before being burnt, Rogers exhorted the spectators to stand firm in the faith he had preached and for which he was prepared to suffer and die. His reaction to the flames is said, remarkably, to have been that he washed his hands in the flames, as though it had been in cold water, and held up his hands to heaven until the flames overcame him. His ashes were collected and treated by his supporters as martyr's relics.

John Rogers was the first of almost 300 martyrs to die for their faith in three years under Bloody Mary, assisted enthusiastically by 'Bloody Bonner'. Archbishop Cranmer himself would be executed in 1556. At the time of Rogers' death, the French Ambassador to Queen Mary's court wrote that his execution confirmed the alliance between the Pope and England, although even he acknowledged the support and love of many at the execution for Rogers, recording that 'even his children assisted at it, comforting him in such a manner that it seemed as if he had been led to a wedding.'[13] Clearly a remarkable man.

John Rogers is remembered by a plaque erected by Birmingham Civic Society, on an industrial unit, in High Street, Deritend. There is also a black metal plaque below. A further black metal plaque identifies this as the site of St. John's Church, a chapel of the parish of Aston, which was founded in 1381, re-built in 1736, and demolished in 1947, having been damaged in an air raid in 1940.

---

11   *John Rogers (Bible editor and martyr)*

12   Foxe, Chapter 16, cited in *John Rogers (Bible editor and martyr)*

13   Van Dorsten, 1962, p.10, cited in *John Rogers (Bible editor and martyr)*

Rogers is also remembered in many publications recording the history of the Reformation and in books and on websites recording the struggle for religious tolerance and freedom.

A white Carrara marble bust of John Rogers was unveiled at St. John's Church on 20th October 1883, by the Lord Mayor, Alderman William White. This followed a campaign to raise funds by public subscription, begun in 1870, that finally succeeded in raising the £140 necessary. When St. John's was demolished in 1947, the bust and tablet were moved to Aston Parish Church, St. Peter and St. Paul, in Witton Lane, Aston, where they can still be seen.

Blue and further plaque, High Street, Deritend, Birmingham, B12 0NB

Bust in Aston Parish Church, St. Peter and St. Paul, in Witton Lane, Aston, Birmingham, B6 6QA

There is a further memorial to John Rogers at Babson College, 231, Forrest Street, Wellesley, Massachusetts, USA. The College is dedicated to developing entrepreneurs and Rogers is an ancestor of its founder, Roger W. Babson.

In the middle of John Rogers' life, in 1525, another Birmingham resident was making a gift of significant generosity that would benefit many thousands of people over five centuries, and continues to do so today. This was William Lench.

WILLIAM LENCH

'The Moor Street tanner whose generosity lives on
after five hundred years'

Very little is known of William Lench, and without his single known act of generosity, it is likely he would never have been known to us. What we do know is that he was a tanner, who lived with his wife Agnes in Moor Street, although it was known as Mole Street in Lench's day. Birmingham had a thriving market for leather, including a Leather Hall at the end of New Street where it joins High Street.

As he and his wife had no children, rather than provide a bequest or endowment to a religious order, such as the Gild of the Holy Cross, which he lived near, he decided to convey his property, freehold land and buildings bought from the proceeds of his business, to nineteen trusted friends (including the Master of the Gild) by a Deed of Gift, in the ancient form of a Feoffment. A feoffment is defined by the Oxford English Dictionary as '(in feudal law) a grant of ownership of freehold property to someone.'

This was compiled on 11th March 1525 in Norman-French, the legal language of the time. It names each of the nineteen friends, and lists Lench's possessions, which were extensive. These included 'my lands, and tenements, meadows, fields and pastures, rents and services in…Birmingham,…Dudston [modern-day Duddeston],… Aston…, Bordesley…, Little Bromwich…, and …in Saltley,' all areas of Birmingham. He commits that 'I, the said William Lench, and my heirs will maintain for ever by these presents against all men, and the said lands and tenements.' The purpose is stated, in his will of 24th March 1525, as being 'after the decease of me, the said William Lench, and Agnes, my wife…to distribute in works of charity, for the health of the foresaid William Lench's soul and [of] Agnes, his wife'.[14]

Lench died in 1525 and Agnes several years later, although the precise dates are not recorded.

The dissolution of the monasteries under Henry VIII would remove the Gild of the Holy Cross and the Gild of St. John in Digbeth, and would have taken William Lench's Trust, had he made his bequest through the church. Fortunately, he did not, and the Lench's Trust continues to the present day and its website describes what happened next. In 1540, a Declaration of Trust appointed twelve trustees to oversee the application and distribution of the income and profits from the land,

---

14 Arthur Musgrove, *The History of Lench's Trust, Birmingham 1525-1925* (Birmingham: 1926), pp.1-2

property and services which had been inherited. They decided on two objects for the expenditure – the repair of 'the ruined ways and bridges in and around the town of Birmingham' and 'in bestowing the same on the poor living within the said town, where there was the greatest want'.[15] Hutton includes a description of the operation of this trust, along with several others, in the 1780s. He berates the original trustees who, in his view, neglected the proper stewardship of this trust, allowing it to become 'too bulky for support' and it required an order from the Court of Chancery to move its stewardship to twenty Birmingham residents, who ensured its growth to the value of £227 5s, a considerable sum in Hutton's time. These residents were clearly businessmen and therefore creditable to Hutton, a successful and wealthy businessman himself: 'The man who can guide his own private concerns with success, stands the fairest chance of guiding those of the public.' As well as giving 'a pittance to the poor widows', Lench's Trust also had 'a power of distributing money to the necessitous at Christmas and Easter, which is punctually performed'. Hutton's record includes the names of trustees at the time of writing (noting that three have died in post), and includes the name of the 'bailiff Lench', a steward chosen from among them each year, then one Thomas Colmore.[16]

As required, the Trust spent its income on establishing, running and maintaining almshouses for the poor alongside spending on highways, bridges and roads for the next three hundred years, helping thousands of people in that time. When Birmingham was incorporated in 1838, and a full Town Council was elected, the trustees decided to leave the physical infrastructure work to the Corporation and instead devote the Trust's resources to looking after the poor. This was effected through a combination of providing housing in almshouses and the payment of stipends, which we would recognise more as a form of pension. This was almost a century ahead of government moves to provide pensions to the elderly, which did not commence until 1911.

The first almshouses provided were in Digbeth in 1639, followed by further building in 1688, in the countryside, on the corner of Steelhouse Lane and Lancaster Street. These apparently at the time offered 'an extensive and beautiful view of the country'.[17] The trust has had several other sites in the past, at Conybere Gardens in Highgate (where the foundation stone remains), Ravenhurst Street in Deritend, Hospital Street in Newtown, and in Ladywood.

---

15 *Our History*, no date
16 Hutton, *An History of Birmingham*, pp.197-9
17 *Our History*

The income from the Trust now funds sheltered housing provision at William Lench Court, at 80 Ridgacre Road, Quinton, the appropriately named Tanner's Close in Sutton Coldfield, and Lench's Close in Moseley. Through this work, the generosity of one man five centuries ago, who would never know the people he would help, continues to have significant and lasting effect. He is formally remembered by a blue plaque, at William Lench Court in Quinton.

Blue plaque at Lench's Trust, William Lench Court, 80 Ridgacre Road, Quinton, Birmingham, B32 2AQ

2.

The Growing Town – developing Trade and War towards the Industrial Revolution

Parish records demonstrate that population numbers began to grow again only in the fifteenth century, as the economy diversified from predominantly agriculture. By the end of this century, wealth was less evenly spread, with classes of 'gentlemen' and 'yeomen' apparent.

From the sixteenth to eighteenth century, Birmingham was a town in transition, as the world took recognisable shape and records began to be preserved. Trade developed, based on the natural resources in, or close to, Birmingham – iron, coal from South Staffordshire, and plentiful water, and was substantially driven by the ingenuity and hard work of the population. The market continued to grow, and markets for specific products proliferated in the town centre, for corn, cattle, butter and cheese, leather, fowl and, of course, metal products. This made for a tumultuous and unplanned town centre, with little regulation and no planning.

A contemporary account, by John Leland in 1538, indicates 'There be many smiths in the towne that use to make knives and all mannour of cutting tooles, and many lorimers that make bites, and a great many naylors [sic].'[18] William Camden in 1563 remarks that Birmingham was 'swarming with inhabitants and echoing with the noise of anvils'.[19] The Tudor period was marked in Birmingham by economic development based on a growing population providing the labour required to fulfil the needs of this expanding metalworking industry. This displaced

18 Skipp, *A History of Greater Birmingham – down to 1830,* p.38
19 Chris Upton, *A History of Birmingham*, (Stroud, Gloucestershire: 2011), p.12

the earlier clothing trade, as mills converted from cloth to iron production. As Skipp indicates, this 'began to set Birmingham apart from the average run of urban centres, and presaged the rise of the modern industrial giant'.[20]

Buildings for educating children, entertaining people and civic development appeared, including schools, breweries and Peck Lane prison. The iconic name, Bull Ring, first appeared in 1550, and denoted, unsurprisingly, a meat market by the Manor House and St. Martin's Church. All of High Street was a cattle market, while mercers (merchants) had stalls in Mercer Street (now Spiceal Street), there was a corn market at Corn Cheaping, and horses were traded in Edgbaston Street, near the Old Market Cross. Dairy products were also sold here, so that for some, the Old Market Cross became the Butter Cross.

The range of tradesmen expanded, from the traditional cloth trades of shearing, weaving, fulling and dyeing, to include tanning, using animal skins from local livestock. This became a substantial industry in the sixteenth century, with Tanner's Row its obvious centre. Skipp surmises that the greater production of leather goods may have been the link to the development of ironworking, as saddles and reins required metal parts and ironworking became 'Birmingham's foremost sixteenth and seventeenth century industry'.[21]

The growth in metalworking was rapid, as the national population grew to around 5 million in 1600, rising by another million in the next fifty years. In Birmingham, the population mushroomed from around 1,500 in the middle of the fifteenth century to 5,000 a century later. More people meant more demand for products, and greater supply of labour to produce them. Hutton comments: 'The chief, if not the only manufactory of Birmingham, from its first existence to the restoration of Charles II was in iron: of this was produced instruments of war and of husbandry, furniture for the kitchen, and tools for the whole system of carpentry.'[22]

The structure of industry reflected many Brummies' preference for independent work, as workshops, each with a small number of skilled workers, proliferated. By 1650, one in six households in the town undertook ironworking. Ironmongers provided these 'cottage industries' with raw materials and sold their products locally and increasingly nationally, gaining great wealth in many instances.

While trade progressed, Birmingham became embroiled in the English Civil War, with the Battle of Birmingham at Easter 1643. Prince Rupert, Prince of

20   Skipp, *A History of Greater Birmingham – down to 1830*, p.39
21   Ibid., p.38
22   Hutton, *An History of Birmingham*, p.19

Wales, led a force of 2,000 Cavaliers to punish the residents of Birmingham for their espousal of the Parliamentary cause, and their 'peremptory malice to his majesty'.[23] This followed an incident when King Charles I was dining at Aston Hall, with an assault on the King's baggage-train in October 1642, and a simultaneous attack on Prince Rupert himself at Kings Norton, resulting in the loss of fifty men. Birmingham sided with Parliament and supplied weapons to the Roundheads.

By 1670, Birmingham was the largest town in Warwickshire, overtaking Coventry, with the population of 7,000 rising to more than 15,000 by 1700 and over 23,000 by 1731. Birmingham's dominance in the iron industry, in Britain and in Europe, brought an international steel trade employing more than 45,000 men by the 1730s.

Relative tranquillity at home and the expanding British Empire's wars abroad in the seventeenth and eighteenth centuries drove the rapid growth of metalworking, tanning and clothing. Complementary industries included banking, printing, and improved means of transporting raw materials and finished products, through the development of canals.

Leading Birmingham figures would play prominent roles, as manufacturing became critical to the expansion of the town and nation. Let's begin with the story of a printer, at the forefront of this developing industry. The printed word had already enabled information to be recorded and kept, improving learning, codifying thinking, and offering a medium for record-keeping and the development of literature. John Baskerville's work resonates to this day. He developed an elegant typeface that, although forgotten shortly after his death, was re-discovered and is in common use. Intriguingly, John Baskerville had a remarkable journey, even after death!

JOHN BASKERVILLE

*'The innovative printer whose story did not conclude until
one hundred and twenty-three years after his death'*

John Baskerville was a prominent resident of Birmingham in the eighteenth century, a manufacturer of japanned ware, then a printer and publisher. He was a member of the Lunar Society and was innovative in designing industrial processes, for metal objects and printing presses. His most famous creation, the Baskerville typeface, was revolutionary in its clarity and simplicity. A non-believer who scorned

---

23 Upton, *A History of Birmingham*, p.24

religion, his corpse undertook an extraordinary journey before being put to rest, more than a century after his death.

John Baskerville was born at Sion Hill, Wolverley, near Kidderminster, Worcestershire in January 1706. Although his date of birth is not recorded, he was baptised on 28th January. His father, also named John (who died in 1738), and his mother Sara, or Sarah, were thought to be landowners and farmers.

As a young man, Baskerville was a footman to a priest in Kings Norton, and was asked to help to teach local poor young men to write. Building on this experience, when moving to live in Birmingham in 1726, Baskerville set himself up as a writing-master, in High Street. By 1730 he had become a letter-cutter, as attested by a slate in the Library of Birmingham, measuring 22cm by 27cm. This is a form of advertising, with five lines in three types of lettering (Roman, Italic and Gothic), stating 'Grave stones cut in any of the hands by John Baskervill writing-master'.[24] Unfortunately, there is no surviving attributable example of a gravestone cut by him.

When Baskerville was sixteen, he and his father mortgaged their land at Wolverley to raise funds for John Junior to establish himself in business. Hutton states that 'this son of genius', while he was 'trained to no profession', as well being a writing master, was teaching a school at 'the Bull-ring' by 1737, 'and is said to have written an excellent hand'.[25] By 1742, Baskerville was a 'Japanner', which involved applying layers of a hard, dark varnish, giving a black gloss, to wooden and metal objects, under which designs or pictures could be preserved by the enamel-like quality of the finish. Based on techniques developed in India, China and Japan (from where the name derives), this became established in Europe in the late seventeenth century, becoming extremely popular in the eighteenth century. It was very lucrative for its manufacturers. Baskerville submitted a patent for 'Machinery for Rolling and Grinding Metal plates or Veneers', and established a home, warehouse and workshop at 22 Moor Street in 1740, aged thirty-four. Nine years later, in 1748, he leased eight acres two furlongs north west of the town centre, and built a house, gardens, and workshop which he called Easy Hill, where Baskerville House and the Hall of Memory now stand. He lived here for the rest of his life, although he soon found his 'little Eden' became part of the expanding town.

24 James Mosley, 'Baskerville, John (1706-1775)', *Oxford Dictionary of National Biography*, (Oxford: 2004, updated 2013)
25 Hutton, *An History of Birmingham*, p.*91

As Hutton notes, Birmingham, 'as if conscious of his merit, followed his retreat, and surrounded it with buildings'.[26]

Hutton knew Baskerville personally for twenty-five years, liked him considerably, and thought very highly of his accomplishments. He describes him as a humourist in private life and extremely idle, although 'his invention was of the true Birmingham model, active'. He designed very well but recognised the value of employing others to produce – 'wherever he found merit, he caressed it', and he was 'remarkably polite to the stranger'. Although short in stature, being 'constructed with the light timbers of a frigate, his movement was solemn as a ship of the line'. Baskerville was given to ostentation, with little or no regard for the judgement of others, or as Hutton puts it, he was 'fond of shew'. To advertise his trade, 'his carriage, each panel of which was a distinct picture, might be considered *the pattern-card of his trade*, and was drawn by a beautiful pair of cream-coloured horses'.[27]

By 1750, he decided to develop a business in printing alongside the japanning work which he continued throughout his life. This new 'uncertain pursuit' was slow to generate profit, and Hutton contends that he spent £600, a massive sum, before he produced anything satisfactory, and thousands of pounds 'before the shallow stream of profit began to flow'.[28]

During the 1750s, Baskerville was joined at Easy Hill by Sarah Eaves, née Ruston, a married woman with a son and two daughters. This unfortunate woman's husband had been convicted of fraud and had fled justice, leaving her with no means of support. Sarah was described as his housekeeper, and remained so until her husband died, after which, on 1st June 1764, Baskerville, at the age of fifty-eight, married Sarah at St. Martin's Church. The union produced no children.

In 1756, six years after beginning, Baskerville produced a quarto edition of Virgil, costing one guinea (Hutton notes it is 'now worth several').[29] He later printed Paradise Lost (in 1758), the works of Joseph Addison (1761), the Bible (1763), a translation of Virgil into English (1766), as well as the Book of Common Prayer, and other Latin and English classic works. Baskerville was a convinced atheist, who entertained a considerable disdain of religion, considering believers to be 'ignorant and bigoted people' who followed 'absurd doctrines about which

---

26   Hutton, *An History of Birmingham*, p.*91
27   Ibid., p.*91
28   Ibid., p.*91
29   Ibid., p.*92

they have no more conception than a horse'.[30] However, he was too sensible a businessman to eschew the opportunity for profit by meeting the demands of the religious market.

Baskerville's success in printing was based partly on the style of the typeface he developed, which is still used. This was clearer, plainer and less ornate and florid than other typefaces in use. In the preface to his edition of Paradise Lost, he explained (shown here in Baskerville Old Face):

'Amongst the several mechanic Arts that have engaged my attention, there is no one which I have pursued with so much steadiness and pleasure, as that of *Letter-Founding*. Having been an early admirer of the beauty of Letters, I became insensibly desirous of contributing to the perfection of them. I formed to my self Ideas of greater accuracy than had yet appeared, and have endeavoured to produce a *Sett of Types* according to what I conceived to be their true proportion.' [31]

In wider society, Baskerville was an active member of the Lunar Society, often chairing meetings. As Jenny Uglow describes, that unique congregation of free-thinking innovators, designers, artists, businessmen, engineers, industrialists and scientists came together in the enlightened, free-thinking atmosphere of 1760s Birmingham. These open-minded innovators were not afraid to defy convention with their behaviour, and frequently self-taught expertise, which manifested itself as an independent approach to all aspects of life. Baskerville was older than many of the members, by some twenty years, but he became a close friend of Matthew Boulton in particular, and came to be seen almost as a second father to him.

Birmingham became a beacon for invention and industry in the early years of the Industrial Revolution and attracted interest from around the world. In 1758, Benjamin Franklin, then the agent of the Pennsylvania Assembly in London to argue for the independence of the American colonies, visited Birmingham for the first time. As a printer himself, and a subscriber to Baskerville's Virgil, he was keen to meet the printer. With his son William, the Franklins met distant relatives, and Benjamin commented that all those they met were 'industrious, ingenious working people and think themselves vastly happy that they live in dear old England'.[32] Seven years later, Baskerville sought Franklin's support to sell his typefaces and printing to the French. Then Ambassador to France, Franklin replied discouragingly that the French were badly affected by the effects of the 1756 war, and 'were so far from pursuing schemes of taste, that

---

30   Jenny Uglow, *The Lunar Men: The Friends Who Made the Future*, (London: 2002), p.23
31   Cited in Mosley, 'Baskerville, John (1706-1775)', *Oxford Dictionary of National Biography*
32   Jenny Uglow, *The Lunar Men: The Friends Who Made the Future*, (London: 2002), p.59

they were unable to repair their public buildings, but suffered the scaffolding to rot before them'.[33]

Baskerville was an innovator in all aspects of printing, from design of the presses, to casting and setting the type, and even improving the paper on which he printed. He is credited with introducing brass plates and typefaces, rather than traditional wood, and developing a successful ink for better printing. He produced the ink by boiling linseed oil, then added amber and rosin for a better sheen, and used 'fine-black', to provide the dark purple colour. This was soot, a by-product of glass manufacturing and soldering, so readily available in rapidly industrialising Birmingham. He developed a 'hot-pressing' process, which gave his products an attractive glaze and durability. Baskerville took the secret of this process to his grave, and it is still not fully known how it worked, although it may have drawn on his approach to japanning. He also developed new forms of paper, and printed on wove paper, which was probably invented by his master paper-maker James Whatman.

While these techniques provided high quality products, they were more expensive than many of his competitors. Baskerville often complained about lack of use of his printing services by London booksellers, that 'the Booksellers do not chuse to encourage me, tho' I have offered them as low terms as I could possibly live by'.[34] There does seem to have been some resistance to the use of his printing, based on issues of style. Following Franklin's second visit to Birmingham in 1760, the American related how a gentleman complained that Baskerville was 'a means of blinding all the readers in the nation'. This extraordinary claim was based on his view that the typeface did not have 'that height and thickness of stroke which make the common printing so much more comfortable to the eye'.[35] While this might not be a widely held view, it does confirm that you cannot please everyone. Baskerville himself interpreted this as prejudice against work produced outside London in general, and by him in particular. This must have been irksome, because of its impact on profits, but also as an insult to his pride.

In Birmingham, however, Baskerville was much loved and appreciated, and with Boulton and Samuel Garbett, the button and hardware manufacturer, was appointed as one of seventy-six Street Commissioners to oversee the improvement of Birmingham's streets and highways, as the town expanded and re-developed. As a notable person, Baskerville was visited in 1760 by Dr Alexander Carlyle, a

33 Hutton, *An History of Birmingham*, p.*92
34 Mosley, 'Baskerville, John (1706-1775)', *Oxford Dictionary of National Biography*
35 Ibid.

Scottish minister visiting friends in Birmingham. He described his visit to Easy Hill, and Baskerville himself as 'a great curiosity'. After dining, while one of his companions thought Baskerville 'a man of genius', Carlyle himself dismissed the great printer and Birmingham celebrity as 'a prating pedant'.[36]

Despite this unflattering depiction, in 1761, Baskerville was appointed to the post of High Bailiff of the Manor of Birmingham, the highest civic office. Although he complained about lack of income, he was not without influence, and arranged a loan of £3,500 for Boulton, later increased to £10,000, to help develop his Soho Manufactory.

Baskerville died at home in Easy Hill, on 8th January 1775, aged sixty-nine, leaving most of his property to his wife, with the charitably selfless provision that she should retain his estate if she married again 'which If She Chuse I wish her happy equal to her merit'.[37] He left detailed instructions for his burial, which sets off an extraordinary story surrounding his remains which continued, unfeasibly, until 1898, one hundred and twenty-three years after his demise.

Baskerville was decidedly not religious, and his will required that his body be interred in the conical base of a former windmill in the grounds of his home, adapted to function as a mausoleum. The strength of his rejection of religion was conveyed in instructions to inter him in his newly painted and refurbished mausoleum: 'it is a whim for many years Resolve'd upon, as I have a Hearty Contempt for all Superstition the Farce of a Consecrated Ground the Irish Barbarism of Sure and Certain Hopes &c I also consider Revelation as it is call'd Exclusive of the Scraps of Morality casually Intermixt with It to be the most Impudent Abuse of Common Sense which Ever was Invented to Befool Mankind [sic].'

Clearly wishing to avoid any sense of equivocation, he composed his own epitaph for posterity:

'Stranger, Beneath this Cone in Unconsecrated Ground, a Friend to the Liberties of Mankind Directed his Body to be Inhum'd. May his Example contribute to Emancipate the Mind from the Idle Fears of Superstition and the Wicked Arts of Priesthood.'[38]

His wife Sarah died on 21st March 1788, and her tombstone remains in the south east corner of St. Philip's churchyard, near the entrance in Temple Row, opposite Cherry Street.

---

36 Bunce, *History of the Corporation of Birmingham: with a Sketch of the Earlier Government of the Town, volume 1*, pp.54-5

37 Mosley, 'Baskerville, John (1706-1775)', *Oxford Dictionary of National Biography*

38 Ibid.

As regards the late Baskerville himself, his remarkable after-death story began when the old windmill base was demolished, as Thomas Gibson, an iron merchant with premises on Cambridge Street, built canal wharves for his business. Baskerville's coffin had not been removed, as originally thought, and when the canal wharves were expanded in 1820, the lead coffin was exposed. It was moved to Gibson's warehouse and incredibly, five months later, was opened, as reported in Aris's Birmingham Gazette on 28th May 1821. This describes Baskerville's corpse as 'in a singular state of preservation… wrapped in a linen shroud very perfect and white. The skin on the face was dry and perfect… eyes gone…but eyebrows, eyelashes, lips, and teeth remained.' It said that the body gave 'an exceedingly offensive and oppressive effluvia strongly resembling decayed cheese'.[39] Even more grotesquely, it is claimed that ghoulish spectators were charged a shilling each to view the remains and that a surgeon who stole a piece of the shroud died a few days later! In any event, after eight years in the warehouse, in 1829, Job Marston, a plumber, moved the coffin to his shop in Monmouth Street, at the end of the present day Colmore Row, where it meets Snow Hill.

There were stories that Baskerville was then buried in the grounds of a chapel in Cradley, that he had been interred in a St. Philip's vault, or even that he had been secretly interred in Mrs Baskerville's grave. Fifty years later, the truth was revealed in a letter to the Birmingham Weekly Post on 22nd November 1879. This account, based on evidence from Marston's widow, indicated that in 1829 Marston had been refused permission to inter Baskerville in St. Philip's, as the deceased was a self-proclaimed atheist. Marston had been allowed to move the coffin to vault 521 in the catacombs at Christ Church, at the junction of the present Victoria Square and New Street. This was done with the surreptitious connivance of George Barker, a solicitor and churchwarden of Christ Church, who had left the key to the catacombs where Marston could find it, without explicitly giving permission for the interment. The vicar of Christ Church, Canon Wilcox, had the register of the vaults checked and found that no name was listed against vault 521. He arranged for the vault to be opened, with an audience comprising the Mayor, local notables and the press, on 12th April 1893. Examination of the coffin revealed Baskerville's name, appropriately set out in typeface letters soldered to the coffin, and the legend 'Died 1775' marked in pinpricks, as well as chalk writing confirming 'Removed 1829'. Even more remarkably, the coffin was opened and the body, not surprisingly, had decomposed dramatically in the intervening seventy-two years. After closing

39   Vivian Bird, *Portrait of Birmingham, 2nd edn.,* (London: 1974), p.110

the coffin, the vault was resealed, with confidence that the mystery of the resting place of Baskerville's corpse had been solved.

As Vivian Bird explains, this was not the end of the matter. Technically, Canon Wilcox had broken the law by disturbing the coffin without Home Office permission, leading to a question being asked in the House of Commons. On 17th April 1893, Home Secretary Herbert Asquith told the House he had concluded that it was not in the public interest to take any further steps, and so Baskerville seemed to have found his final resting place. This was confirmed by a tablet on the north wall of Christ Church that read: 'In these catacombs rest the remains of John Baskerville, the Famous Printer'. This was signed by the Mayor and others present at the exhumation.

Sadly, bizarrely, this was not the end of Baskerville's journey. Five years later an Act of 1897 authorised the demolition of Christ Church, having fallen into disuse as people moved out of the town centre. As no-one claimed Baskerville's coffin, it was moved with the other 600 interred there to Warstone Lane Cemetery, and was placed in a vault beneath the chapel. The tablet from Christ Church was also placed there, recording the date, 26th February 1898. This must have been a nightmarish procession: 'In order not to disturb the city unduly, the transfers took place at night, an endless procession of funeral coaches making their slow progress out to the Jewellery Quarter.'[40]

The chapel in Warstone Lane was demolished in 1953, but thankfully the graveyard remained and the catacombs were undisturbed. So there John Baskerville lies, an avowed atheist, after being moved from his chosen, self-created, secular resting place, to warehouse, to shop, and between two pieces of consecrated ground. A petition to Birmingham City Council to remove his remains to unconsecrated ground was refused in April 1963. It is hard to imagine that he would have been at all happy about this sequence of events and outcome.

Although not his own epitaph, Hutton's summary of John Baskerville perhaps serves us best in giving a picture of the man, his motives and his life. Baskerville was 'This son of genius' who 'during the twenty-five years I knew him, though in the decline of life,…retained the singular traces of a handsome man.' While acknowledging that he 'exhibited a peevish temper, we may consider good-nature and intense thinking are not always found together…Taste accompanied him through the different walks of agriculture, architecture, and the finer arts'. Before roundly criticizing the nation for not buying Baskerville's printing presses after

---

40   Upton, *A History of Birmingham*, p.140

his death (they were sold to a literary society in Paris for £3,700 in 1779), he concludes that 'Whatever passed through his fingers, bore the lively marks of John Baskerville'.[41]

John Baskerville is remembered in the naming of Baskerville House, in Centenary Square, Broad Street, and in a plaque erected in 1956 on the building, to the right of the main entrance.

In front of the building is the 'Industry and Genius' sculpture by David Patten, of Portland Stone, depicting characters in the Baskerville typeface. The typeface punches are in the possession of Cambridge University Library, having been discovered in Paris and presented to the university in 1953. Worldwide, his legacy can be seen in the works produced using his typeface and, of course, by its continuing use.

John Baskerville, by James Millar, 1774, from the Birmingham Museum and Art Gallery

'Industry and Genius' sculpture by David Patten, outside Baskerville House, 2, Centenary Square, Broad Street, Birmingham, B1 2ND

Birmingham's growing population was codified in Bradford's Plan, published in 1751. This listed the names of the eighty-six streets in the town, recorded that there were 4,170 houses in those streets, and 23,688 inhabitants in those houses. By 1769, the town had grown again, to 6,025 houses accommodating more than 30,000 people.

The second half of the eighteenth century saw the emergence and development of manufacturing as an identifiable industrial sector nationally and particularly

---

41   Hutton, *An History of Birmingham*, pp.*92-3

markedly in Birmingham. The best known example is the Soho Manufactory opened in 1764 when Boulton formed a partnership with John Fothergill. This was the first example of all production processes taking place in one building, so that the works was a series of separate workshops benefitting from common sources of supply of materials, warehousing, distribution, marketing and management. The ability to streamline processes meant that better quality goods could be produced for lower cost, driving expansion from local into national, and international, markets. Boulton's partnership with James Watt and William Murdock resulted in these men becoming extremely wealthy. They were very influential in local society, able to afford enlightened working practices, such as well-ventilated workshops, and a social insurance scheme for workers and their families when such benefits were very rare.

As would be expected, this rapid growth of trade needed appropriate arrangements for financing. Birmingham became an important provider of financial services and had an involvement in the establishment of several big banks that continue today. The most notable of these was Taylors & Lloyds, which became today's Lloyds Bank, internationally known and respected.

The name derives from Sampson Lloyd, an ironmaster, who set up a joint venture in Dale End, in 1765, with John Taylor, a manufacturer of buttons and metal goods.

SAMPSON LLOYD

'The local iron master who became a banker
whose name lives on in Lloyds Bank'

Sampson Lloyd was born in Birmingham, on 15th July 1699, the son of Sampson Lloyd (born 1664, died 1725) and his second wife, Mary, née Crowley, whose father Ambrose was an ironmaker in Stourbridge. Sampson Junior had an older brother and younger sister, as well as four half-sisters from his father's first marriage. Both Sampson's parents were Quakers, his father coming from a Welsh well-to-do family, from Dolobran. Sampson Senior moved to Birmingham in 1698 and became the owner of a slitting-mill in Bradford Street, which used the River Rea to power the machinery to produce nails, iron bars, and other metal products on a wholesale basis. Lloyd may have been seeking a more tolerant environment in which to live, in respect of his religion, to escape the more hostile attitudes he had found in Wales. He had in fact been born in prison, his parents having been incarcerated because, as Quakers, their principles did not allow them to swear an oath of allegiance to Charles II. Although imprisoning Quakers had ended in 1672, attitudes often remained unwelcoming at best. Birmingham had a reputation as a town of tolerance, respect and progressive thinking, and this may have been a factor in his decision to live here.

Sampson Lloyd Junior was apprenticed to a brass-wire manufacturer, Thomas Sharpe, in Bristol, but he returned home in 1720 as a result of ill-health. Working in the family business, he expanded it to own more of the supply chain, including other mills, forges and furnaces. Lloyd married a Quaker heiress, Sara Parkes, in 1727, aged twenty-eight, and they had one son before Sara's death in 1729. His second marriage, on 17th September 1731, was to Rachel Champion, daughter of Nehemiah Champion, an ironmaker from Bristol. They had three sons and two daughters. Large numbers of children were common in the Lloyd family, as evidenced by his sons Sampson (born 1728) having seventeen, and Charles (born 1748) having fourteen children.

For three decades, the business prospered and grew. The period was one of considerable opportunity for manufacturers, as the British Empire expanded particularly in North America and India. Birmingham was famously described by Edmund Burke as 'the great toy-shop of Europe', producing toys (meaning small metal objects), trinkets, ornaments and a wide range of other metal products. Profits grew rapidly by meeting the demand for metal for swords, guns, cannon, buttons for uniforms, and other needs of the British Army, during the Seven Years' War (1756 to 1763). One estimate is that more than three quarters of a million consignments of arms were made in Birmingham in the last twenty-five years of the eighteenth century. There is an inescapable irony, in that the Lloyds' wealth expanded, in part at least, based on supporting wars, when their religion was definitively pacifist. This is a paradox to which we return later, in the life of Samuel Galton Junior in Chapter 5.

By 1742, Lloyd was wealthy enough to purchase, at the cost of £1,290, a large Elizabethan manor house in the countryside outside the centre of Birmingham. This was an estate called 'Owen's Farm' and consisted of fifty-six acres of land in the manor of Bordesley. He built a Georgian mansion called 'Farm', now a Grade II listed building. This house still exists in modern Sparkbrook, an excellent example of Georgian style. Farm Park and the nearby Dolobran Road are reminders of the Lloyd family. Lloyd lived both here and in his house in Edgbaston Street, in the town centre, close to his ironworks. The growth of the town to surround the house led to the family moving later to the more fashionable Edgbaston Grove.

Shortly after peace was declared in 1763, Sampson Lloyd was in his sixties, a time when most people are considering retirement. His business legacy was assured but it was then that he embarked upon another business venture that was to secure recognition of his family name from then to now. He was sixty-six in 1765 when he formed a partnership with John Taylor, a button maker and manufacturer of what might now be termed fancy goods, including japanned ware, and elegant snuff boxes. Both he and Taylor involved their eldest sons, also called Sampson Lloyd and John Taylor, with each contributing £2,000. After six years, each received £2,500 in profits.[42]

John Taylor Senior was born in 1710 or 1711 and came from humble beginnings, starting work as an artisan cabinet-maker. He established a factory in what is now Union Street and by 1755, his business had progressed to such an extent that he was described as 'Mr Taylor, the most considerable Maker of Gilt-metal Buttons and enamell'd snuff-boxes'.[43] He also invested in property and rebuilt Bordesley Hall at a staggering cost of £10,000. By 1765, he had amassed considerable wealth, having forty-three properties, generating an annual income of £872. It is interesting that he is little known now, perhaps because his name was no longer associated with the bank after 1852.

Lloyd was attracted to working with such a leading business light, and the partnership was formed, with the bank being called 'Taylor & Lloyds', with its premises at 7, Dale End. Initially the staff numbered two bank clerks, at an annual salary of £80.[44]

This was a further period of growth for Birmingham, with the population of 25,000 doubling by 1780. The Taylor & Lloyds Bank was the first in Birmingham, and one of the first outside London. Hutton describes how commerce operated before the creation of the bank and how it changed the way business was undertaken:

'Perhaps a public bank is as necessary to the health of the commercial body, as exercise to the natural... Few places are without: Yet Birmingham, famous in the annals of traffic, could boast no such claim. To remedy this defect therefore, about every tenth trader was a banker, or, a retailer of cash. At the head of whom were marshalled the whole train of drapers and grocers, till the year 1765, when a regular bank was established by Messrs. Taylor and Lloyd, two opulent tradesmen, whose credit being equal to that of the bank of England, quickly collected the shining rays of sterling property into its focus.'[45]

---

42 T.R. Gilbert, J.B. Boothroyd, *The Lloyds of Lloyds Bank,* Supplement to *The Dark Horse* (Lloyds Bank Staff Magazine: June 1951), p.3

43 Polly Hamilton, 'Taylor, John (1710/11-1775)', *Oxford Dictionary of National Biography,* (Oxford: 2004, updated 2013)

44 Gilbert, Boothroyd, *The Lloyds of Lloyds Bank,* p.5

45 Hutton, *An History of Birmingham,* p.83

The bank was successful, having 227 customers, mainly business traders and manufacturers, by 1775. They opened a bank in London, securing a necessary link to trade in the capital, with Lloyd's son-in-law Osgood Hanbury founding the Hanbury, Taylor, Lloyd and Bowman bank in 1770 in Lombard Street.

Sadly, both John Taylor and Sampson Lloyd would not live much longer. Taylor died in Bath on 27th March, 1775, and is buried in a family vault in St. Philip's Cathedral. Taylor had left his family a considerable legacy, due to his 'extraordinary Ingenuity and indefatigable Diligence', according to Aris's Birmingham Gazette on 3rd April 1775.[46]

Sampson Lloyd died on 30th November 1779, at the age of eighty, and was buried in Bull Lane, a Quaker cemetery. He left partnerships in the ironworks and banking businesses to his three eldest sons, and his fourth son John became a partner in the Hanbury, Taylor, Lloyd and Bowman bank in 1790. He also left a tobacco business.

Banking continued to be a major part of both families' business interests, and gradually the Lloyd family dispensed with the ironworks and foundry to concentrate on banking exclusively. With the death of James Taylor in 1852, John Taylor Senior's grandson, the Taylor family withdrew from the bank and it became Lloyd's & Company. Lloyd's descendants achieved the continued development of the business, so that it is now one of the 'Big Four' British clearing banks. His descendants achieved positions in public life, one being an MP (also

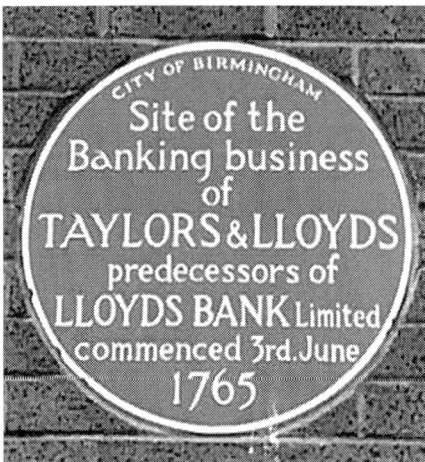

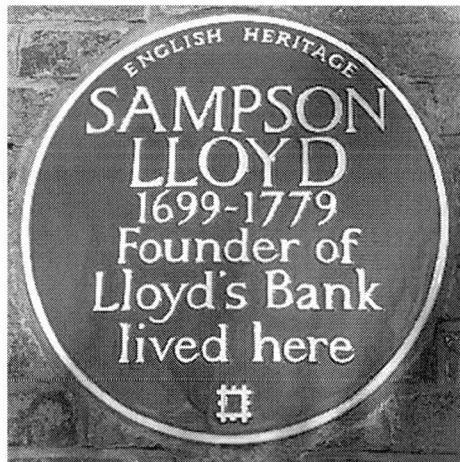

Blue plaques at 64, Dale End, Birmingham, B4 7LS and Lloyds Farmhouse, Farm Park, 139, Sampson Road, Sparkbrook, Birmingham, B11 1HH

46   Hamilton, 'Taylor, John (1710/11-1775)', *Oxford Dictionary of National Biography*

called Sampson), one Lord Mayor of Birmingham (John Henry, 1901-02), and another, Charles, his grandson, being memorialised by a bust at the General Hospital in 'the recognition of a lifetime's work for the welfare and prosperity of that institution'.[47]

Sampson Lloyd's memory is not prominent in Birmingham, being mainly marked by two blue plaques: one was erected by English Heritage, part of its Outside London Series, in 2003, at Lloyds Farmhouse in Sampson Road; the second was erected by the City of Birmingham, appropriately, between Pound Palace and Cash Generator, at 64, Dale End.

Sampson Lloyd II, unknown artist, from the Birmingham Museum and Art Gallery

As well as effective financing, growing businesses needed an effective means of transporting raw materials to and from their factories, throughout the country and the world. Birmingham was by happy accident at the centre of the country's road infrastructure, which was struggling to accommodate the substantial growth in goods and passenger traffic. The town was a natural stopping off point for travellers going north to south and west to east, and back again. Hutton stated that 'From Birmingham, as from a grand centre, issues twelve roads that point to as many towns; some of these, within memory, have scarcely been passable'.[48] As Bunce notes 'Birmingham had communication by means of carriers' carts with one hundred and sixty-eight other towns, ... the whole of the intervening country being thoroughly covered by this means of conveyance'.[49]

The first solution pursued was improvement of roads. During the early eighteenth century, these carried a considerable and increasing amount of traffic. The weight and volume of carts and carriages severely damaged the roadways, as these became hollowed out and rutted, adding further risk of accident and injury. As early as 1692, Digbeth had 'become a holloway, very dangerous and much

47 Gilbert, Boothroyd, *The Lloyds of Lloyds Bank,* p.10
48 Hutton, *An History of Birmingham,* p.262
49 Bunce, *History of the Corporation of Birmingham: with a Sketch of the Earlier Government of the Town,* volume 1, p.49

out of repair… by reason of the daily passing of great numbers of waggons, carts and other carriages, loaded with coals, ironwares and other ponderous goods'.[50] Hutton reported: 'Where any of these roads led up to an eminence, they were worn by the long practice of ages into deep holloways, some of them twelve or fourteen yards below the surface of the banks, with which they were once even, and so narrow as to only admit one passenger'.[51] These worn down thoroughfares are still seen in names locally, such as Holloway Head, Birmingham and Drews Holloway, Halesowen.

As local parishes bore the cost of maintaining roads, they were maintained to very different standards, with a complete absence of planning or oversight between and across areas. To raise funds for road improvements, turnpike roads were introduced, and users were charged to travel on these roads, with the receipts theoretically paying for repairs. As these spread across Birmingham and the Black Country, they helped with business expansion, and with leisure travel. By 1731, it was possible to take a coach from Birmingham to London for one guinea (twenty-one shillings). As well as money, the eighteenth century traveller needed time, as the journey took two and a half days, falling to just nineteen hours by the 1780s. A pistol may have been advisable, to guard against the risk of highway robbery by desperate and well-armed mounted thieves, who might make them 'stand and deliver'.

The volumes of traffic were very high, with fifty-two services offered from Birmingham to London, and sixteen to Bristol. As each coach carried only six people, this meant congestion on deteriorating roads. For business, this was neither quick nor sustainable, and entrepreneurs began looking for alternatives. The solution was the development of a system of inter-connected canals, giving a massive transformative impetus to trade and manufacturing, as it opened access to rivers and sea-ports. When fully developed, from Birmingham in the centre of the country, it was possible to bring in raw materials from almost anywhere in the country, and from abroad, and to sell products in these areas as well. Although transportation remained slow, the major advantage of canals was the weight each vessel could carry, far in excess of the capacity of carriages using roads. Over thirty years, the expanding canal network linked Birmingham to Bristol, London, Liverpool and Hull, so trade could literally flow in all directions on the 'Silver Cross'. Individual businesses built their own wharves and branches as off-shoots from the main canals, as seen with the disturbance of the late John Baskerville.

---

50 Skipp, *A History of Greater Birmingham – down to 1830*, p.46
51 Hutton, *An History of Birmingham*, p.20

At the height of their use, there were more than 550 such privately built branches and basins in Birmingham and the Black Country, all providing access to the thirty-three miles of canals.

Canals were immediately attractive to businessmen as improved transport, but also as an investment opportunity. Most prominent businessmen took full advantage to expand their businesses and their personal fortunes. Many of those appearing in this book from this period, including James Keir and Samuel Galton Jnr, had no expertise in canals (unlike Watt who worked on canal surveying in Scotland before coming to Birmingham), but they held shares in canal companies, established by Act of Parliament and operated in a fiercely competitive market place. The expectation of large profits drove investment rapidly and canal companies were profitable, although their investors could not have foreseen the development of railway and motorised transport that would render canals largely unused for business by the late nineteenth century.

Development of new canals proceeded rapidly and ubiquitously from the 1770s. It is argued that they made the definitive contribution to the expansion and industrialisation of Birmingham. Sir Frank Price, Lord Mayor, wrote in July 1969: 'It is a fact that Birmingham was launched into the powerful industrial position it now enjoys by the decision made 200 years ago to extend the canal system from the Black Country right into the heart of the city.'[52]

In January 1767, a meeting was held at The Swan Inn (near the junction of High Street and New Street), by a group of local businessmen. The focus was on the feasibility of cutting a canal from Wolverhampton to Birmingham so that coal could be brought easily and relatively cheaply from Black Country collieries into the town's factories. James Brindley, an engineer based in Leek, Staffordshire, had developed expertise in surveying and cutting early canals and was commissioned for this project, so was present at this meeting. His survey to build a canal to join the Staffordshire and Worcestershire Canal (which went from Great Hayward to the River Severn) was presented on 4th June, as announced in Aris's Gazette on 15th July 1767. The cost was to be £50,000, an enormous sum, of which £35,000 was already secured. Each canal development required parliamentary approval, taking a further year, with the Act of Parliament passed on 24th February, and royal assent on 26th July 1768. This caused great rejoicing in Birmingham with church bells rung in celebration. The cutting of the canal progressed, but costs were higher than predicted. In fact, the canal cost £100,000, double Brindley's

---

52 Bird, *Portrait of Birmingham*, p.73

original estimate, and the first part, from Paradise Street to Wednesbury, opened on 6th November 1769. Further extensions linked this to the Staffordshire and Worcestershire Canal, at Autherley Junction, by 1772, extending its length to over twenty-two miles. The original shares, at £140 each, proved an extremely sound investment, being worth more than £1,000 by 1792. Its completion was heralded in verse by John Freeth, the Birmingham poet and an investor himself, in his poem 'Inland Navigation: An Ode':

'Then revel in gladness, let harmony flow,
From the district of Bordesley to Paradise-Row;
For true feeling joy in each breast must be wrought,
When Coals under Five-pence per hundred are bought.'[53]

This reflected the reduction in costs that better transport brought and optimism for the expansion of Birmingham's trade across Europe.

James Brindley was central to the development of the canal system locally, being the lead engineer on many canal developments, and training many other engineers, as well as inspiring others who followed him, including Thomas Telford. Although he made an impact in every part of the country, he is included here as the impact of canals on Birmingham helped to change how its businesses operated, bringing employment, wealth and prosperity, enabling the town to grow further very rapidly.

JAMES BRINDLEY
'The Father of the Canals … who made water run uphill.
Britain's first civil engineer'

James Brindley was born in 1716 (no precise date is recorded) in Tunstead, Wormhill, north of Buxton, Derbyshire. His father, also James (1684-1769/70) married Susannah Bradley (1695-1779) in Chesterfield on 25th June 1716, and Susannah is said to have been the stabilising influence in the lives of James and his six younger siblings.

The family moved to a farm at Lowe Hill, Leek, owned by Richard Bowman of Stockley Hall, Tutbury, an uncle of James Senior, who originally bought part of the farm from Richard and later inherited it entirely, in December 1727. It also accommodated Ellen, Richard's sister and James Senior's mother.

---

53   Bird, *Portrait of Birmingham*, p.75; Upton, *A History of Birmingham*, p.88

The children were educated at home, and probably attended school at the Quaker Meeting House in Leek. Although able to read and write, Fairclough notes that James's spelling in his notes is phonetic, indicating a lack of formal education.[54] He showed more ability in the practical application of learning than in education for its own sake. Young James constructed rudimentary mills out of wood and tested them out in local streams.

At seventeen, in 1733, James Junior began an apprenticeship with Abraham Bennett, who manufactured mills and wheels. Although experiencing some problems initially, having built a cartwheel with the spokes leaning in rather than out, Brindley enjoyed his work and was successful. As Harold Bode records, he impressed a mill-owning client so much in 1735 that Bennett was persuaded to allow James to repair his machinery at a silk mill in Macclesfield which had been damaged by fire. Brindley was meticulous in his approach, and although this was commendable, Bennett found the time he took infuriating, complaining 'Thou knows that firmness of wark's the ruin o' trade [sic]!'[55]

Brindley's dedication was evident in his response to his employer's failure to survey properly work to be done in constructing a new paper-mill at Wildboarclough. Bennett got drunk on his visit to a similar mill at Smedley, on the River Irwell, and returned without an adequate assessment of how the work should be undertaken. Brindley took his own decision to rectify this, walked twenty-five miles to Manchester on a Saturday evening, and presented himself to Mr Appleton, the Smedley Mill owner the next day. Brindley surveyed the mill and then walked back to Macclesfield. Bennett found Brindley working on the design of the new paper-mill on Monday morning and the work was completed successfully.

Brindley's role in Bennett's business grew, until he was effectively in charge. When Bennett died in 1742, Brindley moved to Mill Street in Leek and set up his own wheelwright business, having wound up Bennett's affairs. Given Leek was a small market town, it was inevitable that he would travel to undertake work on site. He undertook one commission in Leek which still stands. In the 1750s, he re-built the town's corn-mill, on the River Churnet. This required construction of a new mill race, in addition to the mill itself, and a bridge. Although the bridge is now

---

54   K.R. Fairclough, 'Brindley, James (1716-1772)', *Oxford Dictionary of National Biography, vol. 7* (Oxford: 2004), p.659

55   Harold Bode, *James Brindley: An illustrated life of James Brindley, 1716-1772, 2nd edn.,* (Aylesbury, Buckinghamshire: 1980), p.6

closed to traffic, it and the mill remain, 'as sturdy as on the day it was built',[56] some two hundred and eighty years ago. The mill operated until 1944, was purchased by The Brindley Mill Preservation Trust in 1972, and is now a museum.

Brindley's business continued to grow, so he rented additional premises from the Wedgwood family in 1750 to operate as a millwright in Burslem. His work on effectively draining a flooded pit, at Wet Earth Colliery, or Gal Pit, in Clifton, near Manchester, enhanced his reputation as 'the Schemer', who could make any task successful. As the pit was 158 feet deep, he became known as 'the man who made water run uphill'.[57] Brindley's approach to solving problems was to retire to bed to think issues through, which led to a solution. This could take up to three days for complex issues and he retained details of processes and calculations in his excellent memory.

Having worked on mills in Ashbourne, Congleton and Trentham, Brindley came to Birmingham and the Black Country in 1756 to study Newcomen's atmospheric steam engine, including the one which has been reconstructed at Dudley's Black Country Living Museum. Having seen this operating, he built one in Little Fenton, Staffordshire.

By now, Brindley's ingenuity had enhanced his reputation and he was the leading engineer of the time. His ability to include several functions in the mills he designed can be observed in the workings of the flint mill he constructed at Tunstall, Staffordshire, in 1757. This enabled the mechanical grinding of flint, used in pottery making, by constructing a water wheel to power the stamping machinery, in place of hand-grinding and hammers. Simultaneously, the motion of the water wheel drove a crank which moved slide rods operating pumps to drain a mine two hundred yards away. The durability of his mechanical applications is seen in the fact that his system continued to operate well for fifty years.

Given his expertise in the use and control of water for industrial purposes, it is not surprising that Brindley was asked to survey the building of a canal. In 1758, his first survey was for a canal to link the Rivers Trent and Mersey, and although he confirmed its feasibility, it was deemed to be too expensive and the project did not proceed. Another canal project, however, would make Brindley's reputation in this new specialist area, bringing him a great deal of work, and significant wealth – the Bridgewater Canal.

Francis Egerton, third Duke of Bridgewater, had inherited considerable estates including coal mines in Worsley, near Manchester. He obtained the required Act

---

56 Bode, *James Brindley: An illustrated life of James Brindley, 1716-1772*, pp.9-10
57 Ibid., p.14

of Parliament in March 1759, which authorised the construction of a canal from Worsley to Salford, where coal was sold. From 1st July 1759, Brindley took forty-six days surveying the route, until October, and proposed that the canal should join another planned canal, from Manchester to the Trent and Mersey Canal. As this differed from the premise of the 1759 Act, Brindley travelled to London, five days on horseback, to present evidence to a Parliamentary Committee and a revised Act was passed in early 1760.

The Worsley to Manchester Canal included a considerable feat of engineering, the Barton Aqueduct. Instead of using several locks to lower the level of the canal to the River Irwell, Brindley built the largest aqueduct constructed in Britain to that date. It was 200 yards long, 12 yards wide and its three arches stood 39 feet above the Irwell. The centre arch span was 63 feet, and it attracted considerable attention. When it opened on 17th July 1761, crowds formed to see the incredible sight of sailing boats cross it, high above the river. The Barton Aqueduct remained in use for one hundred and thirty-three years, until 1894. Although successful, canal construction was expensive, with the Worsley Canal costing a huge 1,000 guineas for every mile built.

Brindley's other major innovation in canal building was the technique of 'puddling clay', a watertight clay-based material used to line canals, ensuring that they did not leak into the countryside. The process involves chopping clay or loam with a spade, and mixing it with a small amount of water to produce a plastic type material. Coarse sand or grit may be added to prevent rodents excavating it. The puddled clay was used as a lining for the sides and bottom of the canal, ten inches thick at the sides and three feet thick at the bottom, built up in layers. Puddle clay has to remain wet to retain its waterproof properties, so it is crucial that the canal structure is always filled with water, or the puddle clay would dry out.

Brindley's approach was to follow the natural landscape, termed 'contouring', to avoid excessive earth moving, which was done by hand and therefore labour intensive and expensive. It did, however, result in canals being longer than a direct route would have created. A striking example of this is the decision to build twelve locks (six ascending, six descending) on the Wolverhampton to Birmingham Canal to climb the hill at Smethwick. This was done in preference to tunnelling beneath the land, but resulted in problems in sustaining the water supply to maintain the system. It was overcome initially by Boulton and Watt building the Smethwick engine, one of the earliest steam engines, in May 1779, which pumped the water back up the hill, a height of thirty-one feet. It operated until 1891, a remarkable piece of engineering, the oldest steam engine in the world, and can still be seen operating at the Thinktank Science Museum, at Millennium Point, Birmingham. This approach had its critics, even from its early years of use. Hutton notes that Birmingham is at the same level as the pits with which the canal connects, so 'what benefit then would accrue to commerce, could the boats travel a dead flat of fourteen miles without interruption?' He answers his own question – trade would increase, journey times would reduce, along with costs, and the waste of water.[58] This system remained until the 1820s, when Thomas Telford tunnelled through the hill, cutting out the locks and shortening the journey by two miles and three hours.

Brindley's successes brought involvement in further canal projects, including attendance at Parliament to secure approval. In one Committee meeting, in January 1762, he used a large cheese to explain how an aqueduct works, as an 'ocular demonstration', or visual aid, and drew in chalk on a Committee Room floor to explain the working of a lock.

To some contemporaries, used to educated men leading significant change, Brindley's lack of erudition and polish could be off-putting. Dr John Aiken wrote in 1795 that Brindley was 'in appearance and manners as well as acquirements a mere peasant. Unlettered and rude of speech, it was easier for him to devise means of executing a design, than to communicate his ideas concerning it to others'.[59]

For those interested in outcomes and profitability, he was seen differently, described as 'the great Mr Brindley, who handles rock as easily as you would plum pies, and makes the four elements subservient to his will…when he speaks, all ears listen, and every mind is filled with wonder, at the things he pronounces to be practicable'.[60]

In private life, Brindley remained unmarried until 1765. He had however fathered a son with Mary Bennett, of Burslem. John was baptised on 31st August 1760 and remained with his mother, retaining her name. He was the great-great-grandfather of Arnold Bennett, the famous novelist and chronicler of the life of the Potteries.

On 8th December 1765, Brindley married Anne Henshall, daughter of John Henshall, a land surveyor, and business associate of Brindley since 1762, in Newchapel, near Tunstall, Staffordshire. Brindley was forty-nine, and Anne only nineteen. After the wedding, they moved into Turnhurst Hall, Newchapel, bought jointly with Brindley's brother John, Anne's brother Hugh, and Thomas Gilbert. The estate included the Golden Lion Colliery, and was conveniently located near

---

58   Hutton, *An History of Birmingham*, pp.267-8
59   Cited in Bode, *James Brindley: An illustrated life of James Brindley, 1716-1772*, p.22
60   Ibid., p.38

to his Burslem workshop and the construction site of the Grand Trunk Canal. Brindley built an experimental lock on the estate, the width of which was dictated by the 'starvationers', the boats used at Worsley mine, later called narrowboats. This decision determined the width of locks in virtually all of Brindley's canals and had far-reaching consequences, requiring the use of narrowboats throughout the English canal system.

Anne helped manage the business, using her superior writing skills. Her brother Hugh became Brindley's assistant and later general manager of the Trent and Mersey Canal Company.

In February 1768, an Act of Parliament, promoted by those local businessmen who met at the Swan Inn, approved the canal from Birmingham to Wolverhampton, which would be twenty-four miles long. Brindley was appointed the Engineer and Surveyor at £200 per year. The investors supported the scheme and it was completed in September 1772, just nine days before Brindley died.

In the mid-1760s, Brindley developed a scheme to link the ports of London, Bristol, Liverpool and Hull by constructing a 'Grand Cross' of canals to join together the Rivers Thames, Severn, Mersey and Trent. The first canal built was originally 'The Canal from the Trent to the Mersey', but Brindley suggested naming it 'The Grand Trunk Canal', to describe its function of providing connections. Extensions to Coventry, Derby and Birmingham were also planned.

Josiah Wedgwood was at the first public meeting to discuss the Grand Trunk Canal at Wolseley Bridge, Staffordshire, on 30th December 1765. He commented that Brindley presented the case 'with such extraordinary lucidity of detail as to make them clear to the dullest intellect present'.[61] Wedgwood was so impressed that he committed £1,000 to expenses and a large number of shares.

The Grand Trunk was approved by Parliament on 3rd May 1766, and work began at Brownhills on 26th July 1766. Wedgwood cut the first sod, which Brindley took away in a wheelbarrow. As Surveyor-General, Brindley was paid £200 per year, his brother John was a member of the management committee, with Wedgwood as unpaid treasurer. Hugh Henshall was paid £150 per year as Clerk of Works. Wedgwood was so convinced of the benefits of the enterprise that he relocated his pottery business to alongside the canal, building the world-famous 'Etruria', named after decorated pottery discovered in Pompeii.

The Canal was a major undertaking, with 76 locks, 160 aqueducts and 213 road bridges along its ninety-three miles, and Brindley expected to complete it by

---

61   Bode, *James Brindley: An illustrated life of James Brindley, 1716-1772*, p.30

1772, but was delayed by problems in constructing a tunnel through Harecastle Hill, near Stoke-on-Trent. This is notable, as it was the first tunnel constructed for transport purposes in Britain. At one and three quarter miles long, it required considerable engineering to make it flat for its whole length. It was finished in May 1777, five years after Brindley's death. It had no towpaths, so boats were poled or legged through, at 1s 6d per boat. Legging required boatmen to lie on their backs, on top of the goods carried, and push their feet against the tunnel walls to propel the narrowboat.

Sadly, Brindley saw only two arms of his Grand Cross completed, the Grand Trunk and the Staffordshire and Worcestershire Canals, as he died at the early age of fifty-six in 1772.

In that year, Wedgwood commissioned Brindley to survey a canal from his Etruria factory to Froghall in the River Churnet valley, to be called the Caldon Canal. In September 1772, while undertaking this survey, Brindley was caught in a heavy downpour and soaked to the skin, catching a chill. Taken to an inn in the village of Ipstones, unfortunately, and avoidably, he was put into a damp bed, which exacerbated his illness. He became very ill and was taken home to Turnhurst, where Dr. Erasmus Darwin attended him and diagnosed diabetes. Remarkably, he received and advised visitors who were having problems with their canal project while lying in what would be his death bed. Brindley did not recover, and as Wedgwood recorded on 28th September: 'He died on 27th inst. about 12 at noon, after giving him something to wet his mouth, he said, "It's enough, I shall need no more", and shut his eyes, never more to open.'[62]

Brindley's widow Anne, only twenty-six, was left with two daughters, Susannah and Anne. Anne Senior remarried in 1775, to Robert Williamson, one of Brindley's assistants, and they had seven children. Williamson died in 1799, while Anne survived, a widow again, until 1826.

James Brindley was buried at St. James's Church, Newchapel, Staffordshire on 30th September 1772. The church was rebuilt in 1880 as a memorial to him. He is remembered throughout the country, in a wide range of plaques in Wormhill, Birmingham, Leek, Stone, Stoke-on-Trent, Worsley, Sutton (near Macclesfield), and on his grave at Newchapel, with a timeline detailing his life and achievements. Unfortunately, this records his date of death inaccurately, as 25th September. Another expansive epitaph, with an ironic final twist, was published in 'The Chester Courant', on 1st December 1772:

---

62 Bode, *James Brindley: An illustrated life of James Brindley, 1716-1772*, p.45

'JAMES BRINDLEY lies amongst these Rocks,
He made Canals, Bridges, and Locks,
To convey Water; he made Tunnels
for Barges, Boats, and Air-Vessels…
He knew Water, its Weight and Strength,
Turn'd Brooks, made Soughs to a great Length…
There ne'er was paid such Attention
As he did to Navigation.
But while busy with Pit or Well,
His Spirits sunk below Level;
And, when too late, his Doctor found,
Water sent him to the Ground.'[63]

The variety of memorials to Brindley is remarkable, more than dedicated to any other subject in this book. They include the well in Wormhill; streets named after him (in Birmingham and Etruria, Stoke-on-Trent); statues (an excellent example at Coventry Canal Basin, and in Etruria); residential developments close to canals (James Brindley Basin in Manchester and James Brindley Wharf in Kidderminster); the Brindley Arts Centre, Runcorn; the James Brindley Science College and the Brindley's Lock public house, in Stoke-on-Trent; the James Brindley Schools, Birmingham, providing education for children in hospitals; and a wooden coal barge at Walkden, Salford, on the Bridgewater estates. Brindley's sculpted face looks down on his Old Main Line Canal from the wall of the Energy Centre of the International Convention Centre in Broad Street, Birmingham. The largest memorial is the adjacent commercial, residential and leisure development, Brindley Place. There are further, less substantial, memorials: in 2009, the Royal Mail issued a First Day Cover, and there was even a James Brindley vegetarian pizza offered by the Stable Restaurant in John Bright Street, although this is no longer available!

This range of memorials is unusual, but recognises the contribution he made to many communities, by linking them and providing access by canals. Of course, the greatest memorial is the collection of canals he left, covering 365 miles, which continue to give the opportunity for leisure activities in England's beautiful countryside, albeit not their original purpose. Brindley was involved in twenty-three canal schemes, only five of which were not completed by him or his associates.

---

63   Cited in *James Brindley*, no date

Known as 'The Father of the Canals', he left a legacy of trained engineers who continued to extend the canal network according to his principles, and frequently using his surveys. He is remembered as the first civil engineer in a country famous for its excellence in this area.

His collaborator and friend Josiah Wedgwood wrote two days before he died that James Brindley was 'a valuable friend, and … one of the great Geniuses who seldom live to see justice done to their singular abilities, but must trust to future ages for that tribute of praise and fair fame they so greatly merit from their fellow mortals'.[64] It seems that the future ages have appropriately remembered James Brindley's singular abilities.

Blue plaque at the Star Inn, 21, Stafford Street, Stone, ST15 8QW

Statue of James Brindley, Coventry Canal Basin, 10a, St Nicholas Street, Coventry, CV1 4LY

Canal development and expansion in and around Birmingham continued through the nineteenth and into the early twentieth centuries, with ten waterways built. Five were developed by Birmingham Canal Navigations, with others cut by companies named to reflect the routes their canals pursued: the Worcester & Birmingham (1815), the Stratford upon Avon (1816), the Dudley (1798), the

---

64   Bode, *James Brindley: An illustrated life of James Brindley, 1716-1772*, p.45

Warwick & Birmingham (1800) and the Birmingham & Warwick Junction (1840). These canals attracted industrial development, with factories, depots and wharves built on their banks, so that by 1839, there were around 70 steam engines and more than 120 wharves along one stretch of canal in Birmingham. By the end of the nineteenth century, the Birmingham Canal Navigation system carried 8.5 million tonnes of goods.

Canals continued to be an important element of trade until the middle of the nineteenth century, but decline set in as railways and motor transport expanded. Despite increases in canal miles built, this competition signalled a significant decline which accelerated after World War I. The canals fell into disrepair and disuse, and as redevelopment took place, many were filled in and covered by commercial or housing developments. Those remaining are now used primarily for leisure purposes, through pleasure trips and boating holidays.

Birmingham clearly changed substantially over the years leading up to the end of the eighteenth century, with changes driven by the growth of trade and business. But what sort of town was Birmingham in these days? How had the burgeoning of trade affected its people, its geography, how it was governed, and what did people do for entertainment?

The first history of Birmingham, by William Hutton, was published in 1782. Rightly called 'the first historian of Birmingham', Hutton's account is detailed, entertaining, and illuminating.

The life of William Hutton himself deserves detailed attention.

WILLIAM HUTTON
'Birmingham's first historian, now, ironically, largely forgotten'

The life of William Hutton, Birmingham's first historian, was long, eventful and remarkably productive, given that he had little formal education. He began work as an apprentice in a silk mill, before being apprenticed to his uncle as a stocking maker, then working as a journeyman in this trade, in Nottingham. Aspiring to better his station in life, he taught himself bookbinding, and set himself up as a bookbinder and bookseller in Birmingham in 1750.

Marrying in 1755, he settled permanently in Birmingham and became a prosperous paper dealer, then invested in land and property. He became one of the foremost inhabitants of the town, with public office following. At the late age of fifty-six, he began writing history and wrote fourteen books between 1781 and 1808, including histories of Birmingham and Derby, his life story, and tales of the extensive tours he took with his wife and daughter. He was extremely fit, walking many miles every day, for work and pleasure, and this secured an unusually long life, as he died just before his ninety-third birthday in 1815.

Hutton's works are a treasure trove and are extensively quoted. Quotations from 'An History of Birmingham' use the expanded second edition, published in 1783, and include his spelling, punctuation and italics to capture the flavour of his commentary.

Let's begin with Hutton's life. William Hutton was born on 30th September 1723, in Full Street, Derby, a middle child of nine to his father William Hutton (born 1691, died 1758), a woolcomber, and his first wife (of three), Anne. Complaining of harsh treatment in his early life, the family was beset by poverty. His mother's reaction at his birth was less than loving: 'my mother observed, I was the largest child she ever had, but so very ordinary (a softer word for ugly), she was afraid she should never love me.'

This changed as he grew, and he comments that 'I had no cause to complain during the nine remaining years of her life.'[65] She died on 9th March 1733, five weeks after giving birth, yet again. Hutton experienced the nasty, brutish and short nature of life very early, as the family's poverty was so severe that Hutton was sent aged four to live with an uncle, a grocer and bachelor at Mountsorrel, and 'three crabbed aunts' who lived together at Swithland. He was treated harshly, with little love: 'I can recollect numberless instances of insult, but not one civil thing they ever said.' He was called 'ugly' by them, and says, forlornly and with resentment: 'They might have considered that this, and other evils, were out of my power to remove.'[66]

Returning to the family home in 1728, his father's welcome was less than effusive: 'My father, who had not seen me for fifteen months, received me with only two words, and those marked with indifference, "So, Bill".'[67]

Hutton did not receive much of a formal education, but was taught to read by his father, whom he describes in a rare complimentary view as well-informed, and 'by far the best speaker I ever heard in low life, and nearly the best in any life.'[68] Attending school between the ages of five and seven, Hutton experienced further harsh treatment, when a teacher, appropriately named Thomas Meat, tried to inculcate learning by beating 'my head against the wall, holding it by the hair,

---

65   William Hutton, (1816) *The Life of William Hutton*, (Studley, Warwickshire: 1816), p.1
66   Ibid., p.3
67   Ibid., p.4
68   Ibid., p.183

but never could beat any learning into it; I hated all books but those of pictures.'[69] Fortunately for us, his view later changed.

At home, he was required to look after the family, including his father, even though he was not the oldest. At the age of six, options for him to begin work were considered, including winding quills for a weaver or stripping tobacco for a grocer, but it was concluded that he was too young. This was only a brief respite, as the next year, 1730, he began working at a silk-mill. Too short to reach the machinery, he was forced to wear pattens (shoes or clogs with raised soles or iron rings). He was 'by far the least and the youngest' of the 300 people employed. For seven years, he endured harsh, demanding conditions, rising at 5am, being caned by the master, and 'the constant companion of the most rude and vulgar of the human race'.[70] Although he had not experienced formal education, he had informal teaching from a former schoolmistress who lived with the family and was greatly influenced by Catherine, his older sister.

His lack of education is often evident in his writing, in his sometimes rough use of language. His autobiography, published after his death in 1816, has the gloriously lengthy title of 'The Life of William Hutton, F.A.S.S. including a particular account of The Riots in Birmingham in 1791, to which is subjoined, The History of His Family, written by himself, and published by his daughter, Catherine Hutton'. F.A.S.S. is the acronym for a Fellow of the Antiquarian Society of Scotland, to which he was elected after the publication of his 'An History of Birmingham' in 1782.

This 'Life' is divided into anecdotes from individual years, providing short, highly readable episodes. He acknowledges his humble beginnings in the 'Preface', saying 'I have only the history of an individual, struggling, unsupported, up a mountain of difficulties'.[71] This is plain speaking and draws us to him in a bond of trust, giving confidence in his story. Writing from his prodigious memory, even at the age of seventy-five, he says he is 'carrying my life in my head.' This is well-known among his family and friends: 'Those who know me are not surprised,'[72] and this is reinforced by his daughter Catherine. Some commentators have doubted his accuracy, as Carl Chinn identified in his introduction to Hutton's 'Life', but he draws attention to the importance of Hutton's capture of the then spirit of Birmingham, and occasional inaccuracies should not detract from the value of

---

69 Hutton, *The Life of William Hutton*, p.5
70 Ibid., p.6
71 Ibid., p.xxv
72 Ibid., p.xxv

the work. As Professor Chinn indicates, Hutton 'was an intelligent, thoughtful and perceptive man whose work has stimulated and made easier the researches of later students of Birmingham.'[73]

When Hutton wrote his History, there was no standard template or accepted style of history writing to follow. He was an innovator, writing from experience and heart, and we lose little by giving him the benefit of the doubt. Although he incorrectly concludes that the Metchley Park Roman settlement was the work of the Danes, Chinn's conclusion is unequivocal: 'Read Hutton. Read the life of the man who was our first historian. Above all, read the words of a man who drew deep into his being the essence of Birmingham.'[74]

Hutton mentions the birth of Sarah Cock, on 11th March 1731, at Aston upon Trent, six miles from Derby, as this child would become his wife twenty-four years later, and would 'be my faithful and dear companion, and love me better than herself.'[75]

A few days after his mother's death in 1733, his father sold up and took three of his children and moved in with a widow, who had four children of her own. Incredibly, Hutton was not taken, leaving this nine year old boy in a desperate position, and Hutton strangely does not explain where, or with whom, he lived: 'My mother gone, my father at the ale-house, and I among strangers, my life was forlorn. I was almost without a home, nearly without clothes, and experienced a scanty cupboard.'[76]

At the end of the silk-mill apprenticeship, he carved 'W.H. 1737' into a top rail at the mill, which he saw again in 1790, fifty-three years later. He had no regret at leaving 'that place, for which I had a sovereign contempt…which gave me a seven years' heart-ache'. He began another apprenticeship, to his uncle George, a stocking-maker in Nottingham. This ended in 1744, when Hutton was twenty-one, but he stayed with his uncle until his death in 1746.

As an adolescent, he could not afford to dress as well as he wished to engage with young women, having to earn five shillings and tenpence a week before he could take any money, which was not always possible, especially as he had to make up any shortfall himself. By 1741, he was prospering more, and gently satirises the preening of his younger self: 'The girls eyed me with some attention; nay, I eyed myself as much as any of them.' This happier phase of his life was interrupted by

73 Chinn, Carl, Introduction to *The Life of William Hutton*, (Studley, Warwickshire: 1998), p.xvii
74 Hutton, *The Life of William Hutton*, p.xxiv
75 Ibid., p.6
76 Ibid., p.9

an argument he had with Uncle George 'upon a mere trifle', which 'caused me to run away, blasted my views, sunk me in the dust, and placed me in a degraded point of view, from which I did not recover for five years.'[77]

Given the dramatic nature of this momentous incident, Hutton cleverly changes the form of the narrative from short annual memories to 'The History of a Week', written from memory thirty-eight years later. He utilises this technique to great effect again later, when describing the four days of riots in July 1791. This difference in style strongly emphasizes the importance of these days within the overall tale, as it takes up nine pages.[78] The argument was prompted by Hutton working below the level required, as he acknowledges: 'five days had passed, and I had done little more than the work of four.' As the argument developed, Hutton confesses that he was surly, dismissive and recalcitrant, so his uncle thrashed him. Despite his uncle's attempt at conciliation the following day, Hutton behaves as an offended teenager: 'I thanked him with a sullen *no*.' He decided to leave, being 'much more hurt in mind' than physically, and ran away, stealing money as he left: 'I found ten shillings, I took two, and left eight.' He set out, 'a lad of seventeen, not elegantly dressed, nearly five feet high, rather Dutch built, with a long narrow bag of brown leather,' and acknowledges that he had 'a spacious world before me, and no plan of operations.' He walked to Derby, Burton and Lichfield, sleeping in a barn and leaving his belongings there, only to find that on his return from walking around the town, they had been stolen. This generated, unsurprisingly, a crisis for this headstrong seventeen year old. He had no alternative but to sleep in the street 'upon a butcher's block'.

Advised by a stranger to go to Walsall to find work as a stocking-maker, he discovered that he had been misled as there were no stocking frames there, and he pushed on to Birmingham, passing, to his surprise, women working as nailers in blacksmiths' shops in the outskirts.

He approached the town from Handsworth Heath, and was clearly entranced by both the sight of Birmingham and its people. Seeking employment, he was suspected of being what he was, a runaway apprentice, and failed with the three stocking-makers in Birmingham. His last discussion was with Francis Grace, who knew his family in Derby. Ironically, although refused employment, Hutton would marry Grace's niece, Sarah Cock, fourteen years later, inherit his house in New Street, and write his 'Life' at the same counter at which he stood, distraught and desperate, thirty-eight years earlier.

Later that day, at 7pm, Hutton was resting on the north side of the Old Cross, when he was approached by two young Brummies in aprons. Seeing his dishevelled state, they took pity on him, bought him beer, bread and cheese at the Bell Inn in Philip Street, and obtained him lodging for the night. So he stayed his first night, 14th July 1741, in Birmingham, 'the seat of civility'. From there he travelled, always on foot, to Coventry, Nuneaton, Ashby-de-la-Zouch and then back to Derby, arriving there on 18th July, having failed to find work. Going to his father's home, he was reconciled with his Uncle George the following day, but had to make up for his losses which took him two years to pay off.

Hutton reluctantly continued working as a stocking-maker with his uncle in Nottingham, during which time he taught himself to play a dulcimer he made himself from a large trunk, 'one of the relics of my family'. Clearly very skilled with his hands, he was determinedly self-taught in playing this instrument, taking six months to learn.

On leaving his apprenticeship at Christmas 1745, he had saved no more than seven pounds after fourteen years' work, and had to make his own way in the world. In 1746, he drew closer to his sister Catherine, who encouraged him to read and learn. He began to acquire book-binding skills, again learning the techniques himself. As 'money was wanting', Hutton demonstrated his resourcefulness, by buying 'three Volumes of the Gentleman's Magazine, 1742, 3, and 4….I fastened them together in a most cobbled style. These afforded me a treat.' He learned all the skills of book-binding from observing a 'shabby bookseller': 'it is a wonder and a fact that I never saw him perform one act but I could perform it myself, so strong was the desire to attain the art.' The first book he bound was 'a very small one, Shakespeare's Venus and Adonis.' He also bought a binding press from the bookseller, and improved its function easily, to the bookseller's chagrin: 'This proved for 42 years my best binding press.'[79]

His Uncle George died in his arms in September 1746, with Hutton surprised at the affection he held for him: 'I was ignorant how much I loved him till my sorrow for his death informed me.'[80] On a visit to his father, Hutton reflects the latter's lack of care for him: 'My father, being elevated with liquor, and by my arrival, rose in extasy [sic], and gave me the first kiss, and, I believe, the last, he ever gave me.'

He began writing verse, which 'gave no offence' and stayed on his shelf 'till the rioters burnt them in 1791.' In 1749, encouraged by his sister's loan of three guineas, Hutton walked 125 miles in three days to London, to obtain the materials

---

79 Hutton, *The Life of William Hutton*, p.30
80 Ibid., p.31

he needed to set up as a book-binder: 'three alphabets of letters, a set of figures, and some ornamental tools for gilding books; with leather, and boards, for binding.' Although he walked around the capital for three days, before the three day walk home, he was far less impressed by London than Birmingham. He proclaimed that he met prejudice from Londoners, because he was poor and because of his 'Northern voice'. He was less than complimentary: 'London surprised me; so did the people, for the few with whom I formed a connexion deceived me, by promising what they never performed.'[81]

By now he had decided that his long term goal was to establish himself in business in Birmingham, as a book-binder and bookseller, and as a preliminary step, he set up shop in Southwell, a 'despicable' market town fourteen miles from Nottingham. Every Saturday, Hutton walked to his shop starting out at 5am, carrying up to thirty pounds of books, opened the shop at ten o'clock, ate bread, cheese and drank half a pint of ale, took from one to six shillings, closed the shop at four, and walked five miles back. This required strength, determination and fortitude: 'Nothing short of a surprizing resolution and rigid economy, could have carried me through this scene.'[82]

The following year, 1750, Hutton achieved his aim and established himself in Birmingham and was impressed again with the people: 'I must again confess, I was pleased with the active spirit of the people.' On the 11th April, he rented a shop at No.6, Bull Street and 'prepared for a total change of life.' His sister's former employer, Mr. Ambrose Rudsdall, a Dissenting minister, kindly allowed him to purchase part of his library as stock for his shop on 13th May, the sale secured by a promissory note, as Hutton did not have the one pound and seven shillings required. This enabled Hutton to fill his shop with the two hundred pounds in weight of books thus obtained. He entered Birmingham on 25th May, and although lonely for the first year, by then he had saved £20, and was reconciled to his life. He began to gain friends 'when a few young men of elevated character and sense took notice of me.'[83]

The following year, Hutton moved into a shop on High Street, next door to Mr. Grace, and continued to prosper, so that by 1752, he had 'a smiling trade'. Business was not without problems, and he candidly relates how he opened a shop in Bromsgrove, did not turn a profit for two years, and so closed it. His writing of verse continued, with some printed in magazines and periodicals.

---

81   Hutton, *The Life of William Hutton*, p.36
82   Ibid., p.37
83   Ibid., pp.37-42

1752 brought Sarah Cock to be her uncle Francis Grace's housekeeper, next door to Hutton. Coming across her regularly, he described her as 'a little, neat, delicate creature, and rather handsome' but 'she seemed to dislike me, which caused a shyness on my side, and kept us at a distance.'[84] By 1754, the relationship had warmed, and he describes charmingly how they became closer, so that by November, Hutton candidly told Sarah 'that I perceived a growing affection for her, and should take no pains to check it.' Their intimacy increased, and by Christmas 'our hearts had united without efforts on either side.' Hutton was clearly entranced, saying 'nature had given to few women a less portion of deceit.' Sarah's uncle was, however, alarmed at the prospect of losing his housekeeper and took Hutton with him to Moseley on the pretext of collecting a debt in 1755. Having scolded Hutton all the way and indicating his aversion to the match, the settlement of the debt in Moseley put Mr. Grace in a good humour and he agreed to the marriage on the way back. As Hutton the businessman wryly observed: 'Such are the wonderful effects of money.'[85]

Having now accrued £200, Hutton was eligible for a young woman of good family, but visited his sister, whom he had not seen for four years, to obtain her blessing. When he told Catherine the fortune offered by Sarah's parents was small, at £100, she replied, 'A fortune is a trifle; what is the woman?' Hutton answered: 'To my wish.' Catherine's clinching judgement was: 'Then she has a fortune within her.'[86]

Hutton and Sarah married in June 1755, at St. Philip's Church, and he expresses his happiness in all aspects of his marriage for the first time: 'No event in a man's life is more consequential than marriage; nor is any more uncertain. Upon this die his sum of happiness depends.' It was clearly a very happy marriage: 'I found in my wife more than ever I expected to find in woman.'[87] Throughout the rest of 'Life', he returned constantly to the love they shared and how greatly he felt her loss.

The next year brought the birth of his daughter, Catherine, who 'has been the pleasure of my life to this day.' His son Thomas followed in 1757, and they moved into the next door house owned by Mr. Grace, who had died in February, and converted their original home into a warehouse. By this time, Hutton had begun to trade in paper and did so successfully for forty years, 'and acquired an ample fortune.' After the birth of his third child, a second son born on 2nd July, he states

---

84   Hutton, *The Life of William Hutton*, p.43
85   Ibid., p.45
86   Ibid., p.46
87   Ibid., p.47

that as a happy family man, 'I had now three to nurse; all of whom I frequently carried together in my arms. This I could not do without a smile.'[88]

1758 brought investment in a paper mill business, with which he admits he became obsessed, and the death of his father, which he describes in bald brevity: 'Dec. 13, my father died.' There is no further comment.

Having continued to try to build and develop his paper-mill for more than a year, Hutton enters 1760, described as 'a melancholy year'. This entry defines the precariousness and sorrow that could fall so easily upon a family, as a result of poor health. In truth, the family experienced a catastrophic catalogue of illness during this period, and suffered the dreadful loss of a child. When pregnant with their fourth child, Sarah developed jaundice, and 'Her life was despaired of, and I unhappy.' His second son, who is not named, was taken ill, and after four weeks, 'on the 19th of May, we lost him.' The very next day, another son was born. Then, his eldest son contracted measles, then small pox, and before he recovered, Hutton's daughter caught both, as did the new born baby as well. Hutton himself then succumbed to jaundice, and describes taking a bolus, a single dose of medicine, which was so large it had to be cut into seventeen large pills to ingest! Now Sarah was fearful he would die, and 'to preserve my life, ran the utmost hazard of her own.'[89] He did not recover until Michaelmas, the end of September. What a dreadful year for any family to endure, reflecting the hazards of life in the late eighteenth century.

By 1762, Hutton finally gave up on the paper mill, having lost, he estimated, around £1,000 in total. Through hard work, however, his fortunes slowly recovered, to the extent that by 1766, his life was successful and happy, with more leisure time: 'Trade was successful; we enjoyed our little pleasures, and lived happily.'

Hutton had an obsessive side to his nature which became evident in business, and can be perceived as the more unfortunate consequence of his earlier described perseverance and fortitude. Obsessed with buying land and property, he was very successful. In the midst of his improved business life, however, disaster strikes his family again, and in early 1767, he and his wife were ill, and their fever was caught by one of their sons, who received 'ignorant treatment of the apothecary', 'languished from the 15th March to the 3rd April, and then departed….We were inconsolable for the loss of this lovely boy, which was followed by daily tears.' He could not bear to look at his late son's things and he and his wife did not mention him for ten years, 'though he was not one day out of either of our thoughts'.[90]

---

88   Hutton, *The Life of William Hutton*, p.48
89   Ibid., pp.49-50
90   Ibid., p.53

On 8th April 1768, Hutton is chosen to be an Overseer of the Poor, and was understandably proud of being 'elevated beyond my ancestors….They had rather been *the poor* than *overseers of* the poor.' He could not resist adding that his property was worth £2,000, making him very wealthy. He threw himself into this unpaid work, taking on extra work from his colleagues. While he disliked taking money from the poor, he greatly enjoyed helping those in distress. In this year, he led the town's opposition to the Lamp Act, to protect his two properties 'which formed the gate-way entering New Street' and he was successful. Within two years, however, he demonstrated his businessman's instinct for financial advantage, and supported the amendment to the Lamp Act, which brought the demolition of his New Street houses, with him securing compensation for this. The following year Hutton purchased land at Bennett's Hill, near Washwood Heath, and built the country house in which he wrote his life story twenty-nine years later.

Re-appointed as Overseer of the Poor in 1770, he became a Commissioner of the Court of Requests in 1772, a role in resolving small 'causes', which were disputed claims up to forty shillings in value. He relished this effective form of public service: 'there cannot be a more useful service rendered to the public, than that of doing justice between man and man.' Hutton devoted two days a week to this, displaying his obsessiveness again, and stayed on the court for nineteen years, handling more than 100,000 cases. The next year, 1773, he was chosen as a Commissioner of the Lamp and Street Act. Hopeful of making major changes, he quickly became frustrated at the corruption he saw, with fellow commissioners furthering their own interests and supporting, or not punishing, transgressions of their friends. Hutton demonstrates an admirable conscience: 'A rich man also was favoured beyond a poor one.' He soon gave up this role, as he 'lost some friends, and declined attendance.'[91]

Hutton continued to trade successfully, until 1779, 'another year of misfortune', prompted again by health concerns in his family. His wife's decline in health gave him most concern, described as 'the beginning of the worst of my afflictions, the indisposition of my dear wife, from which she never returned into health', and Sarah would gradually decline over seventeen years, until she died. His daughter Catherine had a nervous complaint leading to 'great debility' for years. His own health suffered, and he developed a gum infection leading to an abscess, fever, and boils. While ill, he was cared for by his son 'with the most filial care.' In business, he experienced problems with attorneys and lost a great deal of money,

91   Hutton, *The Life of William Hutton*, pp.56-7

which led him to renounce buying more land: 'Thus I have gone through a year, replete with the largest number of calamities, though not the greatest, that ever occurred to me.'[92]

Perhaps as a distraction from these problems, he spent nine months of 1780 writing his 'An History of Birmingham'. He attests that he wrote 'with dread' as he felt he did not have sufficiently ability, but was reassured by those around him: '*Rollason* the printer was pleased with it, and shewed it to Dr. Withering, who pronounced it the best topographical History he had ever seen.' Seventy-five copies were sold, and as ever, Hutton relates the profit made, £40. To his credit, he recognised his own limitations: 'To venture into the world as an Author, without having had a previous education, was a daring attempt.' He was pleasantly surprised by the reaction of readers: 'This was afterwards considered the best book I ever wrote. I considered it in a less favourable light.'

In the next two years, he re-wrote his 'History', enlarging it, including descriptions of places of antiquity around Birmingham in the second edition, published on 22nd March 1782. On his election as a Fellow of the Antiquarian Society of Scotland, he commented, tongue in cheek, that 'A man may live half a century, and not be acquainted with his own character.' It seems he had been an antiquary without ever suspecting it![93]

Towards the end of 1783, aged sixty, Hutton suffered a serious illness, inflammation in the bowels. By now, he was wealthy enough to receive the best medical care but again complained about the apothecary, 'who was as unacquainted with the disorder as myself.' After two days, he was treated by Dr John Ash, who bled him several times a day, but advised his family and friends he would die. However, by noon on Sunday, Hutton had begun to recover and relates Ash saying to him, comically: 'You are as safe as a bug in a rug.' Hutton's wife sat up three out of four nights with him, even though she was ill herself. His entry for the next year confirms that both he and his wife continued in poor health, and he confirmed his belief that he owed his life to Dr Ash's care.[94]

Travel alleviated their concerns, and as they could afford it, they travelled often. In 1785, Hutton and his wife travelled to Buxton and through the Peak District, visiting his beloved sister Catherine for what would be the last time, as she died in 1786, aged sixty-seven. Hutton recorded what must have been a most distressing conversation with his continually ailing wife, who identified a replacement for her,

---

92 Hutton, *The Life of William Hutton*, pp.62-4
93 Ibid., p.66
94 Ibid., p.67

in the event of her death, which she expected soon. Hutton's was 'affected' and states: 'If her dear shade should hover over me, and observe my action, it will never see another in those arms which have enfolded her. I have now, July 19, 1798, lost her two years and a half, and have never thought of offering that violence to her memory, or my own feelings. Can a cure be found for the man who has lost half of himself?' He remained true to his darling wife for a further seventeen years, until he died. He published his second book, this year, 'The Journey to London', which was 'price two shillings and sixpence.'[95]

The next few years consisted of trips, to Buxton again, Aberystwyth and Shrewsbury, Blackpool, Manchester, Bosworth, and Halstead in Leicestershire, with several books published. He extended his house at Bennett's Hill, as the air was beneficial for Sarah's health, incurring further cost, 635 guineas, in 1790 when he added a coach house, carriage and horses, as his wife's asthma caused difficulty in walking. This required him to buy a few extra yards of land from his neighbour, whom he clearly felt used this to his advantage, prompting a rather bitter comment that 'Pride may induce the Philosopher and the Divine to expatiate upon the dignity and the excellency of man, but we take advantage of each other.'[96]

By 1791, he was happy in his family and work, having stopped buying land, keeping his money in his existing businesses, reducing risk. He had 'no pressure upon the mind', except his wife's ill health.[97]

However, a major event was about to take place, which would seriously worsen his wife's health, change his perspective on the goodness of Birmingham people, and destroy his home and his equanimity and peace of mind.

---

95   Hutton, *The Life of William Hutton*, p.69
96   Ibid., p.72
97   Ibid., p.73

3.

Riot! – Four tumultuous days in Birmingham, 1791

William Hutton's happy family life and contentment in business was shattered during four days beginning on Thursday, 14th July 1791: 'a calamity awaited me I little suspected: the Riots in 1791, which hurt my fortune, destroyed my peace, nearly overwhelmed me and my family, and not only deprived us of every means of restoring to health the best of women, but shortened her days.' He wrote the history of 'that most savage event at the time', within three weeks, but his family opposed its publication, so in 1798 he included in his 'Life' 'with exactness the manuscript copy' of his 'Particular Account of the Riots at Birmingham in 1791'.[98]

The section has its own heading page, entitled 'A Narrative Of The Riots In Birmingham, July 14, 1791, Particularly As They Affected The Author' and covers 25 pages of the total of 146, one sixth of the full content. The riots were clearly the most momentous event of his life, from which he emerges as angry, bitter and damaged, even seven years later.

Hutton's Dedication to 'The Lovers of Riot' ensures he puts their disgraceful behaviour front and centre of the reader. This begins ironically, congratulating them on their 'refined taste for pleasure', but quickly excoriates them as akin to cannibals, who 'devour others to feed yourselves; or, like the destroying angel, scatter destruction without the control of human laws.' His final sentence oozes with contempt and fury: 'You have discovered a conciser way of acquiring property than by the antiquated mode of industry. Yours is the right to take what property you please, destroy the rest, and laugh at the sufferer.'[99]

---

98   Hutton, *The Life of William Hutton*, p.73
99   Ibid., p.77

The Preface conveys bewildered resentment at the lack of gratitude for his public service in The Court Of Requests. His reward for kindness and fairness in judging cases was dreadful: 'For this were my houses destroyed, my person insulted, and my life threatened.' Written three weeks after the riots had taken place, it remains powerfully and understandably raw. He acknowledges that this, his eighth book, is written from the heart, not the head. He is bewildered by the rioters' motives, having experienced harmony in Birmingham for forty years, and recalls with chagrin his description of Birmingham in his 'History', that 'celebrated the mild and peaceable demeanour of the inhabitants, their industry, and hospitality.'[100]

Given Hutton's clear and forceful anger, it is best perhaps to draw on other historians for a view of the reasons behind, and the progress of, the riots, and their ending and outcomes, before returning to Hutton's perspective. Chris Upton, Vivian Bird and Jenny Uglow among others have written accounts, and the main events can be summarised briefly below.

The background to the riots lay in the debate about the nature and benefits, or otherwise, of the French Revolution in 1789. Debate about the monarchy's responsibility to provide for a nation's people might have been inflammatory on its own, given the concern and fear from those in government that such sedition might lead to a revolution in England. It was exacerbated by the fact that many Dissenters, opposed to the dominance of the Church of England in the governance of the country, supported changing how the country was structured, favouring a republic. Religion and politics were entangled irrevocably, hence the rioters shouting their allegiance, to justify their actions, to 'The Church and King'. The riots were also known as the 'Priestley riots', after Dr. Joseph Priestley, who lived locally and had preached at the New Meeting House Chapel from December 1780. Priestley was a prominent proponent of republicanism and eschewed all opportunity to moderate his message, gaining a reputation nationally for powerful and stringent invective against the monarchy and machinery of the state.

The spark that ignited the flame which exploded into a widespread conflagration, metaphorically and literally, was the decision to create a Constitutional Society in Birmingham, the first act towards which was the publication of a handbill in London and Birmingham promoting a dinner at Dadley's Hotel, on Temple Row, on 14th July 1791, the second anniversary of the storming of the Bastille. This was aimed at wealthy anti-establishment figures, as the cost was five shillings,

---

100 Hutton, *The Life of William Hutton*, p.81

including a bottle of wine. The handbill contained inflammatory language, calling Parliament 'venal', Prime Minister Pitt 'hypocritical', and attacking the clergy as 'legal oppressors'. It stated that the Crown was 'too weighty for the head that bears it'. It protested that it was not promoting civil unrest, but could not maintain this stance even to the end of the paragraph, calling on sympathisers to keep the peace only until 'the Majority shall exclaim, The Peace of Slavery is worse than the War of Freedom. Of that moment let Tyrants Beware.' This was hardly likely to calm establishment fears and although Dissenters locally disowned the handbill, the damage in the mind of the public was done.

There was controversy in Birmingham about whether or not this dinner should go ahead, given the reaction to its publicity, and Priestley himself decided against attending, although several friends, fellow members of the Lunar Society, did so among the eighty-one attendees.

A mob assembled in St. Philip's Churchyard to defend 'the Church and King', and although the dinner finished at around five o'clock, from eight o'clock onwards they started to break the hotel's windows, believing Priestley was inside. On finding this not to be the case, the alcohol-fuelled mob attacked the nearby Unitarian churches, with the Old Meeting House in Philip Street being razed to the ground. The fire engines were slow to arrive, as the vicar of St. Martin's had ordered the key to the shed in which they were housed to be hidden, and even when they did, the mob forced them to direct their hoses only onto buildings around the chapel, leaving the chapel itself to burn down. Hutton's account includes an accusation that magistrates dining at the Swan Inn encouraged the mob's anger, as they 'huzzaed *Church and King,* waving their hats, which inspired fresh vigour into the mob'. An attorney, John Brooke, suggested the mob went to the 'meetings', a reference to Dissenters' houses of prayer. Following this, the New Meeting House was attacked and ransacked, then burnt, all within half an hour. This accusation of establishment connivance is compounded in Hutton's mind by the fact that the magistrates could have mobilised the military to quell the riot, but signally failed to do so.

Having gutted Priestley's New Meeting House Chapel, they moved on to attack his home at Fair Hill, Sparkbrook, close to 'Farm', the home of Sampson Lloyd. The Priestleys had been playing backgammon, but wisely fled an hour earlier, having been told of the mob's destruction in the town and anticipating the worst. Bird intriguingly states that: 'Priestley himself, unrecognised, moved about the fringe of the mob as it wrecked his home, flooded his cellars and got drunk on his wine.'[101] In his 'Appeal to the Public on the Subject of the Riots in Birmingham', published in 1792, Priestley himself wrote: 'It being remarkably calm; and clear moon-light, we could see to a considerable distance, and being upon rising ground we distinctly heard all that passed at the house, every shout of the mob, and almost every stroke of the instruments they had provided for breaking the doors and furniture.'[102] He witnessed the destruction of his precious laboratory, its equipment, and the littering of streets with books from his cherished library. There seems little doubt that had they remained, the Priestleys would have been seriously injured or, in all probability, killed. Hutton highlights the inescapable irony of Priestley's discovery of oxygen saving lives of thousands, 'and, in return, he can scarcely preserve his own.'[103]

The riots continued the following day, the mob going on to wreck the dungeon in Peck Lane, off New Street, and then the properties of other free-thinkers, including Hutton's shop, and Baskerville's former home at Easy Hill. They moved on to surrounding areas, including an attempt to ransack Edgbaston Hall, the home of Dr Withering, who hired prize-fighters to defend his property. Boulton and Watt had taken the precaution of arming their workers at the Soho Manufactory as a precaution, but it was not required.

These extensive unchecked riots lasted for four days, until the anger of the mob dissipated, but more particularly were ended by the arrival of the 15th Regiment of Dragoons from Nottingham, with reinforcements of cavalry from Lichfield the next day. Twenty-seven houses and four meeting houses had been attacked during those days of unbridled lawlessness. The Times printed what would now be termed 'fake news', a cartoon showing Priestley and other radicals drinking 'treasonous toasts' at the dinner, but of course Priestley, and others depicted, did not attend. George III is quoted as being pleased that Priestley had suffered 'for the doctrines he and his party have instilled, and that the people see them in their true light'.[104] Upton states only twelve people were tried (Uglow has seventeen) at Warwick Assizes, for their riotous behaviour. Only four were convicted, two of whom were later pardoned. In his account, Hutton reported a joke that reinforced this undue leniency, with a foxhunting gentleman declaring, as the hounds closed in on their quarry 'Nothing but a Birmingham jury can save

101 Bird, *Portrait of Birmingham*, p.93
102 Uglow, *The Lunar Men: The Friends Who Made the Future*, p.442
103 Hutton, *The Life of William Hutton*, p.89
104 Uglow, *The Lunar Men: The Friends Who Made the Future*, pp.445-6

him now!'[105] Leniency did not apply to the two not pardoned, as Francis Field and John Green were hanged.

It is ironic that the riots were known not only as 'the Church and King riots' but also 'the Priestley riots', given that the eponymous alleged cause did not attend the dinner. However, newspapers took the harsh view that although law and order should be respected, the victims had really brought the riots upon themselves by their outrageous opinions and statements!

Hutton sets out the reasons behind the riots at the beginning of his Narrative,[106] and describes five occurrences which disturbed the 'delightful harmony of this populous place.' These include an attempt to include Dr Joseph Priestley's 'polemical works' in a new library, which the clergy opposed; and the alleged republicanism of Dissenters, perceived through their attempts to repeal the Test Act 1673 which prevented Dissenters from seeking public office, a nakedly discriminatory law. The third cause is the controversy prompted by Priestley's writings. Hutton asserts that arguing with Priestley became, for those ambitious in the Church of England, 'the road to preferment'. Some Dissenters felt discomfort with elements of Priestley's opinions, particularly 'some warm expressions, which his friends wished had been omitted.' The fourth cause is the inflammatory handbill which 'operated upon the mind, like a pestilence upon the body. Whatever it touched, it poisoned.' However, he protests against the unjust reaction of the establishment and rioters: 'If it *was* fabricated by a Dissenter, is it right to punish the whole body with fire and plunder? This is visiting the sins of one man upon another.' It was later found that the handbill, printed in London, had been scattered under a table at an inn in Birmingham. The final cause is, unsurprisingly, the dinner at Dadley's Hotel. While he describes it as an 'inoffensive meeting', he concedes that it became 'an error by being ill-timed'. He powerfully contrasts the peaceable nature of the Revolution (executions by guillotine did not take place until the Reign of Terror between June 1793 and July 1794) with the riots, and claims that 'more mischief was done in the Birmingham riots, than in overturning the whole French government.'

His outrage is clear as he abhors the statements of the Church in justifying the actions of rioters as supportive of the King, and re-asserts the right of any man to choose his own religion: 'It is the privilege of an Englishman to walk in darkness if he chuses.'[107] Most strikingly, the Narrative conveys Hutton's consternation and

---

105 Hutton, *The Life of William Hutton*, p.104
106 Ibid., pp.81-4
107 Ibid., p.86

perplexity at being targeted by the rioters himself. On Friday 15th July, learning of events overnight from a servant, he walked into Birmingham, but 'I was not under the least apprehension of danger to myself.' Hutton was greatly surprised that John Ryland's home at Easy Hill was attacked and burned, given the nature of the man that Ryland was, and that he did not attend the dinner. Indeed, Hutton observes that Ryland was 'a friend to the whole human race', to whom 'an obelisk ought rather to have been raised to his own honour, than his house burnt down'.[108]

Hutton is approached by 'a person' who told him his 'house was condemned to fall.' Even having witnessed mindless destruction, he did not give credence to this, as he could not understand what harm he had caused to anyone. 'Being no man's enemy, I could not believe I had an enemy myself.' He thought that local people, after forty years, 'esteemed me too much to injure me' but concedes that 'I drew from fair premises false conclusions.' He reflects that it seemed he was guilty of two faults, being a Dissenter and 'an active Commissioner in the Court of Requests.' When the mob entered New Street, a friend heard one rioter say 'If you will pull down Hutton's house, I will give you two guineas to drink, for it was owing to him I lost a cause in the Court.' 'The bargain was instantly struck, and my building fell.'[109]

Hutton and his son Thomas made efforts to buy off the mob, in paying the leaders to protect their property. In response, Hutton was 'seized by the collar on both sides, and hauled a prisoner to a neighbouring public house, where, in half an hour, I found an ale-score against me of 329 gallons.' His son 'purchased the favour of *Rice*', one of the leaders who gave assurances of safety and his ability to control the mob. Rice however betrayed his promise and joined the destruction of Hutton's New Street properties, and led the mob next morning in destroying his country house at Bennett's Hill. Hutton's bitterness about this betrayal was compounded by the fact that this was proved against Rice at his trial, but a soldier provided an alibi that Rice was drinking with him in a public house.

At Bennett's Hill, the mob attacked three times and were again bought off by his son, but, treacherous again, on the fourth occasion, they 'completely ravaged my dwelling' from 9pm at night to 8am the next morning, so that Hutton has to 'write this Narrative in a house without furniture, without roof, door, chimney-piece, window, or window-frame.' In his destroyed home, he found wood shavings, chips, and faggots with three hundredweight of coal, in a kitchen, ready to be lit. His furniture had been carried upstairs, thrown through windows and smashed,

108 Hutton, *The Life of William Hutton*, p.90
109 Ibid., pp.90-1

with anything that survived the drop smashed by three 'bludgeoners stationed below for that service.' His ordeal was not over, as the next day, Saturday 16th July, there were 'fresh calamities'. Rioters returned at 4am, threw out and burned the furniture he had saved, and 'the house expired in one vast blaze.' Hutton is surprised that the women were as bad as the men, stealing his furniture and making sure all the buildings, including his new coach house, were burned down.[110]

Eventually, the military restored order after four days of tumult, and Hutton went back to Bennett's Hill, where the ruins were still burning. There were fifty rioters there so he had to hide, and beg for water at a cottage. This led him to consider the ravages of fortune and circumstances: 'How thin the barriers between affluence and poverty!' 'In the morning of the 15th I was a rich man; in the evening I was ruined.' He returned to Birmingham on Monday 18th, and met friends who had secured some of his property which 'had paved half the streets in Birmingham.' He commented that he was offered homes by seventeen men, sixteen of whom followed the established Church, 'which indicates that I never was a party man.'

In concluding the narrative, Hutton reflects on the most apparent cause of the riots, and the legal process which followed at Warwick Assizes. He sets out in full the eighteen toasts made at the dinner, the first being 'To The King and Constitution', so hardly revolutionary. His purpose is to make plain that: 'The sum total of the above toasts amounts to this, a solicitude for the perfect freedom of man, arising from a love of the species.'[111] This does seem to be a fair conclusion.

Hutton describes the process of justice which followed as: 'a mere farce, a joke upon justice, and truly laughable.' Many of the accused were given false alibis, or simply lied, and were aided to avoid justice. Hutton names them, the only real justice he felt he could achieve, as: 'By the false lenity of the court, villainy became triumphant.' Sufferers were abused in the streets during these trials. He comments that while some of the establishment wanted the victims recompensed, others were indifferent, and the 'bigoted part of the clergy' alleged the Dissenters' sufferings were too mild, calling them 'wholesome correction' and wanted tragedy to befall them again.

The issue of the authorities' complicity in fostering the riots remained an active one, and numerous affidavits allegedly provided evidence that those with authority had been at least neglectful. Conspiracy theorists had their suspicions confirmed when the Prime Minister, William Pitt the Younger, refused to take note of these sworn statements.

110 Hutton, *The Life of William Hutton*, pp.91-4
111 Ibid., pp.105-6

Hutton felt the injustice of the riots themselves, but also of the supposedly fair and equitable process of justice, and closes his record of those dreadful events, unequalled in Birmingham's history before or since, with the sad statement that: 'with a tear I record the sorrowful thought, that there appeared afterwards no more repentance on one side, than there had been faults on the other.' This represents the 'End of the Narrative of the Riots of July 1791. Written in August that year'.[112]

WILLIAM HUTTON
A life resumed

Hutton now returns to describing annual events, by concluding 1791. His confidence in the nature of mankind has been shattered, as he reflects on his nineteen years of public service, but 'the return I met with…convinced me that the nature of the human species, like that of the brute creation, is to destroy each other.' His experiences led him to withdraw from public life, and spend the rest of his life with 'my little family, and amuse myself with the book and the pen.'

He notes that fifty years ago, he came to Birmingham as a 'runaway 'prentice, a forlorn traveller, without money, friend, or home', but the events of 1791 'left me in a more deplorable state of mind than at the former period.' As Sarah's disorder was exacerbated by the stress and loss, Catherine took her to near Bristol for the Hot Wells. Hutton stayed in Birmingham to sort out his business and properties, and bought a cottage next to Bennett's Hill for £300, which he occupied from 18th December, while he re-built his own house.

The following year records the process for compensating the victims, and Hutton details the fifteen claimants, including himself and Thomas. Complaining that his losses were greater than his claim, he records that his loss was £8,243. 3s. 2d, and his claim was £6,736. 3s. 8d., but he was awarded only £5,390. 17s., as those compensated had to pay for the cost of the trials. Hutton was further affronted by the resentment exhibited by the jury throughout, saying that 'every insult was offered to the sufferers that the malice of an enemy could contrive', and 'The sum allowed was paid with as much reluctance as if the sufferers had destroyed their own property'.[113]

Hutton's 'Life' from 1792 to 1812 is dominated by concern for his ailing wife, details of travels and walks with his wife and later Catherine, and the publication of further books. As we know, Sarah was the love of his life, and his expressions of concern from 1793 to 1796, when she died, reflect this. His feelings are powerful,

---

112 Hutton, *The Life of William Hutton*, p.107
113 Ibid., pp.111-2

as he describes seeing her die: 'Grief stops the pen. The scene is affecting. I am undergoing a second death. I can stop the pen, but not the tear.'[114]

Hutton tries to deal with his grief through poetry. In 1802, he includes a poem in which he contemplates what makes a happy life, based on his own family circumstances. 'A Day' was dedicated 'To DR. WITHERING, who inquired How I spent my Time':

> 'When Aston steeple strikes my eye,
> It steals for her I lov'd a sigh.
> An intercourse, now lost, I mourn,
> How to forget I ne-er can learn.'[115]

The year 1804 begins 'with melancholy reflections upon the loss of an excellent woman', in a poem written on the ninth anniversary of her death, 23rd January:

> 'O! I mourn the day I lost thee,
> As the year winds round its way,
> Many a sigh and tear thou cost me,
> Sorrow never sleeps a day.'[116]

When Thomas married on 5th September 1793, just before his father's seventieth birthday, Hutton transferred the businesses to him, retaining land and property for his own income, sufficient to sustain a comfortable lifestyle for the rest of his life. Hutton remained very active, undertaking many excursions with Catherine, to help preserve her health, visiting Barmouth, Wales in 1796, Shifnal and the Wrekin in 1797, and Buxton and Caernarvon in 1799. In 1801, they undertook a remarkable excursion to Cumberland, and particularly Hadrian's Wall. This exemplifies how fit Hutton remained, even at the age of seventy-eight. He and Catherine went to the Lake District, with Hutton making a diversion to see Hadrian's Wall. They travelled to Penrith, his daughter on horseback, and Hutton walking, his obstinately preferred mode of transport.

At Penrith, they went their separate ways, Catherine turning left to the Lakes, and Hutton continuing to Carlisle to Hadrian's Wall. Incredibly, Hutton, an old man, walked the length of the Wall and back, in one week and six hours, 'melted

---

114 Hutton, *The Life of William Hutton*, p.115
115 Ibid., p.127
116 Ibid., p.136

with a July sun, and without a drop of rain.' Returning to Birmingham, they arrived on 7th August, 'after a loss on my part of perhaps one stone of animal weight by perspiration, a lapse of thirty-five days, and a walk of 601 miles.' He went on to publish 'The History of the Roman Wall', and reported that he was frequently stopped in the street, as 'so long and singular a journey on foot was, perhaps, never wantonly performed by a man of 78', and it 'excites the wonder of the town.'[117]

Further excursions included Derby, Matlock, Kedleston, Leicester and Fotheringay in 1802, and annual visits to Scarborough from 1803 to 1805. On the last of these, he complained of difficulty walking and states that 'I believe it will be my last.' Further annual excursions followed, and despite a diagnosis of cancer requiring surgery to his thigh in February 1807, he visited Bosworth Field in July and Coatham in North Yorkshire in 1808 and 1809, and Redcar in 1810. By 1811, he was, at last, feeling his age. Noting that at the age of eighty-two, he thought himself 'a young man', who 'could, without much fatigue, walk forty miles a day', now, at the age of eighty-eight, 'I have felt a sensible decay' and 'The strings of the instrument are, one after another, giving way, never to be brought into tune.'[118]

From 1798, the annual entries include references to the effects of time on his body, as Hutton begins to face the prospect of death. In that year, he considers ending his narrative, thinking that life will 'probably roll on in silence to its ultimate period, which cannot be far distant', symbolised in his loss of the pen with which he has written his 'Life' to date. In a thoughtful, equally symbolic, footnote, Catherine notes that 'This pen was afterwards found, and is kept as a relic'. In 1803, he describes humorously an issue of ageing: 'One lesson however I must learn, to eat without teeth.' Poignantly, he feels alone in terms of his contemporaries, as he has seen whole generations be born, live, and die: 'Thus I am become a stranger to the world which I have long known.'

His reaction to a notice published in the Monthly Review of The Gentleman's Magazine announcing he has died is gentle and tongue in cheek. His letter to them, confirming he remains alive, closes with: 'I am, with sincere respect, Yours, till a second death,' and provides them with a poem dated 12th August 1807, published in the next issue, which contains the lines:

'The wonder consists, when a man is no more,
He should still write his name though a *dead*-man.'

---

117 Hutton, *The Life of William Hutton*, p.121
118 Ibid., p.145

The publishers' affection is evident in their response: 'we will engage, if he requires it, never again to state an event which we hope is yet distant, till we have, in like manner, *his own certificate of it.*' It is possible to hear Hutton chuckling at this.[119]

In 1808, for posterity, he lists the fourteen books he has published, by title and date, noting with evident, justified pride: 'Some of them have since risen to double their original price.' The next year he returns to his sense of coming to the end of life and the problems old age brings: 'The infirmities of age inform me that I am drawing towards a conclusion.'[120]

His final entry in 1812 includes a memory of a service in a meeting house in Nottingham in 1742, in which the minister mused that all there would be dead within sixty years. Hutton comments 'Seventy years have elapsed, and there is more reason to conclude that I am the only person left.'

The last sentence of his 'Life' is confusing, as he states: 'This day, October 11th, is my birth-day. I enter upon my ninetieth year, and have walked ten miles.' While his walking ten miles is hard to contest, we know from the first page of his 'Life' that he was actually born on 23rd September 1723.[121] So this extensive, eventful and enthralling life ends with an enigma.

He lived in fact until Wednesday, 20th September 1815, three days short of his ninety-third birthday, and died from pneumonia. He was buried in Aston Parish churchyard on 26th September.

Hutton's final three years are described by Catherine, in the 'Conclusion'. She describes this as 'the melancholy task of laying the cap-stone on the building' of Hutton's life, whom she calls both 'father and friend.' Her summary of Hutton is clearly written from the great depths of her love and regard. She states that the predominant feature of his character was 'love of peace'. He always acted the part of mediator and conciliator, as we have seen, especially at the Court of Requests. Catherine recalls him teaching his children that a man should 'relinquish a part of his right' in a quarrel: *the giving up an argument was meritorious*, and that *having the last word was a fault.*' He was generally silent on religion and politics, although she acknowledges that he made his views plain in the wake of the riots. These views she presciently thought 'will be found too liberal for the present day.' Hutton's conduct towards his children was 'admirable'. He allowed them a greater degree of liberty than customary, but if transgressing, he only needed to

---

119 Hutton, *The Life of William Hutton*, pp.140-1
120 Ibid., pp.142-3
121 Ibid., p.146

use a single word to correct them. He strongly inculcated the need to confess an error, saying: 'A fault acknowledged was not merely amended: in his estimation it almost became a virtue.'[122] Catherine is certain that his devotion to exercise, particularly walking, prolonged his life. This is a message which modern medicine and science has validated.

Catherine ends by describing Hutton physically. His face conveyed 'sense, resolution, and calmness', and he had a keen eye when animated or irritated. We are left with a pleasant image: 'Such was the happy disposition of his mind, and such the firm texture of his body, that ninety-two years had scarcely the power to alter his features, or make a wrinkle in his face.'[123]

This assessment is largely reflected by the content of Hutton's 'Life'. William Hutton was clearly a remarkable man, whose long life was lived through distinct phases, from apprentice to entrepreneur, wealthy Birmingham luminary, land and property owner, dedicated public servant, and author of histories, travelogues and poems, before the events that shattered his belief in mankind. The traumatic nature of those days in July 1791 would leave its mark on anyone, and it is testament to his determination and resilience that he recovered his businesses and willingness to help people. He shows a similar single-minded focus on writing his history and other books from 1780.

Hutton's 'Life' displays the nature of the man: observant, clear-eyed, with a sharp memory, quoting precise days, dates and monetary amounts from fifty years before. He is honest and balanced in his descriptions and recollections (the only detraction from this being his flimsy justification for stealing a small amount of money from his uncle, which leaves a tiny doubt).

A major theme is the happiness of family life, in contrast to his own childhood and obviously poor relationship with his uncaring father. In his early life, making his way, Hutton shows resourcefulness, ingenuity, and great manual skill, allied to his relentless pursuit of being able to support himself, in which he succeeds spectacularly. What attracts the reader to him is his continuous sympathy with those in poverty around him, as he draws attention to the precarious nature of life, and how close people always were to penury and disaster. This is further reinforced in 'An History of Birmingham', as he describes many of the institutions which benefit the poor and sick, including charitable trusts, the General Hospital and the Workhouse. It is William Hutton's clear persistent humanity that makes him a compelling figure in Birmingham's history.

122 Hutton, *The Life of William Hutton*, pp.165-6
123 Ibid., pp.146-166

Unfortunately, apart from the blue plaque at Waterstones bookstore in High Street, there is no public memorial to him in Birmingham, and this feels like an unforgiveable oversight. It is no mean achievement that two of his books are still read over two hundred years since his death. This is unusual, and while they are not great literature, they are essential and entertaining reading for any student of Birmingham history. William Hutton is certainly the first person I would invite to my fantasy dinner party of historical figures.

Blue plaque at Waterstones Bookshop, 24, High Street, Birmingham, B4 7SL

William Hutton by unknown artist, 1780, from the Royal Armouries Collection

4.

A Portrait of Birmingham in the late eighteenth century

William Hutton remarks in the Preface to his most famous book that: 'no such thing ever appeared as *An History of Birmingham*. It is remarkable, that one of the most singular places in the universe is without an historian', and that a town that manufactures almost everything had not manufactured a history of itself.[124]

Hutton's 'History' is a highly personalised account, lacking a definitive structure, and moving easily between history, anecdote, digressions (which, given his dedication to walking, he calls appropriately 'peregrinations'), descriptions of buildings and institutions, governance, current affairs and his own particular hobby-horses. So what sort of a place was Birmingham, as described by Hutton, in the late eighteenth century?

Hutton gives his first impressions of Birmingham in 1741, its vibrancy conveying the deep impression it made on this young man of seventeen:

'St. Philip's Church appeared first, uncrowded with houses, (for there were none to the North, New Hall excepted) untarnished with smoke, and illuminated with a Western sun. It appeared in all the pride of modern architecture. I was charmed with its beauty, and thought it then, as I do now, the credit of the place….'[125] 'I had been before acquainted with two or three principal towns. The environs of all I had seen were composed of wretched dwellings, replete with dirt and poverty; but the buildings in the exterior of Birmingham rose in a style of elegance. Thatch, so plentiful in other towns, was not to be met with in this. I was surprised at the place, but more so at the people: They were a species I had never

124 Hutton, *An History of Birmingham*, p.x
125 Hutton, *The Life of William Hutton*, p.20

seen: They possessed a vivacity I had never beheld: I had been among dreamers, but now I saw men awake: Their very step along the street shewed alacrity: Every man seemed to know and prosecute his own affairs: The town was large, and full of inhabitants, and those inhabitants full of industry. I had seen faces elsewhere tinctured with an idle gloom void of meaning, but here, with a pleasing alertness: Their appearance was strongly marked with the modes of civil life: I mixed with a variety of company, chiefly of the lower ranks, and rather as a silent spectator: I was treated with an easy freedom by all, and with marks of favour by some: Hospitality seemed to claim this happy people for her own, though I knew not at that time from what cause.'[126]

Birmingham was cramped, vibrant, and tumultuous. Ancient streets and passages were crowded with people, and there was no area designated for shopping: 'In a town like Birmingham, a commodious market-place, for we have nothing that bears the name, would be extremely useful,' but he concludes that: 'We are not easily drawn from ancient custom, except by interest.' He reports that foodstuffs were sold in the Bull Ring, meat in Spiceal Street, and flowers and shrubs in Moor Street and Philip Street (the latter where the statue of Bully now stands). Animals were traded in the 'beast-market' in Dale End, pigs, sheep and horses in New Street, cheese from 'one of our principal inns', and 'fruit, fowls and butter…at the Old Cross.' Goods were sold everywhere: 'it is difficult to mention a place where they are not.' Decisions had to be made quickly: 'much business is transacted in a little time; the first customer is obliged to use dispatch, before he is justled [sic] out by a second: to *stand all day idle in the market place*, is not known among us.'[127] Brummies found the town's ambience positively uplifting: 'it is easy to give instances of people whose distinguishing characteristic was idleness, but when they breathed the air of Birmingham, diligence became the prominent feature.'[128]

A successful businessman, Hutton includes extensive details of manufacturing. After all, the town housed Boulton and Watt's Soho Manufactory, and before long was known as 'the city of a thousand trades.' He describes makers of buttons, buckles, guns, leather, steel, nails, bellows, thread, brass, hackney coaches, and Baskerville's printing. Hutton's friend has the distinction of being the only individual, except Lords of the Manor, named in the 'Contents'.

Contemporary sources confirm the range of trades operating in Birmingham. The Directory of Birmingham, the 'Tradesman's True Guide or Universal

126 Hutton, *An History of Birmingham*, pp.63-4
127 Ibid., pp.230-2
128 Ibid., p.58

Directory' published by Sketchley and Adams in 1770, provides fascinating details of prominent people and industries. Ninety trades are listed, with the number of purveyors of each trade, plus a 'Miscellaneous' category which indicates 'about' 300 people practise these unspecified activities. The numbers operating range from two to 285 (the latter predictably publicans), with most between two and twenty, confirming the proliferation of small independent workshops and businesses.

Many trades, with strange sounding names, have disappeared: chaffing dish makers, cock founders, curry comb makers, gimblet makers, lapidaries, nut crack makers, peruke makers, and stilliard makers. In 1878, Bunce indicates that the 'Miscellaneous' category includes many now extinct trades, including 'buckle cutter, silver caster and bluer, fire-shovel bit maker, heckle maker, paste moulder, harrateen (?) [sic] maker, ink-horn maker, steel convertor…&c.'[129] While Bunce is perplexed, 'harrateen' is apparently a coarse woollen cloth, the term last recorded in 1739.

Hutton describes trade as praiseworthy and patriotic: 'acquiring a fortune – A laudable motive!' Wealth through business had advantageous effects throughout society: 'the great advantage of private fortune, and the greater to society, of softening and forming the mind, are the result of trade.' Consequently, the lower ranks of society 'bask in the rays of plenty.' This is an early version of the doctrine of 'trickle down economics': 'the preservation of private wealth, tends to the preservation of the State.' Hutton is not, however, blind to businessmen's faults, characterising trade as 'a line of minute deceits.'[130] Even a trusted friend deceives him while selling a horse, but he accepts this with equanimity.

Surprising passages reflect an understanding of environmental issues, ahead of their time. Hutton acknowledges the health impact of the physical environment, articulating supposedly modern ideas about the impact of sunlight, good air and clean water when describing the Lamp Act. He recognises the link between lack of sunlight, as buildings were built higher, and 'sickness and inconveniency'… 'The narrower the street, the less it can be influenced by the sun and the wind, consequently the more the dirt will abound.' Stagnant water was recognised as 'extremely prejudicial to health.'[131]

Hutton describes the British system of governance with something approaching reverence: 'that excellent system of polity, which shines, the envy of the stranger, and the protector of the native.' While it may not be perfect, it nevertheless

129 Bunce, *History of the Corporation of Birmingham, vol. 1,* pp.55-58
130 Hutton, *An History of Birmingham*, pp.59-*67
131 Ibid., pp.99-101

'stands higher in the scale of excellence than that of its neighbours.' Within this, 'Birmingham…is a sparkle of the first *water*, and of the first *magnitude*.'[132]

The extent of what we call local government is very slight, for a population estimated at 25,032 in 1780, and for Hutton, preferring a 'less is more' style of government, this is a major advantage. There are only two acting magistrates: 'we are a body without a head', and the style of government is virtually 'as the Saxons left it.'

Hutton includes nine pages about the Court of Requests, and states forcefully: 'Law is the very basis of civil society, without it man should quickly return to his original rudeness; the result would be, robbery and blood.' The Court provides 'an easy, and expeditious method of ending dispute, and securing property.' An Act of Parliament in 1752 established the Court 'for the recovery of debts under Forty Shillings', which met on the first floor of the Old Market Cross building in Edgbaston Street every Friday morning.[133]

The Lamp Act 1769, amended in 1773, provided 'for lighting and cleaning the streets of Birmingham, and for removing obstructions that were prejudicial to the health or convenience of the inhabitants.' The seventy-six commissioners appointed, and the 700 lamps installed to prevent 'many unfortunate accidents', were the first attempt at local government, recognising the need to take care of people, beyond the needs of businesses.[134]

Bunce, over a hundred years later, gives detailed perspective to the actions of the Street Commissioners. While the Gild of the Holy Cross was 'a kind of local government', the establishment of Street Commissioners is the 'First Regular Local Government.' The growing complexity of town life has led to 'a natural result that the more thoughtful of the inhabitants should endeavour to establish a system of local government of a more regular character, and with powers in some degree proportionate to the necessities of the place.'[135]

The Act remained until Birmingham became an incorporated borough in 1838, but was extended in 1773, 1784, 1801, 1812 and 1828, and each time, the Commissioners' powers, and often their number, was increased. Each Act specified named properties for demolition, for better control, transport, communications, hygiene and light. How rates were set and collected was updated, with a sliding scale according to property value. Exemptions were established, including from property

---

132 Hutton, *An History of Birmingham*, pp.84-5
133 Ibid., pp.*99-99
134 Ibid., pp.99-105
135 Bunce, *History of the Corporation of Birmingham, vol. 1,* p.67

rates for those exempt from paying the poor law rate, separately administered and collected (Second Act, 1773). The Third Act, 1801, introduced a requirement for new houses and properties to meet Commissioners' strictures on the level and line of streets, and to pave the street in front of them. For this, an exemption for ten years applied.

Other regulations prevented buildings encroaching onto streets, on pain of financial penalties and demolition. Given the extent of such encroachments listed in three of the Acts, it seems Brummies showed consistent inventiveness in obstructing the streets! The Lamp Acts introduced street cleaning and lighting, and streets in front of houses could be swept and rubbish removed by 'scavengers' for an annual fee. Other restrictions controlled trades carried out on the streets, and increased requirements on carts, carriages and other transport, including hackney coaches and sedan chairs from 1801. Initially requiring horses to be led by 'a halter or cord', rather than riding, this expanded to include charges made, and the maximum width of cart and carriage wheels.

Bull-baiting, a popular pastime, was prohibited in 1773, along with bonfires, and 'discharging any squib, serpent, rocket, or other fireworks whatsoever in any public place.' Thatch or straw roofing was prohibited in 1812. The First Act guaranteed the Lord of the Manor's rights, but subsequent acts concentrated on protecting townspeople. A Night Watch was introduced in 1773, and by the Fifth Act, 1828, Commissioners were empowered to 'appoint such number of able-bodied watch-house keepers, night constables, watchmen, patroles [sic], street keepers and other persons…sufficient for the protection of the inhabitants, houses, and property, streets and other places, by day and by night.'

Penalties for breaches figured in each Act, and some misdemeanours resulted in prison, although the sentence seems disproportionate to the crime: breaking a lamp led to jail for a month, and three months if more than one lamp was broken.

The powers for planning of the town grew over time. Initially based on demolition to free up streets and thoroughfares, successive Acts added powers of setting boundaries, naming streets, numbering houses, and letting contracts for road building and repairs. The Commissioners dictated the location of markets, and the type of produce sold. The Fifth Act, 1828, provided for laying out new streets, and empowered Commissioners to 'widen, open, extend, and alter streets', and to 'erect and build one or more market house or houses' and 'a corn exchange'. By the last Act, the powers were general, rather than specific, noticeably moving towards conferring powers allowing Commissioners discretion, rather than demolition or construction of specific buildings.

The Fifth Act authorised building a Town Hall, with capacity for 3,000 people for public meetings, and accommodating officers. This was funded by a specific Town Hall Rate of no more than sixpence in the pound, levied on property valued at fifteen pounds or more. This Act demonstrated the Commissioners' consciousness of the need for improved health care, providing that the Town Hall be reserved 'at special times' to host music festivals and turned over to the Governors of the General Hospital for what became the fund-raising Triennial Music Festivals for the hospital. Dr John Ash, founder of the General in Summer Lane in 1779, was a Commissioner from 1769.

Street Commissioners were named in the Acts, a parade of the great and the assumed to be good in the town. Their powers to appoint people of their choosing to any vacancy ensured only the 'right' type of person became a Commissioner. The 1769 Act indicated that Commissioners 'were debarred from in any way benefiting [sic] personally by holding offices of profit under the Act' and were required to meet their own expenses. While a laudable attempt to secure probity, there was no requirement to act in public view, no legal liability, nor any means of overseeing Commissioners' decisions.

Although the Town Council was created in 1838, it was 1851 before the Birmingham Commissioners, and counterparts in Deritend and Bordesley, and Duddeston and Nechells, were abolished, and their powers transferred to the local authority. Before then, Commissioners were responsible for a major improvement, the planning and partial implementation of a town sewerage system, which remains the basis of its drainage. By 1848, a third of the town's streets had sewers, and the scheme was completed by the Town Council after 1851.

Many improvements were made by Commissioners from 1769 to the early 1830s. Within the restrictions on them, particularly in the first thirty years, they tried to deliver fairness and justice, sensible development schemes, better living conditions, safety of the townspeople, and punishment for criminality. Joseph Sturge, even while asserting the right of the newly elected Town Council to govern, acknowledged their success. In 1838, he concluded it was: 'an act of justice to say that few bodies had, upon the whole, more economically applied the funds at their disposal for the safety and general improvement of the town.'[136] The successive Acts demonstrated a gradual building on achievements, as experience was gained and civic bankruptcy avoided, evident from the move to less specific actions and more general powers, and the increased confidence in limits for borrowing against the public purse.

---

136 Bunce, *History of the Corporation of Birmingham, vol.1*, p.148

Notions of representative democracy were gaining ground, fostered by Revolutionary France and the United States of America. In Britain in the early nineteenth century, it became increasingly obvious that groups of influential men (they were exclusively male) could not carry the confidence of those providing the money for public benefit. 'No taxation without representation' was a familiar cry for American independence, and underscored the political agitation that led to the Great Reform Act, 1832. The result was that by 1833, Commissioners were increasingly seen as: 'a self-elected body, which was felt to be out of harmony with the new development of the representative principle.'[137]

As Brummies debated this, an application for a charter to establish the town as a corporation was developed, but delayed by the national government's recognition of problems with the probity of Commissioners, and a recognition that other forms of governance also required a better solution for effective local government. A Commission of Enquiry in 1833 examined systems of local government across England, and its report was damning for Commissioners: 'There prevails… among the inhabitants of a great majority of the incorporated towns a general… distrust of the self-elected municipal councils,…a discontent under the burthen of local taxation, while revenues are diverted from their legitimate use, and are sometimes wastefully bestowed for the benefit of individuals, sometimes squandered for purposes injurious to the character and morals of the people.' Bunce concluded: 'No indictment could well be more comprehensive.'[138] The outcome was the development of a single model of governance and locally, an application for incorporation of the town under the Municipal Corporations Act 1835.

Towards the end of the eighteenth century, the greater sense of society's responsibilities for those in need led to provision of a workhouse in 1730 (extended by an infirmary in 1766 and workshops in 1779), and the General Hospital itself in 1779. The support provided through the workhouse, on 14th April 1781, was for about 5,240 people, a high percentage (10.5%) of the 50,000 townspeople. The poor of Birmingham were well served by the workhouse and the community around them: 'the wretched of Birmingham are not made more so by ill treatment, but meet with a kindness acceptable to distress.' In describing the workhouse's impact, Hutton articulated a powerful argument for community support of the elderly and infirm: 'if he is arrived at the western verge of life, when the powers of usefulness decline, let him repose upon his fortune; if no such thing exists, let

---

137 Bunce, *History of the Corporation of Birmingham, vol.1*, p.97
138 Ibid., p.98

him rest upon his friends, and if this prop fail, let the public nurse him, with a tenderness becoming humanity.'[139]

Schools in Birmingham included the Free School, on the site of the Gild of the Holy Cross, becoming the Free Grammar School of King Edward VI in 1552, the original of those famous schools. The Charity School was commonly called The Blue School from the colour of the uniforms. Established in 1724, in a building in St. Philip's Churchyard, it taught ninety scholars overseen by a governor and a governess, 'both single'. Hutton described how Dissenters established their own school on the pattern of the Charity School twenty years previously, which educated eighteen boys and eight girls: 'the boys are innured [sic] to moderate labour, and the girls to house-work.' This was funded by annual subscriptions, 'willingly paid, thankfully received, and judiciously expended.'[140]

Birmingham was a complex, populous, almost frantic place of activity and industry, constantly looking forward, but making initial efforts to ensure those left behind were cared for. Trade was key to individual and collective prosperity and well-being, and as the town threw itself headlong into the Industrial Revolution, Hutton was confident of success: 'I have often mentioned an active spirit, as the characteristic of the inhabitants of Birmingham. This spirit never forsakes them. It displays itself in industry, commerce, invention, humanity, and internal government. A singular vivacity attends every pursuit till compleated [sic], or discarded for a second.'[141]

Birmingham was a populous town, where fortunes were made, but where poverty, disease and want presented a daily challenge for many. This is a modern, seemingly insoluble, challenge for cities, but there are thankfully always some who use their talents and wealth to help those less fortunate. An early pioneer of improving health care in Birmingham was Dr John Ash, a successful physician in Birmingham and London, who was central to the founding of Birmingham General Hospital. He was well-known and respected in Birmingham society, counting Dr William Withering a close friend, and on good terms with members of the Lunar Society.

JOHN ASH
'The founder of Birmingham General Hospital in Summer Lane'
The date of birth of John Ash is not recorded but he was baptised in Coventry, Warwickshire, at St. Michael's Church, on 25th July 1722. His father, Joseph Ash,

---

139 Hutton, *An History of Birmingham*, pp.215-222
140 Ibid., pp.203-14
141 Ibid., p.361

was a brewer, married to Anna. He was educated initially at King Henry VIII School in Coventry and then went to study at Trinity College, Oxford, receiving his BA in 1743, and his MA in 1746.

Wanting to pursue a medical career, he studied and achieved his MB in 1750 and his MD in 1754, and then established a practice in Birmingham, taking up residence at 9, Temple Row, in 1752. Temple Row was an attractive address to have, being described in 1726 as 'lofty and elegant and uniform,…and inhabited by People of Fortune.'[142] His practice became large and prosperous, providing an annual income of £25,000. William Shenstone, the Halesowen poet, and Hutton were two of his well-to-do patients.

His most notable, long-lasting achievement in Birmingham was the founding of Birmingham General Hospital. He organised a public meeting on 4th November 1765, bringing together local prominent people to pursue the building of an infirmary. This group included Boulton, Sampson Lloyd and Baskerville. Despite this high profile and well-connected support, it took fourteen years before the hospital opened, in Summer Lane, on 20th September 1779, now marked by a blue plaque on the Network West Midlands building.

As well as providing considerable financial support, Ash was the senior physician in the General. An early member of medical staff was Dr William Withering. Dr William Small, a Scot recently returned from teaching in Virginia, USA, who had shared Ash's consulting rooms since 1766, was also on the staff.

John Ash was wealthy from his practice and built what is described as a 'sumptuous house', called 'Ashted', in north Birmingham, on land owned by Sir Lister Holte, MP for Lichfield from 1741 to 1747, who lived at Aston Hall. Ash built this large imposing house in 1771, and it was surrounded by gardens, fields and orchards. Ash never moved into this house but continued to live in Temple Row. He later sold the Ashted lease to John Brooke, the attorney alleged by Hutton to have been complicit in stoking the flames of the 1791 riots. The house had a cupola added and in 1791 became the Church of St. James the Less, as Brooke developed the estate. The church was badly damaged by bombing in the Second World War and demolished in 1956. The area in which it was built is in the ward of Nechells today, and it is the origin of the name of Ashted, as in Ashted Circus. Brooke's tenure is recalled by Great Brook Street, originally part of the estate, which leads off Lawley Middleway (A4540) from Dartmouth Circus.

---

142 Skipp, *A History of Greater Birmingham – down to 1830*, p.49

Ash believed that life could be improved for the local population, and was active in the life of Birmingham, being a governor of King Edward VI School, one of the original investors in the Birmingham Canal in 1768, and one of the Lamp Act Street Commissioners.

It seems he suffered from mental health problems, described as 'temporary mental derangement.' This first became apparent in 1781, and Withering took on more of his consultations in the practice, which had declined in size. This may have affected his mental state and 'hurt his spirits.' He became a Fellow of the Royal College of Physicians in 1787 and a fellow of the Society of Antiquaries. He joined the Dilettanti, an exclusive society established as a gentleman's club in 1734, which attempted to purify the public's taste by supporting classical learning, and contemporary 'high brow' art forms, such as Italian opera. Horace Walpole in 1743 had a more disparaging view, describing it as: 'a club, for which the nominal qualification is having been in Italy, and the real one, being drunk…'[143] Sir Joshua Reynolds was a member, and this is presumably where he and Ash met. It was certainly for the wealthy, privileged and ennobled, and continues today. On 8th November 1787, Ash was elected Fellow of the Royal Society.

He left his General Hospital appointment on 17th December 1787, and the next year went to Bath. He subsequently moved his practice to London, in Brompton Row, Knightsbridge, and continued to practise successfully. He is said to have overcome his mental health problems by disciplined study of mathematics and botany.

He held several offices in the Royal College of Physicians alongside his practice. He also published a paper 'Experiments and Observations to investigate by Chemical Analysis the properties of the Mineral Waters of Spa, Aix'.[144]

As well as being well regarded for his medical expertise, Ash was active in wider London society, being the founder of a social and literary club called the Eumelian, a pun based on his name, from a Greek word meaning 'with an ashen spear'. Its members, including Reynolds and James Boswell, met at the Blenheim Tavern in Bond Street.

Reynolds painted Ash's portrait between April and July 1788, at the cost of £210 to the Hospital Governors, and it was displayed in the General Hospital Board Room, Steelhouse Lane, for many years, until the services there were transferred to the Selly Oak and Queen Elizabeth Hospitals in 1995. The portrait's background

---

143 Joan Lane, 'Ash, John (bap. 1722, d. 1798), physician', *Oxford Dictionary of National Biography*, (Oxford: 2004, updated 2013)
144 Ibid.

includes the foundation block of the medical school, which became part of the Queen's Hospital (later Birmingham Accident Hospital), in Bath Row. To secure his legacy, the painting was acquired by Birmingham Museum and Art Gallery, where it remains on display.

Ash died in Knightsbridge on 18th June 1798 and was buried in St. Mary Abbots Church on 26th June. In 1965, the University of Birmingham Medical School named a lectureship in his memory. In Birmingham, a blue plaque erected by the City of Birmingham is located at the rear entrance to the former House of Fraser store in Temple Row. No. 9 was his home from 1752 to 1769.

Dr John Ash, by Joshua Reynolds, 1788 from Birmingham Museum and Art Gallery

Blue plaque at rear entrance to the former House of Fraser store (next to no. 43), Temple Row, Birmingham, B2 5LS

The appreciation of the need to protect more vulnerable members of society, epitomised by Ash, was reflected in the establishment of several hospitals in Birmingham in the early nineteenth century. By 1819, three further institutions to help the poor and sick had opened. The General Dispensary was founded in 1793 in Temple Row, close to Ash's home, and by 1818 had cared for 37,139 'sick' patients, 6,223 midwifery patients and had carried out 13,964 'vaccine inoculations', including for smallpox. On 4th January 1815, the Institution for the Instruction of the Deaf and the Dumb opened in Church Road, Edgbaston with capacity for forty people. This became the Royal School for Deaf Children in Calthorpe Road. The General Institution for the Relief of Persons Labouring under Bodily Deformity opened on 24th June 1817. From 1888, this would be known as the Royal

Orthopaedic Hospital.[145] This was followed by the establishment of The Institution for the Cure of Diseases of the Eye in April 1824 in Cannon Street, which, after expansion and several moves, is now the Birmingham and Midland Eye Centre on the City Hospital site. A Fever Hospital opened at the corner of Bishopsgate Street and Bath Row in 1828. All of these attest to the growing sense of community in Birmingham, and the need to provide effective and organised care, beyond the ability of family members, for the sick and afflicted members of society.

145 Hutton, *An History of Birmingham*, pp.370-3

5.

Dissent and Discovery in late eighteenth century Birmingham

The last years of the eighteenth century brought a seismic shock to the settled order of the major imperial powers, as the earthquake of the 1789 French Revolution reverberated through the long-established governing structures of monarchy and aristocracy. While many abhorred this affront to the natural and divinely-dictated order of society, those with a progressive frame of mind saw opportunities for freedom and democracy to be explored in, and applied to, Great Britain. As a town usually welcoming of dissenting voices and radical thinking in religion, politics and civil discourse, it is not surprising that Birmingham became a location for such debate and action.

Debate was the cornerstone of an association of like-minded men drawn from differing backgrounds and interests, who became famous nationally and internationally as 'The Lunar Society'. Despite its name, this was not a formal organisation, and no records of meetings held or decisions made were kept. It was much more an opportunity for men who had achieved prominence and wealth in their chosen careers, from the 1770s onwards, to meet and talk about their interests. They exchanged ideas, undertook experiments, ate and drank, and frequently helped each other to develop their pet projects, whether in business or not. This assistance might be suggestions or advice, but often resulted in formal business arrangements or partnerships. These enabled expertise to be pooled to mutual benefit, through patenting new discoveries, leading to manufacturing of new products and their commercial exploitation.

Most members lived in or near Birmingham and travelled to meetings, often at Boulton's Soho House, or Samuel Galton Junior's Barr Hall at Great Barr.

Meetings were arranged for days on which a full moon shone, making travel easier (hence the name 'lunar'). They playfully called themselves 'Lunaticks' after the term was coined by Galton's butler, and it conveys the fact that having fun was as important as debating the artistic, political and scientific issues of the day. While these friends did not always agree, there was only one serious dispute between members, between William Withering and Erasmus Darwin.

Entrance to the group was by personal introduction, or recommendation from an existing member, to preserve the integrity of the group, and its expansion only to those with a similar cast of mind and interests. These included engineering, chemistry, metallurgy, geology, botany, education, the arts, and political thinking and theory. Nowadays, such individuals meet and debate in formal structures, including universities, professional associations, and thinktanks, but these were not available to men who dissented from the established Church in England, as most of these did. The Corporation (1661) and Test (1673) Acts prohibited dangerous, free-thinking radicals from entering the two English universities, any profession, or public life. What was remarkable was the extent and brilliance of the achievements of the Lunar Society members, the quality of the intellectual debate, and the resulting practical application of ideas. This was the Age of Enlightenment, when it was possible to encompass the sum total of human knowledge. It is probably true to say that this has not been possible since, and is certainly impossible in the modern age.

Each major figure involved in The Lunar Society is remembered in Birmingham by a remarkable memorial at an unexpected site. The Asda Superstore in Queslett, Great Barr, has erected around its car park perimeter nine 'Moonstones'. Each is a sandstone monolith carved with a member's name, and a symbol or picture which represents the most well-known of his achievements. The nine are Matthew Boulton, Erasmus Darwin, Samuel Galton Jnr, James Keir, William Murdock, Joseph Priestley, James Watt, Josiah Wedgwood, and William Withering. The site is appropriate as it is close to where Barr Hall, Samuel Galton Jnr's home, still stands in Fish Pond Way, although it is now derelict and closed.

Let's return to the aftermath of the French Revolution, and begin with the most dramatic story concerning a 'Lunatick' – Dr Joseph Priestley.

JOSEPH PRIESTLEY
*'Radical thinker, innovative chemist, discoverer of oxygen,
and a dangerous friend to know'*

Joseph Priestley was an educated, thoughtful, innovative thinker and often controversial writer who spent eleven years in Birmingham, and made a significant impact on the town and its history. Although his stay was relatively short, his many achievements and influence were felt across the world for many decades. One of the leading figures in the Enlightenment, a friend of powerful and influential figures, and an unrivalled polymath, Priestley is credited with the discovery of oxygen and other gases. His disputatious nature and radical dissenting views provoked outrage leading to riots in Birmingham, as we have seen. He was a minister and theologian, prolific author, politician, scientist, moral and natural philosopher, teacher and educator, grammarian, historian and inventor.

Joseph Priestley was the first of six children of Jonas Priestley (born 1700, died 1779), a finisher of cloth, and his first wife Mary, née Swift, the daughter of Joseph Swift, a farmer and maltster from Shafton, near Wakefield. Joseph Priestley was born on 13th March 1733, at Fieldhead, Birstall, near Leeds, West Yorkshire. His parents' family grew rapidly and from the age of one, Joseph lived with his grandfather on his mother's side, staying there until she died in 1739 when he was six years old. Returning home, he stayed for two years until his father re-married in 1741, when Joseph went to live with his uncle and aunt, John and Sarah Keighley, at Old Hall, Heckmondwike, three miles away. John died in 1745 but Joseph stayed with his aunt, who provided him with educational opportunities in the hope that he would become a minister in the dissenting tradition.

At Batley Grammar School, he learned Latin, Greek and Hebrew, later learning Arabic and Aramaic in the small village school until 1749. Highly intelligent and intellectually able, he learnt Italian, French and German at the age of sixteen in preparation to travel abroad for the benefit of his health, and to work as a translator for his uncle, a merchant. He had been diagnosed with consumption (pulmonary tuberculosis) but recovered, and continued his studies independently. He developed a stammer which he learned to overcome through reading 'very loud and very slow every day.' Being from a dissenting Calvinist family, Priestley was prohibited from attending Oxford or Cambridge, although his talents suggest he would have flourished in such an environment. Religion was extremely important in his family, and by the age of four, he memorised, and could repeat, all 107 questions and answers in the Westminster catechism. From the age of seventeen, he led family prayers, going to prayer meetings at the chapel, and attending services twice on Sundays.

Instead of university, Priestley attended the dissenting academy at Daventry from September 1752, aged nineteen. He flourished, learning classical languages, history, English literature, rhetoric, mathematics, chemistry, anatomy and natural philosophy, as well as studying the Bible in detail. He also learned how to weigh opposing views to formulate a considered and argued opinion, and soon believed that the truth could only be discerned as a result of the conflict of differing ideas. This approach stayed with him throughout life as he pursued his interests, often resulting in him being thought to be overly disputatious.

His appearance was slight, his demeanour eager, and he had 'a long nose, bulging eyes, and gentle mouth'. He walked with 'a kind of disjointed, bird-like trot'. This unattractive description concludes by indicating he had a lopsided face, so that his two profiles looked like they belonged to different people! In conversation, he talked very quickly, seemingly keen to make his point, but this may have been a consequence of his stammer.

Priestley was brought up as a Calvinist, and took religious issues and the idea of his potential salvation or damnation very seriously. It is said that his anxiety and terror that he had not experienced a fundamental religious experience led to his stammer. Priestley himself said that 'I felt occasionally such distress of mind as it is not in my power to describe, and which I still look back upon with horror.'[146] Over time, he developed his thinking to reject this vision of inevitable damnation and seek out a rational basis for faith and belief. His religious views differed from those of his family, as he came to deny the doctrine of the Holy Trinity. When his brother Timothy informed his Aunt Sarah of his radical liberal thinking, she consequently withdrew her financial support, a schism with his family which was never resolved.

His world and religious views were heavily influenced by David Hartley's book, 'Observations on Man, his Frame, his Duty and his Expectations', published 1749, and he developed an approach to life which synthesised his faith and science, believing that social change would come from all ranks of men and women becoming knowledgeable about the world and its potential, and the opportunity for mankind to become perfect. This would bring the state of happiness made possible by God's Providence. He therefore rejected religious and political doctrines which he felt defied rationality and science, which led him into conflict with many in society and the established Church.

On graduating from Daventry, Priestley moved to Needham Market, near Ipswich, to support the chapel minister, but he was not welcome, due to his Yorkshire accent and stammer. His time there was unhappy, the stress exacerbating his stammering. His friends tried to secure him a post at a new dissenting academy in Warrington, Lancashire, but the report of his 'hesitation' in speaking put

---

146 Uglow, *The Lunar Men: The Friends Who Made the Future*, pp.71-3

them off, and instead a relative secured him the post of minister to the chapel in Nantwich, and he moved there in September 1758. In a sympathetic environment, he learned to control his stammer and opened a successful school, which continued until 1846. He taught a wide curriculum to boys and girls, and bought scientific equipment, including an air pump and machine for generating electricity, to help his pupils' experiments. Following this success, he was offered a post at the Warrington Academy which had rejected him three years earlier, joining them in September 1761, moving into a new house provided by the academy in May 1762. He was ordained as a minister that same month, and on 23rd June, married Mary Wilkinson, aged nineteen, an ironmaster's daughter. Mary was able to speak her mind, with a 'penetrating glance', but was well read and a fiendish organiser, for which Priestley was grateful, as it allowed him to concentrate on his work and writing. Their first child Sarah, named after his aunt, was born on 17th April 1763.

While at Warrington he published 'The Rudiments of English Grammar' in 1761, followed the next year by 'A Course of Lectures on the theory of Language and Universal Grammar'. The first book was particularly successful, its nine editions establishing Priestley as an influential and important grammarian. He updated the Academy curriculum to meet the practical needs of students, preparing them for working lives in civil and commercial life. This was markedly different from traditional education, which generally prepared students for entry into the professions, but Priestley felt students would derive greater benefit from more pointedly focussed and practically based studies, including natural history and modern history, rather than the classics. Priestley published two charts, historical timelines, to help students put historical individuals and events into perspective and context. 'The Chart of Biography' was published in 1765 and 'The New Chart of History' followed in 1769, with 'Descriptions' alongside it. These remained popular for decades, well into the nineteenth century, in England and the USA. The expected publication of 'The Chart of Biography' and his lectures led to him being awarded an honorary Doctorate of Law (LLD) by Edinburgh University on 4th December 1764.

During his time at Warrington he expanded his scientific experiments, and began his major work on a history of electricity, as the first part of his history of experimental philosophy. Through friends at the 'Club of the Honest Whigs', at St. Paul's coffee house, he was introduced to Benjamin Franklin, the American colonies' representative in London and then the pre-eminent authority on electricity in the country and arguably the world. These two astonishing men, who changed the world in very different ways, became great friends, with Franklin indicating that first impressions of Priestley could be off-putting: 'To strangers he was cold and reserved; but where he was intimate, no man indulged to more pleasantry and good humour.'[147] Franklin, among others, supported his application to become a Fellow of the Royal Society, and Priestley became FRS on 12th June 1766. The next year, he published his hugely successful book 'The History and Present State of Electricity, with Original Experiments', said to be the first exposition of the inverse square law of electrical force, which ran to more than 700 pages, five editions in England, and translations into French and German.

Shortly after this, Priestley moved in September 1767 to be minister of Mill Hill Chapel, Leeds, indicating that his move was in part for reasons of his wife's poor health, as well as returning home. Sadly the break with his family was not repaired. While in Leeds, the Priestleys had two more children, Joseph Junior in July 1768, and William in May 1771. He devoted his time mainly to his religious duties, although he also helped to organise a circulating library and gave sermons in aid of charitable organisations, schools and the infirmary. Publications on religious issues followed and he published pamphlets and established a journal for theological thinking in 1768, the 'Theological Repository'. Despite his efforts, contributing a third of the articles, this was unsuccessful, running for only three years. Between 1772 and 1774, he published 'Institutes for Natural and Revealed Religion' which outlined his approach to radical dissent so successfully that it became the standard work on explaining Unitarianism. Reiterating his belief that God was benevolent, not vengeful, man could and should aspire to perfection through awareness of his place in God's scheme. He approached religion, science and politics from the standpoint that rational analysis could prove the rightness of his theories. In the preface to 'Experiments and Observations' in 1772, he wrote: 'The rapid progress of knowledge…will, I doubt not, be the means, under God, of extirpating all terror and prejudice, and of putting an end to all undue and usurped authority in the business of religion as well as of science.'[148]

These publications, and fame from his grammatical and scientific works, meant that he was now well known for his radical views. His tendency to reply to attacks reinforced his profile nationally, as a leading thinker in religious, scientific and political issues. While at Leeds, he published works on education, the principles of good government, libertarian approaches to the American colonies, reform of the established Church, and his objections to Dissenters being described and treated as 'tolerated criminals'. He continued to publish on scientific issues, including five

---

147 George Goodwin, *Benjamin Franklin in London,* (London: 2016), p.74
148 Uglow, *The Lunar Men: The Friends Who Made the Future*, pp.76-7

papers to the Royal Society, and started his books on the history of experimental philosophy, beginning with 'The History and Present State of Discoveries Relating to Vision, Light and Colours' (known as 'Optics'), in 1772.

He conducted chemical experiments and pursued investigations into what was called 'fixed air' and its applications, partly because of his fortuitously living next to a brewery which provided him with carbon dioxide. In 1772, he published 'Directions for Impregnating Water with Fixed Air' which in effect invented soda water. He did not exploit this commercially, and it was picked up by one J.J. Schweppe, who manufactured a range of carbonated drinks from this method, making his fortune, so Priestley is the de facto father of the fizzy drinks industry.

In June 1773, in financial difficulties, Priestley accepted the post of companion, librarian, and tutor to the children of William Petty, second earl of Shelburne, at Bowood, near Calne, Wiltshire. This post included a salary of £250, and minimal teaching duties, allowing Priestley to concentrate on his own interests and writings. This productive period resulted in six volumes of 'Experiments and Observations on Different Kinds of Air', the first volume published in 1774. This identified Priestley's successes in isolating nitric oxide, ammonia, nitrous oxide, sulphur dioxide, and most importantly oxygen, which he termed 'dephlogisticated air', and enabled the development of thinking by others around photosynthesis. In 1773, the Royal Society awarded Priestley the Copley Medal in recognition of this pioneering work.

During the years from 1773 to 1780, Priestley enjoyed himself, and had his fourth child on 24th May 1777 (named Henry at Shelburne's request). Becoming more closely involved in liberal dissenting politics, he supported attempts to repeal the Corporation and Test Acts which prevented Dissenters from participating in public life. In 1774, he published a pamphlet openly attacking the government on this issue and its approach in managing the American colonies. He continued to engage in debates with others on subjects as diverse as metaphysics, politics, religion, philosophy, and most notably for posterity, science, and he regularly published papers and books, including one describing his discovery of gases, including oxygen, in 1775.

In 1778, Shelburne became leader of the Whig Party and re-married in 1779, after which the relationship between the two families seems to have cooled. In search of a supportive and sympathetic environment for his views, and the company of a progressive, scientific community, Priestley moved to Birmingham, a magnet for free-thinking pioneers during the Enlightenment. He accepted an offer from the New Meeting House Chapel in Moor Street, one of the largest and wealthiest dissenting churches in England. Priestley became minister there in December 1780, receiving a salary of £100 to amplify his pension from Shelburne of £150 per year.

As a well-known and visible radical thinker, it was inevitable that Priestley was asked to become a member of the Lunar Society. Unsurprisingly, he revelled in the companionship and debates of the Lunar luminaries and used his scientific knowledge to support some of these new friends in their endeavours, developing new methods of production or scientific applications in their industries. Well-known in Birmingham, he befriended Hutton, whose daughter Catherine joined his chapel and expressed her admiration for Priestley. Confirming his ostensible lack of charisma, she saw this as a positive attribute: 'I look upon his character as a preacher to be amiable, as his character as a philosopher is great….He is not what is called an orator; he uses no action, no declamation; but his voice and manner are those of one friend speaking to another.'[149]

Priestley continued to preach, and taught around 150 adults and children in his congregation, supporting Sunday schools which combined bible studies with basic numeracy, literacy and job skills.

A major issue during these years was his continuing dispute with Antoine Lavoisier who opposed his conclusions about phlogiston. Eventually, Lavoisier would be proved correct, and his work formed the basis of the structure and functioning of modern chemical thinking, but Priestley doggedly argued against Lavoisier for the rest of his life. He continued to publish his series of 'Experiments and Observations Relating to Various Branches of Natural Philosophy', with further volumes in 1781 and 1786, and an abridged version in 1790. 'Lectures on History and General Policy' appeared in 1788, with seven editions in England, and again, translations into French and German.

He published two volumes of a controversial work, 'An History of the Corruptions of Christianity' in 1782, which argued forcefully against the doctrines of Christ's divinity and the Virgin Birth, that Nazareth was Christ's birthplace, and that the early church was in fact Unitarian in nature. These arguments infuriated the established Church of England hierarchy and their opposition led an unrepentant Priestley to publish further books in 1786, rebutting their criticisms and driving home his points. In the political sphere, he exacerbated the antipathy of the establishment by writing in support of repealing the discriminatory

---

149 Robert K. Dent, *Old and New Birmingham: A History of the Town and its People,* (Birmingham: 1880), p.221

Corporation and Test Acts, including an open letter on the subject to the Prime Minister, William Pitt the Younger.

In 1785, Priestley published 'The Importance and Extent of Free Enquiry', including an incendiary passage on the approach needed to develop the number of Unitarian churches: 'We are, as it were, laying gunpowder, grain by grain, under the old building of error and superstition, which a single spark may hereafter inflame, so as to produce an instantaneous explosion; in consequence of which that edifice, the erection of which has been the work of ages, may be overturned in a moment, and so effectually as that the same foundation can never be built upon again.'[150] While clearly figurative, this provoked a national debate and earned Priestley the epithet 'Gunpowder Joe', evoking in popular consciousness acts of revolution and destruction of the existing order. Already known as a supporter of independence for the American colonies, achieved in 1783, Priestley supported the French Revolution in 1789, expressing his enthusiasm for this in his 'Letters to the Rt. Hon. Edmund Burke' in 1791. Burke, an Irish statesman, and political and philosophical thinker, attacked the effects of the French Revolution and defended the monarchy, the state and the Catholic Church. It was therefore a short step from establishment anger at Priestley's views to his depiction as a revolutionary, wanting to overturn the established order of Church and King. Fostered by establishment figures, this spilled over into popular discontent with him, and the causes he espoused. As the mood darkened, sermons attacking Priestley were preached at St. Philip's Church, and the slogan 'Damn Priestley' was daubed on Birmingham walls. In Parliament, Burke spoke against him during the third debate on repealing the Test Act, which was lost by twenty votes in May 1791. Burke quoted extracts from Priestley's subversive commentaries, and political cartoons labelled him 'Dr Phlogiston: the Priestley politician or the Political Priest' on 1st July 1791.

His political approach included views that are mainstream and we take for granted today, including the separation of religion and state, people having rights, with the ideal state being created 'which good sense, and the prevailing spirit of commerce, aided by Christianity, and true philosophy, cannot fail to effect in time.'[151] While this may seem uncontroversial now, other elements of his political platform were more contentious, when viewed through the lens of the role of the established Church in society, and the wars and revolutions which had recently occurred in Europe in which England had been involved. He espoused the idea that there should be no established Church, nor colonies, and that public money

---

150 *Joseph Priestley,* no date
151 Uglow, *The Lunar Men: The Friends Who Made the Future,* p.440

spent on defence could instead be spent on public works. In Birmingham, there was unrest at increases in rates, and these were blamed on Dissenters.

These concerns and antagonisms erupted literally, in response to the proposal to create a Constitutional Society in Birmingham, and specifically, on the publication of the handbill promoting the infamous dinner at Dadley's Hotel on 14th July 1791. Given the likelihood his presence would incite violence, Priestley himself did not attend, although several friends did, one of whom, James Keir, offered the toast.

The rioters were initially intent on finding Priestley specifically, and it is clear that he and his family were in mortal danger, and may well have been killed, had they been discovered. Having narrowly escaped the mob attacking his home at Fair Hill, Sparkbrook, Priestley and his family were understandably traumatised, and fled. Priestley never returned to Birmingham after the night of 14th July 1791. While Mary was taken in by Samuel Galton Junior, Priestley himself fled to Worcester, and then moved to Clapton, Hackney, in London to preach at the Gravel Pit Meeting House. His suffering had attracted international support and he was granted citizenship of France, and offered a place in the French National Convention, which he declined. He continued to publish, including his 'An Appeal to the Public on the Riots in Birmingham' later that year, which was re-printed three times. He lectured on history and natural philosophy at Hackney New College, and carried on his long running argument with Lavoisier, publishing a further pamphlet in 1793. However, he felt increasingly isolated, and feared the growing attempts by the government to silence liberal Dissenters.

Priestley's sons had already moved to the United States, and on 8th April 1794, he and his wife took passage arriving in New York on 4th June, where they were met by Joseph Junior. Priestley was made very welcome in America, as an enlightened friend of the United States, unfairly treated by his country of birth. He settled with Mary at Northumberland in Pennsylvania, and they built a house. Sadly his son Henry died on 11th December 1795, followed by his mother, Mary, on 17th September 1796.

Priestley met George Washington and became a friend of Thomas Jefferson, who regarded him as 'one of the few lives precious to mankind'. He continued to publish on all his favoured subjects, and attracted controversy again, particularly in an argument with President John Adams. This brought the threat of prosecution, but that disappeared when Jefferson became the Third President in 1801. As well as offering advice on the establishment of a college for Virginia, Priestley dedicated a book to him in 1802, stating 'Tho' I am arrived at the usual term of human

Joseph Priestley, engraving by Charles Turner, after painting by Henry Fuseli, 1783

life, it is now only that I can say I see nothing to fear from the hand of power, the government under which I live being for the first time truly favourable to me.'[152]

His daughter Sarah died in 1803, and the following year, Priestley died at home in Northumberland, Pennsylvania, on 6th February, aged seventy. He was buried alongside his family in the Friends' burial ground at Riverview Cemetery. His son Joseph Junior returned to England in 1812, remaining until he died in 1863. Priestley's granddaughter returned to Birmingham to marry, and this branch of the family subsequently included Hilaire Belloc, the author.

Joseph Priestley was a controversial and compelling figure, but his innovation, intelligence, optimism for the future of mankind, and indeed his discovery of several gases, is unfortunately no longer well known. He is memorialised in many of the towns where he lived, as well as having an asteroid named after him, '5577 Priestley'. The American Chemical Society's most prestigious award is the Priestley

Blue plaque at the Church of St Michael and St Joseph, New Meeting House Street, Birmingham, B4 7UD

Priestley Moonstone, Asda Superstore, Old Horns Crescent, Queslett, in Great Barr, Birmingham, B43 7HA

152 Robert E. Schofield, 'Priestley, Joseph (1733-1804), theologian and natural philosopher', *Oxford Dictionary of National Biography*, (Oxford: 2004, updated 2013)

Medal. In Birmingham he is remembered by a statue in Chamberlain Square (currently removed due to redevelopment works), by the naming of Priestley Road, Sparkbrook, and by one of the Lunar Society Moonstones at the Asda Superstore in Great Barr. This includes a depiction of laboratory equipment. There is a blue plaque, erected by the Birmingham Civic Society and the Royal Society of Chemistry in 1980, on the side of the Church of St Michael and St Joseph, New Meeting House Street.

JAMES KEIR

'The most famous resident of West Bromwich that nobody knows'

One of Priestley's friends present at the infamous dinner, a fellow Lunatick, James Keir, was the son of Scottish landowners, who moved to Birmingham after leaving the army, became a rich, famous and successful chemist, businessman, and industrialist, and an author. Engaged in politics, he was a key figure among Dissenters in Birmingham and his Tipton alkali and soap factory became a model of industrial progress, attracting visitors from around the country and the world. Despite this, very few people have heard of him.

James Keir was born on 29th September 1735 in Edinburgh, the youngest of eighteen children. His father John Keir (born 1686, died 1743) was a landowner in Stirlingshire, and his mother Magdaline (née Lind, born 1691, died 1775) was the sister of a Lord Provost and MP for Edinburgh. With John Keir being a town councillor in Edinburgh, this was a wealthy and respected family.

Although his father died when he was aged eight, James Keir was educated, initially at Edinburgh High School from 1742 to 1748, and then privately, before studying medicine at Edinburgh University from 1754. It was here that he met and formed a lifelong friendship with Erasmus Darwin, who was influential in Keir's decision to move to Birmingham.

In 1757, Keir curtailed his studies and joined the army aged twenty-two, to fulfil his dream of seeing the world. His eleven year military career in the 61st Regiment, now the Gloucestershire Regiment, included spending time in the West Indies during the Seven Years' War (1756 to 1763). He rose through the ranks to become a Captain on 23rd June 1766. Although successful, while serving he demonstrated the intellectual and scientific interests which would shape his future life. He wrote a treatise on the art of war, which unfortunately was burnt accidentally at his publishers, and a pamphlet to support the sale of army commissions. Keir rose at four every morning to read the classics and translate the works of Polybius, the ancient Greek historian on military and constitutional issues. He used this mode of learning through translation later in life when translating Pierre Joseph Macquer's 'Dictionnaire de Chymie' into English, published anonymously in 1766. As Uglow identifies, Keir states in the Preface: 'I thought I could not take a better method of fixing in my mind a knowledge of chemistry, than by employing the leisure which I then possessed, of making a complete translation, and giving it to the public.'[153] A congenial man, Keir formed a friendship with Alexander Blair, a fellow officer, with whom he would establish his most successful commercial venture in Tipton.

Keir left the army in 1768, as he felt the lack of intellectual stimulation from his fellow officers, but he was also severely affected by contracting yellow fever. Uglow reports that when in the West Indies, having seen many colleagues die from the fever, their bodies tossed into shark-infested waters, he was close to a similar fate, a doctor having concluded that he had died. In this peril, Keir scribbled a note asking for antimony, an ancient remedy suggested by Paracelsus, which was administered to him on the basis that he was going to die in any case. Remarkably, he recovered.

Having survived this, and seeking intellectual society and opportunities to make his fortune, he was drawn to Birmingham and the Black Country. He visited in 1767, spending time with his friend Erasmus Darwin, and Darwin's friends in the Lunar Society. Given Birmingham's growing reputation as a centre for debate and dissension, experimentation and industrialisation, this was a perfect fit for Keir. He remained in the area until his death in 1820.

He initially pursued the development of metal and chemical processes capable of industrialisation, including the development of malleable but non-corrosive metals, and the production of sulphuric acid, sodium carbonate and caustic soda. However, deciding that they would not return sufficiently high profits, Keir turned his attention to an existing local industry which could be profitably developed, glass-making. In 1770, a lease became available on a glass house making white flint glass at The Holloway, Amblecote (opposite the War Memorial Athletic Ground, now home of Stourbridge FC). Keir took on the lease for Holloway End Glasshouse, moving into the house on site. He formed a partnership with Samuel Skey (whose Bewdley business produced vitriol), and John Taylor (Hutton's friend, an established manufacturer of metal goods). The works produced glassware, including windows, wine glasses and decanters, and glassware for chemical experiments, the latter supplied to Boulton's Soho Manufactory. In 1772, a laboratory was set up so Keir could explore and manufacture alkalis, and the

---

153 Uglow, *The Lunar Men: The Friends Who Made the Future*, p.156

company developed the production of nitric acid. Keir was 'urbane and financially astute' in his business ventures and became an investor in the new Stourbridge Navigation Company from 1775. This built a canal link to Amblecote, part of the Staffordshire and Worcestershire Canal.

His personal life was also developing to his great satisfaction. On 10th October 1771, he married Susanna Harvey (born 1747, died 1802) at St. Philip's Church. One of his Lunar Society companions, Dr. William Small, described his happiness, with a hint of jealousy: 'Mr Keir has turned glassmaker at Stourbridge and has married a beauty.'[154] This was a match made of love, but Susanna was also the daughter of a Birmingham ironmaster, and Keir turned to the development of industrially useful metals in the next few years. They had two children, although sadly, Francis, a boy, died in infancy; Amelia was born in 1780.

His experimentation continued and he published a paper in the 'Philosophical Transactions' of the Royal Society in 1776, entitled 'On the Crystallizations observed on Glass'. This was the result of observing that crystals formed as glass cooled slowly, and he developed the notion of this being applicable to all materials that changed from liquid to solid. He followed this in 1777 with his 'Treatise on the Different kinds of Elastic Fluids or Gases'. It is said that this article introduced the use of the word 'gas' into the chemical lexicon, in place of the previously prevalent use of 'air'. He was working again on Macquer's revised edition of his 'Dictionnaire de Chymie', and in fact Keir published his English translation, complete with notes and annotations to the previous edition by Keir which Macquer had gratefully included, before the French edition itself appeared!

Gregarious and helpful, Keir was co-operative and unassuming. His 'Treatise on Gases' states that 'Knowledge is important, but whether the discovery is made by one man or another is not deserving of consideration.'[155] His preference for working with friends and like-minded people, rather than in competition, led him into many collaborations, including with Wedgwood on improving the glazes he used for his pottery. Having known Boulton and Watt since 1768, he was amenable to Boulton's suggestion in 1778 that he manage the Soho Manufactory for a quarter of the profits, rather than a salary. Keir sold his share in the Amblecote glass works and moved to Winson Green. Boulton was frequently absent and had neglected the proper management of the works, as Keir found 'great abuses',[156]

154 Uglow, *The Lunar Men: The Friends Who Made the Future*, p.162

155 Ibid., p.241

156 Barbara M.D. Smith, 'Keir, James (1735-1820), chemist and industrialist', *Oxford Dictionary of National Biography*, (Oxford: 2004, updated 2013)

and that 'considerable amendments in the economical part were requisite.'[157] Keir made the necessary changes, and increased efficiency and profitability, although this did not bring the offer of a partnership, as initially discussed.

In 1779, while still at Soho, Keir developed a metal alloy, from copper, zinc and iron which could be forged and wrought whether hot or cold. He felt that this alloy, called 'Eldorado', perhaps with optimism for the riches it might generate, had great potential for sheathing the hulls of boats and ships, as well as providing a non-corroding material for bolts and nails, and he took out the sole patent in 1779. It was tested by the Royal Navy for three years but they decided not to use it for the purposes Keir proposed. It was used to produce metal window frames and these were installed in Soho House and are still visible. Once more Keir was ahead of his time, as Eldorado was virtually identical to Muntz (or Yellow) Metal that George Muntz, a famous metal manufacturer from Birmingham, patented in 1832, and which was used for sheathing ships' hulls instead of copper, including notably the Cutty Sark.

While at Soho, Keir helped Watt develop a paper copying machine in 1780. Taking a design by Darwin, Watt patented this as a press-copier under the name James Watt & Co. As well as Boulton, Keir held a quarter stake in the business, and his role was to advise on the chemical composition of the ink used for the original letter, and to develop the technique of providing a mirror image of a document through pressing tissue papers through rollers. The page was then so thin that its content could be read by simply turning over the page. This revolutionised the previously laborious process of copying documents by hand: within a year, sales in Great Britain and abroad had reached more than 150. Upton notes that thousands of these copies are retained in the Boulton and Watt Archive in the Central Library, Birmingham. This method of copying remained popular until made obsolete by the invention of carbon paper in the early nineteenth century.

By 1781, Keir decided to pursue further opportunities to make his fortune, with yet another collaborator, his Army friend, Alexander Blair. This was to prove the most lucrative and successful of Keir's ventures, as he and Blair created a factory on the site of Bloomsmithy Mill, Tipton. Sited in Bloomfield Road, alongside the Birmingham Canal, the twenty acre site included a building of 20,000 square feet, and initially produced alkali, red and white lead, and the alloy Keir had patented, Eldorado. Keir used his chemical expertise to develop a better process for producing alkali, using percolation, which was more suitable for making soap, rather than

---

157 Uglow, *The Lunar Men: The Friends Who Made the Future*, p.291

glass. The scale of operations was vast, with soap pans fourteen feet wide and very deep, large cast iron vats, with two steam engines, water wheels and fire engines on site. By 1800, the factory was producing one million pounds in weight of soap each year. The size and profitability of the Tipton works made it famous world-wide as a model of modern manufacturing, like the Soho Manufactory. A nearby road was named Soap Factory Road, although that has now been shortened to Factory Road. It made Keir very rich and he took the secret of its chemical composition to his grave. It has been claimed that the easy availability of cheap soap contributed to the improvement in the health status of the population towards the end of the eighteenth century.

Although keen to implement new processes, Keir was a very patient man. His daughter Amelia said her father employed 'the aid of a chemical agent (for which he always expressed the highest respect, and the functions of which in natural operations were, he thought, greatly underrated) Time.'[158]

His final business venture saw him purchase Tividale Colliery, in partnership with Blair, and Blair's father, in 1794. The mine was also located alongside the Birmingham Canal, near what is now Kiers [sic] Bridge Close, at the rear of today's Cleton Street business park. Keir used his experience of operating a mine for an article in 1798 describing the geology and mineralogy of Staffordshire, where Tividale was then located. In February 1811, Keir provided the Geological Society with 'An Account of the Strata in sinking a Pit in Tividale Colliery', along with relevant specimens.

In 1790, Keir moved home to be closer to his factory, to Finchpath Hall, Hill Top, West Bromwich. The house was opposite Hawkes Lane, off Hill Top itself, and he lived there until his death.

Being a pioneering chemist and successful industrialist, Keir was well-respected in society, and was elected to the Royal Society on 7th December 1785, on the same day as his Lunar Society colleagues and friends Boulton, Watt, Withering and Galton Junior. Over many years, he contributed many papers to this organisation, including 'Remarks on the Principle of Acidity, Decomposition of Water, and Phlogiston' in May 1788 (having worked with Priestley). A later paper in 1790 provided the basis for the discovery of the electro-plating process. Keir had also published the first part of his own 'Dictionary of Chemistry' in 1789, but this was discontinued after only the letter 'A', as he became disillusioned with the controversy over the theory of phlogiston, following Lavoisier's publication of his

---

158 Uglow, *The Lunar Men: The Friends Who Made the Future*, pp.164-5

theories on the nature of oxygen. He returned to the theory and application of chemistry when he published his 'Dialogues on Chemistry between a Father and his Daughter', addressed to his beloved Amelia, in 1805.

Keir was a consummate polymath, and wrote extensively on many issues. As well as his unpublished (burned) treatise on the art of war in the 1760s, he is said to have written a 'Dictionary of the Art of War Ancient and Modern' in 1792, although this is not provable as no copy has survived. 'The Martial Character of Nations' appeared in 1793, followed in 1803 by 'Reflections on the Invasion of Great Britain by the French Armies; on the Mode of Defence; and on the useful application of the National Levies'.

He published memoirs of two members of the Lunar Society, Thomas Day, author of 'Sandford and Merton' (in 1791), and Boulton (in 1809). A poet himself, for his own amusement, he helped Darwin improve his poem 'The Botanic Garden' in 1787. This was in addition to being a member of the Society of Antiquaries and the Society for the Encouragement of the Arts, Manufactures and Commerce, reflecting his broad range of interests and ability to articulate cogent and forceful opinions on them all.

He was an enthusiastic member of the Lunar Society, often chairing meetings, holding his own by his knowledge and accomplishments, and his friendly and welcoming nature. In 1799, Sir Humphrey Davy, on one of his regular visits to Birmingham to discuss issues with Lunar Society members, said: 'Mr Keir is one of the best informed men I ever met with, and extremely agreeable.'[159] Others described him as 'the man of the world, the finished gentleman who gave life and animation to the party.'[160] He was a tall and imposing man, personable and affable, as well as patient and calm. His loyalty was evident in the care he showed for Dr William Small, who, prior to his death at Soho House on 25th February 1775, was visited constantly by Keir, who 'loved him with the tenderest affection.'[161]

Given the challenging times in Europe, these qualities were to be tested. It is no surprise that Keir had firm views about contemporary politics, and as a confirmed Whig, he sympathised with the revolutions in America and France. As other Lunar Society members did, Keir believed strongly in the democratic power of learning and knowledge. While the issue was divisive in the Society and the country generally, Keir was unequivocal: the 1789 Revolution was the 'sole *triumph of Reason*'…'having been the effect of the gradual illumination

---

159 Uglow, *The Lunar Men: The Friends Who Made the Future*, p.483
160 Ibid., p.36
161 Ibid., p.249

of the human mind over a whole nation, by *Philosophy* shewing that the true end of Government is the happiness of the Many and dispelling the baneful *prejudices* which established the tyranny of the *Few*, and which were the relics of the ignorance of barbarous ages.'[162] Like others, he saw no great issue with the decision to create a Constitutional Society in Birmingham, and the publication of the handbill promoting the dinner at Dadley's Hotel on 14th July 1791. Although controversy was sparked by the disparaging tone of the handbill's language, Keir attended the dinner and even proposed the toast. Keir wrote a pamphlet in 1792 defending himself and Priestley, and condemning the riots, under a pseudonym, entitled 'A letter from Timothy Sobersides, extinguisher-maker, at Wolverhampton, to Jonathan Blast, bellows-maker, at Birmingham'. Typically, given his inherent concern for others, he tried to obtain justice and compensation for the destruction of Priestley's house.

In later life, Keir suffered from rheumatism which restricted his ability to go out from 1804 onwards, although he continued to socialise with Lunar Society colleagues when he could. He was present at the final allocation of the Lunar Society library in 1813. He suffered a loss of personal possessions on 19th December 1807 when his Hill Top home burned, while Keir himself was staying at Alexander Blair's home at Hilton Park. After his death, Amelia's home, Abberley Hall, Worcestershire, was also destroyed by fire in 1845, and a significant portion of Keir's correspondence was lost.

Keir's beloved wife Susanna died suddenly on 20th November 1802, a few days after their granddaughter was christened. Keir wore Susanna's wedding ring on a black ribbon around his neck from then onwards. Keir derived much pleasure from his grandchildren, born to Amelia and her husband, who had come to this country from Geneva as Jean Louis Moilliett, and later naturalised his forenames to John Lewis. Moilliett was a successful banker whose Moilliett and Sons Bank was later merged with Lloyds Bank.

As Keir aged and declined, he withdrew from business, and gave up his interest in the soap factory in 1811. During his long decline into poor health, Keir may have suffered from dementia, as Amelia wrote that the visits she made frequently were unhappy, as she saw 'his superior mind gradually departing and his body suffering', and Keir often did not recognise her.[163]

James Keir died in his sleep, peacefully, aged eighty-five, on 11th October 1820, and was buried in the churchyard at All Saints Church, Charlemont, West

---

162 Uglow, *The Lunar Men: The Friends Who Made the Future*, p.436
163 *James Keir: Member of the Birmingham Lunar Society*, no date

Bromwich on 19th October. His modesty was evident in his will, in which Amelia was 'precluded from erecting a monument by his particular desire.'[164]

It is unfortunate that there are very few monuments to James Keir, despite his large personality and considerable achievements. He has been described as 'the greatest man the parish (of West Bromwich) has known as a resident.'[165] It is therefore perplexing that, apart from misspelled road and canal bridge names, the only monument is the Lunar Society Moonstone at the Asda Superstore, in Great Barr. This includes, appropriately, a carving of crystals. This seems hardly sufficient given the scale of his impact on the Birmingham and Black Country area.

James Keir with granddaughter Amelia Moilliett, by L. de Longastre, before 1820

Keir Moonstone in the car park of Asda Superstore, Old Horns Crescent, Queslett, in Great Barr, Birmingham, B43 7HA

Although not present at the dinner in July 1791, the Edgbaston home of one member of the Lunar Society was seriously threatened by the rioters, and was only saved by William Withering and his staff arming themselves and fighting them off. Withering deserves to be remembered for much more than this, as he was the physician who discovered the medicinal properties of the foxglove, and developed the medicine digitalis. This had a transformative impact on the treatment of heart disease and has therefore benefitted many thousands of people over the last three centuries.

---

164 *James Keir: Member of the Birmingham Lunar Society*

165 Reverend S. Lees, quoted in W.E. Jephcott, 'James Keir, Hill Top's Most Famous Man', 2nd March 1945

WILLIAM WITHERING

*'A polymath, a Lunatick, the inventor of digitalis,
and the foe of Erasmus Darwin'*

William Withering was born in Wellington, Shropshire on 17th March 1741 (although his memorial monument states 28th March), the second child of a surgeon and apothecary, Edmund Witherings (born 1713, died 1769), and his wife, Sarah Hector (born 1708, died 1789). William's mother came from a doctoring family, her father George having delivered Samuel Johnson, her uncle Brooke practising in Lichfield, and her uncle George and cousin Edmund being surgeons.

Educated at home, William studied classical languages with a local priest, and was instructed in 'just moral sentiments and genuine principles of religion' by his parents.[166] He was apprenticed in 1758 to a doctor or apothecary, and in 1762, aged twenty-one, moved to Edinburgh to study medicine at the University, qualifying in 1766. Withering was enthusiastic about anatomy and chemistry, but ironically, given later discoveries, found botany 'disagreeable'.[167] His final year thesis was 'De Angina Gangraenosa' (malignant putrid sore throat). Withering joined the Freemasons in Edinburgh. Having qualified, he toured Europe, visiting a large hospital in Paris, but this was curtailed following his travelling companion's sudden death.

In 1767, he set up practice in Stafford, and was one of the first two physicians appointed to Stafford Infirmary, which opened in 1766. Here he met his wife, Helena Cooke (born 1751), when she was his patient. The daughter of Stafford's town clerk, George Cooke, she was an amateur botanical artist and later illustrated his work. They married on 12th September 1772, and had three children, Helena, born 1775, who died a few days later, William, born 1776 and Charlotte, born 1778. As a married man with a family, Withering needed to earn more than the £100 per year his Stafford practice provided, and he moved to Birmingham, at the invitation of Erasmus Darwin, and from May 1775, worked at Birmingham General Hospital, alongside its founder, Dr John Ash. This gave him the opportunity to work with a wider range of diseases and conditions.

He left his family with cousins in Tettenhall, Staffordshire and initially lodged at the home of Mr Wheeley, a coachmaker, at 10, The Square, now Old Square. He later moved next door to Ash, in Temple Row, into the house previously occupied

---

166 Jeffrey K. Aronson, 'Withering, William (1741-1799), physician and botanist', *Oxford Dictionary of National Biography*, (Oxford: 2004)

167 M.R. Lee, 'William Withering (1741-1799), a biographical sketch of a Birmingham Lunatic', *JLL Bulletin: Commentaries on the history of treatment evaluation*, 2005

by the doctor he replaced, the late Dr William Small. His family joined him, and his earnings increased ten-fold, to over 1,000 guineas in 1776, rising to £2,000 by 1780, making it one of the largest practices outside London. He moved home again, in 1786, to Edgbaston Hall, outside the town, and stayed there until just before his death in 1799. He was wealthy enough to retain his Temple Row house as consulting rooms, and occupied 15, The Square as a town house.

When the General Hospital, funded by public subscription, opened in 1779, Withering was one of the physicians treating diseases including dropsy (oedema, often associated with heart failure) and scarlet fever, an outbreak of which occurred in Birmingham in 1788. He offered free care to poor patients in his daily clinic in Birmingham (said to be two or three thousand consultations per year) and in Stafford, which he supported until a successor was appointed.

Withering was also a member of the Lunar Society. As one of these enlightened scientists, philosophers and innovators, he believed that a man should know everything there is to be known. He became interested, and expert, in a number of fields.

His interest in botany began in Stafford and in 1776, he published in Birmingham 'The Botanical Arrangement of All the Vegetables Naturally Growing in Great Britain'. This major book, of two volumes published in 1787, a third in 1792 (produced with his friend Jonathan Stokes), and running to 836 pages, was the first British book to use the Linnaean system (a method of classification to enable the identification, grouping and naming of organisms in a standardised manner). It was so popular that there were three editions during his life, with his son producing four further editions under the title 'An Arrangement of British Plants', the last, fourteenth, edition being published in 1877. Withering's approach was different from previous publications, as it combined the idea of species with establishing a hierarchy of organic life. This work brought him election as a Fellow of the Linnaean Society in 1789, and the plant Witheringia solanacea was named after him. He was known in Europe as 'the English Linnaeus'.[168]

Unsurprisingly, given his painstaking cataloguing, Withering is described as meticulous and precise, obsessive in his approach, but he could be stubborn, ambitious, reserved and wary. He was ill at ease socially, wary of opposition and determined to defend his own conclusions. These traits contributed to conflicts in later years, between him and two Lunar Society friends.

Withering is best known for discovering the healing properties of the foxglove plant, digitalis purpurea, known clinically as digoxin. He published his approach

---

168 Lee, 'William Withering (1741-1799), a biographical sketch of a Birmingham Lunatic', *JLL Bulletin: Commentaries on the history of treatment evaluation*

and observations in 'An Account of the Foxglove and some of its Medical Uses; with practical remarks on the dropsy, and some other diseases' in 1785. The story of his observation of its use by 'Mother Hutton', an old woman practising as a folk herbalist in Shropshire, was invented for a marketing campaign for digitalis in 1928. In reality, travelling to Stafford Infirmary in 1775, while the horses were being changed, Withering was shown a herbalist's recipe, which had been provided for a woman who Withering had seen and had concluded was in extremely poor health. He was astonished to find out later that she had recovered, and from examining the recipe he determined that digitalis was the active ingredient from more than twenty ingredients. While the foxglove was poisonous, it had been used in medicine for hundreds of years. In his book, Withering writes that 'when given in very large and quickly repeated doses, [it] occasions sickness, vomiting, purging, giddiness, confused vision, objects appearing green or yellow, increased secretion of urine, with frequent motions to part with it, and sometimes inability to retain it, slow pulse, even as slow as 35 in a minute, cold sweats, convulsions, syncope (*loss of consciousness from fall in blood pressure*), death.'[169] Although this was hardly promising, there were reports of remarkable successes using digitalis, and this gave Withering hope that experimenting with different approaches, forms of the plant, and dosages, might prove successful.

Withering was the first to isolate and identify its active effects as a treatment for dropsy (oedema), in powdered or liquid (boiled) form, after experimenting on some of his poor patients unsuccessfully. His colleague and friend Dr Ash informed him in 1776 of a case of dropsy which had been successfully treated with digitalis. On enquiry, Withering worked out that a very high dosage had been given, probably twelve times the usual dose, and he pursued its use more rigorously. His detailed and meticulous experiments and observations on 163 patients established the effects of digitalis as the active component, and that the dried powdered leaf form was five times more effective than the plant's fresh leaf.

In 1776, he used digitalis to treat a patient of Dr Erasmus Darwin. She had suffered many difficulties, including pain, persistent coughing, and was distended with fluid, being both thirsty and unable to pass water. Although apprehensive about the potential effects, Darwin encouraged Withering to try and it succeeded dramatically, with the woman recovering, having produced eight quarts of water within a day.

---

169 Uglow, *The Lunar Men: The Friends Who Made the Future*, p.275

He observed the effects of differing doses on patients with cardiac failure, including its diuretic properties and side effects, which he indicated should lead to stopping its use and re-starting with a smaller dose. As well as improving care for dropsy sufferers, this approach, of close clinical observation, meticulous recording of effects and side effects, and change in the clinical approach as a result, followed by further close observation, has become a standard tenet of medical practice, followed to this day. This approach led to sustained high success rates in his treatments.

Withering developed an interest in geology and mineralogy, analysing heavy ore from Alston Moor, Cumberland. He was unable to isolate the new element he felt might be within it, but this was achieved by others and the element barium carbonate was named 'Witherite' in his honour. There is a specimen of witherite in the Matthew Boulton mineral collection at Birmingham Museum and Art Gallery with a label in Boulton's handwriting, stating 'given me by Dr. Withering'.[170] After presenting his work to the Royal Society, Withering was elected as a Fellow in 1785. He developed expertise in mineral water analysis, working in Staffordshire, Sutton Coldfield, and Europe (Spa in Belgium, Pyrmont and Seltzer in Germany). Following analysis of waters in Caldas da Rainha near Lisbon, in 1795, the Portuguese Academy of Science elected him a foreign corresponding member for his findings, which he published in English and Portuguese.

As a member of the Enlightenment, Withering had a wide range of scientific and social interests, and was active in both the Society for Promoting the Abolition of the Slave Trade and the Lunar Society. In this latter group, he met Darwin and Stokes, as well as Boulton, Watt, Baskerville, Priestley, Wedgwood, Samuel Parr, Galton Junior and his son Samuel Tertius.

Withering was a very methodical, meticulous and careful individual, described as 'a punctilious man of high moral rectitude', lacking imagination and shy to the point of not being comfortable socially.[171] His professional pride, or obsessiveness, had its detrimental side as he became embroiled in two long-running disputes with members of the Lunar Society, Erasmus Darwin and Jonathan Stokes. Originally friends, problems arose when Darwin claimed in print that he had first observed the healing effects of digitalis, and Stokes claimed that he had authored the second edition of 'The Botanical Arrangement of All the Vegetables' in its entirety. Withering later complained that Stokes, having borrowed a large number of his books, had returned them with many illustrations cut out!

---

170 *William Withering*, no date

171 Aronson, 'Withering, William (1741-1799), physician and botanist', *Oxford Dictionary of National Biography*

The dispute with Darwin was particularly galling for Withering. Darwin had published his late son's thesis on 'Pus and Mucus', in 1780, including descriptions of treatment of five cases with digitalis. One of these was identifiably the woman Withering treated in 1776, but Darwin failed to acknowledged this. This had been published in advance of Withering's book in 1785, and infuriated him.

The argument with Stokes included another affront by Darwin, who published his 'System of Vegetables' in 1783. This large work, in two volumes, almost 1,000 pages, identified almost 1,500 plants. In the Preface, he thanked those who had helped him, but, perhaps conscious of their strained relationship, said that 'Dr Withering …has…rendered many parts of his work unintelligible to the Latin scholar.'[172] This was a direct criticism of Withering's development of a scheme of pronunciation of plant names that he believed Darwin stole from him, through intelligence gained disingenuously by members of the Lichfield Botanical Society, who visited Withering and with whom he shared his progress. Darwin criticised Withering as a 'pseudo-botanist' who had corrupted the science. These arguments dragged on for years, even being continued by Withering's son after his father's death, and ruptured friendships between them and other Lunar Society members.

It is wrong to believe that Withering and other men of the Enlightenment lived in a cocoon of academic study and research. They lived, on occasion, in dangerous times. Following the French Revolution, in 1789, the Lunar Society became associated with revolutionary ideas, including extending the electoral franchise and was perceived by some as republican and anti-monarchist. As seen earlier, this led to the 'Church and King', or 'Priestley', riots in Birmingham in July 1791. As Priestley's close friend, Withering's home Edgbaston Hall, now the home of Edgbaston Golf Club, was attacked. Withering had had the house's contents removed to Edgbaston Old Church, and hired prize-fighters, who, with his servants, engaged in hand to hand fighting with rioters and drove them off, with one man being killed. Sensibly, Withering had stayed at his home in The Square during the riot.

Having contracted a fever in 1776, Withering suffered with haemoptysis (coughing up blood from the lungs or bronchial tubes), and experienced ill health each winter. This was one motivation for moving to Edgbaston Hall, hoping the air beyond the busy town centre would be beneficial for his health. In 1790, he deteriorated, having developed pneumonia with pleurisy, and contracted pulmonary tuberculosis. This forced his retirement from the General Hospital

172 Uglow, *The Lunar Men: The Friends Who Made the Future*, pp.381-2

in 1792. Although he wintered in Cintra, near Estoril, Portugal to alleviate the disease's effects, he continued to decline and moved to his new house, The Larches, Sparkbrook, previously owned by Priestley, on 28th September 1799. This proved too much for him and he died on 6th October, aged fifty-seven. He was buried at Edgbaston Old Church on 10th October 1799, his funeral attended by hundreds of people, and his monument in the church includes a bust and a carving of a foxglove.

William Withering, engraving by W. Bond, after painting by Carl Frederik von Breda, unknown date

A true man of the Enlightenment and a polymath, he is remembered in the William Withering Chair in Medicine at the University of Birmingham Medical School, and in the annual William Withering Lecture. He has a Lunar Society Moonstone at the Asda Superstore, in Great Barr, which includes a depiction of a foxglove. A blue plaque was erected by the Birmingham Civic Society, 1988, at the main entrance of Edgbaston Golf Club. In July 2011 a public house was named after him in his birthplace, Wellington, Shropshire.

Blue plaque at Edgbaston Golf Club, 25, Church Road, Edgbaston, Birmingham, B15 3TB

Withering Moonstone in the car park of Asda Superstore, Old Horns Crescent, Queslett, in Great Barr, Birmingham, B43 7HA

The tensions involved in balancing the requirements of religious faith and being a successful businessman were undoubtedly first experienced during the Enlightenment, and continue to worry successful entrepreneurs with a social conscience. Many enterprising businessmen of the age certainly had a sense of the social responsibility that their wealth placed upon them, a dichotomy explored more in the next two chapters. For one member of the Lunar Society in the 1790s, Samuel Galton Junior, this was a difficult and contemporary challenge in reconciling his Quaker faith, with its emphasis on pacificism, and his business interests, the most important and profitable of which was gun-making.

SAMUEL GALTON JUNIOR
'The successful gun manufacturer who followed a pacifist religion'

Samuel John Galton was born into a Quaker family in Duddeston, Birmingham, on 18th June 1753. His father, Samuel Galton Senior (born 1720, died 1799), was a gun-maker, owning a factory in Steelhouse Lane. He wanted a good Quaker education for his son, and sent him to the renowned dissenting Warrington Academy, in Lancashire.

With his education completed by 1773, at the age of twenty, his father made Galton Junior manager of the Steelhouse Lane factory, and a full partner a year later. The family lived in Galton House which was replaced in the twentieth century by the Gaumont Cinema, well-known to older Brummies. The Gaumont Cinema ceiling included a tribute to the Lunar Society, with its depiction of 'star-spangled heavens, with a central moon, and the signs of the Zodiac surrounding it.'[173]

Being involved in business, the Galtons naturally knew other business people and industrialists. Galton Junior got to know Boulton, Watt, and Keir and then, through the Lunar Society from 1781, other members, including Withering, Wedgwood and Thomas Day.

The business was very successful, and Galton Senior and Junior became very wealthy as the British Empire demanded substantial military arms and munitions for expansion and defence, being involved in virtually continuous wars during the eighteenth and early nineteenth centuries. Birmingham was the leading source of armaments for the government, and was known as 'the small arms arsenal of the world'.[174] Sketchley's Directory of 1767 lists sixty-two workshops producing guns or armaments, particularly in the gun-making area of Steelhouse Lane, Whittall Street, St. Mary's Row and Weaman Street. Samuel

173 Bird, *Portrait of Birmingham*, p.115
174 Ibid., p.56

Galton Senior had a proof-house for testing gun barrels in his factory, like the one which still exists in Banbury Street, opened on 16th March 1814, during the Napoleonic wars.

Well-to-do and well-connected, in 1777 Galton Junior married Lucy Barclay, daughter of Robert Barclay, of Ury, Kincardineshire, Scotland, an MP from 1788. The marriage was happy and eight children were born, beginning with Mary Anne Galton. Another daughter followed, and then two sons, one being Samuel Tertius, before another daughter. Three further sons included John Howard.

Galton Senior moved into Duddeston House, in an out of town area. Its four acre lake, with exotic water fowl provided 'scenes of perfect and luxuriant solitude',[175] a far cry from where the current Galton Street meets Duddeston Mill Road, alongside railway lines.

Galton Junior's rapidly growing family needed more space, and in 1785, he took on the ninety-nine year lease of Barr Hall in Great Barr, although the family left in 1797. Barr Hall was frequently used for the monthly meetings of the Lunar Society. It later became St. Margaret's Hospital and treated patients with mental health problems from 1910 until the 1990s, prior to partial demolition on the site to provide housing in 2006. It was at Barr Hall that Galton's butler is said to have first coined the term 'lunaticks' about this group of free-thinking industrialists, artists, naturalists, doctors and philosophers.

Mary Anne, who became a well-known author, Mary Anne Schimmelpenninck, after her marriage to a Dutch nobleman, wrote on historical and religious subjects, and provides insight into her father's enlightened view of education: he 'wished me to be a philosopher; and used to instruct me in the rudiments of science.'[176] It would not be expected however that the daughters would join the business, as these matters were restricted to sons only!

The range of interests of the diverse group that was the Lunar Society intrigued Galton Junior, as Mary Anne makes clear: 'My father's insatiable thirst for knowledge made his books, his laboratory and other appliances for scientific research more attractive to him than general society. He had a large folio blank book in which he…set down stray pieces of knowledge….Information on diet, on training, on pugilism, on horses, on building, the various resistances of timber &c, &c,…the book…was entitled the Book of Knowledge; it was alphabetically arranged, and formed many volumes.'[177]

---

175 Bird, *Portrait of Birmingham*, p.115
176 Uglow, *The Lunar Men: The Friends Who Made the Future*, p.313
177 Ibid., p.352

Sadly these volumes have disappeared but Galton's scientific interests resulted in a paper to the Royal Society in April 1781. Entitled 'Experiments on the Prismatic Colours', it proved that when the colours in Newton's prism were rotated, they created white, which as Uglow notes, was a discovery commonly dated a quarter of a century later. This was instrumental in Galton's election to the Royal Society on 7th December 1785, the same day as fellow 'lunaticks' Boulton, Watt, Keir and Withering.

Galton's interest in natural philosophy, what we now term the natural world, led him to publish several volumes on birds and quadrupeds, beginning in 1786 with the first of three volumes of 'The Natural History of Birds: containing a variety of facts selected from several writers for the amusement and instruction of children, with copper plates'. While originally intended for his own children, the work was published anonymously initially, by Joseph Johnson, a friend of Priestley. Peter Allen describes the complex publishing history of this work in his fascinating article. By 1789, the third volume appeared, and was well received by critics. It is the first example of a natural history book written specifically for children. Given the success of this, and as an early member of the Linnaean Society from 1788, Galton developed a work on mammals. 'The Natural History of Quadrupeds, including all the Linnaean Class of Mammalia: to which is prefixed, A General View of Nature, for the instruction of young persons' took years to produce, due in part to the author's ill health. It appeared at last in 1801, with Galton having employed an unknown writer to complete the volumes. There is only one copy of this work in existence and it was not well-received at all, unlike his 'Natural History of Birds', to the extent that copies were not published or sold after 1806. The Preface to this work demonstrates a great deal of sensitivity on Galton's part to criticism of him:

'From experience, I have learnt that none are so circumspect, but that their diligence sometimes fails them, and they are liable to error. This consideration has enabled me to support the scoffs of the ignorant and malicious, who like grinning Satyrs, and chattering Monkeys, have beset me in my progress.'[178] While this was clearly in response to critical views of his work on natural history, it is worth questioning whether or not it also reflected the intense and distressing debate he had been subjected to within the Quaker family.

In 1789, Galton, with Boulton and Priestley, had welcomed to Birmingham Olaudah Equiano, a former slave whose autobiography engendered considerable

---

178 Peter Allen, 'The Extraordinary Natural History Books of Samuel Galton Jnr.', *historywm*, no date

interest in the growing campaign against slavery. Galton's fortune was built on selling guns around the world, which obviously were used in armed conflict. They were supplied to those involved in the slave trade, and in the British Empire's defence of slave merchants. These people traffickers captured slaves in Africa and transported them to the plantations in the Americas and West Indies, where they were required, by force of arms, to work, live and die.

This apparent contradiction, of supporting pacifism through active Quakerism, while profiting from the instruments of misery, began to preoccupy the Religious Society of Friends more forcibly as tensions rose in Europe, in the days after the French Revolution and the succeeding wars. In 1790, the Religious Society of Friends issued guidance nationally, in its Yearly Meeting Epistle: 'If any be concerned in fabricating or selling Instruments of War, let them be treated with in love; and if by this unreclaimed, let them be further dealt with as those we cannot own. And we intreat [sic] that when warlike preparations are making, Friends be watchful lest any be drawn into loans, arming, or letting out their Ships, or Vessels, or otherwise promoting the destruction of the human Species.'[179] In assessing the character of Galton Junior, his reaction to the pressure on him to abandon his lucrative business as an expression of his faith is instructive. It would cause him and the family considerable difficulty.

By 1792, the Birmingham Meeting of Quakers, to which the Galtons belonged, had questioned openly the moral and religious correctness of accepting donations from members whose wealth was built on the arms trade. On 8th March 1795, the Meeting in Tamworth appointed three members, Sampson Lloyd, the banker, Samuel Baker and Joseph Gibbins to meet with the Galtons to pursue the concerns they had 'respecting the Inconsistency thereof [of involvement in the manufacture and trade of firearms], with our religious principles'. After several meetings, they reported to the Meeting on 8th July 1795, that as Samuel Galton Senior 'has relinquished the business & declined receiving any further emolument from it, the minute as far as respects his case is discontinued.'[180]

While Galton Senior's continued membership was secured, the same was not the case for his son. In fact, Galton Junior decided to provide a detailed statement of his views to the meeting on 13th January 1796, an extremely strong defence, which bears some examination. It is an extraordinary document, with the tone of the address by turns embattled, resentful, dismissive and appealing. Galton Junior performs intellectual gymnastics to justify the continuation of his trade, but the

179 *Faith & Disunity: Samuel Galton and the Quakers*, 22 March 2018
180 Ibid.

undeniable undercurrent of simmering anger culminates in his rejection of the expected conclusion to disown him as a Friend.

Beginning by addressing 'Respected Friends', and acknowledging the 'candid and liberal conduct' of 'my Worthy Friends, Sampson Lloyd, Samuel Baker and Joseph Gibbins', it soon descends into suspicion and defensiveness: 'I am very solicitous that you should comply with this request [to preserve this letter in the records], in order that my Children, or others, who may feel an interest in the Event, may have an opportunity hereafter, of informing themselves of the Circumstances, and of the motives of my conduct.' In an approach unlikely to gain much sympathy, he disparages the process to which he is subject 'because from the rules of your discipline, I am precluded from every other Mode of Defence.'[181]

Galton sets out his argument, moving from 'FACTS' to 'OBSERVATIONS' (Galton's capitals). An early FACT is that his family: 'and lastly, my Father and myself, have been engaged in this Manufactory for a period of *70 years without having before received any Animadversions on the part of the Society*' (Galton's italics). He indicates that he inherited the family fortune and the capital invested in the business, and that 'the Manufactory… appropriated Mills, Erections, and Apparatus [are] not easily assignable, or convertible to other purposes.' He comments that he has personally been involved only since 1777 (although he was a partner from 1774) and this was not queried by the Society until 1790. He strangely argues that his involvement is: 'not a matter of *choice*…and there has *never been a time*, when I would not have withdrawn from it, could I have found a proper Opportunity of transferring the Concern.' While this acknowledges the validity of the concerns, Galton then veers back onto the attack: 'I am convinced…THAT THE MANUFACTURE OF ARMS IMPLIES NO APPROBATION OF OFFENSIVE WAR – THAT THE DEGREE OF RESPONSIBILITY THAT HAS BEEN IMPUTED TO THAT MANUFACTURE DOES NOT ATTACH – AND THAT IN ITS OBJECT, OR ITS TENDENCIES, IT NEITHER PROMOTES WAR OR INCREASES ITS CALAMITIES.' This use of capitalisation is seen as a modern phenomenon, 'shouting' in texting and tweets, conveying anger and indignation. The train of thought here is one of the arguments used today by the National Rifle Association in the USA to justify the availability of weapons, that it is the person who fires the gun who is culpable, not the manufacturer or owner.

Galton expresses outrage at being assumed to 'encourage the *Practice* or the *Principle* of War', rather than his being simply a legitimate businessman engaged

---

181 *Letter from Samuel Galton, jnr to the Friends of the Monthly Meeting in Birmingham,* no date

in 'the acquisition of Property.' While arms are used for 'Offensive War', they are 'equally applicable to the purposes of DEFENSIVE WAR, to the Support of the CIVIL POWER, to the PREVENTION OF WAR, and to the PRESERVATION OF PEACE.' By the Quakers' application of this rationale, the barley farmer, brewer, importer and distiller of alcoholic drinks is equally responsible for intemperance, disease, vice and misery. Therefore, the manufacturer of firearms is not 'the cause of war', but 'a consequence'. Galton makes the frankly unsustainable claim that: 'Neither can it be admitted that the Calamities of War have been increased thereby – *all History*, both sacred and profane, proves the reverse – Those horrid Contests, since the invention of fire arms, are universally allowed to be *less sanguinary*, and *less ferocious.*' Really?

He cites examples from scripture to argue that the use of arms and weapons is supported in the Bible: 'does not Jesus Christ speak in high terms of Approbation of the Centurion? (whose Profession was Arms).' He challenges his accusers to examine their own behaviour: are they without the sin of relying on firearms? 'When your houses are beset, and invaded, by *Thieves* and *Murderers*, do you not call on the Civil Magistrate, and is he not obliged to *use Arms* against armed Ruffians?' He then quotes examples of Quakers, involved in the arms trade for over a century, who have been allowed to remain as Friends 'without any Censure from the Society.'

Galton's argument encompasses the whole financial system as an enabler of war, and concludes that anyone involved in business, or who pays taxes, is vicariously equally responsible for war. He ends by arguing that it is unreasonable for him to withdraw from his business and places the blame for any rejection of him by the Society on those who judge him: 'if I should be disowned – I shall not think that *I* have abandoned the Society, *but that the Society has withdrawn themselves from their antient* [sic]*, tolerant Spirit and Practice.*'[182]

This is an extraordinarily argumentative approach from someone trying to argue that he should be allowed to remain in the Society. He understandably feels that the world has changed around him, rendering his respectable business something undesirable and profane, which as a committed Quaker, must have deeply hurt. His arguments about hypocrisy in the use of the products of war and slavery have some validity. The Meeting of Friends was reluctant to exclude Galton, but unsurprisingly, given the guidance and change in attitudes, they were unable to accept his arguments. At the following meeting, on 10th February 1796, it was agreed not to accept further donations from Galton, as 'we cannot admit his arguments as substantial & 'tis

---

182 *Letter from Samuel Galton, jnr to the Friends of the Monthly Meeting in Birmingham*

matter of real concern to us that he sh[oul]d attempt to vindicate a practice which we conceive to be inconsistent with our religious principles & this meet[in]g directs the Preparative M[eetin]g of Birm[ingha]m, not to receive any further collection from him while he continues in the practice of fabricating & selling Instruments of war as a testimony of our disunity therewith.'[183]

Further overtures were made through members visiting Galton in attempts to persuade him to change his mind and renounce his business, but these were unsuccessful. On 9th March 1797, Galton was prevented from attending future meetings. The Regional Meeting was informed of the position and they also sent representatives to try once more to change Galton's position, and to persuade him to give up his business, all to no avail. Eventually on 19th August 1796, seven years after the initial guidance from the national organisation, and after repeated, frequently heated, discussions, meetings and cases made for and against, Galton was disowned by the Society of Friends, albeit with a route to re-join included in the judgement.

Samuel Galton's reaction has not been recorded but he continued to attend worship and did contribute financially to a Quaker school at Ackworth, Pontefract, Yorkshire, and to the Yearly Meeting, so the rigour with which the exclusion was enforced is in doubt.

He remained in touch with colleagues in the Lunar Society, and was the first to offer assistance to Priestley, taking his wife into protection in the aftermath of the July 1791 riots. Mary Priestley was a close friend of Lucy Galton and stayed with them during the four days of riot. This placed the Galtons at considerable risk themselves but Galton was consistently supportive of Priestley. He encouraged the traumatised preacher to return to Birmingham in September, promising to meet him to demonstrate public support for him, and asked him unsuccessfully to attend the Lunar Society's next meeting at Barr Hall. Following Priestley's move to Clapton, Galton sent him money to help him.

Amid these changes and tumultuous events, Galton purchased the Warley Hall estate in 1792 for £7,300 and commissioned Humphrey Repton, the landscape architect, to create what is now Warley Woods. Galton also saved Lightwoods Park, Bearwood from further building development.

Samuel Galton Junior and his son, Samuel Tertius Galton, continued to run the arms business, before they both moved into banking. This was more acceptable to the Quakers, and in accordance with the minute of the meeting on 19th August, 1796, Galton Junior was restored to the Society of Friends.

---

183 *Faith & Disunity: Samuel Galton and the Quakers*

His activities with the Lunar Society continued, although many of his friends were reaching the end of their lives in the early 1800s. When the Lunar Society was wound up in 1813, they held a lottery to determine who would curate the Society's library, and Galton Junior won, taking all the books home. He lived in quiet retirement for almost twenty years, and died aged seventy-nine, having seen the Great Reform Act enacted, on 19th June 1832, the only Lunar Society member to do so. He was buried in the Quaker cemetery in Bull Lane. In his will, he left £300,000, a massive fortune.

His descendants included several notable people, including his grandson Sir Francis Galton, son of Samuel Tertius and Frances Darwin, daughter of Erasmus Darwin. Sir Francis invented the science of fingerprinting in criminal detection and the now discredited 'science' of eugenics. Another grandson, Sir Douglas Strutt Galton, son of John Howard, was an engineer, a Captain in the Royal Engineers, and became Secretary to the Railways Department, Board of Trade and Director of Public Works and Buildings, contributing, as a supporter of Florence Nightingale, to improved hospital design and construction.

Galton Junior is remembered in the dedication of Galton Bridge, across a Smethwick canal. Built by Thomas Telford in 1829, this was the highest single span bridge in the world, at 151 feet. Telford's new canal crossed the loops created by Brindley, and cut through the hill at Smethwick, and included building Edgbaston Reservoir at Rotton Park. The bridge stands 71 feet above the canal, which reduced the distance from Birmingham to Wednesbury by two miles and travel time by three hours. This New Main Line overcame chronic congestion, but Brindley's original canal was retained as a series of loops and branches from the new canal, allowing businesses to retain access and flourish.

The bridge was dedicated to Galton as the largest shareholder in the project. While initially a road bridge, it is now accessible only to pedestrians, and listed as a Grade I building. The adjacent railway station is named Smethwick Galton Bridge. This still attractive bridge is best viewed from the station platform for the line from Birmingham to Stourbridge.

Galton and his family are remembered in the names of roads in Bearwood, around Warley Woods. As well as Galton Road and Barclay Road, Abbey Road and Abbey Crescent (as well as Abbey Infant and Junior schools) are named after Warley Abbey, built by Hubert Galton, one of his sons, and demolished in 1975. Hadzor Road is named after Hadzor House, the family seat from 1821. A blue plaque erected by Smethwick Local History Society in 2000 at Abbey Junior School, Abbey Road, near Warley Woods, records Galton Junior's creation of the park and woodland. He is memorialised by one of the Moonstones for Lunar Society members at the Asda Superstore in Great Barr. This notes that meetings were held at the nearby Barr Hall. Galton's Moonstone depicts 'Experiments on Colours by Mr. Galton'.

Samuel Galton Jnr, by unknown artist

Galton Moonstone in the car park of Asda Superstore, Old Horns Crescent, Queslett, in Great Barr, Birmingham, B43 7HA

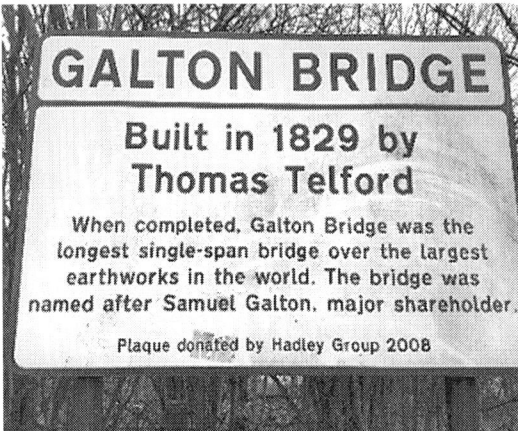

GALTON BRIDGE

Built in 1829 by Thomas Telford

When completed, Galton Bridge was the longest single-span bridge over the largest earthworks in the world. The bridge was named after Samuel Galton, major shareholder.

Plaque donated by Hadley Group 2008

Galton Bridge, Oldbury Road, Smethwick, B66 1HU

6

Thinking and Acting for Others – Social Conscience, Political Consciousness and Philanthropy in early nineteenth century Birmingham

As the eighteenth century became the nineteenth century, two men were born within two years who would develop and implement methods of working and treating people with illnesses that would resonate far beyond Birmingham. Born in 1799, George Bodington revolutionised how 'consumptive' patients were treated. His methods informed a new national approach on treating tuberculosis, including its development as a medical specialty. In the second year of the next century, William Sands Cox was born. He trained as a surgeon, before teaching medical students in Birmingham, establishing the first medical college outside London. This would become, first, Queen's College, and later, the Medical School of the University of Birmingham almost a century later.

GEORGE BODINGTON
'The pioneering physician who revolutionised the care of tuberculosis'

George Bodington was born in 1799 to a wealthy landowning family, in Calverton, Buckinghamshire. His family had worked the land in Cubbington, near Leamington Spa, Warwickshire, since the time of Henry VIII. He attended Magdalen College School in Oxford, and decided to pursue a career in medicine. He was apprenticed to a Mr Syer in Atherstone, and then transferred to Mr Wheelwright, a surgeon in London. He studied at St. Bartholomew's Hospital and

125

achieved the Licentiate of the Society of Apothecaries in 1825. He married Ann Fowler, from a prosperous local family, at this time. He achieved the Licentiate of the Royal College of Physicians in Edinburgh in 1859. He moved to Birmingham to practise as a physician and general practitioner in Hillaries Road, Erdington, from 1825. In 1836, he rented the 'White House' in Maney, Sutton Coldfield, as the location to develop effective treatments for 'consumptive' patients. He purchased the Driffold House Lunatic Asylum in 1836, and moved his family there, as well as accommodating patients with mental health problems.

He developed an interest in pulmonary consumption, now termed tuberculosis. In the 1830s, treatment was harsh and cruel for patients, as well as substantially ineffective. Sufferers were bled, cauterised, given mercury-based treatments, purges and emetics, and virtually starved, while kept in rooms from which fresh air was deliberately excluded as much as possible. Rich patients were sent to foreign towns and ports, but experienced the same regime there, often dying far from home and family.

Bodington saw this treatment regime as 'helpless and meagre', 'the utter uselessness of which is so well-known and so obvious.'[184] He published an essay addressed to the President and Council of the Central Board of Health, London, in 1831 which attacked the established treatment of Asiatic cholera, indicating his willingness to oppose conventional medical thinking. He followed this in 1840 with his most well-known publication, his essay 'On the Treatment and Cure of Pulmonary Consumption'.

This eighty page treatise identified the contemporary approach to treatment, which included the use of the drugs digitalis and tartar emetic. He was scathing about the closeting of patients in airless rooms, which forced 'them to breathe over and over again the same foul air contaminated with the diseased effluvia of their own persons.' As we now know, he was correct that this exacerbated patients' difficulties rather than helping to overcome the disease. He felt that this regime resulted in an attitude of 'desperate hopelessness' from both patients and doctors. His approach was set out, based on five case studies. These represented a radically different approach, based on 'the most important remedial agent in the cure of consumption, that of the free use of a pure atmosphere; not the impure air of a close room, or even that of the house generally, but the air out of doors, early in the morning, either by riding or walking;…therefore riding or carriage exercise should be employed for several hours daily, with intervals of walking as much as the strength will allow of, gradually increasing the length of the walk until it can

---

184 R.Y. Keers, 'Two forgotten pioneers: James Carson and George Bodington', *Thorax* (July 1980)

be maintained easily several hours every day.' Bodington addressed the issue of poor weather, and denied that exposure to cold air would be deleterious to these patients' health, arguing that the reverse is true: 'The application of cold pure air to the interior surface of the lungs is the most powerful sedative that can be applied, and does more to promote the healing and closing of cavities and ulcers of the lungs than any other means that can be employed.'[185]

Modern medical practitioners have indicated that two of these patients may have been suffering from lung abscesses, and the other three from tuberculosis, but the essential point is that all five recovered well following Bodington's regime. A young tool-maker from Erdington progressed from breathlessness and exhaustion to return to work and was taught how to use natural treatments when symptoms returned. Bodington described the care of a sixteen year old woman, whose family opposed his regime until she was close to death. Fortunately, it was not too late and she recovered very well under Bodington's care, writing to a doctor in Switzerland, sixty-six years later, that she was still well. This woman was Hannah Fowler from Birches Green, Erdington, Bodington's niece.

He cared for these patients at Driffold House, giving them the opportunity to receive clinical care based on 'the free use of a pure atmosphere' inside, but more effectively in the open air. This approach was combined with a nutritious diet, 'of mild, fresh animal and farinaceous food, aided by the stimulus of a proper quantity of wine, having regard to the general state and condition of the patient.'[186] He avoided using drugs, believing more in the curative impact of nature itself. He opposed the popular use of digitalis and tartar emetic, but occasionally used morphine as a sedative, when required. Bodington established his home as a sanatorium, then a novel approach, but which became the standard mode of treatment and care for tuberculosis patients throughout the world, until the development of antibiotics.

At the end of the essay, he proposed developing a specialised branch of medicine, in larger towns and cities, to treat consumptive patients. For the poor, he felt that hospitals should be established, allowing access to open air, with provision for outdoor exercise, including gardening and farming for convalescent patients, alongside riding and walking. This approach was not taken up, unfortunately, and it was not until 1886, four years after Bodington's death, that a National Tuberculosis Scheme was proposed, which was also recommended in the Astor Report in 1912.

---

185 Keers, 'Two forgotten pioneers: James Carson and George Bodington', *Thorax*
186 Ibid.

This prescient essay was poorly received by the medical establishment. The Lancet was harsh in its rejection of Bodington's approach, giving an outline of the principles set out, 'without expending any portion of our critical wrath on his very crude ideas and unsupported assertions.' This was hardly fair-minded and it had a considerable impact on Bodington. He was greatly disheartened, and decided to stop treating patients with tuberculosis within three years. It was only in 1857 that the Journal of Public Health and British Medical Journal published articles supporting his approach, seventeen years after the essay was initially published.

Bodington changed the nature of his home and sanatorium to deliver care and treatment for mental illnesses, developing Driffold House as an asylum. His thirty years of care for patients with mental health problems was virtually overlooked by commentators, although it is referenced in his obituary in the British Medical Journal on 11th March 1882. Although licensed 'for the reception of insane persons, 25 in number, male and female, whereof 5 to be parish pauper patients,' the census of 1851 records eleven 'lunatics' residing at Driffold House, and six staff, including Bodington and his family.[187] He provided careful and humane care to 'lunatics', at a time when this was unusual, but is entirely consistent with his general approach to providing care. He continued to do so until his retirement in 1866, when he passed responsibility for running the asylum to his eldest son, Dr George Fowler Bodington. George had been trained at Queen's College, and would later be a founding member of the Birmingham Medical Institute, serving as one of its early presidents. Driffold House, which stood on the corner of the road of the same name and Wyndley Lane, closed in 1884 and has now been demolished. By the 1881 census, Bodington was living at Manor Hill, close to Sutton Park, and his two daughters ran a girls' boarding school there. Of the nine pupils identified as residents, five were Bodington's nieces.

In his early life, and in his retirement, Bodington participated in civic life, being elected as a councillor (for life, as was then the custom) to Sutton Coldfield Corporation. He was a magistrate and served as Warden (Mayor) from 1852 to 1854. He stood for Parliament, unsuccessfully, in 1859. A man of strong opinions and convictions, he was able to express them in the political as well as the medical sphere. He was a Protectionist in terms of trade issues and strongly advocated his chosen political positions. For many years he was a member of the Birmingham and Midland Counties branch of the British Medical Association.

---

187 Roger Lea, *George Bodington: Pioneer Physician Treating TB and Mental Illness*, (2013)

George Bodington as a young man, 1830, hand coloured photograph, unknown artist, reproduced by kind permission of Tim Boddington

Blue plaque on flats at the corner of Gravelly Hill and Hillaries Road, at Erdington, Birmingham, B23 7PE

Garden with a commemorative plaque between Maney Corner and the Birmingham Road (A5127), B72 1QR

George Bodington died on 5th February 1882, aged eighty-three. His obituary in the British Medical Journal ensured his legacy was acknowledged, indicating that the author was 'glad again to claim for a general practitioner the high credit of having been the first, or among the first, to advocate the rational and scientific treatment of pulmonary consumption.'[188] The Lancet's obituary acknowledged

188 'Obituary', *British Medical Journal*, (11 March 1882), p.362

its error in 1840. Keers comments that 'his only error lay in being wise before his time.'[189]

The buildings which Bodington used for his clinical practice have now gone. The White House was demolished in 1935, to make way for shops and the Odeon cinema. However, George Bodington is remembered by a blue plaque erected by the Birmingham Civic Society on the second floor of a block of flats on the corner of Gravelly Hill and Hillaries Road, Erdington. It was originally erected on 14th April 1956, on his former medical practice, 165, Gravelly Hill, which was subsequently demolished. On 6th June 1953, the Royal Town of Sutton Coldfield unveiled a garden with a commemorative plaque in Bodington's honour, between Maney Corner and the Birmingham Road, an appropriate open air space, a short distance from where his sanatorium was located.

WILLIAM SANDS COX

'The determined, or stubborn, surgeon who founded Birmingham's
first medical school, and The Queen's Hospital,
later Birmingham Accident Hospital'

William Sands Cox was born in 1801, the eldest son of Edward Townsend Cox (1769-1863), an established surgeon in Birmingham, and was educated at King Edward VI Grammar School. His medical education reflected his privileged background, beginning at Birmingham General Hospital, working with his father, and then progressing at Guy's and St. Thomas's Hospitals in London from 1821 to 1823, and the École de Médecin in Paris in 1824. By then, he had been admitted as a Member of the Royal College of Surgeons. Appointed as a surgeon to the General Dispensary, Cox was ambitious to establish a medical school and having visited several in Great Britain and on the continent, he advertised in Aris's Birmingham Gazette on 7th November 1825 'a course of ANATOMICAL DEMONSTRATIONS with Surgical and Physiological Observations.'[190] These commenced on 1st December 1825, with nineteen students, at his father's house, at 24, Temple Row. A requirement for entry was being an Anglican.

In 1827, aged twenty-six, Cox became joint surgeon to the infirmary in Birmingham, with his father. Key to the school's success was obtaining the support of senior members of the local medical establishment, including Dr Edward Johnstone, physician to the General Hospital from 1779 to 1801. Johnstone later founded the Provincial Medical and Surgical Association, with Cox's active support,

---

189 Keers, 'Two forgotten pioneers: James Carson and George Bodington', *Thorax*
190 *History of the University of Birmingham Medical School, 1825-2001*, no date

and this became the British Medical Association. Cox's school grew rapidly, with him lecturing on anatomy and surgery, and as the curriculum developed in the first three years, Cox's achievement impressed local colleagues. At a meeting on 15th April 1828, it was agreed to establish the Birmingham School of Medicine and Surgery. This opened on 28th October 1828, and was immediately recognised by the Royal College of Surgeons of England, the Society of Apothecaries of London and the Royal College of Surgeons of Edinburgh.

The organisation's success necessitated a move in 1829 to a new building in Brittle Street. One of the school's pupils was Francis Galton, later Sir Francis, the grandson of Galton Junior. A further move took place as the expansion of the Great Western Railway required the Brittle Street site to develop Snow Hill Station, and the Medical School moved to what became Queen's College, built on land purchased by Cox's father. A new frontage, completed in 1904, still stands in Paradise Street, opposite the Town Hall. It was an undoubtedly successful organisation, with every student in the first eight years passing the Royal College of Surgeons' examination in London.

In 1836, King William IV became patron of the Medical School, allowing it to be known as 'The Birmingham Royal School of Medicine and Surgery'. However, there were concerns about the effectiveness of the teaching facilities in the Workhouse Infirmary, and it proved impossible to use those in the nearby General Hospital, as Cox's insistence on controlling all teaching was unacceptable to them. Undeterred, Cox resolved to establish his own hospital, and with funding from a wealthy private patient, he set up and opened a hospital within a year, without any outstanding debt, on 28th October 1841, in Bath Row. Cox was senior surgeon, later becoming consulting surgeon. Following a petition to Queen Victoria, the hospital was known as Queen's Hospital, with room for 130 patients. Staff appointed were required to undertake clinical teaching. In 1843, Queen Victoria granted a Royal Charter to the medical school, establishing Queen's College. That same year, Cox was elected Fellow of the Royal Society, becoming the school's first Dean of Medicine.

Cox wanted to develop Queen's College further, expanding its curriculum to include architecture, civil engineering, law, literature, arts and theology, in addition to surgery and medicine, thereby establishing a provincial Anglican university. The curriculum expanded initially to include the arts in 1847 and theology in 1851, and he used a public subscription of £1,050 in 1857 to fund scholarships and the College's museums. He was influenced by leading Anglican clergymen, the Reverend Samuel Warneford, Rector of Bourton-on-the-Hill, Gloucestershire, and the Reverend James Law, Chancellor of the Diocese of Lichfield. Warneford in particular influenced the exclusion of Roman Catholics, Jews, and Non-Conformists, which created considerable tensions in a town as open and diverse as Birmingham. Cox's personality created further difficulty, given his requirement to be in control of all aspects of the institution. In his role as Principal of the College from 1858 to 1859, according to the Birmingham Daily Post on 28th December 1875, 'he was autocratic in his mode of conducting both institutions, and as his administrative faculty was by no means equal to his creative power, and to the readiness with which he gave and obtained money, the college and hospital both became involved in a succession of serious quarrels between the founder and his associates.'[191] The high cost of expanding the curriculum, and competition from a rival medical school, Sydenham College, at 12, St. Paul's Square, meant that the College began to fall into debt. The General Hospital also began to expand, supported by Sydenham College, and became very successful, developing expanded premises in Summer Lane in 1858.

As debts grew to £10,000 by the 1860s, the Queen's College was in considerable difficulty, and facing bankruptcy. In an increasingly acrimonious atmosphere, Cox's colleagues appealed to the Charity Commissioners, who required the separation of the hospital and college, as enacted in the Queen's College (Birmingham) Act 1867. This was unacceptable to Cox, so he resigned and had no further involvement with either the College or the Hospital.

Having left Birmingham in 1863, when his father died, Cox retired to Bole Hall, near Tamworth, with his wife Isabella, and also lived at Leamington, and at Glass House, Kenilworth. In retirement he published the four volume 'The Annals of Queen's College' in 1873, which added to his numerous articles in the London Medical Gazette and several books on medical procedures throughout his career.

He died in Kenilworth on 23rd December 1875 and is buried in Aston Parish Church. His will included legacies to several medical institutions, but not Queen's College or Queen's Hospital. Instead, he left £3,000 plus his medical books and instruments to Moreton-in-Marsh cottage hospital, two bequests of £3,000 to endow dispensaries in Tamworth and Kenilworth, and £12,000 for the same purpose in Birmingham. Further bequests funded scholarships at King Edward VI School in Birmingham and Guy's Hospital, London. As well as a magistrate and deputy lieutenant of Warwickshire, Cox was a committed Anglican, and his legacies included funds to complete the building of a church in Birmingham.

---

191 G.T. Bettany, revised by Patrick Wallis, 'Cox, William Sands (1802-1875)' *Oxford Dictionary of National Biography*, (Oxford: 2004, updated 2012)

His estrangement from the institutions he founded and developed was a sad end to his career and was unfortunate, given his central role in founding both a medical school and a significant hospital in Birmingham. He is described as irascible and impatient of having to deal with the views of others, but this could be seen as focussed and determined entrepreneurship, which led to substantial achievements. While the Medical School may well have been founded even without him, it is clear that it happened earlier than otherwise and for this, he deserves to be remembered as a pioneer with great enthusiasm and drive from an early age, being only twenty-four when his 1825 advertisement appeared in Aris's Birmingham Gazette.

He is remembered through the Sands Cox Society at the University of Birmingham Medical School, which also displays several portraits, and by a blue plaque erected by the City of Birmingham, at the rear entrance to the former House of Fraser store in Temple Row. A further blue plaque was erected on the building that housed the Birmingham Accident Hospital, commemorating the Queen's Hospital, and is visible on Bath Row.

William Sands Cox by Thomas Herbert Maguire, 1854, from the collection of the National Library of Medicine, USA

Blue plaque at the rear entrance to the former House of Fraser store, Temple Row, Birmingham, B2 5LS

The effects of the French Revolution continued to infect political thinking in Great Britain early in the nineteenth century, prompting growing agitation for an expansion of the electoral franchise and a greater level of representation in

Parliament for the less well off. This came particularly from expanding industrial towns like Liverpool, Manchester, Sheffield and, of course, Birmingham, as demand grew for direct representation rather than through the often remote and unconnected county towns. In the case of Birmingham, representation was by MPs elected in Warwickshire. Pressure grew for the abolition of 'rotten boroughs' where populations had declined, but MPs were still elected, often by very small numbers of people. Towns which had become major centres of population argued against the corruption often associated with these anachronistic arrangements and saw their opportunity to take over these seats in the House of Commons. The new political consciousness was embodied in Birmingham mainly by one man, Thomas Attwood. Born in Halesowen, Attwood was originally a banker and middle class Tory, who changed his views significantly. He came to be seen as so radical, by establishment Tories and the aristocracy, that he seemed to threaten revolution. A skilled and incisive orator, he would be called 'the most influential man in England' and was a major force behind securing the passage of the Great Reform Act of 1832 which enabled his return as one of the first two Members of Parliament for Birmingham.

THOMAS ATTWOOD

'Radical thinker, persuasive orator, 'the most influential man in England', who became Birmingham's first Member of Parliament'

Thomas Attwood was born on 6th October 1783, at Hawne House in Halesowen, then Shropshire. He was the son of Matthias (born 1746, died 1836) and Ann, née Adams (born 1752, died 1835). Ann was from Cakemore, near Halesowen. There were ten children, seven sons and three daughters. Thomas's grandfather, George, began mining iron ore in Halesowen in the mid-eighteenth century and opened steel furnaces at Corngreaves in 1771, before opening steel, copper and rolling mills in Birmingham by 1797. Matthias and his brother James continued this success in coal and iron making, and Matthias became a partner in the bank of Spooner, Attwood, and Co. Ltd, in New Street. All the male children of Matthias and Ann were successful, as bankers, ironmakers, High Bailiffs of Birmingham (Thomas, 1811; George, 1827), MPs (Thomas from 1832; Matthias Junior, from 1819 to 1847), glassmaker and philanthropist. This was therefore a wealthy and influential middle class family of entrepreneurs and industrialists.

Thomas attended Halesowen Grammar School, now Earls High School, before attending Wolverhampton Grammar School. In 1799, he began work at the family bank. He married a farmer's daughter, Elizabeth Carless (born 1784 or 85, died

1840), from Lower Ravenhurst Farm, on what is now the Moor Pool Estate, Harborne, on 12th May 1806. Their union produced three children, George de Bosco (born 1808), Thomas Aurelius (born 1810) and Angela. From 1823 to 1846, they lived at The Grove, Harborne, and the grounds of the Georgian house became Grove Park after the house was demolished in 1963.

Attwood's work in banking gave him experience of issues facing commerce and manufacturing. He became an influential figure in Birmingham politics, becoming High Bailiff in 1811 at the age of twenty-eight. This was the highest local government office at the time. Nationally, he opposed the monopoly of the East India Company, provided by Parliament to allow exploitation of foreign trade opportunities across the British Empire. Attwood felt these restrictions on Midlands businesses were increasing unemployment, and he joined the campaign to remove the legislative advantage afforded to the East India Company. This included leading a Birmingham delegation to Parliament in 1812, to give evidence to the Select Committee investigating the issue. His evidence contributed substantially to the House of Commons deciding to end the Company's monopoly, and he was lauded by local artisans and businessmen, who raised £300 and presented him, on his thirtieth birthday, with an engraved silver cup, designed by Birmingham artist, Samuel Lines. This successful campaign encouraged him to consider economic policy more widely and he developed proposals for reforming the currency.

At this stage of political development, he was definitely a middle class Tory, believing in 'Church and King' and that men of property were best-placed to make decisions in Parliament that would affect the rest of the population. He stated in 1822 that universal suffrage was to be opposed as it 'would necessarily lead to the right of sitting in Parliament without the qualification of property.'[192] He certainly abhorred violence in pursuit of political aims, and always retained this view, although some of his views would change and develop in the light of experience.

In 1816, he published the first of seven pamphlets on currency reform, 'The Remedy, or, Thoughts on the Present Distress'. The distress was an economic crisis, which he argued could be alleviated by better management of the money supply. Proposing an argument that is now mainstream economic thinking, following Keynesian principles, his premise was that the lack of available money reduced the general population's spending, which limited demand, leading to under-production. This 'underconsumption' could be overcome by expanding

---

192 Clive Behagg, 'Attwood, Thomas (1783-1856)', *Oxford Dictionary of National Biography*, (Oxford: 2004, updated 2009)

production to meet the current need by the government issuing paper-based currency as required. Today, this is 'quantitative easing'. He expounded that the results would be high wages and increased profits as people spent more of their higher income. This argument was not well-received, and although it gained widespread support in Birmingham, it was not supported by the government or the rest of the country. He was derided as a 'currency crank' and 'crude inflationist'. The future Prime Minister Benjamin Disraeli dismissed Attwood as 'a provincial banker labouring under a financial monomania.'[193] Despite a supportive public petition of 40,000 signatures, Attwood's proposals were rejected by Lord Liverpool's Tory government.

Considerable social upheaval followed the Napoleonic Wars, and calls for social change were resisted by the government, with the established political classes fearful of the example of the 1789 revolution in France. Pressures increased on the poor, prices and the population rose substantially, while wages fell, and unemployment grew rapidly, as less labour was required due to increasing mechanisation. The Spitalfields riots in 1816 and the Peterloo Massacre in 1819 are two of the better known examples of the ensuing division and strife, as the government sought to repress dissent and agitation, and preserve the status quo.

Attwood came to believe, during the 1820s, that the economic reforms he propounded could only be achieved through changing the nature of those involved in decision-making in Parliament. He advocated that middle class men of property and business should be engaged in debates on policy formulation and in running the government. These individuals were usually involved in business and commerce in the rapidly expanding towns, like Birmingham. Attwood joined the campaign to reform 'rotten boroughs', to ensure large towns would be represented by MPs drawn from people like him. At the time, the two MPs representing Birmingham were elected to a Warwickshire constituency, clearly not reflecting the changed demographics and growth of the manufacturing towns. By 1830, there were fifty six rotten boroughs, each with less than fifty voters, and each sent two MPs to Parliament. In contrast, there were no MPs to represent the people of Leeds, Manchester, Sheffield and Birmingham, which had a combined population of over 540,000. The seats in rotten boroughs were sold by auction, with advertising in newspapers, and were purchased by rich men, frequently with no connection to the area which the seats 'represented'.

193 *Thomas Attwood*, no date

Although Attwood's political views became more radical, he was by no means a revolutionary, and his initial efforts in 1827 involved support for a private member's bill to transfer representation from East Retford, a rotten borough in Nottinghamshire, to Birmingham. Attwood felt the reasonableness of the argument would succeed, but when it failed, and he observed the success of a public campaign in 1828 for electoral emancipation for Roman Catholics, he committed to a popular campaign to secure both his cherished currency reform and larger parliamentary reform. His first public commitment to the cause of reforming Parliament was in May 1829, during a remarkably long, three-hour speech to a crowd of between 4,000 and 5,000. A petition of 8,000 signatures was organised, but this was rejected by Parliament.

The Tory Party had been in government since 1807, and the long tenure of Lord Liverpool was followed by brief tenures as Prime Minister by George Canning and Viscount Goderich, before the Duke of Wellington became Prime Minister on 22nd January 1828. All these governments had remained obdurate to calls for reform, including Wellington, whose military tendency was to crush dissent. The Whig Party indicated they would support political reform if in government, encouraging radicals to organise further.

Attwood and others established a permanent group to campaign actively for reform, the 'Birmingham Political Union of the lower and middle classes of the people'. Its formal title was 'The Political Union for the Protection of Public Rights'. On 14th December 1829, a set of rules was agreed between activists, meeting at the Royal Hotel, New Street, and these were set out to a meeting at Beardsworth's Repository For Horses and Carriages, Balsall Street, in Birmingham's market district. A staggering 80,000 people attended on 25th January 1830, and the proposed rules for the Birmingham Political Union (BPU) were approved by a majority of twenty to one. The BPU adopted the slogan 'I'm backing Britain', with this appearing on a Union Jack badge.

The first annual meeting of the BPU on 26th July 1830 was chaired by Sir Francis Burdett, a Radical MP. Initially, the Union argued the case for better representation for manufacturing industries through direct representation of the large towns, and Attwood was keen to confirm that its proposals did not include universal suffrage or annual parliaments, although it did include a commitment to secret ballots from December 1830.

He argued that common interests and objectives for change existed between working men and their employers, his rhetoric referring to both 'productive capital' and 'productive labour'. He stated: 'the interests of masters and men are, in fact, one. If the masters flourish the men flourish with them; and if the masters suffer difficulties their difficulties must shortly affect the workmen in a threefold degree.'[194] His views ensured that men from the middle class, not the working class, populated the Union's controlling council, affirming his belief that leaders who effected change were always 'men of wealth and influence.'

Despite a modest membership of only 6,000 people in August 1830, the election of a minority Whig government under Earl Grey on 22nd November 1830 ensured Attwood and his fellow activists in the BPU had a concrete cause around which to coalesce and Attwood became 'the most influential man in England.'[195] He was now in a position to ensure public support for the changes proposed by the Whig government.

The example of the BPU was copied throughout the country, with many areas adopting the Union's rules wholesale, and by the end of 1830, there were twenty-seven affiliated unions. Attwood frequently addressed large open air meetings, attendance at which was estimated at times to be a remarkable 200,000. He had a strong and occasionally violent rhetorical style, designed to generate strength of feeling in support of parliamentary reform. The BPU campaigned for shorter term parliaments from the existing seven year term, to increase accountability to electors, and abolition of the need to own property to become an MP, extending its availability to ordinary people. To ensure this was a viable option for working people, they campaigned for payment of MPs from the public purse. A further demand was the extension of suffrage to all who paid taxes, either locally or nationally, through direct or indirect taxation.

Another attempt to provide Birmingham with parliamentary representation was made in February 1831, with the rotten borough of Evesham the target, but this also failed. This seemed immaterial, in light of the national developments taking place. Lord John Russell, a leading Whig and Liberal, Prime Minister twice during the early part of Queen Victoria's reign, introduced a Reform Bill in the Commons on 1st March 1831. He had tried to move the abolition of individual rotten boroughs a few years earlier, transferring their representation to larger towns, as supported by Attwood in 1827 and 1831. This broad-based and encompassing Reform Bill was vehemently opposed by Tories in both Houses, but pressure from the general population was growing, sustained by Attwood and his fellow activists. They repeatedly petitioned Parliament to support the Bill, with eighty petitions being presented to the Commons on a single day, 4th October 1831. Although

---

194 Briggs, quoted in Behagg, 'Attwood, Thomas (1783-1856)', *Oxford Dictionary of National Biography*
195 Brock, quoted in Ibid.

committed to securing change by peaceful means, frustration grew when the Reform Bill failed to pass the Commons. The Duke of Wellington even asked King William IV to return him to power to repress the civil unrest militarily. As the protests were peaceful, the King wisely did not agree.

As Grey led a minority government, he resigned and called a general election and was returned to power with a large majority, thereby making the prospects of success much brighter. This time the Commons passed the Second Reform Bill in July with a majority of 140, but despite widespread public support, as displayed at a Union-led meeting on Newhall Hill, with 15,000 people on 3rd October 1831, the Lords rejected the Bill again on 8th October. Widespread riots and serious disturbances followed, in London, Birmingham, Bristol, Derby, Exeter, Leicester, Nottingham, Sherborne and Yeovil. The Commons tried again in December 1831, only for the Bill to be rejected again by the Lords. In the prevailing febrile atmosphere, in November, Attwood announced that the BPU would arm its members, ready to fight for reform. This was not carried through, after being declared illegal by royal proclamation, and efforts continued to pass the Reform Bill in Parliament. In March 1832, the Reform Bill passed the Commons again and was sent to the Lords once more. Attwood addressed a meeting of an astonishing 200,000 people, from forty of the now hundreds of Political Unions across the country, on 7th May 1832, at Newhall Hill. Known as 'The Great Gathering of the Unions', this had a carnival-like atmosphere, with a final procession four miles in length, Attwood himself, as depicted in an oil painting, being brought into the centre of the meeting, in a carriage pulled by working men. In his speech, Attwood claimed that they 'had united two million men peacefully and legally in one grand and determined association to recover the liberty, the happiness, and the prosperity of the country.' Exerting maximum pressure on the Lords by demonstrating overwhelming public support for the Bill, he said: 'I would rather die than see the great bill of reform rejected or mutilated.'[196] Despite this 'Gathering of the Unions', and the march of 500 businessmen and middle class professionals in support of Attwood, the Lords voted down the bill once more, on the same day. Grey approached the King and asked him to create sufficient new peers to overturn the Tories' Lords majority, to ensure the Bill became law. When he refused, Grey resigned again on 9th May, and Wellington was asked again to form a government.

This constitutional crisis is seen as the time when Great Britain came closest to revolution and events moved very quickly, during the 'Days of May', as

---

196 Wakefield, quoted in Behagg, 'Attwood, Thomas (1783-1856)', *Oxford Dictionary of National Biography*

this period became known. Civil unrest grew quickly, with news of Grey's resignation reaching Birmingham on 10th May. Membership of the BPU rose very quickly, with threats of an organised campaign to withhold tax, alongside a run on gold at the Bank of England. In response, the military was mobilised to garrison towns across England, with Birmingham garrisoned by the Scots Greys, 'booted, saddled, and loaded with ball cartridge.'[197] There were attacks on the property of Lords known to have voted against the Bill, and petitions were presented to Parliament from all over the country. Attwood claimed that the whole country could be mobilised within one hour, and it is clear from contemporary accounts that the upper classes were very frightened. Queen Adelaide had the 'fixed impression ...that an English revolution is rapidly approaching, and that her own fate is to be that of Marie Antoinette.' While historians describe the country as being 'within an ace of revolution', a Whig MP, Edward Littleton, stated that it was in 'a state little short of insurrection', and a clergyman, Sydney Smith, rather more graphically described 'a hand-shaking, bowel-disturbing passion of fear.'[198]

In Birmingham, it was rumoured that Attwood would be arrested on Wellington's authority, and as workers went on spontaneous strike, 100,000 people gathered on Newhall Hill, where Attwood denounced Wellington, describing his 'incompetency to govern' and invoking the Bill of Rights as justification for the 'right to arm'. These febrile times meant that Attwood was surrounded at home by armed guards.

In the event, Wellington, described by Grey as a man who 'didn't understand the character of the times', was unable to form a government, and King William IV recalled Earl Grey as Prime Minister on 15th May 1832. Attwood travelled to London to meet him and was made a freeman of the city. The King now reluctantly agreed to Grey's demand for the appointment of Whig-supporting peers, and even wrote to existing peers, without Grey's knowledge, to warn them of the consequences of further resistance. Rather than see a permanent change in the balance of the upper chamber, the Tory majority in the Lords abstained when the Reform Bill was sent again by the Commons, and it was passed, becoming The Representation of the People Act, 1832, given royal assent on 7th June 1832. It is more popularly known as The Great Reform Act.

For Attwood, this was the crowning moment of his career, and he was called 'King Tom' by William Cobbett, the journalist, MP and author of 'Rural Rides'.

---

197 Bird, *Portrait of Birmingham*, p.97
198 *Days of May*, (no date)

The Times newspaper called the BPU 'the barometer of the reform feeling throughout England', confirming the roles of Attwood and Birmingham at the centre of these turbulent political times. The Act gave two MPs to Birmingham, and in the election on 12th December 1832, Attwood became an MP, along with Joshua Scholefield, a fellow activist from the BPU. They were unopposed, as the Tories were unable to find anyone willing to stand against them. Attwood was subsequently re-elected on 7th January 1835. In this election, Attwood and Scholefield were opposed by Richard Spooner, a Conservative, who uncomfortably was Attwood's banking partner. During a Town Hall meeting, the crush in the gallery was so great that the front of it collapsed, with people falling onto those beneath. Attwood and Scholefield were both returned with substantial majorities. The 1837 election was similarly dramatic, the Tory headquarters in the Royal Hotel being attacked by a mob, breaking windows with stones, and in return, being pelted with roof tiles by those inside. The riot went on all night, until soldiers arrived next morning from West Bromwich and Coventry to restore order.

Despite electoral successes, Attwood was unable to secure support for his ideas on currency reform. The length of his speeches in the House may have put off other members, and as an independent he became increasingly disappointed in his inability to make a substantial impact, in contrast to his leadership of the BPU. The Union itself, having achieved its objective, became much less of a force, and was disbanded amidst acrimony in June 1834.

Attwood continued to champion Birmingham, and campaigned for the town to become an incorporated borough, under the Municipal Corporations Act of 1835. This did not incorporate any of the towns at a stroke, but it did allow unincorporated towns to petition Parliament for incorporation. This would mean towns were governed by town councils, with councillors elected by ratepayers, although aldermen could still be appointed for six year terms. Elections to councils were held each year, with one third of members elected each year to represent specific wards, ensuring three year terms, consistency and continuity. Each borough had to appoint a paid town clerk and treasurer, who were not members of the council, and accounts were to be published and audited.

In Birmingham, there were distractions which held up the application for a Charter of Incorporation for two years. Political parties took opposite sides in the debate, as 'the desire for a Corporation existed only amongst the Liberal party', with the Tories stridently opposed, and the Whigs being 'passive, if not active, sympathisers.' A petition was submitted to the Privy Council for incorporation, on Wednesday 1st March, 1837, 'a date which deserves honourable remembrance in the history of Birmingham.'[199]

To support incorporation, Attwood revived the BPU in May 1837, seeing it as a vehicle to overcome local Tory opposition, through reviving the alliance between working people and the middle classes. Initially, Attwood supported household, rather than universal, suffrage, and set out his proposals on this basis. He had lost none of his rhetorical power, declaring at a meeting in June 1837: 'we have against us, the whole of the aristocracy, nine-tenths of the gentry, the great body of the clergy, and all the pensioners, sinecurists, and bloodsuckers that feed on the vitals of the people.'[200] Nonetheless, his attempt to revive the Union was beginning to founder on his refusal to pursue universal suffrage, as this was now the objective of the majority of working people in Birmingham, and certainly of the increasingly powerful Chartist movement. A meeting in October attracted no more than 2,500 people, a far cry from the hundreds of thousands on Newhall Hill. Recognising greater public momentum was needed, he changed his view and in January 1838, he announced his support for universal suffrage 'and if ever I uttered a word against it I now altogether retract it.'[201] This had the desired effect, and thousands rallied to the cause.

The application was agreed, and Birmingham became an incorporated borough in 1838, with Manchester and sixty others around the country. In Birmingham, this was seen as a natural extension of the democratic principle from national to local government: 'thus the Reform Act of 1832 received its necessary and natural complement.'[202] In the first council elections on 26th December 1838, many BPU candidates were elected. The 1835 Act introduced the local government system of governance which applies, with amendments, today. This was another major victory for Liberalism in the town, although it would not be the last. The twin successes of securing two MPs and self-government through the Charter of Incorporation introduced the era of Radical Liberal domination of Birmingham politics that lasted for almost a century.

This campaign had brought Attwood back to wider attention and he was now welcomed publicly into the Chartists' organisation by its leaders. He was revered as the one who made the Great Reform Act possible, and spoke to a large rally in Glasgow on 21st May 1838. This meeting agreed the need for a national

---

199 Bunce, *History of the Corporation of Birmingham, vol.1*, p.104
200 John Simkin, 'Thomas Attwood', *Spartacus Educational*, (1997, updated 2020)
201 Behagg, 'Attwood, Thomas (1783-1856)', *Oxford Dictionary of National Biography*
202 Bunce, *History of the Corporation of Birmingham, vol.1*, p.104

petition to endorse the People's Charter's six demands, set out in 1837. These were universal manhood suffrage; annual parliaments; secret ballots; equal election districts; payment of MPs; and abolition of the need to own substantial property to become an MP. It was proposed that the petition be agreed at a national Chartist convention in London, after which Attwood would present it to Parliament.

To pursue this, Attwood spoke at a meeting of 150,000 people at Newhall Hill in August 1838, which began the process of collecting signatures. Acknowledging that this campaign may be as difficult as the Reform Bill campaign, Attwood, as a 'Moral Force' Chartist, believing in change through non-violent means, proclaimed 'No blood shall be shed by us; but if our enemies shed blood – if they attack the people – they must take the consequences on their own heads.'[203] This was a doctrine of resistance and self-defence, but many middle class supporters were dismayed by the arguments for physical force, advocated by the newly elected working class representatives on the Union's governing council. The Birmingham middle class delegates all resigned, leaving Attwood feeling this to be a very different form of political movement from the one he had felt most comfortable leading.

When presented to the Commons on 14th June 1839, the national petition had 1,280,958 signatures, a remarkable achievement. Attwood argued for the Charter's six points but eschewed 'talk of physical force or arms'. Unfortunately, the petition was rejected by Parliament, by 235 votes to 46, and Attwood was castigated for the failure by Chartists. Riots followed in Birmingham, for two weeks in July 1839, and the BPU ceased to be an effective force.

Attwood's continuing attempts at reform had failed both locally and nationally, and his disillusion and failing health led him to resign from Parliament in December 1839, at the age of fifty-six. He moved to Jersey for his health, but sadly, on 26th April 1840, his wife Elizabeth, who had been ill for some time, died. His distress was compounded the next year, when the family bank, run by brother George, had to be dissolved to meet debts of £12,000. Attwood returned to The Grove in Harborne, his only further foray into public life being a short-lived and failed attempt to bring productive capital and labour together to address the economic crisis in August 1843 through the non-political National Union or General Confederation of All Classes. This attempt to recreate the previously successful campaigning style failed by November, as Attwood could not attract political support for it.

---

203 Behagg, 'Attwood, Thomas (1783-1856)', *Oxford Dictionary of National Biography*

On 30th June 1844, Attwood, now sixty years old, married an old family friend, Elizabeth Grice. They moved to Allesley, near Coventry, in 1848, and then to Ellerslie, the home of Edward and Walter Johnson, doctors practising the Water Cure, in Abbey Road, Great Malvern in 1855, to seek treatment for his 'creeping paralysis', most probably Parkinson's Disease. He died there, aged seventy-two, on 6th March 1856 and is buried in Hanley churchyard, Upton upon Severn. By this time he was no longer well known and few obituaries appeared, even though, as the one in The Birmingham Journal claimed: 'Twenty five years ago there was no more popular man in the British Empire.'[204]

He was remembered in Birmingham, however, with his statue erected in Stephenson Place on 7th June 1858, funded by public subscription. This Grade II listed statue recorded his founding of the BPU and was moved to Calthorpe Park in 1925, and then in 1975 to Sparkbrook, near The Larches, his former home from 1808 to 1812. It was unfortunately vandalised and removed into storage for renovation in 2012. A second statue, in bronze, of Attwood reclining on the steps in front of the former Birmingham Library, with several pages of his writing, was erected in 1993 and removed into storage in 2016 for the duration of the redevelopment work on Paradise Circus and Chamberlain Square.

Although Hawne House has been demolished and replaced by housing, Attwood Street, off Hawne Lane, is named in his honour. The nearby Cherry Orchard Avenue and Cherry Street recall the cherry orchards that were part of Hawne House's gardens. A further memorial occupies each side of the entrance to The Scrolls, a park on Stourbridge Road, Halesowen, named after the two concrete rolling scripts which have lead letters fixed to them, the words being taken from his speech to the 'Great Gathering of the Unions' on Newhall Hill on 7th May, 1832:

"Peace, Law, Order,
God is our guide!
No sword we draw;
We kindle not war's fatal fires.
By union, justice, reason, law,
We claim the birthright of our sires,
And thus we raise from sea to sea,
Our sacred watchword – Liberty!"
'Thomas Attwood. Reformer. b. Halesowen, 1783.'

---

204 Bird, *Portrait of Birmingham*, p.95

Thomas Attwood, engraving from painting by possibly George Sharples, 1832

His legacy, in representation for Birmingham in Parliament, and extending the vote to more than fifty per cent of the population, is a considerable and memorable one. He was possibly the first to recognise, and utilise effectively, the general population in pursuing a set of political objectives, through passion, commitment and the ability to move crowds by powerful force of argument. As the Birmingham Journal's obituary stated: 'He was the leader of the most formidable confederacy that the kingdom ever saw; with no weapons but the will of the people,

Blue plaque at Crescent Tower, 63, Brindley Drive, Birmingham, B1 2NJ

Green plaque at Ellerslie, Abbey Road, Great Malvern, WR14 3HL

he used that power with wisdom, temperance, and firmness, and brought the nation safely through a crisis as perilous as that which was consummated at Runnymede or Edge Hill.'[205]

Thomas Attwood is further remembered by a blue plaque, erected by Birmingham Civic Society on Crescent Tower, Brindley Drive. The plaque is visible from Cambridge Street. A green plaque, erected at Ellerslie, in Great Malvern, records the fact of Attwood's death there in 1856.

205 Bird, *Portrait of Birmingham*, p.95

JOSEPH STURGE

'He laboured to bring freedom to the negro slave, the vote to
British workmen, and the promise of peace to a war-torn world'

While consciousness of the plight of those dispossessed within the developed nation of Great Britain drove Attwood, one of his contemporaries, Joseph Sturge, born ten years later, was motivated by the undeniably cruel and demeaning treatment of black slaves, transported from Africa to the nascent United States of America. So successful in business that he could retire at the age of thirty-eight to concentrate on humanitarian and religious issues, and motivated by his Quaker faith, he campaigned relentlessly for the abolition of slavery and founded the British and Foreign Anti-Slavery Society in 1839.

Joseph Sturge was born into a large middle class farming family in Elberton, Gloucestershire, on 2nd August 1793, the fourth child of Joseph Senior, and his wife Mary Marshall, from Alcester, Warwickshire. They had twelve children, six boys and six girls. The family were Quakers and Joseph Junior's religious beliefs shaped his actions from his earliest days. Having attended school at the local market town, Thornbury, South Gloucestershire, for a year, Joseph became a boarder at Sidcot School, near Winscombe, Somerset, run by the Religious Society of Friends. As his later philanthropy demonstrated, Sturge certainly followed the ethos of caring for and supporting others, exemplified in the school motto 'Sic vos non vobis', translated as 'Thus do ye, but not for yourselves.'

Aged fourteen, Joseph joined his father in farming and later farmed on his own. His independence of thought and adherence to the pacifist tenets of his religion led him in 1813 to refuse to serve in the militia, or even to identify a proxy to serve on his behalf, as was permitted. The penalty for this was the confiscation of his flock of sheep, which were sold to pay his fine. In 1814, at the age of twenty-one, he moved to Bewdley, Worcestershire, and established himself in business, as a corn factor, selling corn on commission. This was not particularly successful, and in 1822, he joined his brother Charles in Birmingham to create a large and successful grain-importing business. He also worked in partnership with other family members, investing in the expanding railways, and joined the board of the London and Birmingham Railway, and in the development of new docks in Gloucester.

The family fortunes grew rapidly, so that by 1831, Joseph was rich enough, at the age of only thirty-eight, to retire and leave the running of the business to Charles, so that he could concentrate on matters which interested him much more: public life, political campaigning and philanthropy, in pursuit of the teachings of his faith.

He married Eliza Cropper on 29th April 1834. Eliza came from a Quaker and merchant family much like his own, but their happiness was short-lived, as Eliza died giving birth, in 1835. Joseph was heavily influenced by his younger sister Sophia, who professed 'idolatry' of Joseph. Although describing herself as a chronic invalid, she was Joseph's housekeeper in Bewdley, leaving on his first marriage in 1834 to become a governess. Sophia was the bookkeeper of the family firm, J. and C. Sturge, for a time. She returned to her housekeeper and supportive campaigning roles in 1835, after Eliza died, living at Wheeleys Road for the rest of her life. She died of her illnesses in 1845, and was attended in her final days by Joseph.

Sturge at the age of fifty-three was married again, on 14th October 1846, to Hannah Dickinson from Coalbrookdale, Shropshire. Hannah was much younger than Sturge, by twenty-three years, and also from a Quaker family that combined entrepreneurial flair with religious and financial philanthropy, being the granddaughter of the master ironmaker, Abraham Darby. Her sister, Mary Darby Dickinson, had married Joseph's brother, Charles, and the closeness of the families had led to their falling in love. This marriage, which took place at the Coalbrookdale Quaker Meeting House, was happy, with five children, a son and four daughters. Hannah was a great support to Joseph's public life, and had invested in the grain business at a critical time to avert a financial crisis, thus enabling them to continue with their efforts to improve the lot of poor and enslaved peoples. Joseph and Hannah lived originally in Monument Lane (now Road) in Ladywood, and then moved to 64, Wheeleys Road, Edgbaston, living there from the time of their marriage until their deaths (Joseph in 1859, and Hannah on 19th October 1896). Hannah continued active philanthropy after Joseph's death, and is said to have died herself during 'one of those acts of unobtrusive kindness in which she found so much pleasure.'[206] Their children, most notably daughter Sophia, continued the family tradition of philanthropy and public service into the twentieth century.

The Sturges supported the Anti-Slavery Society from its establishment on 31st January 1823, as the 'London Society for Mitigating and Gradually Abolishing the State of Slavery throughout the British Dominions'. This organisation included William Wilberforce and Thomas Fowell Buxton who had many links with the Quakers and led the abolitionist campaign in the House of Commons. Locally, Sturge pursued abolition through the weekly paper he established, 'The Philanthropist'. While trading in slaves had been abolished in 1807, slavery still existed for many thousands of Africans transported to the colonies to work on

---

206 Alex Tyrell, 'Sturge [née Dickinson], Hannah (1816-1896)', *Oxford Dictionary of National Biography*, (Oxford: 2004)

plantations. The plantation owners argued that slavery was essential to ensure the financial viability of their businesses, and advocated that children of slaves should be used as slaves, thus ensuring the continuation of the 'property' rights on which their business model was based. In the first few years, while many argued against this position, its leaders, as the full name of the Society indicates, did not want to foment disorder and riot, hence the emphasis on gradual change. Sturge's sister Sophia was one of the founders of the Birmingham and West Bromwich Ladies Society for the Relief of Negro Slaves, in the 1820s, as an auxiliary organisation to the Society, and this formed part of a national campaign by women for the immediate abolition of slavery.

The arguments advocating gradual changes to how slavery operated became anathema to those with more radical approaches, such as Sturge, and he and others who shared his view began to agitate within the Society itself for the immediate abolition of slavery. Sturge believed in the 'political agency of ordinary people' which today would be called direct action. In May 1831, Sturge and his colleagues secured agreement from the Society to take the argument to the whole country through petitions, public meetings, and challenges to election candidates to state their position on the issue. They formed the Agency Committee, within the Society, to campaign for immediate abolition. The argument over which approach to pursue continued, and public shock at the violence used during a rebellion of slaves in December 1831, in Jamaica, provided further impetus to the cause of the advocates of immediate abolition.

By March 1832, tensions had increased to such an extent that the Agency Committee declared itself independent. There was considerable agitation politically for giving the vote to a much broader range of propertied individuals in Great Britain, and this was secured in the Great Reform Act of 1832. This success in changing how democracy operated clearly encouraged abolitionists, who organised a national campaign to convince the government to abolish slavery. This was successful, and the British Emancipation Act was passed on 28th August 1833. At the end of this process, however, the government sought to mitigate the impact on plantation owners by replacing slavery with an unpaid and temporary (although for twelve years) indentured apprenticeship for any slave aged six and above. They also offered compensation, from a £20 million fund, to slave owners for the loss of their 'property'. The members of the Agency Committee saw compensation as indirect support for, and participation in, continued slavery. Although the Anti-Slavery Society was disbanded, Sturge and others continued to campaign against this indentured apprenticeship, seeing it as slavery by another name.

Sturge dedicated himself to campaigning against this extended form of slavery, undertaking two trips to the West Indies to see for himself how it operated. His first trip in 1834 involved discussions with apprentices themselves, and plantation owners, and led to his publication of the 'Narrative of Events since the First of August 1834', in which he described the experience of 'James Williams', a pseudonym for an indentured apprentice. This description was given authenticity by the support of two free African-Caribbeans and six apprentices and included an introduction by an English Baptist minister. Sturge undertook a further visit from November 1836 to April 1837, and in 1838, he published 'The West Indies in 1837'. This description of the iniquities of the system of indentured apprenticeship was popular and Sturge combined its publication with giving seven days of evidence to a House of Commons Committee investigating the issue, and a public lecture tour. His efforts and those of fellow campaigners for immediate, complete emancipation were successful as the temporary apprenticeship system was abolished, and full emancipation throughout the British Empire was enacted in legislation on 1st August 1838.

Sturge had also been actively involved in local public life, becoming a councillor for St. Thomas's ward in the first elections to the Town Council on 26th December 1838, being appointed as an alderman at the same time. His brother Charles was elected to represent Edgbaston ward, defeating the Tory candidate, Richard T. Cadbury. Both Joseph and Charles refused to acknowledge the part of the oath that required them not to criticise the established Church of England. As Quakers, they were unable to do so, but were still allowed to take up their elected offices by their radical colleagues on the Council. In later years, this requirement, as well as that of being a Christian, was removed from the oath. Joseph is said to have opposed the building of Birmingham Town Hall (1832 to 1834) as he objected to its potential use for religious oratorios.

Sturge continued to support the freed former slaves, with gifts of money to develop schools, missionary expeditions with Baptists, and settling former slaves in towns, one of which was named Sturge Town after him. These were 'free' towns, outside the control of plantation owners. He was honoured by a marble monument near Sturge Town, in a Baptist chapel in Falmouth, Jamaica, in 1839. Later in life, he bought an estate in Montserrat in the West Indies to prove that free labour was both morally and economically viable.

His attention turned to abolishing slavery throughout the world and he founded the British and Foreign Anti-Slavery Society in 1839, and organised the World's Anti-Slavery Convention in London in 1840. Further conventions were held in Brussels in 1843 and in Paris in 1849. This organisation continues today as Anti-Slavery International and is acknowledged as the world's oldest human rights organisation.

Slavery was still legal in the United States, but was an issue that was a major reason for the American Civil War twenty-five years later. In 1841, Sturge travelled throughout the US to look at how slavery operated. He travelled with a poet, John Greenleaf Whittier, and published a narrative describing this visit in 1842, 'A Visit to the United States in 1841'.

Within Great Britain, Sturge was anxious to campaign for universal suffrage, and established the Complete Suffrage Union, and became involved in the Anti-Corn Law League, as well as the Freehold Land Society. This became the leading friendly society in Birmingham. Sturge gave prominence to the complete suffrage campaign, using the slogans of 'County Votes for Working Men' and 'Freeholds for the People' to secure both voting rights and accessibility to property security. He tried to secure the support of the Chartist Movement and the League for Universal Suffrage, but their objectives were not fully aligned, and he was unsuccessful.

In Birmingham, Sturge was remarkably active. He provided the first public park in the town, public baths and washhouses, and established the Reformatory School Movement which provided reformatories for young delinquents, beginning with three converted cottages in Ryland Street. He supported greater learning, donating his library of 3,000 books to the Polytechnic Institution when it was established in Steelhouse Lane in 1843. Unfortunately, this closed in 1848. By then, Sturge had successfully set up yet another movement, this time to provide adult education, in which cause he opened the Severn Street Adult School in 1845. Sturge felt that Sunday Schools, although useful in teaching children, left adults with nowhere to go to access learning, to improve their minds and their ability to earn money and support themselves. He persuaded fellow Quakers to teach young men aged fourteen and over, but the appeal of the school grew rapidly, with adult men beginning to attend, so an adult division was set up. This was so successful that a separate school for women, the 'Girls' British School', was opened in 1848 in Ann Street (now Colmore Row). Although concentrating on basic skills of reading, writing and encouraging religious awareness, provision expanded to include evening schools, lending libraries, and social events, including tea parties, day excursions and meetings to encourage temperance. By 1860, there were 654 men and 300 women attending, with many leading Quakers teaching, including George Cadbury. As a Quaker himself, Sturge was of course supportive of, and involved in, the Birmingham Temperance Society.

Sturge stood for parliament on a platform that included complete suffrage on three occasions, in 1842 (Nottingham), 1844 (Birmingham, following the death of Joshua Scholefield) and in 1847 (Leeds). He was unsuccessful each time. However, Sturge was not daunted by a lack of immediate success and became involved in a movement for 'people diplomacy', a modern-sounding attempt to ensure the use of arbitration to avoid war arising from international conflicts. As well as helping to organise peace conferences in the late 1840s in several major European cities, he tried to persuade the governments of Denmark and Schleswig-Holstein to resolve their territorial dispute by arbitration. He was unsuccessful in 1854 in a similar attempt to secure arbitration between Great Britain and Russia, with the Crimean War following. To pursue the cause of arbitration, Sturge supported the establishment of the Morning Star newspaper in 1856, and visited Finland as an ambassador of the Society of Friends, offering financial relief for the famine caused there by Royal Navy gunboats during attacks in the Crimean War.

The wide range of movements and causes he espoused was remarkable, emanating from his 'practical benevolence towards men in general', although this was extended explicitly to include women, as we have seen. He clearly 'had by nature a strong sympathy with all who were in need'[207] and devoted his energies and efforts to these many causes full time after his retirement from business, until his death twenty-seven years later.

Joseph Sturge died from a heart attack, aged sixty-five, on 14th May 1859 at home in Wheeleys Road. He was buried in the graveyard of the Quaker Meeting House in Bull Lane. At his funeral, John Bright MP eulogised that 'there was about him a ripeness and goodness which is rarely seen.'[208]

He is remembered by a statue which stands outside the Marriott Hotel at Five Ways, Edgbaston, a short distance from the site of his home in Wheeleys Road. The statue was unveiled in front of 12,000 people on 4th June 1862, and was restored in 2007 following an appeal by Birmingham Civic Society, with support from Birmingham City Council and the Sturge family. The statue was re-dedicated by the Lord Mayor, Councillor Mike Sharpe. The restoration included replacing the left hand which had fallen off in 1975. In 1925, a bronze plaque was added which encapsulates perfectly Joseph Sturge's life's work of bringing peace and equality to all: 'He laboured to bring freedom to the Negro slave, the vote to British workmen, and the promise of peace to a war-torn world.' A blue plaque

---

207 Victor Skipp, *The Making of Victorian Birmingham*, (Studley, Warwickshire: 1996), p.111
208 Ibid., p.111

was erected on flats at Edencroft, 64, Wheeleys Road, Edgbaston by Birmingham Civic Society, on 24th March 2007.

Portrait of Joseph Sturge by Alexander Rippingille, from Birmingham Museum and Art Gallery

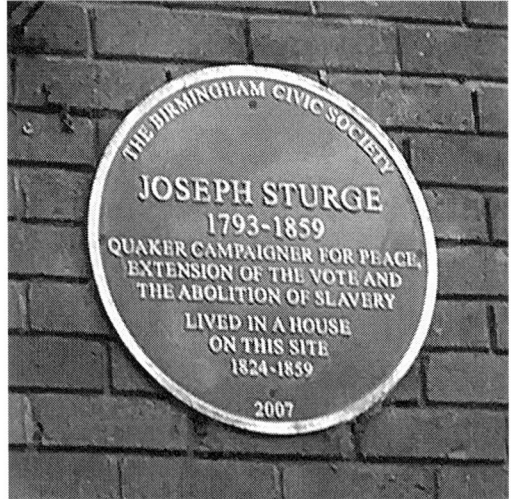

Blue plaque on flats at Edencroft, 64, Wheeleys Road, Edgbaston, Birmingham, B15 2LW

Statue, with plaque, of Joseph Sturge, in front of Marriott Hotel, Five Ways, Edgbaston, Birmingham, B16 8SJ

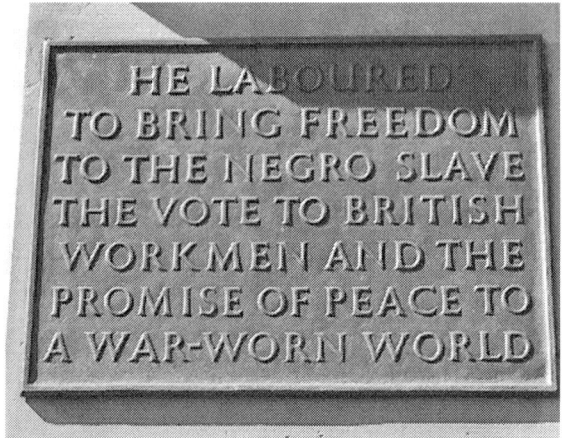

7.

A Portrait of Birmingham in the mid-nineteenth century

In the wake of the Industrial Revolution, Birmingham's population grew substantially, as it attracted workers to its burgeoning industries. As the centre became crowded, rich townspeople moved from Edgbaston Street, The Square and Temple Row into surrounding developments, such as the Ashted suburb and the 'Summer Hill Estate', advertised in 1790 as 'a range of elegant and uniform building, comprising fifteen houses, along the declivity of a beautiful hill.'[209]

Birmingham industries grew so rapidly it became 'the city of a thousand trades' by 1870, when Kelly's Directory listed 953 trades or companies. Innovation was evident, as the number of patents registered demonstrates, from 71 in the 1820s to 265 in the 1840s, one every fortnight. Watt's steam engine powered industrial processes, making travel, and migration, easier as railways spread across the country. The Railway Age arrived inauspiciously in Birmingham, at Vauxhall, named after the nearby pleasure gardens, a temporary station constructed to meet the first train, from Liverpool, with thirty-six passengers in six coaches, on 9th July 1837. The permanent station, Curzon Street, was opened in 1839. The site of Vauxhall Station is now Duddeston Station.

As railway companies were established, the lines came into the area now called Heartlands, creating a confusing and congested tangle of arrival points, with the need for a cab ride from each terminus into the town centre. Before long, a town centre railway station, New Street Station, was confirmed by Act of Parliament

---

209 Skipp, *A History of Greater Birmingham – down to 1830*, p.73

on 3rd August 1846. The required clearance of the town's worst housing, in the Froggery, took with it Birmingham's first synagogue and theatre. The station, with the largest iron and glass roof in the world, operated from 1852, although it formally opened on 1st June 1854. The railways gave the town the name of its most elegant shopping location, the Great Western Arcade, built above the tunnel linking Snow Hill and Moor Street Stations.

As Birmingham was at the centre of the country, as with the development of canals, the expansion of railways created an 'Iron Cross', replacing Brindley's 'Silver Cross'. Local business benefitted considerably, with reduced delivery times for raw materials and finished products. As seen above, as the Victorian era started, there was growing recognition of the need for more co-ordinated and stringent planning and oversight of local government to benefit all residents.

The solution was radical reform. Birmingham's petition under the 1835 Municipal Corporations Act was agreed and its Charter of Incorporation was granted on 1st November, 1838. This Charter, received on 5th November, was treated with reverential respect, and kept safe by the first Town Clerk appointed, William Redfern: 'It was a precious deposit: he revered it as the foundation of our local rights and liberties – it was our Magna Charta [sic].'[210]

Birmingham expanded, encompassing Edgbaston, Deritend and Bordesley, and Duddeston and Nechells. The Act enfranchised male burgesses with property valued at £10 or more. Birmingham Town Council, or 'the Corporation', had a mayor, sixteen aldermen and forty-eight councillors elected from thirteen wards. There was a public reading of the Charter on 5th November, in the Town Hall. On Boxing Day, the first forty-eight councillors were elected, meeting for the first time on 27th December. Liberal domination meant that all forty-eight councillors were Liberals, as were the sixteen appointed aldermen, and the Mayor, William Scholefield, Joshua's son.

Once elected, the people's representatives, the Town Council, should have made rapid progress on the issues facing the population. This was far from the truth, regrettably. Although establishing the Council, the government had not repealed the legislation giving powers to the Street Commissioners. They strenuously resisted the Council's attempts to co-ordinate and centralise local government in one body, for a further fractious and divisive thirteen years. This extraordinary tale of delay, disruption and hostility between the Council and the three groups of Commissioners, in Birmingham, Deritend and Bordesley, and Duddeston and

210 Bunce, *History of the Corporation of Birmingham, vol.1*, p.169

Nechells, allowed the disgraceful condition of the town to persist long after it should have been resolved. This complete failure of coherence and sense extended entirely avoidable health dangers, disease and death for years, an egregious example of the dominance of sectional, partisan politics.

For four years, tortuous arguments raged in the town, the courts and Parliament to confirm which powers the Council actually had, and the extent to which they could be exercised. Local Conservatives opposed the Council on every issue, and called for the abolition of the Corporation, blaming it for the state of the town in 1842. Considerable poverty persisted, as a result of depression caused by the Corn Laws, which meant low wages. 'Extensive distress prevailed among the artisan and trading population', and rates rose punitively to 8s. 9d. in the pound. Reverend Timothy East, at an anti-corn law meeting, said that in visiting cottages in the town, he had scarcely found 'any person who could tell him the price of meat per pound: this article of food having literally fallen out of the dietary of the poor.'[211]

The government's concerns about Birmingham radicalism meant they were content to see these extreme elements curtailed. Locally, the government was denigrated as 'idle, careless, apathetic, doing nothing to vindicate its own work', no longer friends and allies, as 'lukewarm friends could scarcely be regarded as other than adversaries.'[212] It was apparent that further legislation was needed, and a change of government was key to progress. When Melbourne's Whig government fell, Birmingham Conservatives anticipated victory, as Sir Robert Peel became Conservative Prime Minister on 30th August 1841. They were sorely disappointed, however, as government legislation confirmed the powers of newly incorporated towns. The Charters Confirmation Act of 12th August 1842 confirmed the Council's powers, the transfer of the police force to the Corporation, and authorised the construction of prison and court buildings. Met with jubilation by local Liberals, this ended all arguments: 'and thus the long and bitter contest which had existed in Birmingham to invalidate the Charter came to an end' and 'after nearly four years of contention, Birmingham acquired the uncontested right of self-government.'[213]

So, what were the major issues that the empowered, validated and vindicated Town Council needed to address?

Population growth was driven in part by migrants from the rest of the country and abroad, including Italy and Ireland, coming to Birmingham for work and a

---

211 Bunce, *History of the Corporation of Birmingham, vol.1*, p.277
212 Ibid., pp.246-50
213 Ibid., pp.284-6

better life. They found depressing slums, in courts of back-to-back houses, in the town centre. These were built quickly and shoddily, without effective sanitation, alongside factories, workshops and even graveyards. Many houses and courts contained metal-working workshops, blacksmiths, or even pigsties, a less than healthy atmosphere for living. The population rose considerably to 232,638, with more than 50,000 living in 2,000 such courts in the centre.

As required by the government, under the terms of the Public Health Act 1848, the Corporation commissioned an independent inspection of Birmingham, undertaken in 1849, by Robert Rawlinson, a distinguished civil engineer. In 1844, he worked on Brindley's Bridgewater Canal, and developed a reputation as a sanitation expert, designing a scheme to bring fresh water to Liverpool from Wales. With the Public Health Act, he became a government inspector. Rawlinson visited Birmingham in February and May 1849, producing his 100 page report by the end of that month. This 'thorough personal examination of the town'[214] is invaluable in describing Birmingham's multiple problems.

Rawlinson details Birmingham's substantial growth in the first half of the century, with 520 trades, divided into twenty separate professions. There were 2,600 varieties of occupation, which are 'advantageous to the population; it tends to a more equal and general diffusion of wealth amongst the master manufacturers, and the means of acquiring it in moderation amongst the workpeople.' In contrast to Manchester and Liverpool, there were 'few, if any "millionaires"' in Birmingham, because of the sizeable class of 'master tradesmen whose wealth tends to comfort rather than ostentatious show, and there is a race of workpeople comparatively independent and self-relying.' Echoing Leland, Camden and Hutton, he confirms the adaptability of Brummies: 'any form of trade or occupation might and may be commenced and carried on without local restriction or interference: the only question to be answered rests with the individual, "Can he make it pay?"'[215]

Wages were higher than in many areas. A man earned between thirty and forty shillings per week, but women, always disadvantaged in pay, earned only ten to fourteen shillings. Rawlinson noted that: 'Many of the men work in garrets in their own houses, and have several boys under them.'[216] He compliments the relationship between employer and employee: 'In no place will there be found more freedom of intercourse between the employer and the employed, or more

---

214 Bunce, *History of the Corporation of Birmingham, vol.1*, p.302
215 Ibid., p.306
216 Rawlinson, quoted in Ibid., p.309

general intelligence and comfort amongst the workpeople, or more forethought and kindness from the employer for the employed.'[217]

Although trade was thriving and expanding, the population was far from healthy. Rawlinson asserted that high wages led many workmen into bad habits, and they were 'often drunk and improvident.' He ascribed the blame to working women, displaying a Victorian, disapproving mindset: 'The habit of a manufacturing life once formed in a female, she generally continues it, and her children are left in comparative neglect....To this may be traced the premature death of many children, and accidents from fire are very frequent.' No evidence is quoted for this unreasonable slur in a report rightly hailed as so significant in Birmingham's history.

Allotments and gardens could not compensate for the crowded insanitary conditions in the centre. Rawlinson depicts dreadful living conditions, caused by the state of the water supply and lack of drainage and sewerage. Water was available from private wells, public wells in Lady Well, Digbeth, Jamaica Row and Allison Street, private water carts, or the Waterworks Company which supplied only a third of the town, and only on three days per week. The problem was that the water was polluted, or 'vitiated', as overcrowding led to 'middens, cesspools, and graveyards', and material from these leaked into the rivers, especially the Rea, from which supposedly fresh water was drawn. Even the water sold by the private carts or Waterworks Company, thought to be pure by residents, was drawn from the same polluted sources. Disgracefully, the cost of supposedly pure water was an astonishing forty-one times more expensive than it would be with 'a proper scheme of water supply.' The effects were potentially fatal: 'This vitiated water frequently, when used, produces dysentery and death.' The mortality rate, although comparable to other large towns, was 26.5 per 1,000 population in 1847 and had risen to 30 per 1,000 in 1848, although 'infant mortality is very considerable.'[218]

The six graveyards in the centre, covering fifteen acres, were 'full to repletion' but gruesomely, no record of burials was made, so the sexton, trying to locate space for new burials, used a 'boring rod' to probe the earth, exposing 'half-decayed bodies.' More problematically, the graveyards were surrounded by housing, 'built in on all sides, so that any effluvium or evaporation that arises must inevitably be carried upon and through these dwelling houses.'[219]

---

217 Rawlinson, quoted in Bunce, *History of the Corporation of Birmingham, vol.1,* p.307
218 Ibid., pp.313-4, 305
219 Ibid., pp.315-6

Sewerage and drainage was non-existent in two thirds of the town, and not effectively connected where it did exist, as the responsible authorities competed for governance. Rawlinson details eight bodies within the town's circumference, with responsibilities for roads, lighting, sanitation and health: three sets of Street Commissioners, three sets of Surveyors of Highways (Deritend, Bordesley, Edgbaston), the Guardians of the Poor of Birmingham, and the Corporation. Their responsibilities frequently overlapped, with 'no general plan of the district', 'no power to levy a common rate', even though it was obvious that: 'Nature has combined the whole [district] so as to render one set of sewers imperative.' For example, Birmingham Commissioners built sewers, but lacked legal authority to enforce the installation of drains and connection to sewers by householders. The Bordesley Surveyors actively thwarted attempts of the Deritend Surveyors to connect their sewerage systems, so Bordesley, being higher, flooded Deritend regularly with foul water and sewage. These eight authorities employed fifty-five officers (nine solicitors, four surveyors, thirty-eight collectors, and four clerks and treasurers), administered thirteen different rates – for the poor, highways, lamps, scavengers, gas, water, Town Halls, so that the embattled rate payer 'receives no apparent advantage…in the bitterness of confused agony and despair.'[220]

Two further reports, appended to Rawlinson's, are by 'eminent surgeons' Mr Hodgson and Mr Russell, and gave distressing details of areas of the town, including specific streets. The living conditions of the poor are appalling. Many courts are 'covered with pools of stagnant filth', and one in Sheep Street is a 'specimen case': 'There are 12 houses in it; one-sixth of its surface is covered with water, this runs into a cistern, from which it is pumped into a well.' In Masshouse Lane, in a court with poor drainage: 'the water, mixed with the ashes and filth from the dust-hole, extends itself up the court to the fronts of the houses, to approach which, to see patients, I have been obliged to walk on bricks placed for the purpose, and the poor have been unable to prevent the filth from running into their houses….The common practice is that the manure is mixed with ashes and rubbish, and there it lies till the place is full. Disputes occur as to the liability to remove it, till it over-runs the seats [of the privvies], runs into the courts, and gives rise to noxious exhalations.' Children 'convert the courts into closets' and many privvies have no doors, so women are 'subjected to the annoyance of laughing and derision from the men….Ordure is…often kept in the houses, and emptied anywhere at nightfall;…the door is opened, and it is thrown out.' This disgusting

---

220 Rawlinson, quoted in Bunce, *History of the Corporation of Birmingham, vol.1,* pp.316-9

situation also applied in well-to-do districts, like Edgbaston: 'In the Hagley Road the water-closets…absolutely discharge themselves into the road. In the Bristol Road the same thing takes place.' Rawlinson concludes: 'the baneful effects of the atmospheric impurities…are a disgrace to civilisation.'[221]

His summary makes thirteen recommendations, proposing one governing body empowered to implement the Public Health Act. Overfull graveyards should be closed, and a better water supply and a 'perfect system of sewers' provided. Health would be improved by proper drainage for houses, courts, and yards, with a constant water supply under pressure to replace the wells and pumps. All water and waste matter should be taken away by new drains, and courts and passages should be paved, regularly washed and disinfected. The rates needed to fund these improvements are detailed, with savings 'generally, but to the labouring man especially, of many times the amount to be paid.' He recommends provision of public parks and pleasure grounds, and that 'sewage manure may be applied to the agricultural land'. He concludes, with understated exasperation, that 'a consolidation of the conflicting powers exercised within the borough would produce great economy.'[222]

This detailed, damningly comprehensive report should surely have been a call to action. Instead, it was 'vigorously and even bitterly criticised, many of its conclusions were disputed, and its recommendations were contested.' The Street Commissioners engaged in a further, year-long, campaign, with 'a vehemence which seems very strange when looked back upon from this distance of time',[223] which successfully delayed the application of the Public Health Act to the town. Displaying a dexterity in legislation sorely lacking previously, the Corporation by-passed the issue of the Public Health Act and developed a Parliamentary Bill which identified the Council as the final arbiter of improvement proposals and actions.

Parliament passed the Birmingham Improvement Act 1851 on 24th July. Coincidentally, the Prime Minister was Lord John Russell, the same who, as Home Secretary, commissioned the 1833 enquiry into the activities of Street Commissioners. Bunce was delighted: 'Thus, after thirteen years of almost incessant conflict, the triumph of the representative principle was finally and firmly achieved; and there was established in Birmingham an united, complete, and unfettered system of local government, based upon the will of the inhabitants themselves, and adequate to all the purposes of public improvement, sanitary

---

221 Hodgson, quoted in Bunce, *History of the Corporation of Birmingham, vol.1*, pp.323-8
222 Rawlinson, quoted in Ibid., pp.328-331
223 Ibid., p.331

reform, and general administration.'[224] The Council immediately organised itself into departments with specified purposes, establishing Committees for Finance, Assessment, Rate and Appeal, Estates and Public Buildings, Watch, Public Works, Markets and Fairs, Lunatic Asylum, Baths and Washhouses, and General Purposes.

By the mid-nineteenth century, Birmingham at last had the people and organisational framework to deliver significant and lasting change. Unfortunately, it took a further twenty-two years before a driven, self-confident and ambitious local politician emerged, through the Corporation, to take the town forward. In the interim, the people of Birmingham received great kindness from two individuals, with widely different backgrounds, who preferred to remain in the background while using their wealth for everyone's benefit.

While the fame of Thomas Attwood and Joseph Sturge rested on their ability to effect change through political campaigns, Birmingham in the second half of the nineteenth century saw remarkable acts of kindness and philanthropy from two unassuming and publicity-shy individuals. Both Josiah Mason and Louisa Anne Ryland were phenomenally wealthy, the former through inventiveness and hard work, the latter by inheritance. Rather than revel privately in their wealth, they used it as a force for good in the community, to the benefit of many people so much less fortunate than themselves.

JOSIAH MASON

'The successful and innovative businessman, a shy and retiring philanthropist, who changed the lives of many thousands of children and students through his patience, kindness, and fortitude'

Born two years after Sturge, in February 1795, Sir Josiah Mason was a remarkable man who made a significant, now largely unremarked, contribution to business, employment, education, and society in Birmingham. This poor young man became enormously wealthy through hard work, application and innovation. A major figure in Birmingham's metal making industries, he became the world's largest manufacturer of pens and nibs, and nickel goods. He pioneered electroplating, with his products used throughout the UK, Europe and the world.

He became a major provider of education and employment opportunities to the most disadvantaged, establishing Mason Science College in Birmingham, which provided practical and vocational training and education to generations of students. Twenty years after his death, this became the University of Birmingham,

---

224 Bunce, *History of the Corporation of Birmingham, vol.1*, p.338

respected around the world for the excellence of its educational programmes. For all this, he was not well-known in his adopted city, declining to enter politics or seek fame.

Josiah Mason was born into a family of two generations of carpet weavers, in Kidderminster, Worcestershire, on 23rd February 1795. Baptised on 27th March at St Mary's and All Saints Parish Church, on today's St. Mary's Ringway, he was the third of five children of Josiah (christened 16th May 1766) and Elizabeth, née Griffiths, (born 1761) from nearby Dudley. They married on 9th August 1790 at St Mary's, and their son William was born on 1st July 1791, with Hannah born 30th March 1793. After Josiah Junior, there were two more children, Elizabeth, born 1798, and Richard in 1802. Josiah Junior outlived his siblings by a considerable number of years, as Hannah died aged just five, and William at only twenty-one. Elizabeth and Richard lived to forty-four and forty-three respectively, but all Josiah's siblings would be dead by 1846, thirty-five years before his own death.

Josiah's early life was undoubtedly hard, the family being poor, but Josiah grew up in a happy home, close to his grandfather, who combined skills of mechanical invention and repair, on looms and weaving machines, with musicality and humour, a social and apparently committed smoker. His father and grandfather worked in Kidderminster carpet factories, the industry that dominated the town, with his father later becoming a factory clerk. His mother kept a clean and careful home, out of necessity with five children. She ran a small grocer's shop, selling tea and loaf sugar, and later bread from a small bakery, from their house in Mill Street, outside the town centre, near surrounding countryside. The baking oven was apparently used to cook Sunday dinners for local people. Josiah's early efforts, from the age of eight, to help the family's income involved a variety of enterprises, including selling bread rolls ('Joe's rolls') and cakes, bagging copper coins in five shilling packets, for which he charged one old penny for every pound's worth, and selling fruit and vegetables from panniers carried by his donkey, called Admiral Rodney. Josiah was told by his father to keep information about his finances to himself: 'Joe, theist got a few pence, never let anybody know how much theist got in thee pockets.'[225]

Josiah attended a dame school next to his home and attended the local Unitarian Sunday School, learning to read and write and then reading theology, history and science books. Clearly Josiah needed a more profitable trade than selling foodstuffs door to door and aged fifteen, he tried shoe-making. Using good quality leather

---

225 Brian Jones, *Josiah Mason 1795-1881: Birmingham's Benevolent Benefactor,* (Studley: 1995), p.8

hoping to make good profits, it allowed him to help his mother and family care for William at home, a poorly child throughout his short life. However, he could not charge enough to cover his costs and return a reasonable profit: 'I found I couldn't make it pay, and must become bankrupt. So I gave it up.'[226] He tried a variety of trades including carpenter, blacksmith, housepainter, and carpet weaver, working as a weaver for two years, earning one pound a week, having paid to rent his own loom and a child to help him.

On a visit to stay with his uncle Richard Griffiths at Christmas 1816, he decided to settle in Birmingham, to explore its possibilities. Richard managed the Aston Flint Glass Works of B. and W. Gibbins in Bagot Street, off the current New Town Row. Josiah impressed his uncle with his application, working hard at labouring and other manual tasks, including feeding and emptying the furnaces. He clearly impressed his cousin, Annie, Richard's daughter, as they married on 13th August 1817, in Aston Church. They were married for fifty-two years, until Annie's death in 1870. Josiah was asked to investigate a gilt toy and jewellery business in which his uncle had invested. Having done so, his uncle's partner left Birmingham, and Josiah became the manager of the business in Legge Street, moving into a house with Annie in Bagot Street, near the factory.

Josiah worked hard to understand the industrial processes and products involved and was successful in managing the business for the next five years. He attended the local Unitarian Belmont Row Chapel, opened by John Wesley in 1790, and developed social and business contacts. He was shocked and gravely disappointed when his uncle sold the business, which Josiah had made successful, without his knowledge to Richard Bakewell, a manufacturer of mathematical instruments in Loveday Street. Although angry and upset, Josiah continued to run the business at an annual salary of £300 while seeking other employment.

Through another member of Belmont Row Chapel, Mason met Samuel Harrison, who had invented split ring keyholders and was looking for someone to manage and develop the business. Mason impressed him with his preparedness to 'get his hands dirty', and Harrison offered him a job. Mason invested his twenty pounds savings in the business, and moved into a rented home in Lancaster Street, attached to the factory. His application and assiduous approach (he returned to work immediately after his and Annie's wedding ceremony) ensured this enterprise grew, with the Masons surviving on money from profits to cover living expenses, rather than a salary. When Harrison wanted to retire, Mason tried and failed

226 Bird, *Portrait of Birmingham*, p.122

to raise the £500 required to buy the business. Harrison, who trusted without question the integrity of his determined employee, generously agreed to let Mason buy the business by instalments of £100, with the first instalment paid in August 1823, the last in 1824.

Mason developed the factory's processes, improving the production of keyholders, initially by using stamping machines and later producing the bevelled split rings which are still used for key rings. He produced steel pen nibs, which had been invented by Harrison, who supplied his friend Joseph Priestley with the 'Magnum Bonum' nib, the first produced in Birmingham, in 1780.

Demand for pen nibs grew dramatically, as trade expanded rapidly in the early nineteenth century, and as the written word became more important in all aspects of life, with steel pen nibs increasingly preferred to quills. Pen manufacturing was very important to the Birmingham economy, with over 1,000 people employed in eight major firms. It rapidly became the centre of the industry and dominated world-wide supply.

John Thackray Bunce, editor of the Birmingham Daily Post for thirty-six years, and Mason's contemporary and first biographer in 1882, tells how Mason saw slip pens in Peart's Bookshop in Bull Street in 1829, and bought three for his own use. In the evening, he set to improving the design, convinced he could improve it. Having done so, he sent it the next day to James Perry, a leading pen-maker in London. Perry was so impressed that he immediately travelled to Birmingham, arriving at 8am two days later at the Lancaster Street factory, to discuss the production of Mason's designs. This started a remarkable business relationship between Mason and Perry, with Mason becoming the sole manufacturer of 'Perryian' pens for the next forty-six years. While Perry patented new designs in 1832 and 1836, with the innovation of a small hole above the hammered split in the nib, Mason improved and automated production and the figures are remarkable. From producing twenty gross (2,880) of pen nibs in 1829, employing twelve people, Mason became the largest producer in this growing industry. By 1849, it delivered 65,000 gross nibs weekly (9,360,000), reaching 98,000 gross weekly (14,112,000) by 1864.[227] By 1881, ninety-three percent of pen makers in England and Wales were located in Birmingham.

A price list for the factory at 36, Lancaster Street, the 'Wholesale Price List of Mercantile Pens', offers a wide variety of pen nibs. Twenty-three different types are listed, the script thicknesses being 'Extra Fine', 'Fine', 'Medium' and 'Broad'.

---

227 Jones, *Josiah Mason 1795-1881: Birmingham's Benevolent Benefactor*, p.29

Costs were similarly divergent, from 9d. per gross for the Ready Writer and Rib Pen types, to 2s. per gross for the Patent Ink Regulator Pen, available in the four script types. There were pens made for specific professions, including a Banker's Posting Pen (Extra Strong), a Counting House Pen (three thicknesses), and a Solicitor's Pen (Medium or Broad) at 1s. 4d. per gross. For the more fashionably-minded, a Ladies' Fountain Pen sold for 1s. per gross, in Fine, naturally.[228]

By 1870, Mason employed more than 1,000 people, using ten tons of Sheffield steel, making 100,000 gross (14,400,000) nibs weekly. This phenomenal growth was fuelled by demand from Europe and North America, and required expansion of the Lancaster Street factory, so that by 1875, it took up two acres, rose five storeys and was 'the largest pen factory in the world'. It was unusual in employing a high proportion of women and girls in semi-skilled roles. Some women worked at home, as sub-contractors, sewing the pens made onto cards for display and transport and were known, unsurprisingly, as 'carders'.

Mason, perhaps remembering his father's advice to keep his affairs to himself, kept secret the precise details of how the nibs were produced. Mason's improvement on Perry's pens was to slit them with a press and die instead of cracking them with a hammer after hardening. He pioneered the use of gas generators and was at the forefront of introducing the use of electricity in manufacturing processes.

For all this, Mason was not well-known outside his immediate business, non-conformist and social circles, a primary reason being that he did not use his name on the products he produced for partners or customers. Even as the sole producer for Perry, it would not be visible to anyone that the Lancaster Street works were the source of the product. He provided pen nibs and other articles to both Joseph Gillott and Somerville and Company, also based in Birmingham, from 1856 to 1870. Even when Mason bought this company, it continued to trade as Somerville and Company.

Mason socialised with his business contemporaries. One of these, George Richard Elkington, and his cousin Henry, patented in 1840 a commercial application for using cyanides of gold and silver in electroplating. Until then, the process of applying silver onto copper was achieved through a long, slow, and therefore expensive process, limiting its use to expensive items for wealthier customers. Boulton and Watt were succeeding with this at the Soho Manufactory, but the Elkingtons were working with a Birmingham surgeon, John Wright, who discovered a method using electricity to spread silver evenly, durably and

228 Jones, *Josiah Mason 1795-1881: Birmingham's Benevolent Benefactor*, p.36

importantly, quickly, over a base metal, such as copper or nickel. Alexander Parkes, an inventor employed by Elkington would go on to be recognised as the first to invent plastic materials (India rubber rings). He developed this plating technique under patent for use with copper, silver and gold. A factory and showroom was built in Newhall Street by Elkington in 1838. This produced 'articles of taste' – vases, Greek urns and sculptured figures, as objets d'art. By 1843, this technique had been developed so that Parkes could electroplate natural objects, even flowers, with silver. When Prince Albert visited the Newhall Street factory, he was presented with a spider's web covered in silver by Parkes, a remarkable feat.

Mason began working with the Elkingtons in 1840, agreeing a partnership on 29th March 1842 and the new Elkington, Mason and Company occupied the factory which was later for many years the home of Birmingham Science Museum, before its move to Millennium Point as the 'Thinktank'. Mason invested £27,500, with Elkington committing £55,000, so Mason owned a third of the company as the junior partner. Wright was not a partner but received an annuity for many years. Originally, Mason kept a low profile but 'the great and incessant call for money in the business needed my personal care.'[229]

While the Elkingtons saw their electroplating innovation as a method to compete with Boulton and Watt, it was Mason who saw the potential to extend this into other markets. Seeing potential to take on the tinplate, silver and japanning industries, he expanded the range of electroplated products to include cheap everyday items affordable by working people, such as knives, forks, spoons, jewellery and toys. The business grew rapidly, and another factory was opened in Brearley Street.

As use of the business's products grew, additional warehouses and showrooms were opened in Liverpool and London, and foreign customers and potential partners became interested. Alfred Krupp, the German industrialist, came to the factory, to offer them his invention of a machine for rolling metal blanks for spoons and forks, which would substantially speed up production. Turning down the exorbitant asking price, Mason offered Krupp £10,000 and the machine was duly bought and installed at Brearley Street. Krupp later established the Essen steelworks, a significant part of German production in both world wars in the twentieth century.

In 1849 and 1851, two exhibitions were used to promote Mason's products. The first, smaller exhibition was in Bingley House, Broad Street, called 'An Exhibition

---

229 Bird, *Portrait of Birmingham*, p.123

of the Manufactures of Birmingham and the Midland Counties', which Prince Albert attended. The larger and well-known Great Exhibition in 1851 offered the opportunity to put on display a large range of products, and included the magnificent Great Exhibition Shield, made specifically for the event.

As markets developed across Europe and North America, so the influence, and income, of Elkington, Mason and Company grew. The company continued to cast public works of art, including statues. These included a bronze statue of Sir Robert Peel, unveiled on 27th August 1855 before a crowd of 15,000 people. Peel died in 1850, three days after being thrown from his horse. Originally cast to commemorate Peel's role in the repeal of the Corn Laws in 1846, it was erected at the junction of Congreve Street and Ann Street (now Colmore Row). The surrounding railings were appropriately fashioned in the shape of wheat ears. In 1927, it moved to Calthorpe Park, in the vicinity of Thomas Attwood's statue, but in 1963 Peel's was transferred to West Midlands Police College on Pershore Road, where it remains.

There is a further Elkington, Mason and Company bronze statue locally, this time of Prince Albert in his Field Marshal uniform, and with the Order of the Garter. He is seated on his horse Nimrod in Queen Square, Wolverhampton. The unveiling on 23rd November 1866 was the first public event attended by Queen Victoria after the Prince's death, five years earlier in 1861. The square, previously called 'High Green', was re-named 'Queen Square' in commemoration of this event.

Mason secured a patent from the inventive Alexander Parkes involving smelting copper ore to produce purified copper using phosphorous. To make this viable, Mason needed a smelting works, so he secured twenty acres of derelict land in Pembrey, South Wales, near Llanelli, which later became Burry Port. A new works was built, with houses with gardens for factory workers, and production began. Mason also acquired collieries and three brickworks. To secure an engaged workforce, Mason built separate schools for boys, girls and infants in the village, at a cost of £1700, using bricks from his own brickworks. The schools opened to 500 children in August 1855, operating on a non-denominational basis.

A further venture for this never content man was a business producing nickel plated hollow ware, cutlery, buttons, pins, bicycles and lamps, as a cheap alternative for silver, which was resistant to rust or corrosion. A factory was established in the 1850s in Erdington, by the canal in Holly Lane, and was the first nickel factory in the world. The canal bridge nearby has been rebuilt but is still called 'Brace Factory

Bridge', after the works. As with pen nibs and electroplating, Mason became the world's largest manufacturer of nickel.

So, by the 1850s, Josiah Mason was one of the foremost industrialists, not only in the UK, but in the world, becoming extremely wealthy. Unlike most industrialists of his time, who entered politics, or sought ostentatious fame as a demonstration of their wealth and influence, he was reticent and reserved in public. He had genuine concern for providing healthy working conditions and opportunities for education, both where it would serve the needs of his businesses, and unusually, when it would not do so directly.

The difficult, frequently dangerous, and sometimes fatal, working conditions of Britain's industrial era, driven by massive short term growth, has been well-documented. Working practices were largely unregulated, with little legislation to govern working conditions or give protection to working people. Many employers demonstrated scant regard for their employees' health and welfare, secure in the knowledge that those incapacitated, injured, or killed could easily be replaced. Mason was different in this regard as well, as objective reports demonstrate. One of Mason's contemporaries, Samuel Timmins, commented that: 'the occupation is pleasant, the labour light, cleanly, and remunerative.'[230] A factory inspector, J.E. White, reported in 1864: 'This factory [in Lancaster Street] shows that much can be done towards securing healthy workplaces....It fronts onto the street in a crowded and poor part of the town but care has been taken to provide the best modes of ventilation in the workshops, and also up the main staircase, closets free from smell, etc....A marked improvement has been found in the health of the females engaged in one of the shops...since these means have been adopted.... Guards are used to protect the workers from the flying oil and dust.'[231]

In evidence to an enquiry into the contentious issue of children's working hours, one Henry Bore wrote, on Mason's behalf, on 11th June 1875: 'There are about 700 hands subject to the Act employed at these works, and I believe that the majority of these hands would object to any alteration in the hours. The hands under the Act work 50 hours per week (from 8 o'clock to 6). I...can testify that hands earn as much money, and that there is as much work done as under the old system of 59 hours.'[232] Mason had found, as Joseph Chamberlain would at the nearby Nettlefold and Chamberlain screw manufacturing works, that ever longer hours do not of themselves increase productivity and that the reverse can be true.

---

230 Skipp, *The Making of Victorian Birmingham*, p.68
231 Jones, *Josiah Mason 1795-1881: Birmingham's Benevolent Benefactor*, pp.35-38
232 Ibid., p.39

Elkington, Mason and Company offered prizes to workers in January 1853 for innovative ideas in improving processes, an early example of a staff suggestion scheme. Development of skills was encouraged, through indentured apprenticeships, and the pen-making business employed specialist toolmakers, often from boyhood. As one commentator stated 'fifty or sixty young men attend evening classes in the Midland Institute, and take such lessons in design and in the application of science to the different branches of the manufacture as shall fit them for its highest grades of art.'[233] For the time, this was an unusually enlightened approach.

In 1841, aged forty-six, Mason experienced a stomach-related illness, draining him of his usual energy. He travelled to France in July and returned in December, going to Malvern to avail himself of the healing properties of the spa water. He had perhaps learned a useful lesson, as he and Annie, called affectionately 'Tet' by Mason, undertook a 'Grand Tour' from November 1847, travelling to Paris, Tours, Bordeaux, Toulon and Marseilles, and then by sea to Italy, visiting Bologna, Naples, Florence and Rome, arriving in March 1848, when the revolution erupted. Deciding against travelling on to Egypt, they returned to Birmingham and never left the country again. His belief in a caring divinity was reinforced by just missing a train from Paris to Tours, which crashed, killing several passengers. Mason took this as a sign not to worry about being delayed in future, perceiving it as intended to protect him in some way.

When Henry Elkington died on 26th October 1852, the partnership was re-formed between George Elkington and Mason, until George's death, aged sixty-three, on 22nd September 1865. This episode produced a strange anecdote. As George Elkington lay dying at his home in Pool Park, Ruthin, Denbighshire, Mason heard music coming from his chimney at home, foresaw Elkington's death and related this experience to Annie, before the news of his partner's actual death arrived.

After their father's death, Elkington's sons carried the electroplating business forward, leaving Mason to concentrate on the Lancaster Street pen factory and other business ventures, including land purchase in Erdington and Northfield, and other parts of the Midlands, including Sutton Coldfield, Bickenhill and Feckenham. Mason was so dedicated to his work that he operated fully in the businesses until well past what would now be considered retirement age. Mason did not retire until February 1877, aged eighty-two.

---

233 Burritt, quoted in Skipp, *The Making of Victorian Birmingham*, p.134

From the 1850s, Mason began to contemplate how he could use his wealth to benefit others, with a particular interest in helping women and children, perhaps recalling his mother's struggles to make ends meet for a family in straitened circumstances. He saw the opportunity to do good, according to the tenets of his non-conformist faith, which places a duty on its followers to use their skills and resources for the general improvement of people's life chances.

Childless with Annie, he tried to adopt a child, Arthur Harris, whose father, employed as a metallurgist at the Birmingham Mint, had died aged thirty. Jones reports that Mason 'tried to persuade the widowed mother to agree to the adoption by offering a financial inducement, but the offer was refused, much to Mason's annoyance.'[234] Sadly the young man died from a heart condition aged eighteen. Although this attempt to 'buy' a child may not sit well with modern sensibilities, Mason was obviously well-intentioned.

Further experiences of helping individuals did not always end well, with Mason giving a blind man and his friend the money to travel to Liverpool for employment, only to see them both very, perhaps even blind, drunk in Birmingham the following day. Similarly, a woman claiming that she had been discharged from hospital and needed money for food and care was recognised by Mason's foreman as regularly using subterfuges to elicit money, and on Mason's insistence that her bandages be examined, she ran off!

The years 1855 and 1856 were significant in the development of Mason's philanthropy. As well as establishing the Pembrey schools, Mason contemplated helping disadvantaged women and children. Alexander Parkes, in a late night conversation, suggested establishing an orphanage in Erdington. Mason developed a plan within two weeks for thirty almshouses for spinsters and widows, and an orphanage for twenty or thirty children. The size of the orphanage soon increased to accommodate fifty girls. This first building in Sheep Street (re-named Station Street), Erdington, opened in 1858. Richard Bakewell's widow was an early resident, along with orphan girls, preference being given to children in dire circumstances from Birmingham and Kidderminster.

Before this opened, Mason was making proposals for another establishment, an even larger orphanage. On 10th November 1856, Mason wrote to Reverend Dr J.C. Miller, vicar of St. Martin's, confirming that he was 'trustee for various property value about 20,000 pounds at my own disposal for the benefit of orphans.' He set out that 'my idea is that destitute orphans are the objects without reference

---

234 Jones, *Josiah Mason 1795-1881: Birmingham's Benevolent Benefactor*, p.21

to class and feel the importance of giving the preference to girls and early training to be fed, clothed and a sound plain education and trained up for such purposes as the progressive developments of this albeit may indicate for their future employment in society. Say two-thirds girls, one-third boys, half under four years old, some infants.'[235] This appeal requests its addressee to take soundings about wider support for this scheme, and looks forward to further discussions. Mason's remarkable letter, while reflecting his lack of formal education in its phrasing, more importantly speaks forcefully of his desire to use his wealth for the greater good, concentrating support on the youngest and poorest in society, specifically the most disadvantaged, orphan girls. Mason's account of Miller's reaction, when Mason later suggested an investment of £100,000 to him personally, was that he looked him up and down: 'as if I were scarcely to be considered in my senses.'[236] Such a generous and open-hearted offer should surely have engendered an immediate response. None came however for more than three months, perhaps because Mason was not known to Church of England men, being a non-conformist, and not active in polite society or local politics.

Mason's preparedness to commit £100,000 to the project made Miller and his acolytes realise that he was significantly wealthy and dedicated to his purpose. Some more intensive correspondence and meetings followed, but a fundamental stumbling block became apparent. As the benefactor, and a non-conformist, Mason insisted that while scripture should be taught, he would not countenance the teaching of the Church of England catechism. This was apparently a deal-breaker for Miller and his friends. In a final letter of 22nd May 1857, Mason courteously but firmly confirms his intention to pursue the project without the clergy's support: 'I deeply regret that [you] do not feel at liberty to give that unreserved and cordial support to the Institution which you would have done but for the objection I have to the introduction of the Church of England Catechism, as a basis for the religious instruction of the children. I have given my best attention to the earnest advice you gave to me on Tuesday last in such a kind and Christian spirit, but my opinion remains unchanged.'[237] Mason was clearly not prepared to compromise his own principles to meet those of another group, and determined that he could proceed without their help. Mason decided to 'appoint a body of laymen only as trustees' and to leave to them decisions about appointing a chaplain and the manner in which scripture would be taught to the children.

---

235 Jones, *Josiah Mason 1795-1881: Birmingham's Benevolent Benefactor*, p.18
236 Skipp, *The Making of Victorian Birmingham*, p.112
237 Jones, *Josiah Mason 1795-1881: Birmingham's Benevolent Benefactor*, p.59

Mason's Erdington home, Norwood House, had extensive grounds, which he developed to build the orphanage. While the foundation stone was laid privately on 19th September 1860, building work did not begin until 1865. It was completed and handed over to the trustees on 29th July 1869. Costing £60,000, the building was endowed to the value of £200,000, a massive sum, guaranteeing its financial security and independence. It stood on Bell Lane, later re-named Orphanage Road, in recognition of what an important and imposing building it was. Built in an attractive Victorian style, combining architectural beauty and functionality, there were leaded light windows, and dormer windows into the dormitories. One of the towers served as a chimney for the building's flues, while a hot water system provided heat to the rooms on all three floors and steam for cooking, washing and drying. This building included water closets and reflected Mason's skill in modern engineering. The three million bricks used were made on site and decorative stone was used for mouldings, corners and windows. The communal areas were large, the dining room measuring seventy feet by thirty feet, with large rooms for music, sewing and undertaking drill (as part of the intent to instil discipline into the children).

When the larger orphanage opened, the almshouses and small orphanage in Sheep Street were re-modelled to accommodate thirty-one women, each having a furnished room, with coal and gas supplied, and a small annual income. Further additions made included a sitting room, kitchen, storage, and a dormitory for eighteen girls who attended the orphanage for education but were deemed too sick or unable to obtain domestic service employment. It was converted again in the 1880s to accommodate twenty-six elderly women and used until demolished in 1974, making way for a nursery school.

Mason carefully secured the orphanage's future after his death by writing to the Mayor of Birmingham, Henry Holland, on 2nd August 1869: 'After much consideration, I have concluded that the most effectual means of accomplishing my object was to place my trust under the superintendence of my fellow-townsmen, [and] really place in their hands the means of securing the efficient administration of the property, which is already considerable and which, from its nature, must increase with the prosperity of Birmingham.'[238] Mason appointed seven trustees, all required to be gentlemen, Protestants, and living within ten miles of the orphanage. He proposed that the Council should appoint a further seven trustees, who may or may not be councillors, and that the Council would have the right

---

238 Jones, *Josiah Mason 1795-1881: Birmingham's Benevolent Benefactor*, p.64

to appoint any replacements over time. In addition, the whole body of trustees would appoint a replacement for the original seven private trustees, thereby giving effectively the Council a voting majority, and with it control. This was accepted by the Council, and Mason's solicitor, G.J. Johnson, confirmed the arrangements to Richard Chamberlain, Mayor of Birmingham at the time of Mason's death, in a letter of July 1881.

Rules for the 300 children to be admitted to the orphanage were also included in the trust deed. This provided for children to be admitted if they were under nine years of age, and the legitimate child of dead parents, and birth, marriage and death certificates were required. Although children could come from anywhere in the country, preference was given to children from Birmingham and Kidderminster, as Mason never forgot his birthplace. Boys stayed until aged twelve or fourteen, before returning to family or friends, or taking up employment. Girls stayed longer, until sixteen or eighteen, also returning to family or friends, or employment in domestic service. Some stayed to become assistants or teachers in the orphanage.

Children could be excluded in cases of disobedience or misconduct and the rules governing visiting were set out in a document: 'Sir Josiah Mason's Orphanage – Ordinary Visitation days – Rules for Visitors'. To today's observer, these appear unnecessarily harsh and restrictive. Visits 'by three persons only, in one party, between the hours of 3 and 5 o'clock in the afternoon' were permitted only twice a year, on specified days in January and June. While applications for special visits could be requested, 'A Special Order' had to be applied for by writing to the Secretary, stating grounds, and enclosing a stamped addressed envelope for the reply. There were 'Directions as to gifts' indicating that 'for the sake of the health and discipline of the children', no food should be given, apart from 'oranges, nuts, apples and ripe fruit.' Acceptable gifts were 'Balls, bats, tops, books, hoops, marbles, magnifying glasses, scissors, needles, pins, skipping ropes, thimbles, dolls, workboxes, toys of a useful kind, etc.'[239]

The lack of contact with families seems particularly harsh, given the emphasis on the children's welfare, and that they may have returned to those families in due course. Some orphans attested to the sometimes sadistic treatment they received from some staff. While they took the view that Mason was not aware of these actions, there is an unfortunate consistency in their accounts. Such violence towards children was sadly not unusual for the times, and even occurs in contemporary

---

239 Jones, *Josiah Mason 1795-1881: Birmingham's Benevolent Benefactor*, p.67

institutions, but was mitigated by acts of kindness from other staff members, many of whom were fondly remembered.

Orphans described their diet as uninspiring, with breakfast being bread and treacle and occasionally, a slice of bacon, with cocoa in tin mugs. Tea was bread and dripping, also with treacle sometimes, sometimes cake, and cocoa. Dinner could be soup and pudding or meat and potatoes, and at Christmas, one of the trustees provided an orange and two apples for each child.

As well as being fed and clothed, children were educated in reading, writing, spelling, English grammar, arithmetic, history, geography, and scripture. Girls learned to sew, bake, cook, wash, mangle and undertake other domestic duties and were responsible for these around the orphanage. While children ate and played together, they were separated for teaching purposes. Boys were taught shoe-making, like Mason as a youth, and industrial skills. Military-style drill was carried out, alongside physical fitness training. Religious instruction was provided by Wesleyan Methodist ministers in the main and local people could attend services, sitting in a gallery holding 200 people.

The orphanage was successful, and an extension was built in 1874, providing dormitories and a schoolroom, allowing the capacity to reach 500 children – 300 girls, 150 boys and 50 infant boys. Mason was understandably proud of the orphanage and, living next door, was a frequent visitor. He attended the Sunday midday meal, sitting at the head of the large central dining table. Jones has said the children called him 'father' or 'daddy', and, implausibly, that he knew all their names! The accounts of the children themselves paint a very sympathetic picture of Mason, wearing his black double inverness cape, and round felt hat. They could hear him coming, as he used a heavy walking stick, but also from the bells around the necks of his two Skye terriers, Fluff and Rough, who, of course, the children greatly enjoyed. One orphan described Mason's kindly manner and recalls 'a striking personality, tall handsome pink complexion, beautiful white hair and beard, the hair curling upwards from the neck, very prominent blue veins on his temple, very high forehead, very firm mouth, of commanding appearance, a type of man rarely if ever seen today.'[240]

From 1869 to 1881, records show that 406 girls and 246 boys were admitted. 29 girls and 7 boys died, and 175 girls and 114 boys left, returning to family or friends, or finding employment. The orphanage continued and flourished after Mason's death in 1881, and, under local authority control, it was later re-used

---

240 Jones, *Josiah Mason 1795-1881: Birmingham's Benevolent Benefactor,* p.81

as a school until the 1960s. By then, the building was expensive to repair and maintain, and the trustees sold it for £106,000 on 1st January 1964. The proceeds funded accommodation for older people at Mason Court in Olton, and the site of the orphanage is now a housing estate and Yenton Primary School. The site of Norwood House is now Saint Edmund Campion Catholic School and Sixth Form, on Sutton Road.

Although an act of generous philanthropy, the orphanage did not last to the present day, as the state took over its primary function of caring for orphaned children. Another institution founded by Mason does continue, although many do not appreciate that he was its originator and sponsor, as it no longer bears his name. The University of Birmingham, the fourth largest in the UK, is rightly regarded as of excellent quality here and across the world. This institution has had an enormous impact on many thousands of young people, and the whole population, given its contribution to academic study, scientific and medical research and care.

Mason's next effort to help those much less fortunate than himself was a substantial testament to his continuing energy, even though he was now in his seventies. He had already demonstrated his commitment to providing educational opportunities for the poor through building schools in South Wales and in the teaching provided at his factories and orphanages. In Birmingham, the Queen's College had been established in 1828 by William Sands Cox as a residential college for medical students, and other institutions for adult further education had been set up, the Mechanics' Institute in 1826, and the Polytechnic Institution in 1843, but both closed (in 1842 and 1846 respectively), due to lack of resources. In 1854, the Midland Institute was established, for 'the advancement of science, literature and art', and was built in Paradise Street opposite Queen's College, opening in 1855 as part of the 'education quarter' around the Town Hall.

As a businessman in the early 1870s, Mason felt the need for more extensive and well delivered teaching and training in vocational subjects, felt by universities to be below their dignity. While they offered education for its own sake, there was little which prepared young people for specific areas of employment, beyond those already mentioned. Mason's view that education could be pursued by anyone, without direction by any particular religious creed, brought him into conflict with Anglican clergy, as we have seen. It also engendered difficulty with Roman Catholics, as Cardinal Newman somewhat churlishly refused to inscribe two of his books which had been purchased for Mason's College library, in July 1882. Mason's approach was therefore to exclude dogmatic religious teaching by establishing an institution to teach exclusively scientific subjects to meet industry's growing needs, and to improve the lot of ordinary people by making them employable.

Having discussed ideas around scientific education with Johnson, his solicitor, and Dr James Gibbs Blake, his doctor, both of whom were involved in the orphanage, he originally considered buying the Queen's College building in Paradise Street, or adding to the Midland Institute in Edmund Street. These proved too complicated and he resolved finally to establish an independent college. Dr Blake offered ideas from his visits to similar institutions during his travels in Europe and North America.

Having decided on a town centre location, Mason succeeded in securing an acre of land near the Town Hall, bounded by Great Charles Street, Edmund Street, Congreve Street and Easy Row (now part of Paradise Circus Queensway). As with the orphanage, Mason set up a Foundation Deed on 12th December 1870, with the same type of provisions, to endow the college for transfer to the then Mayor of Birmingham, his fellow industrialist, Thomas Avery, with control of appointments of the trustees of the college being exercised by the Council. Mason's stipulation once more was that these would need to be laymen and Protestants, whether councillors or not.

The range of subjects to be delivered were set out in the curriculum, which deliberately excluded theology and literary subjects, and ensured the college concentrated on teaching practical subjects to meet the needs of Midlands industry. Mathematics, Physics, Chemistry, Natural Sciences, Biology, Botany, Zoology, Physiology and Engineering were included. While other subjects were excluded, Mason left further development in the hands of the trustees, again as he had done with the orphanage, wisely recognising that needs would change in the future. English, French and German were added later, as were courses leading to degrees conferred by universities, as educational thinking became more progressive and accessible. Mason required the trustees to review the curriculum and administration of the college formally every fifteen years, at least, so that it would move with the times.

The Deed ensured that admission was open to all, with preference given to pupils from the orphanages (up to a fifth), and further preference given to students from Birmingham and Kidderminster, recalling Mason's place of birth, again as with the orphanages. Determining that admission could not be refused on grounds of creed, race, sex, age or birthplace reinforces the fact that Mason wanted the very poorest in society to have cradle to adulthood equality of opportunity. Students were taught from the age of fourteen to twenty-five, with some older being admitted on an exceptional basis, up to a limit of ten percent of students.

The final Deed was signed at Norwood House, with six trustees attending, on Mason's seventy-eighth birthday, 23rd February 1873. Mason signed this as Sir Josiah Mason, having been knighted in 1872. The foundation stone was laid on 23rd February 1875, Mason's eightieth birthday. The ceremony was short, due to cold and wintry weather, and local notables attended. Joseph Chamberlain, the Mayor of Birmingham, was not there, due to the death of his second wife, Florence. The radical MP, John Bright, gave a speech in which he confirmed the low public profile that Mason had, saying: 'I am sorry to say I know very little of Sir Josiah's early life. I know him by what I have seen and heard only recently, but he has acquired for himself a position…which we can admire and respect.' Mason's reply encapsulates his whole purpose and motivation: 'Trusting that I, who have never been blessed with children of my own, may yet in these students leave behind me an intelligent, earnest, industrious truth-loving and truth-seeking progeny.'[241] Perhaps unsurprisingly, Mason was inclined, as with orphans, to see the students as his surrogate children.

Maintaining his tradition of undertaking major events on his birthday, Mason's Science College was completed on 23rd February 1880, his eighty-fifth birthday, and opened on 1st October. A large opening ceremony at the Town Hall included the Mayor, Richard Chamberlain, and representatives of Birmingham and Kidderminster Councils, and the universities of Oxford, Cambridge and London. Mason handed the key to the chair of the trustees, saying: 'The key of my College is now mine, and I can say that the College is mine, but in a moment I shall be able to say so no longer, for I now present it, and with it, the College, to my old friend, Mr Johnson, on behalf of my trustees, to be held by them in trust for the benefit of generations to come.'[242]

The building itself was another example of fine Victorian architecture, combining beauty and purpose, and made a substantial and imposing contribution to the attractiveness of the education quarter around the Town Hall. It was built from red brick, made in Kingswinford, with Portland, Bath and Bolton Wood stone for the windows. The Daily Mail commented that 'As a specimen of Gothic architecture, it is one of the finest the town possesses.'[243] Electricity was used for lighting the entrance hall and corridors, and the decorative elements included

---

241 Jones, *Josiah Mason 1795-1881: Birmingham's Benevolent Benefactor,* pp.89-91
242 Ibid., p.92
243 Quoted in Ibid., p.93

enamels from Elkington, Mason and Company. Its famous alumni included two future prime ministers, students at the same time (although not thought to have known each other while there), Stanley Baldwin and Neville Chamberlain.

Mason's financial contribution had been enormous, at £170,000 in endowment and building costs (the latter at £60,000), a phenomenally large sum. He gave the College a motto and crest, 'Progress through Knowledge', and an emblem of a mermaid. This is a recurring emblem for Mason, as he was fascinated by a mermaid depicted in a stained glass window when a boy in Kidderminster. It appeared on the badges of prefects and the belt buckles of girls at the orphanage, and a similar window was included in the mausoleum he built for his wife's interment (Annie died on 24th February 1870, aged seventy-eight, after fifty-five years of marriage) in the grounds of Norwood House. The mermaid still appears in the University of Birmingham crest, and a statue of a mermaid which stood at the College for eighty-five years was moved to the Birmingham Students' Union building, where it remains to this day.

In 1892, the Medical Faculty at Queen's College joined the College, and by the following year, there were 556 students attending. In 1898, it became Mason's University College, with control moving to a Court of Governors. Joseph Chamberlain became chair, and lobbied for Parliament to establish the College as a university, and this was enacted on 1st October 1900. Chamberlain became the first Chancellor and the first Principal was Oliver Lodge, knighted in 1902. Mason's Science College building contributed to the provision of education to many thousands of students for more than eighty years until its demolition in 1964 for the development of Paradise Circus.

Mason's final appearance in public was the dinner he hosted for professors and trustees of the College and trustees from the orphanage, and his other charitable organisations, on his eighty-sixth birthday, 23rd February 1881. Visibly unwell, he had difficulty with sight and hearing, and following the conversation. His health declined, with a fall on 11th March, confining him to his bed and the house. Telling friends 'his work was done', Mason bade farewell to Johnson, his longstanding friend, on 11th June, and fell into unconsciousness, dying around 8pm on 16th June 1881. Attended by his great nephew, Martyn Josiah Smith, and his housekeeper, Miss Hannah Winwood, Mason died from 'senile decay', that is old age, according to the death certificate completed by his friend, Dr Blake.

Mason's attention to detail in life was evident in the arrangements for dealing with his death and estate. His funeral was a private and simple ceremony, befitting the man. His coffin was carried from Norwood House by some employees to the orphanage chapel for a short, respectful service. The coffin was carried to the mausoleum in which Annie rested, accompanied by 150 boys and 200 girls from the orphanage. After an abridged burial service, he was laid to rest, with Annie, the coffins adorned by two wreaths. The mausoleum had his instructions for those running his orphanage engraved on a window:

'They will be what you will make them,
Make them wise and make them good,
Make them strong for time of trial;
Teach them temperance, self-denial,
Patience, kindness, fortitude.'[244]

Mason lived a frugal and careful life, walking miles each day, eating plain food, drinking only a little wine, and never smoking, despite his enormous wealth. He gave away more than £500,000 in his lifetime to causes important to him. He worked hard in developing and ensuring effective management of the institutions he loved, especially the orphanage and Mason Science College, as it allowed him, according to his own dictum, to 'Do deeds of love'. The evidence indicates a hard-working, effective businessman throughout his life, whose kind-hearted generosity and concern for the poorest in society was made tangible though the foundations he established. The amount he spent and donated was equivalent to more than four years' worth of the town's income from the rates, a staggering amount. He changed the course and quality of thousands of lives by these means, probably unmatched by anyone else in Birmingham's history.

Sir Josiah Mason, despite his contribution, is not prominently well-remembered in Birmingham. As his name has disappeared, so has the public consciousness of his kindness and achievements. A blue plaque in Paradise Forum, by the now demolished Central Library, will hopefully be restored. A bust of him on a stone pedestal sits on the roundabout at the intersection of Orphanage Road and Chester Road, close to where the orphanage was. This is inscribed simply with his title and name and is based on a statue showing Mason seated, holding the College foundation deed. This stood in Edmund Street for sixty-five years, but was removed due to wear and deterioration in 1951. Two portraits exist, one in the Senate Room at the University of Birmingham (on loan from Birmingham Museum and Art Gallery), and a half-length copy in the university's ownership.

244 Bird, *Portrait of Birmingham*, p.124

The University has mounted his coat of arms, along with those of the Calthorpe family and the University's own heraldry, on a low wall outside the new library at the Edgbaston campus. There is a bust in a ground floor corridor alcove in the Great Hall, showing Mason as a firm and dignified individual, with a truly resplendent beard!

Mason Road joins Orphanage Road in Erdington. In Kidderminster, there is a carved stone plaque on the house in which he was born in Mill Street, and a mall named after him at the Rowland Hill Shopping Centre. The mausoleum at the orphanage was demolished at the same time as the main building, and special permission had to be obtained from the Home Office to move the bodies of Mason and Annie, and the remains of fifty-four children buried in the grounds. They were cremated at Perry Barr Crematorium in 1962. The names of them all were carved on a stone plaque, etched in red, erected in a walled area of the crematorium, named Mason Court, a testament to their memory.

Bust of Josiah Mason on stone pedestal on roundabout at the intersection of Orphanage Road and Chester Road, Erdington, Birmingham

Josiah Mason's coat of arms, outside library, Edgbaston campus, University of Birmingham

Mason is remembered very practically in the work of the Sir Josiah Mason Trust. This trust, a charitable organisation providing accommodation and care services for disadvantaged members of society in Birmingham and Solihull, is the trust originally established by Mason on 29th July 1868. It maintains thirty-six almshouses built in Bell Lane in the 1920s, now called Mason Cottages. Further developments of almshouses followed in Shirley in 1974 and Olton, Solihull in 1979. From the 1980s, the trust has provided care services. This living memorial is undoubtedly the one he would feel to be his most appropriate legacy.

At the laying of the foundation stone of Mason Science College, on 23rd February 1875, John Bright MP offered a fulsome and fitting tribute:

'Whether you consider these institutions dealing with the orphan and the fatherless, or this institution of today [the College], which will make science the common heritage of the people, he has done that, I say, which will give him a name that will be revered in hundreds and thousands of homes. He has shown himself the helper of the forlorn and the helpless, the promoter of that science, of these branches of science especially, upon which we know the future prosperity of your city must be built. I am here to offer my tribute of respect and admiration to one whom we now deem, and one who will by generations to come be deemed, one of the worthiest of the worthy citizens of this great city.'[245]

Clearly, Josiah Mason was reluctant to be well-known by the public, but Louisa Anne Ryland was even more shy and retiring, despite her considerable generosity.

LOUISA ANNE RYLAND
'The wealthy heiress who did not wish her considerable kindness and philanthropy to be known'

Louisa Anne Ryland inherited considerable wealth from her parents and was keen to ensure that those around her, and particularly the place of her birth, Birmingham, benefitted from her remarkable good fortune. She made many gifts and donations, and many bequests in her will to a wide range of health, medical, educational and religious causes, but always indicated that her generosity should not be publicly known. She is barely known at all in the city which benefitted from her generosity, in its parks, hospitals, schools and churches, but it is now surely right that her legacy is acknowledged.

Louisa Anne Ryland was the only child of Samuel Ryland and his wife Anne, née Pemberton. She was born on 17th January 1814, into a wealthy family, at The Laurels, 280, Hagley Road, Edgbaston. This house later became Edgbaston High School for Girls. Samuel's father, John, who died the year his granddaughter was born, became rich through his wire-drawing business in Birmingham, and this wealth was invested in land and property in Birmingham and surrounding areas by Samuel and Anne. They were described somewhat uncharitably as: 'excellent

---

245 Quoted in Jones, *Josiah Mason 1795-1881: Birmingham's Benevolent Benefactor,* pp.89-90

people, but very unrefined and thought much of money. They lived economically and saved enormous sums every year', by the daughter of Galton Junior, Elizabeth Wheeler.[246] While some records state that Anne died in 1815, she did in fact live until 1862, and is buried in Sherbourne, Warwickshire, as is Louisa herself. Samuel died in 1843, leaving Louisa, aged twenty-nine, a vast fortune of more than £1 million. Louisa and her mother continued to invest in land and property, some of which would later be given to Birmingham.

In 1832, the family moved from Birmingham, renting the Priory Estate in Warwick and became prominent members of Leamington society. They moved to the Barford Hill Estate, in Sherbourne, when the Great Western Railway was built across the Priory Estate, and the family became substantial landowners in Warwickshire.

As a twenty year old heiress, Louisa was much sought after company for young men of position and standing. Described in 1834, she had 'simplicity of mind, sweetness of temper, and unaffected manners [which] never fail to charm, and when accompanied by personal accomplishments, are irresistible.'[247] Samuel enjoyed the life of a country gentleman and wanted his daughter to marry into the aristocracy. Apparently, Lord Foley and Lord Blayney sought her hand, and her father favoured Lord Brooke. Unfortunately Louisa had already fallen in love with Henry Smith, later Mayor of Birmingham in 1851 to 1852. He loved her, but the match was refused by her father. Louisa never married, and displayed extraordinary faithfulness to Henry, even though he married someone else (a relation of hers, Maria Louisa Phipson). On her death, Louisa left her fortune to Henry's son, Charles Alston Smith, on condition that he adopted her surname, becoming Charles Alston Smith-Ryland. Perhaps this was Louisa's way of finally claiming the family that she felt should have been hers.

Louisa's governess, Charlotte Randle, became a lifelong friend and her companion at Sherbourne, until Charlotte's death in 1882, aged eighty-eight. Charlotte was an Anglican, and under her influence, Louisa, brought up as a Unitarian, converted to Anglicanism. Louisa was buried alongside Charlotte in Sherbourne Church, which she paid to be re-built in 1864.

Louisa used her wealth to benefit many causes, and prominent among these were gifts to Birmingham, where her family's wealth originated. She gave at least £180,000 during her life, but is thought to have donated much more, as many gifts

---

246 Phillada Ballard, 'Ryland, Louisa Anne (1814-1889)', *Oxford Dictionary of National Biography*, (Oxford: 2013)
247 Ibid.

were made anonymously, as 'a friend of Birmingham'. Notably, Louisa stipulated that her name was not attached to her gifts, preferring anonymity. As an example, it was suggested that her considerable gift of eighty acres of land in Edgbaston should be called 'Ryland Park'. When Louisa refused this, it was called 'Cannon Hill Park', as it remains. Carl Chinn describes how the land, valued at £25,000, was made up of two parcels of land bought by the Rylands, Cannon Hill House in 1788 and the Horse Moors in 1803. Louisa paid £5,000 for the land to be drained, laid out and planted, to a design by John Gibson, designer of Battersea Park, London, before it opened on 1st September 1873. Bunce, in a tone described by Skipp as: 'not wholly inappropriate wonderment' explained that 'several acres were devoted to ornamental gardening, including shrubberies, in which were planted many choice and rare evergreens; large pools, surrounded by plantations and walks, were also constructed; and a carriage drive, nearly a mile in length, was formed round the park. A handsome refreshment room and an entrance lodge were also erected by Miss Ryland. On the margin of one of the pools, a boat-house has been provided, together with a landing stage. There is also a bathing pool.'[248] While the bathing pool is no longer used for this purpose, many of these features are recognisable to any visitor to Cannon Hill Park, and the lodge now bears the single memorial to her in the city.

15,000 people attended the opening, including Louisa herself. The Mayor, Ambrose Biggs, led the crowd in three cheers for Louisa, and each visitor was handed a card with a comment from the generous benefactress which stated: 'Through the bounty of God, I have great pleasure in giving Cannon Hill Park to the Corporation of Birmingham for the use of the people of the town and neighbourhood. I would express my earnest hope that the park may prove a source of healthful recreation to the people of Birmingham, and that they will aid in the protection and preservation of what is now their own property.'[249]

In 1863, Louisa contributed £1,000 towards a public subscription scheme to purchase Aston Hall and Park, although this was not completed until 1884. 'Another noble gift of Miss Ryland'[250] was £4,000, given in 1876 to lay out forty-two acres in what became Small Heath Park, later re-named Victoria Park, on the Coventry Road. For this she was given an illuminated book by the Corporation

---

248 John Thackray Bunce, *History of the Corporation of Birmingham: with a Sketch of the Earlier Government of the Town*, vol.2, (Birmingham: 1885), p.201

249 *Carl Chinn: Heartbreak led to Louisa Anne Ryland's gift to Birmingham*, 9th March 2013

250 Bunce, *History of the Corporation of Birmingham: with a Sketch of the Earlier Government of the Town*, vol.2, p.203

which thanked her for the 'further proof of Miss Ryland's generous interest in the welfare and happiness of its inhabitants.' Once more, Chinn describes how the development of the park proceeded, and notes the contributions made by local contractors in constructing the lodge, refreshment room, bridge, iron railings and carriage drives and pathways. The opening ceremony took place in heavy rain, following a procession from the junction of Cattell Road and Herbert Road, headed by the Hay Mills Band. Queen Victoria visited Birmingham, to lay the foundation stone of the Victoria Law Courts, in Corporation Street, on 23rd March 1887, and as part of the visit, went to the park. Subsequently, the Council sought the Queen's permission for the park to be re-named 'Victoria Park', although it is still known locally, and recorded on maps, as Small Heath Park.

Louisa made many other gifts to Birmingham, to churches, health and medical causes, and educational projects. She and her mother gave land for the building of St. Barnabas's Church (now demolished) in Ryland Street, named after the family, and £10,000 which funded three churches in the city between 1867 and 1869. Her retiring nature was evident again when asked to lay the foundation stone of one of these, writing 'I prefer not to take a prominent position on the occasion.'[251] Louisa was a founder member of the Church of the Saviour Chapel in 1847, where George Dawson developed his 'Civic Gospel'. Further financial gifts followed, including extensive funds to help rebuild St. Martin's in the Bull Ring between 1872 and 1875. She made donations for churches in Warwickshire, including one on the family estate in Sherbourne, and the tower of St. Mary's in Warwick in 1885, which unusually does have a carved dedication on one of its walls recording her generosity.

Louisa gave a house in Sparkhill in 1878 for conversion into the Birmingham and Midland Women's Hospital, leasing the building for a peppercorn rent for forty-two years. Other gifts were made to the Queen's Hospital, later Birmingham Accident Hospital, on Bath Row, the Birmingham and Midland Eye Hospital in Church Street, to the foundation for the Jaffray Hospital, Erdington, and a legacy in her will of £25,000 to Birmingham General Hospital.

The current Birmingham City University School of Art in Edmund Street was originally established in 1843 as the Birmingham Government School of Design, before moving to Margaret Street in 1885, as the first Municipal School of Art, with a contribution of £10,000 from Louisa to support teachers' salaries. Her gift included an endowment to fund a student travel scholarship which is still

---

251 Ballard, 'Ryland, Louisa Anne (1814-1889)', *Oxford Dictionary of National Biography*

awarded today. After a further gift of £10,000 in 1882 to 1884, she again declined public acknowledgement, saying 'that good is done, it is enough for me to have the privilege of doing it.'[252] Nearby, at 9, Margaret Street is the Birmingham and Midland Institute, founded by her cousin, Arthur Ryland, a solicitor, and others, to which Louisa gave £5,000 to fund an industrial fellowship and a further £5,000 towards reducing its debt.

Louisa Anne Ryland died of bronchitis, on 28th January 1889, aged seventy-five, at Barford Hill House, the funeral taking place on 31st January, with servants and labourers from the estate as her pallbearers. Her fortune was estimated to be £2 million, double that she inherited. Her will left most of this to Charles Alston Smith, Henry's son, but also included bequests to around a hundred individuals and institutions, including hospitals, churches and schools, with the proviso that they spend the bequest as she directed. Her reticence for public acknowledgement prevailed to the end, with a note that stated: 'I am ashamed to mention that the idea has occurred to me that it is possible some little memorial of me may be proposed in Birmingham. Now, I entreat that such may not be the case, for I shrink from having any money collected or trouble taken for such a purpose.'[253]

It is not possible to control people's actions after one's death, and there are some discreet memorials and several reminders of her in Birmingham. Cannon Hill Park has a blue plaque placed on The Lodge, at the park

Louisa Anne Ryland, photograph, before 1890, reproduced by kind permission of Birmingham City Council

entrance in Edgbaston Road, and has named its recreational train which runs around the park itself after her. A reredos was erected in her memory in St. John's Church, Sparkhill, and a grateful city named one of its buildings Louisa Ryland House. This houses the City housing and social services headquarters in Newhall Street. Bird states: 'The Ryland family has given more names to Birmingham streets than most of the city's great families.' Many were from the Sherbourne

252 Ballard, 'Ryland, Louisa Anne (1814-1889)', *Oxford Dictionary of National Biography*
253 *Louisa Anne Ryland, 1814-1889,* 31st December 2000

estate, including Northbrook, Coplow, Morville, and Sherbourne. 'Names from the family are perpetuated in several Ryland roads and streets: Alston Street, and in Sparkhill, in Ivor, Phipson, Dennis, Evelyn, Adria, Esme, and Doris roads, while even the old school of the wealthy Smith-Rylands is among them in Eton Road.'[254]

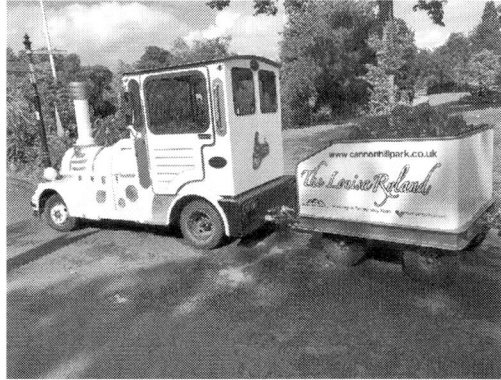

Blue plaque on The Lodge, at the park entrance at 143, Edgbaston Road, Edgbaston, Birmingham, B12 9QA and the Cannon Hill Park children's road train

---

254 Bird, *Portrait of Birmingham*, pp.23-5

8.

From Individual Acts to Corporate Action in the nineteenth century – Birmingham begins to take care of its people

Despite the euphoria around the Birmingham Improvement Act 1851, there is little evidence of significant success by the Council in addressing social and economic issues in the following twenty years. The development of education often relied on individuals or foundations creating schools through philanthropy. This continued until the need to improve literacy led to the founding of the Birmingham Education Society in 1867, through the efforts of Jesse Collings, supported by the Mayor, George Dixon. This pressure led in part to the Education Act of 1870.

Those with radical tendencies, supporting greater expenditure on public services and public health, were seen by some ratepayers as untrustworthy and wasteful. In the 1850s, this desire to keep spending under control was embodied in Birmingham Town Council by a group calling themselves 'The Economists', whose avowed intent was simply to keep the rates down. Led by Joseph Allday, they promoted themselves as representatives of the ordinary struggling ratepayer. Described as 'petit bourgeois councillors',[255] they wanted neither local government provision, nor the rates to increase above the level required to meet the Corporation's legal obligations for funding the police force and poor relief. They argued that social initiatives should be the product of philanthropy, not the result of local government action. Whatever their intentions, they proved incapable of effective management of the Council's budgets, and Allday was replaced by Thomas Avery in 1859.

---

255 Roger Ward, *The Chamberlains: Joseph, Austen and Neville 1836-1940*, (Stroud, Gloucestershire: 2015), p.19

Avery bears a name that every Brummie knows, from the world-famous weighing machines and scales produced by this company over many years. William Avery, Thomas's father, a 'scale-beam maker', inherited a family business, which he developed with his brother Thomas. They re-named the company 'W. & T. Avery'. When William died in 1843, the company was passed on to his sons, William Henry and Thomas Junior. As they fortuitously bore the same forenames as their father and uncle, there was no need to re-name the company! By 1851, their factory in Moat Lane, Digbeth, employed 150 men and boys. Thomas was the driving force, gaining a reputation for hard work and trustworthiness. By 1859, the company had grown rapidly to employ more than 400 people.

Thomas believed that local government could be improved by financial discipline and efficiency, and retired from business in 1864, aged fifty-one, fully turning the business over to William Henry in 1866. He was elected as a councillor for St. Martin's Ward, where his family's factory was located, became an alderman, then Mayor in 1868 and again in 1881. Avery was 'Conservative in party allegiance and Gladstonian in financial management',[256] but had liberal tendencies, and supported the Liberal MP, John Bright, in Parliamentary elections. Avery wanted to maintain downward pressure on the rates, but believed that more could be done with the resources available and is credited with introducing financial discipline into the Corporation, including a more effective accounting system.

Under his leadership, the Council improved drains, widened streets and opened libraries. The major problem remained public health and the poor and insanitary condition of many parts of the town. In an 1869 pamphlet, Avery argued for municipal control of water, writing that: 'Wealth can always take care of itself, but poverty cannot; and surely it is the duty of a wise local government to endeavour to surround the humbler classes of the population with its benevolent and protecting care.'[257] In 1871, Avery chaired a Sewage Enquiry Committee seeking practicable and affordable solutions. This found that only 3,884 houses had water closets, and that 14,500 of the 20,000 middens were draining into the sewers that supported only one-third of the town. This created an 'almost unimaginable difficulty' of collecting excreta which overwhelmed the 140 acre sewage farm at Saltley. The Committee proposed purchasing 800 acres to build a sewage farm with sufficient capacity, but the Parliamentary Bill was opposed by Sir Charles Adderley, the owner of Hams Hall, and other landowners. This prevented the development of

---

256 Peter T. Marsh, *Joseph Chamberlain: Entrepreneur in Politics,* (London: 1994), p.78
257 Bunce, *History of the Corporation of Birmingham: with a Sketch of the Earlier Government of the Town,* vol.2, p.405

an effective solution to the problems of handling sewage for seventeen years, until 1875. As Adderley's legal challenges continued, the debate became figuratively mired in Parliament, while the town continued to be mired in its own excreta, and the Bill failed.

As a response, the Council implemented an alternative system, called the 'Rochdale Pan System'. Over time, as Joseph Chamberlain became the most prominent, articulate and innovative councillor and Mayor, Avery came to sympathise with many of his proposals. He was involved again in 1884 when chair of the Tame and Rea District Drainage Board, 'a work with which the name and labours of Mr. Avery are honourably associated.'[258] He was respected, chairing the Council's Water Committee from July 1875, enabling the purchase of the private Waterworks Company. He opened Shustoke Reservoir in July 1883, its 400 million gallon capacity securing a continuing water supply for Birmingham for years. He chaired the Council committee which established the Shakespeare Memorial Library in 1868. He retired as an alderman in 1892, and died at his home, Beech Lawn, in Church Road, Edgbaston on 17th February 1894.

Avery made a positive and creditable contribution to resolving the town's social and hygiene problems. These issues were so substantial that it would, however, require a bigger personality and forceful direction to resolve them. Fortunately for Birmingham, such a personality came to the fore. Joseph Chamberlain rose rapidly to local, and later national, prominence to become one of the most effective politicians of the Victorian and Edwardian eras, and Birmingham's most famous resident.

JOSEPH CHAMBERLAIN
*'Birmingham's greatest man' and 'the father of modern
Birmingham', 'the most trusted man in England'
and 'the first minister of the Empire'*

The name Chamberlain is well known to Brummies, and is very visible in the city, from Chamberlain Square, including the fountain adjacent to the Town Hall and Council House, to Joseph Chamberlain Sixth Form College in Belgrave Road, to the Chamberlain Clock at Warstone Lane roundabout in the Jewellery Quarter, to 'Old Joe', the clock tower at the University of Birmingham Edgbaston campus. These permanent monuments are forceful reminders of the great affection felt by Brummies for Joseph Chamberlain during and shortly after his life. While many know something of the Chamberlains (there were three of local and national

---

258 Bunce, *History of the Corporation of Birmingham: with a Sketch of the Earlier Government of the Town*, *vol.1*, p.353

significance, a father and two of his sons), it is probable that many are not able to articulate in any detail who they were or what they did.

Joseph Chamberlain, in the second half of the nineteenth century and into the first decade of the twentieth, was a political colossus, enormously well regarded locally but also described as 'the most popular and trusted man in England'[259] and 'the first minister of the Empire.'[260] It is true to say that he was extremely ambitious politically, and personally he could be very charming and urbane, but was also completely ruthless in pursuing his political objectives. While the extent of his legacy as Colonial Secretary from 1895 to 1903 may be questioned, what cannot be doubted is that in his three years as Mayor of Birmingham, from 1873 to 1876, he had a dramatic impact on the town (Birmingham was incorporated as a city in 1889). While this sketch covers the whole of Joseph Chamberlain's career, it will spend most time and attention on his achievements in Birmingham.

Joseph Chamberlain was born on 8th July 1836, at 3, Grove Hill Terrace, Camberwell, in Surrey, the first of eight children, five sons and three daughters, of Joseph (born 1796, died 1874) and his wife Caroline (born 1808, died 1875). Joseph Senior was a cordwainer, or shoe manufacturer, and later invested in a company producing wood screws. Caroline, described as cultured, was the daughter of Henry Harben, a brewer and provisions merchant. Joseph's background in manufacturing and retail (four generations of the family were cordwainers) influenced his political opinions about trade, the value of labour, taxation and indeed the British Empire all his life, first in industry, but then in politics at a local and national level.

The family held Unitarian beliefs, thorough non-conformists, and imbued Joseph with a clear mission to use his talents for his own, and his family's, benefit, but also to provide help and support through his actions to those in need of employment and relief from poverty. Life would challenge his belief in a merciful god, but he retained his connections to this faith throughout his life.

His family, well to do and relatively comfortable, moved from the still rural Camberwell to Highbury Place, Islington when Joseph was ten, in 1846. Manufacturing shoes was profitable, given that the family firm supplied the British Army during a period of regular military conflict around the world in defence, and expansion, of the Empire. The Chamberlains lent their support to the war against Revolutionary France and 'appreciated the blessings of a belligerent state.'[261]

---

259 The Times, quoted in Ward, *The Chamberlains: Joseph, Austen and Neville 1836-1940*, p.54
260 Peter T. Marsh, 'Chamberlain, Joseph [Joe] (1836-1914)', *Oxford Dictionary of National Biography*, Oxford: (2004, updated 2013)
261 Ibid.

Excelling in the plays his mother put on at home, Joseph was lively, clever and thoughtful, and received a good education. He moved from a dame school in Camberwell to an Islington school and was then enrolled in University College School, in Gower Street, Bloomsbury, which was well supported by Unitarians. Joseph excelled and won prizes in both arts and science subjects, and on completing his education, was naturally apprenticed to his father's business.

Chamberlain learnt the business from top to bottom, undertaking and understanding the production processes for shoe-making, before learning how the finances of the firm operated, so that he quickly gained an appreciation of process, and profit and loss. His father's brother-in-law, John Sutton Nettlefold Senior owned a wood screw manufacturing business in Birmingham, and was looking for investment to purchase the British patent for an automated American screw-making machine. Convinced that this would allow him to break into overseas markets, he needed to raise capital to invest in the patent and machinery and premises, as a new factory would need to be built, at Heath Street, Smethwick, with railway and canal links. The agreement involved Joseph Junior, aged only eighteen, moving to Birmingham to become part of the firm of Nettlefold and Chamberlain, so that he could learn more about business, and presumably to ensure that the family's investment was protected. Joseph lodged in Frederick Street, Edgbaston, and was able to walk to the firm's premises in Broad Street.

Joseph was an extremely able and successful businessman. While he controlled the finances and marketing of their increasing range of products, his cousin Joseph Nettlefold managed production. They improved the production, storage, sales and marketing processes, and were known as 'The Screw Kings', as the firm took a major share of the national market. They began developing markets in Europe and North America for their products. By the time of his retirement from business, the firm employed 2,000 people. They invested further up the supply chain, buying ironworks, and produced their own metal supplies for screw production. This company became Guest, Keen and Nettlefold, or GKN, a major employer for thousands of Brummies for many years. The name continues, although it is now part of a global and specialised firm concentrating on driveshafts in the automotive and aerospace businesses.

In an 1866 publication, Chamberlain provided an article setting out his philosophy on the role of factories, which were springing up in and round Birmingham, compared to the plethora of small workshops, located in houses and backyards. The best run factories provided 'healthier work places, regularity of hours, economy of labour, increased demand, lower prices and at the same time higher wages.' His own factory had 'large...airy and well lighted' premises, with a working week of sixty hours with Saturday afternoons off (as well as Sunday, of course).[262]

In 1861, aged twenty-five, Chamberlain married Harriet Kenrick (born 1838), the daughter of Archibald Kenrick of Berrow Court, Edgbaston, an ironmaster in West Bromwich. Harriet's family were Unitarians who became heavily involved in Liberal Unionist politics. On marrying, Chamberlain moved out of his lodgings into a house on Harborne Road, Edgbaston, the garden of which prompted his lifelong love of horticulture. Chamberlain was active in his Unitarian church, which moved from Priestley's New Meeting House, near Moor Street, to the Church of the Messiah, Broad Street. He participated, and held several offices, in the Edgbaston Debating Society, in the late 1850s and early 1860s, where he burnished the oratorical skills which would mark him out as a leading debater in his political career.

His marriage was happy, with a daughter, Beatrice, being born in 1862, and then in 1863, Harriet was pregnant again. This resulted in tragedy, as although Joseph Austen (later known as Austen) was born on 16th October, his mother tragically died a few days later from puerperal fever, a urinary tract infection. Chamberlain was devastated, and could not bear to return to the family home, so moved with his two children to live with Harriet's parents, where their older daughter cared for the children. Chamberlain's response was to devote his time to his work and the broader issues which led to his political career.

Chamberlain, thoughtful and analytical in his approach to business processes, developed an unusual view of production efficiency. He proposed a shorter working day, of a maximum of nine hours, on the basis that this would increase productivity. This creative 'win-win' approach endeared him to employees and trade unions, and improved profits. He offered his suppliers and customers discounts for cash payments, an approach which was widely copied. His ability to bear down on production costs meant that the firm's products were very competitive, and the customer base expanded substantially, with an agreement with a French screw manufacturer to operate in spheres of influence in Europe. The competitive threat of the firm was such that screw manufacturers in the US agreed to pay Nettlefold and Chamberlain a large annual sum simply to stay out of their home market. These experiences convinced Chamberlain of the compatibility, and indeed interdependence, of free trade and imperialism, and this shaped his future actions when in government.[263]

---

262 Ward, *The Chamberlains: Joseph, Austen and Neville 1836-1940*, p.13
263 Marsh, 'Chamberlain, Joseph [Joe] (1836-1914)', *Oxford Dictionary of National Biography*

As his firm grew, so did Chamberlain's business contacts, and he joined the board of the Midland Railway, and the bank of Lloyds, which originated in Birmingham.

In private life, Chamberlain married again in 1868. His second wife was Florence Kenrick (born 1847), Harriet's first cousin. Although described as 'physically never sturdy', they had four children, Arthur Neville (known as Neville) in 1869, Ida in 1870, Hilda in 1871 and Ethel in 1873.

Chamberlain is regarded as 'a prime example of modern monopoly capitalism' and a 'model of Victorian paternalism'.[264] This paternalism took form in his focus on education, initially offering his employees educational and recreational clubs, and profit-sharing for senior members of staff. He came to believe that the system of education needed radical change and reform, as less than half of children were enrolled in full-time education. He wanted free, compulsory education, on a secular basis, without it being controlled by any religious denomination. He stated that: 'it is as much the duty of the State to see that the children are educated as to see that they are fed.'[265]

Joseph supported the creation of the Birmingham Education Society in March 1867, at his Southbourne home in Augustus Road, Edgbaston. This organisation paid the school fees for 5,000 children to receive elementary education. In 1869, he pursued the objective of improved education from a national platform to secure state provision. With friends and businessmen, he founded the National Education League (NEL) in Birmingham. This was the first organisation established by Chamberlain in the public sphere, and set a pattern for how he would generate consensus for radical change, by aligning with like-minded individuals to press for a particular change.

Beginning locally, the NEL had nationwide ambitions. The group campaigned for changes in legislation to ensure schools were fully funded by taxation, operating consistently with each other, and managed by local councils. The objective was to provide every child with literacy and numeracy skills, as well as religious instruction, ensuring improved employability and the ability to contribute to national life more effectively. The system was to be funded by local rates and government grants. The NEL grew rapidly, having more than 140 branches by 1870, mainly in cities and with the support of twenty Trades Councils. The NEL 'served as the pace-setter in what was unquestionably one of the nineteenth century's most crucial social reform movements.'[266]

264 Skipp, *The Making of Victorian Birmingham*, p.159
265 *Joseph Chamberlain*, no date
266 Skipp, *The Making of Victorian Birmingham*, p.160

The campaign brought Chamberlain to national attention for the first time in 1870, and had partial success, as Gladstone's Liberal Government responded by legislating. This new law retained the Church of England as the primary provider of elementary education, which did not sit well with the NEL's non-conformist base. Chamberlain campaigned for further changes, proclaiming that he wanted to 'smash up this gigantic sham called the Liberal Party',[267] but was unsuccessful in achieving widespread political support for a non-denominational basis for education. He had however begun to mark himself out as a left leaning radical Liberal, prepared to act in defiance of the leadership, and campaign against established thinking.

As his interest in broader social issues grew, Chamberlain became more involved in local politics, challenging traditional Liberals in Birmingham on many issues. As a regular contributor to 'The Fortnightly Review', Chamberlain used an article to coin a slogan: 'the Four F's: Free Church, Free Schools, Free Land and Free Labour'. This effectively sums up much of his political philosophy, particularly in respect of domestic policy.

Political effort continued to extend further the franchise beyond the limited range of electors given the right to vote in the 1832 Great Reform Act. The Representation of the People Act 1867, or the Second Reform Act, was enacted on 1st January 1869. This increased the number of men who could vote from one to two million, with every male head of a household eligible to vote by the end of 1868, a considerable extension. This had substantial implications nationally, but meant that locally, there were many more eligible voters, including many more working class men than previously.

In Birmingham, the effect was that those living in the appalling conditions in back to back courts were able to vote, and would surely support candidates prepared to eradicate these problems. As Skipp indicates, on an individual ward basis, the difference in number of voters was huge: while St. Mary's Ward had just 272 burgesses to elect three councillors in 1838, by 1871 that rose almost ten-fold to 2,151. Even more dramatically, the number eligible in Ladywood Ward rose from 152 to 5,943, increasing by a factor of thirty nine.

Birmingham radicals established the Birmingham Liberal Association (BLA) in 1865, and used this to take advantage of this significantly broadened franchise. The intention was to organise effective representative machinery at ward, and then town, level to deliver electoral success. This approach, labelled the 'Birmingham

---

267 Ward, *The Chamberlains: Joseph, Austen and Neville 1836-1940*, p.18

2000' based on its membership, or 'the caucus', as it operated as a single entity, dominated Birmingham politics for the next twenty years. It operated through effective organisation at ward level, enabling those in control of the party at the executive level to direct which candidate to vote for, by every Liberal voter. Given that the three MPs were voted for by all electors across Birmingham, this meant that votes could be allocated across the three Liberal candidates to maximum effect. It worked extremely well in the 1868 General Election, ensuring that radical MPs John Bright, George Dixon and George Muntz were returned, with a combined majority of less than 1,000. Unsurprisingly, this election became known as the 'Vote as You're Told' election. The BLA then applied this approach to local elections.

Birmingham had been controlled on the Council in the 1850s and 1860s by a group of very conservative councillors, known as 'The Economists', led by Joseph Allday until 1859. As the population grew, so the town attracted wealthy industrialists, and these more forward-thinking entrepreneurs began to populate the Council with a very different agenda. Chamberlain, as a forward thinking businessman with the 'right' social reform tendencies, was asked to stand for local office. He was elected unopposed as a councillor for St. Paul's Ward in the Jewellery Quarter in November 1869, and re-elected in 1872.

Chamberlain certainly made an impression on people he met. Smartly dressed, clean-shaven, he had a trademark appearance, characterised by a monocle (for poor sight in his right eye) and three small orchids, or one large orchid, as a buttonhole. These were grown in his greenhouses at Highbury after 1879. Although a mayor in the provinces, he looked like a patrician gentleman or aristocrat and he looked substantially younger than his years. While Skipp describes him as 'pocket-sized, dapper, autocratic, intensely dynamic and ambitious',[268] Marsh simply writes, 'Like his politics, he looked new.'[269]

Chamberlain was elected Mayor of Birmingham in 1873, as part of a sweeping victory for Liberals, as a direct result of the organisational approach of the BLA. He won by a landslide, using expansion of the voting franchise to great effect. Chamberlain had recognised early that the game had changed, and ensured he was not left behind, like local Tories. He wrote: 'The working classes who cannot contribute pecuniarily…are now the majority in most borough constituencies, and no candidate and no policy has a chance of success unless their good-will and active support can be secured.'[270]

---

268 Skipp, *The Making of Victorian Birmingham*, p.159
269 Marsh, 'Chamberlain, Joseph [Joe] (1836-1914)', *Oxford Dictionary of National Biography*
270 Skipp, *The Making of Victorian Birmingham*, p.162

Chamberlain demonstrated his parliamentary ambitions early, and stood in Sheffield at the 1874 general election. Disappointed to be defeated, finishing narrowly third in a contest for two seats, he continued his duties as Mayor, retaining this position for almost three years, a period described as the most famous mayoralty in British history. The 1874 election defeat can therefore be seen as very fortunate for Birmingham and its residents, as they would witness several dramatic and far-reaching changes to the infrastructure and life of the town. As Mayor, Chamberlain promised that the town would be 'parked, paved, assized, marketed, gas and watered and "improved".'[271] He was true to this promise. The pace of change in this period is almost unimaginable, as Chamberlain created a much stronger financial base for the Council, bringing immediate and longer-term health benefits for its population.

So that he could concentrate on his civic ambitions as Mayor, Chamberlain retired from business in 1874, at the very young age of thirty-eight. He could do this because he had been so successful in business. As his father died in 1874, his share of Nettlefold and Chamberlain was the family's share, and amounted to £600,000, a phenomenally large sum. When he disbursed this within the family, Chamberlain himself retained £100,000 which secured affluence for the rest of his life. Coincidentally, thirty-eight was the same age at which Joseph Sturge retired from business to concentrate on larger issues. This was part of a growing trend as: 'A higher standard of public duty was developed. Men who had made fortunes in the town, and had acquired leisure, began to feel that they owed to the community a debt of service, and that in doing work for others they were acquiring for themselves the reward of a loftier and nobler benefit than could result from the mere enjoyment of personal ease.'[272]

No longer having to concentrate on financial security, Chamberlain devoted himself entirely to his local and national political ambitions. He was supported in this by Florence, who edited the articles he wrote for 'The Fortnightly Review'. This began as a broad based periodical, but soon changed into a journal providing a platform for radical liberal views, as a counterbalance to the more conservative editorial stance of newspapers. Florence supported women having the vote, and studied while having and raising her family. The Chamberlains purchased Southbourne, in Augustus Road, Edgbaston, a large brick-built villa, with the £4,000 given by Florence's father when they married. This happy family home

---

271 Ward, *The Chamberlains: Joseph, Austen and Neville 1836-1940*, p.23
272 Bunce, *History of the Corporation of Birmingham: with a Sketch of the Earlier Government of the Town, vol.1*, p.353

became a focus for the development of political ideas in the group of radical friends now working with Chamberlain.

Florence tragically died in 1875, giving birth to a stillborn son. With his mother's death the same year, following his father's the year before, this was extremely hard for Chamberlain to bear, again, and he spent some time abroad, in the Mediterranean. It certainly shook his faith, unsurprisingly, and although he remained a Unitarian, this was based more on the obligation he felt to family upbringing than a strong belief in God's mercy.

On his return, Chamberlain again devoted his time to his civic duties. The period from 1873 to 1876 heralded major achievements in his role as Mayor, changing the nature of Birmingham in a remarkably short period. His style was active leadership, and he was clearly in charge of the Council, in the same way as he was in business. He increased the town's revenue substantially, enabling the development of improved infrastructure and commercial practice, adding to the effectiveness and attractiveness of the town for residents, business investors and visitors. Many of these improvements have persisted and are part of the essential fabric of Birmingham today.

His first action was to take control of the supply of gas to the town. There were two gas supply companies, the Birmingham Gas Light and Coke Company, established 1819, and the Birmingham and Staffordshire Gas Light Company, formed in 1825. The companies generated gas, provided gas lamps in the streets, which they lit each night, charging the Corporation seventy shillings for each lamp. When the cost of providing, running and maintaining these 2,085 lamps was subtracted, the companies made a profit of fifty two shillings per lamp. Surprisingly, the charges made to private customers were higher than those charged to the Corporation.

This duopoly meant considerable profits for the gas companies but meant that the Corporation was unable to influence either supply or costs, with the latter highlighted as 'excessive' in the report of Robert Rawlinson in 1849, made more expensive by the duplication of pipework and lights. Chamberlain believed that if the Corporation were in charge, the income received could be used to finance his further plans for major change in Birmingham. His view was that 'the purchase of the waterworks concerned the health of the town, while that of the gasworks concerned its financial resources.'[273] He chaired the Gas Committee established to take this forward, continuing as chair even after his election as an MP in 1876.

273 Bunce, *History of the Corporation of Birmingham: with a Sketch of the Earlier Government of the Town*, vol.2, p.348

The change in ownership was achieved, without any increase in rates payable, making the scheme popular with voters. After the takeover, at a cost of £1,953,050, the Corporation received a profit of £34,000 in its first year of ownership and operation, rising to more than £420,000. The first ten years of this allowed public works costing £242,000 to be completed, transforming the town, especially the central area. It brought a fall in prices to customers of thirty per cent. By 1884, the Gas Department had laid 500 miles of gas mains, installed 61,000 meters, 600,000 lamps within buildings, and 10,000 public lamps on 320 miles of town roads. The level of light provided was equivalent to 17.19 candles, more than twice the required parliamentary standard. An Exhibition of Gas Apparatus in the Town Hall in June 1878 encouraged customers to buy gas stoves on a system of deferred payments. Annual savings averaged £63,500, with reduced charges to consumers totalling £550,000 from 1876 to 1884, and £235,000 was contributed by the Gas Department to reduce the level of rates payable. This delivered on Chamberlain's promise in a speech in January 1874 of 'the certainty of receiving in a short time considerable sums in relief of taxation.'[274] This stunningly successful approach was admired throughout the country and many towns put similar schemes in place.

Having achieved this, Chamberlain moved on to municipalisation of the water supply, with even more dramatic results. We are lucky to be able to take good sanitation for granted, but this was not the case in Victorian Birmingham. As we have seen in Chapter 7, poor sanitation and lack of water, or poor quality water where available, led to significant ill-health and high levels of mortality in Birmingham, as well as the more immediately noticed foul smell and dirtiness.

To make immediate progress, pending longer term improvements to sewerage and water provision, the 'Rochdale Pan System', also called the Nightsoil Interception System, was introduced in 1874. This improvement on throwing excreta into the streets still sounds appalling from our modern privileged perspective. Bunce described it: 'The method is very simple. Beneath each closet seat is placed a metal pan, capable of affording closet accommodation for a week. In the yard is placed a wooden or iron tub for the reception of dry ashes and vegetable and other refuse from the houses. Once a week these receptacles are cleared of their contents. The closet pans are carried away in closed vans, each containing about eighteen of the pans and holding also about one ton of ashes taken from the ash tubs. The pans in process of removal are covered with close-fitting metal lids, fresh pans being left in their places. The pans are then taken

---

274 Bunce, *History of the Corporation of Birmingham: with a Sketch of the Earlier Government of the Town*, vol.2, p.349

to the Corporation Wharf in Montague Street, are emptied, thoroughly cleansed and disinfected, and are then again ready for use.'[275] Even this measure was only partially implemented, covering one-third of houses by 1876, with 15,992 pans in use. By 1884, there were 38,865 pans emptied each week, totalling 1,922,752 instances of change and emptying. This required 106,864 van loads of excreta to be removed, and 73,871 loads of ashes from the 21,542 ashpits. The Nightsoil Department employed 325 staff, with 109 horses and 61 vans, working out of three depots, in Shadwell Street, Montague Street and Rotton Park.

Although a significant increase in capacity, this meant many areas were still subject to open drains, or middens. Chamberlain chaired a conference in March 1876 which set up the Tame and Rea District Drainage Board, covering Birmingham and surrounding areas. By 1884, this Board's work had delivered an effective sewerage system across the area.

In the intervening years, this awful system of human waste disposal resulted in widespread disease and very high mortality rates. Contagious diseases were prevalent, including smallpox, diphtheria, diarrhoea, and whooping cough, with a mortality rate of thirty deaths per 1,000 people in 1875. In some areas, the death rate was twice the rate in wealthier areas like Edgbaston. Bailey Street was worst of all, with a mortality rate of 97 per 1,000, one in ten dying every year!

Despite Rawlinson's report in 1849, by 1875 there had been no improvement, as set out by Dr Alfred Hill, the Medical Officer of Health for Birmingham, who confirmed that the death rate from infectious diseases was the highest in the country. He remarked on the 'want of ventilation, want of light, want of proper and decent accommodation, resulting in dirty habits, low health, and debased morals on the part of the tenants.'[276]

Chamberlain concurred: 'Many of them do not know what health is; fever, diarrhoea, and other diseases are never absent from these courts for a single day.' There were estimated to be 3,000 preventable deaths annually, with six cases of disease for every death, totalling 18,000 cases of preventable disease. These conditions were so depressing that they explain high levels of drunkenness, and despair. Chamberlain asserted forcefully that: 'Those who die are even happier than those who have to drag out a wretched existence in the courts.'[277]

275 Bunce, *History of the Corporation of Birmingham: with a Sketch of the Earlier Government of the Town*, *vol.2*, pp.141-2

276 Ibid., pp.457-8

277 Ibid., p.464

Chamberlain, confident and ambitious, expected to take radical, effective action, when he became Mayor in 1873: 'The town shall not, with God's help, know itself!'[278] He certainly delivered on this expectation, taking control of the water company in January 1876. He told a House of Commons Select Committee: 'It seems to me absolutely certain that…the power of life and death should not be left in the hands of a commercial company, but should be conducted by the representatives of the people.'[279] The waterworks were purchased for £1,350,000 and the Corporation Water Department was formed. This philosophy underlay his approach of 'municipal socialism', as it became known. The results were impressive, as the Council's Health Committee closed the sources of infected water, with 291 wells closed in the first year, rising to more than 3,000 within nine years, and the supply of fresh water, through connected pipework, to 60,000 houses.

As well as providing health benefits, Chamberlain's actions were clever politics, in pursuit of a principled vision, in which he intended to use his 'considerable amount of business ability and commercial experience' to ensure that 'all monopolies which are sustained in any way by the State ought to be in the hands of the representatives by whom they should be administered, and to whom their profits should go.' This would 'increase the duties and responsibilities of the local authority,…to constitute these local authorities real local parliaments, supreme in their special jurisdiction.'[280] In presenting Birmingham's case to the Lords Committee scrutinising the Water Bill in June 1875, Chamberlain declared: 'we have not the slightest intention of making a profit. We shall get our profit indirectly, in the comfort of the town, and the health of the inhabitants.'[281] He was as good as his word, delivering a framework within which the Council continued to deliver improved services, with successive reductions in the charges made for both gas and water supply. Reservoir capacity increased substantially, the Chamberlain Memorial Fountain was built and connected in 1879, pollution caused to the River Tame by Black Country residents was eradicated through legal action, and a scheme of accredited plumbers to undertake repairs was introduced in 1882. There were regular and repeated reductions in charges, new investment in infrastructure, including more than 145 miles of water mains, and increased levels of water supplied, to 11.5 million gallons in 1883. New supply was provided to

---

278 Upton, *A History of Birmingham*, p.151

279 Bunce, *History of the Corporation of Birmingham: with a Sketch of the Earlier Government of the Town*, *vol.2*, p.409

280 Ibid., p.347

281 Ibid., p.411

47,292 houses, and to 5,309 hydrants in thirteen major thoroughfares. The overall profit generated for the Council was £56,427.

Other Chamberlain initiatives included the establishment of a municipal Fire Brigade in 1875. Previously, services had been operated by insurance companies, but they would only attend fires if the householder or businessman had paid their premiums in full!

The scheme which made the most visible difference, re-shaping the geography of the town permanently, was Chamberlain's 'Improvement Scheme', for which he secured the unanimous approval of the Council. Chamberlain's proposal was to clear the overcrowded and unhealthy central slums to create room for redevelopment. On 27th July 1875, Chamberlain suggested an Improvement Committee to oversee the planning and execution of a grand scheme. The plan took advantage of the Artisans' and Labourers' Dwellings Improvement Act of the same year. This gave powers to local authorities with a population over 25,000 to have properties examined by the Medical Officer of Health and, where deemed unfit for human habitation, to be condemned. It was then the responsibility of the local authority to decide what to do with these properties. Originally, the local authority was required to buy the land, pay for demolition and 'provide for the accommodation of at least as many members of the working class as may be displaced…' but local authorities effectively avoided this provision, preferring to encourage private building, and the clause was removed in 1882.[282] Chamberlain ignored this provision and delivered an urban re-development scheme, not a re-housing scheme. Birmingham was the first town to develop a far-reaching plan for redevelopment using this legislation. Chamberlain's plan was to eradicate the slums completely, and to create a 'great street, as broad as a Parisian boulevard',[283] a mile long, from the middle of New Street (today's Grand Central and New Street Station entrance). On its way, it was to pass through Old Square, to Aston, the site of Aston University today. There were further proposals, including further streets and a rail link through a tunnel, between New Street and Snow Hill Stations, but these were not implemented due to cost.

In October 1875, Chamberlain suggested creating an Improvement Trust to buy properties and land. Financed by a £58,000 loan from the Birmingham Banking Company, guaranteed by the nominated councillors, the trust would sell any acquisitions to the Corporation at cost under the terms of the proposed

---

282 Chris Upton, *Living Back-to-Back*, (Chichester: 2005), p.43

283 Bunce, *History of the Corporation of Birmingham: with a Sketch of the Earlier Government of the Town*, vol.2, p.456

improvement act, but it still represented a gamble for those individuals contributing. Chamberlain set the example by guaranteeing £10,000, with his brother Richard and uncle Arthur committing £5,000 each. The Act received royal assent on 15th August 1876.

Work began in August 1878, taking until early 1882 before the appropriately named 'Corporation Street' reached Old Square. This involved demolition of decayed and poor quality houses in the Minories, Oxygen Street, Lower Priory and Old Square itself, as well as cherry orchards. The cost was enormous, at £1,500,000, and the plan was to offset this by two thirds, through sale of leases in this attractive commercial thoroughfare. Leases sold would allow the building of a coffee shop, a 'Temperance Variety Theatre', a women's hospital, a school, hotels, shops, forty-three public houses, and even the Corporation Street Winter Gardens. Not all of these were completed. Law Courts were provided, originally Assize Courts, which remain in use as the Victoria Law Courts, which were formally opened by the Prince (later King Edward VII) and Princess of Wales on 21st July 1891. Financially, the scheme achieved breakeven point in 1892.

The high cost of this massive regeneration of ninety-three acres of Birmingham did attract some criticism, as it led to an increase in rates of two shillings in the pound, and Chamberlain's determination was described by some as dictatorial (perhaps suggested by his use of the term 'boulevard' which reminded his critics of Napoleon's redesign of Paris). While Corporation Street was derided as 'Rue Chamberlain', this criticism ignored the other improvements, including paving of streets, improved lighting, creation of proper sewers, building of swimming pools and planting of trees and parks. The scheme did not include replacement housing to any real extent, with only 62 houses built as part of the scheme, which had demolished 653 homes. Chamberlain outlined the basis of the scheme and reflected his political philosophy on housing to a Royal Commission in 1884: 'It really consists almost entirely in making provision for the destruction of unhealthy and overcrowded dwellings, and the reconstruction and re-housing of the poor may safely be left to private enterprise.'[284] A weekly newspaper, The Dart, a Liberal supporting paper, although not close to Chamberlain, put a contrary view, with no shortage of wit:

'New Birmingham recipe for lowering the death-rate of an insanitary area. Pull down nearly all the houses and make the inhabitants move somewhere else. 'Tis an excellent plan and I'll tell you for why. Where's there's no person living no person can die.'[285]

---

284 Upton, *Living Back-to-Back*, p.138
285 Ibid., p.44

At the time, there was no requirement in legislation for local authorities to replace housing which had been demolished, and in fact, the Artisans' Dwellings Act 1875 prohibited corporations from building houses themselves, unless they made a compelling case to the government's Local Government Board. They could however contract with private builders to provide such accommodation. Concerns at the failure to replace demolished homes were raised locally, and a Council review reported on 3rd June 1884 that: 'there is ample dwelling-house accommodation for the working classes' and that 'accommodation for the artisan and labouring classes within the Borough, is, generally speaking, in a fairly sanitary condition, and that overcrowding does not exist to any great extent.'[286] The original residents of the central area had little choice but to move to the suburbs as the era of mass council housing building was still many years away, despite a small number (104 dwellings) being built by the Corporation in Ryder Street and Lawrence Street in 1889 and 1890.

Under the Artisans' Dwellings Act 1875, the government had for the first time 'recognised something higher than property.' Chamberlain argued that the Act enabled the Council to buy land and property through compulsory purchase orders, without the need to pay 'solatium' (compensation above market value). This meant it could acquire property which it would not have to use as part of the redevelopment, meaning such land and property could be leased to provide income to the Council, 'and consequently secure for future generations of ratepayers the advantages hitherto secured by a few large landowners in the town.'[287]

The benefits of the Improvement Scheme colour any discussion about the impact Chamberlain had. The first complimentary assessment concerned the much greater value for money for ratepayers. Bunce, the Council's official historian, reported that rates payable in 1849 were 3s. 1d. in the pound to the Street Commissioners, and 1s. in the pound to the Corporation, a total of 4s. 1d. in the pound. By 1878, after introduction of sewerage, drains, improved street lighting and paving, planning control and municipalisation of water and gas, 'the rating for purely municipal purposes is only 3s. 9d. in the pound; thus giving probably more than double the work and advantages of 1849 with a considerably diminished burden on the ratepayers.' He concludes that in comparison to the state of Birmingham described in Rawlinson's report, 'the contrast seems well-

---

286 Bunce, *History of the Corporation of Birmingham: with a Sketch of the Earlier Government of the Town, vol.2*, pp.503-5
287 Ibid., p.457

nigh inconceivable, and might be regarded as incredible, if it were not so formally authenticated.'[288]

Historians have rushed to praise Chamberlain for these improvements, rightly so, and have also attributed a dramatic improvement in the death rate to the combination of the Improvement Scheme in clearing some of the slums and the other sanitary improvements. Bunce recorded that the average death rate in nine named streets for the years 1873 to 1875 was 53.2 per 1,000, falling to an astonishingly improved 21.3 per 1,000 for 1879 to 1881. The reductions seen in individual streets were incredible, with Bailey Street's death rate being cut by seventy-five percent, from 97 to just 25.6 per 1,000. The next worst was Lower Priory, falling by two thirds, from 62.5 to 21.9 per 1,000.[289] It is incontrovertibly the case that there was a dramatic fall in the death rate for the whole of Birmingham. This had stood at 30 people in every 1,000 in 1848. By 1878, this had reduced to 25.2 per 1,000, and to 19.9 by 1901. Its fall from the levels in 1848 was a dramatic improvement by a third, although the average for England and Wales was 16.9 per 1,000. While this is cause for praise of Chamberlain and those who followed him, it is important to note that there remained a considerable gap between Birmingham and other places.

The Mayor had a firm hold over the Corporation and its politics, and it is undoubtedly the case that his determination to develop grand schemes implemented in a short period of time changed the face of the town. These included the Birmingham Museum and Art Gallery and the Council House (the foundation stone was laid by Chamberlain in 1874, and can still be seen in Victoria Square), which, with many lovely redbrick buildings built as part of this scheme, remain in use today. He was elected chair of the Liberal-dominated Birmingham Schools Board in 1873, and combined this role with his mayoralty to develop the provision of free education, including building many schools, under the terms of the Education Act 1870. As Skipp says: 'high Victorian Birmingham really did bear some resemblance to a promised land, a holy city.'[290]

The improved economic performance of the Corporation from these municipalisation schemes allowed it to embark on a more ambitious scheme to secure a long term solution for Birmingham's water needs. Although Chamberlain was not involved, being in central government in 1894 when it began, the Elan

---

288 Bunce, *History of the Corporation of Birmingham: with a Sketch of the Earlier Government of the Town*, vol.1, p.321
289 Ibid., p.484
290 Skipp, *The Making of Victorian Birmingham*, p.187

Valley project was breath-taking in its scale. The Corporation bought seventy acres of land, created reservoirs and built seventy-three miles of pipes, tunnels and aqueducts from the Elan Valley in South Wales, at a cost of £6,600,000. It was opened by King Edward VII on 21st July 1904 and supplied 12 million gallons of water per day to Birmingham residents, and continues to this day.

Chamberlain's major achievement was using the size and financial muscle of the Corporation to ensure rapid and effective change, to benefit local people and deliver permanent improvements. Without a long term increase in the level of rates, Chamberlain set up and serviced loans of more than £5m in his three years as Mayor, compared to £1m in loans across the previous thirty-five years.

This required determined, intelligent, long term vision, and the tenacity to see his ideas through from conception to completion. His substantial and demonstrable successes as Mayor earned him the enduring support and affection of local Liberal Radicals, as well as the general population, as demonstrated by monuments established while he was still alive. These include the Chamberlain Fountain in Chamberlain Square, built in 1880, and the Chamberlain Clock on the Warstone Lane roundabout in the Jewellery Quarter, in 1903. Small wonder that he was revered as 'the father of modern Birmingham.'[291]

As Mayor, Chamberlain established local government in Birmingham as a major modernising force, operating in reality independently of national government. He is credited for creating the notion of 'the City State.' Chamberlain's own view, however, was that this owed more to the work of George Dawson, a non-conformist preacher whose religious beliefs stressed the importance of local democratic government working for the benefit of all, enshrined in his approach of 'the Civic Gospel.'

On his second attempt at becoming an MP, such was his standing in the town, Chamberlain was elected unopposed as one of Birmingham's MPs in a by-election in 1876. Approaching forty years of age, he felt keenly the need to make an impact nationally with his radical form of Liberalism. He remained close to Birmingham issues, however, and in 1879, bought a piece of land in Moor Green, Kings Heath, on which he built his home, Highbury Hall, named after the area of London where he grew up. This was on the edge of the town, and he developed the grounds and gardens, including extensive greenhouses, in which he cultivated many types of his beloved orchid.

Chamberlain won again in Birmingham West in the 1880 general election, defeating the floridly named Frederick Gustavus Burnaby. Burnaby was a

291 Ward, *The Chamberlains: Joseph, Austen and Neville 1836-1940*, p.20

charismatic and highly colourful figure well known in Victorian society, and all but forgotten now. Born in March 1842, the son of a Bedford clergyman, he was educated at Harrow and Oswestry Schools, and privately in Germany. At 6' 4", he was physically very strong and while still a schoolboy, could carry two schoolfellows under each arm upstairs. He joined the Royal Horse Guards in 1859 aged sixteen, and undertook extreme exploits, including hot air ballooning.

Long periods of leave from the Horse Guards and his comparative wealth allowed him to travel extensively for months at a time, visiting Central and South America, Odessa and Tangier. His entertaining travel writing brought him work as a war correspondent for The Times newspaper. He reported on the Carlist rebellion in Spain and General Gordon's campaign at Khartoum in the Sudan. The Russians closed Central Asia to Europeans, as it was a war zone, so Burnaby, in a typically audacious defiant act, travelled to Khiva, in what is now Uzbekistan. Suspected of working for British intelligence, but undeterred by danger, Burnaby related his exploits in his book 'A Ride to Khiva: Travels and Adventures in Central Asia', published in 1876, which made him a famous and much sought after celebrity in Victorian society.

In the book, in which he styles himself 'Fred', Burnaby combines travelogue with anecdotes, and political and cultural commentary. His upper middle class background is evident in tales of derring-do, as he ruminates on the national characteristics of the people he meets, and of the English. His advice on 'How to Catch Sturgeon' leads inevitably to a section on 'The three kinds of Caviare' [sic]. Other highly readable tales include 'A Servant an Encumbrance when Travelling', 'Amorous Females in Search of a Husband', 'Effeminate Boys dressed a little like Women' and the unlikely 'A Camel in Love' called, appropriately, Romeo.

Most of the book is light-hearted and aimed at an audience entranced by tales of the exotic and extraordinary, in far off countries, populated by strange people with odd customs. It was a huge success, with eleven editions in a year. Further publications covered his journeys through Turkey and Armenia. Burnaby's gregarious and outgoing personality revelled in the attention he received and he comments vaingloriously many times on the surprise of women that he was not married.

There was serious intent in the book as well. An avowed Imperialist, Burnaby details his views on the growing menace to British power in the region from Russia. He highlights the potential for further mutinies in 'British India', only nineteen years after the unsuccessful 1857 Indian Mutiny. Fearful of the loss of this important part of the Empire, arguing for a stronger regional presence, Burnaby concludes that Russia will exploit British complacency: 'If we allow her to keep on advancing, the same arms which we might now employ will one day be turned against ourselves.'[292]

He married a rich heiress in Ireland in 1879, and turned to politics, keen to expound his extremely conservative views. Recognising Chamberlain's popularity, Birmingham Tories were keen to have an appealing candidate, and approached Burnaby to stand based on Lord Randolph Churchill's recommendation, and his social popularity. In the 1880 general election, the Tories were better organised, and hopeful of success with this larger than life character, making this a more formidable campaign for Chamberlain. However, the results vindicated Chamberlain's attention to organisation through the caucus system, and the three Liberal candidates were elected. Burnaby and his Tory colleague, Augustus Gough-Calthorpe, the shy and reticent heir to the Calthorpe estate, finished fourth and fifth. The total Liberal votes achieved were 68.3% of the vote, giving a comfortable majority on a respectable turnout of 74.6%.

After his defeat, Burnaby crossed the English Channel, by hot air balloon in March 1882, and later returned to the army, being promoted to Colonel. Despite not gaining permission, Burnaby joined the British forces in Egypt and fought in the Sudan campaign. He was killed in hand to hand combat, by a spear thrust through his throat, in the Battle of Abu Klea on 17th January 1885, aged just forty-two. In Birmingham the Conservatives funded a substantial memorial to Burnaby, a large Portland stone obelisk. This has a carving of his face and the words 'Khiva 1875' and 'Abu Klea 1885' on panels, with just his surname inscribed on it. This stands in St. Philip's Churchyard. Although remembering a war hero and character is understandable, it is strange that such a significant and imposing memorial was erected in Birmingham, to which its subject had a tangential connection, as a losing parliamentary candidate.

Chamberlain was to have a discernible influence on the organisation and success of the Liberal Party, but was also responsible for several considerable and long-lasting schisms. His dogged pursuit of his ideas on Radical Liberalism attracted a significant minority of the parliamentary party, and many Liberals in the country, to support him. Chamberlain was not universally welcomed in the Commons: 'Thus, although he sat on the back benches, a cold, carefully dressed, monocled newcomer to Parliament, he was at once recognised as a politician of the front rank.' This view was shared even by members of his own party:

292 Fred Burnaby, *A Ride to Khiva: Travels and Adventures in Central Asia*, (London: 1876), p.viii

'The House, and particularly the Liberals, had greeted him with bleak suspicion. There was, even at this stage, something chilling and implacable about him.'[293] The extent of the capital's prejudice against anyone from 'the provinces', unless a member of the aristocracy or ruling elite, was reflected by The Times newspaper's surprise at Chamberlain behaving as a gentleman when the Prince and Princess of Wales visited the town in 1874. There were further such comments when the 'Brummagem Robespierre' confounded prejudiced expectations with an elegant and well-received maiden speech on education, his expert subject, in July 1876.

Chamberlain made an immediate impact on national politics, through his re-organisation of the Liberal Party, based on the same structure used to such good effect in Birmingham in the mid-1870s.

The National Liberal Federation was important in the 1880 election victory for Prime Minister Gladstone.

For the 1885 general election, Chamberlain made a number of radical proposals in his first 'unauthorised programme', published without the agreement of the national party. It is hard to imagine this being accepted by the highly centralised political party structures which exist now, but Chamberlain did this regularly before general elections, prompting debate nationally on the issues he wanted to pursue, and wrong-footing both his opponents and, on occasion, his own party. It speaks to his independence of thought, and determined ambition.

As a sign of his growing influence, Chamberlain was appointed to the Cabinet in Gladstone's second government as President of the Board of Trade. This was the first of several Cabinet appointments between 1886 and 1903, although he was at times out of government, due to disputes between him and his party. This has been covered in detail by others, but for this narrative, it is sufficient to note that the controversies in which he became embroiled reinforced the view of Chamberlain as a political force nationally, a potential alternative leader of the party, with influence and power, which was often exercised in an idiosyncratic manner. This placed him often at odds with other Liberals on issues such as Irish Home Rule, which led to a major and permanent schism with the Liberal Party. His opposition to Gladstone's Government of Ireland Bill in early 1886 effectively brought down the government and prompted a further general election. His decision to forge a co-operation pact with the Conservatives made this split permanent, and led Chamberlain to set up his own party, the Liberal Unionists, from June 1886. The strength of this organisation, and the pact with the Conservatives, meant that five Liberal

---

293 Robert Rhodes James, *The British Revolution: British Politics 1880-1939*, (London: 1978), p.39

Unionists and two further Unionists were elected unopposed in Birmingham. On a national level, however, it meant that neither the Liberals nor the Conservatives could form a majority government for the next few years. Chamberlain himself, as the leader of the Liberal Unionists in Parliament from 1891, a sizeable and distinct party in its own right, would not return to government until 1895.

 In late 1887 and early 1888, Chamberlain was sent as the Conservative government's representative to arbitrate in a fisheries dispute between Canada and the USA. While there, he met and fell in love with Mary Endicott, aged twenty-three, the daughter of William Crowninshield Endicott, who was President Grover Cleveland's Secretary of the Army. Chamberlain, aged fifty-one, proposed before leaving the States, telling friends Mary was 'one of the brightest and most intelligent girls I have yet met'[294] and they married in Washington D.C. in November 1888. Mary supported Chamberlain in his political career on their return to England.

Out of national government, Chamberlain pursued the development of educational opportunities locally, and was the prime mover in establishing the University of Birmingham at the turn of the century. The University was formed by bringing together Mason Science College, in Edmund Street, and Queen's College, Birmingham's Medical School, in nearby Paradise Street. Chamberlain saw the need to bring these institutions together to create the first viable red brick university in the country. The Mason University College Act 1897 incorporated Mason University College on 1st January 1898, with Chamberlain as President of its Court of Governors. He told the Governors on 13th January 1898 that: 'to place a university in the middle of a great industrial and manufacturing population is to do something to leaven the whole mass with higher aims and higher intellectual ambitions than would otherwise be possible to people engaged entirely in trading and commercial pursuits.'[295]

A Town Meeting on 1st July debated the issues and within just eight months, £326,500 had been raised for an endowment fund, including £50,000 from Andrew Carnegie, the Scottish philanthropist. Queen Victoria granted a royal charter on 24th March 1900, the Birmingham University Act 1900 was passed, and the Charter for the University of Birmingham was provided to the Court of Governors on 31st May 1900. Chamberlain became the first Chancellor and the first Principal was Oliver Lodge, who was knighted in 1902. Chamberlain raised funds, accruing £500,000 for new buildings, telling Lodge to: 'spend the money now, give people something to see, and I will get the other half million without

294 *Joseph Chamberlain*
295 Bird, *Portrait of Birmingham*, p.125

delay.' He was true to his word. Land in Bournbrook came from Lord Calthorpe: 'to be used solely for the purposes of a university for ever',[296] with a further parcel of land alongside Bristol Road. Building took nine years to complete. The buildings include the beautiful Great Hall and the 325 foot Joseph Chamberlain Memorial Clock Tower, resembling the Mangia campanile in Siena, and known affectionately ever since as 'Old Joe'.

The Medical Faculty opened in Edmund Street on 1st October 1900, and the Science and Arts Faculties the following day. There were initially 700 students and 70 teaching staff. Appropriately, given Chamberlain's involvement in business and politics, Birmingham was the first British university to have a Faculty of Commerce. The University was formally opened by King Edward VII on 7th July 1909, although Chamberlain was unable to attend due to illness.

The 1892 general election brought a further clean sweep for Chamberlain's Liberal Unionists, as they won all seven Birmingham seats, and in Warwickshire, Staffordshire and Worcestershire (known by Chamberlain's opponents as his 'Duchy', given his influence and bearing), the party won thirty of thirty-nine seats. It held further significance for Chamberlain, as he proudly welcomed his son Austen to the House of Commons, elected as MP for East Worcestershire, the constituency in which Chamberlain's Highbury home was located!

Within three years, Chamberlain returned to government as part of a Conservative-Unionist coalition under Lord Salisbury, in July 1895, and he remained in the Cabinet until 1903. The Liberal Unionists gained seventy-one seats and held the balance of power. Having the power to make or break Salisbury's government, Chamberlain chose his Cabinet post, Colonial Secretary, to pursue his policy ideas on preserving and enhancing the Empire. This role has led to him being categorised as an imperialist, and might be seen as a contrast to his earlier social reformist attitudes. His view, however, was that the success of the Empire enhanced the ability to implement social reforms in Great Britain, through increased prosperity, and avoidance of trade tariffs between Great Britain and its colonies.

He was almost immediately embroiled in a scandal, resulting from the Jameson Raid. Dr Starr Jameson had led a force of 470 men, including British soldiers, into the South African Republic, the Transvaal, to attempt to overthrow the government, and replace it with one sympathetic to the Empire. This poorly conceived, fruitless attempt was easily defeated by the Boers, but created

---

296 Bird, *Portrait of Birmingham*, p.126

opprobrium nationally and internationally. Chamberlain was discredited, having given the land in Bechuanaland, from which the raid was launched, to Cecil Rhodes and his supporters. It was alleged that Chamberlain had foreknowledge of the attempted coup, but he always steadfastly denied this. The controversy raged for eighteen months but, partly through ensuring he was on the Select Committee investigating the circumstances behind the Raid, Chamberlain survived.

To secure a strong and effective British Empire, Chamberlain attempted to create a customs union between Great Britain and its colonies, to include advantageous trading terms for both sides. This was his doctrine of 'Imperial Preference', but it was unsuccessful, as the emerging strength of the colonies meant that they wanted to keep their options open for trading with third nations.

Chamberlain was Colonial Secretary during the Second Boer War, which began in South Africa in 1899, and he and his family were memorably attacked in the Commons by David Lloyd George, then a Radical MP in Wales. This verbal assault highlighted the business interests of the wider Chamberlain family, several of whom benefitted from contracts to supply the British Army, saying with characteristic caustic wit: 'the more the Empire expands, the more these Chamberlains contract.'[297]

Lloyd George's animosity to Chamberlain and his family may have prompted the riot against the former at Birmingham Town Hall on 18th December 1901, when he was prevented from addressing a meeting, and forced to escape in a police constable's uniform. Brummies never miss an opportunity to make a few bob, as one resourceful entrepreneur set up a stall selling half house bricks for the rioters to throw!

The military campaign directed by Chamberlain was so successful that on 13th February 1902, at a special presentation at the Guildhall, London, Arthur Balfour, soon to be Prime Minister, heralded him as 'the man who, above all others, has made the British Empire a reality.' The next day, reporting this event, The Times newspaper proclaimed him: 'the most popular and trusted man in England.'[298] How times had changed from 1874!

Although now called 'the first minister of the Empire', he did not take the post of Chancellor of the Exchequer under new Prime Minister Balfour when Michael Hicks-Beach retired, and he became increasingly frustrated with opposition to his

---

297 Ward, *The Chamberlains: Joseph, Austen and Neville 1836-1940*, p.53
298 The Times, quoted in Marsh, 'Chamberlain, Joseph [Joe] (1836-1914)', *Oxford Dictionary of National Biography*

views on tariff reform. He suffered a significant cut to his forehead on 7th July 1902, caused bizarrely by a pane of glass breaking in an accident in a cab on The Mall. Alongside continuing issues of neuralgia and gout, Chamberlain apparently ignored doctors' advice and returned to work before fully recovered.

He and Mary travelled to South Africa in November 1902 to try to persuade the Boer leadership to adhere to the terms of the treaty which had ended the war, and this is the visit marked by the erection in 1903 of the cast iron clock, the Chamberlain Clock, on the Warstone Lane roundabout in the Jewellery Quarter.

On his return, Chamberlain lost a cabinet debate on his doctrine of 'Imperial Preference'. Undaunted, in September 1903 he established a national platform, the Tariff Reform League and Tariff Reform Committee to develop his campaign for tariff reform. Characteristically on his own initiative, without the formal support of his party or government, shortly afterwards he resigned from government to campaign full time on this issue. He toured the country, arguing that decline would follow any failure to protect or expand the Empire. Locally, within 'the Duchy', resistance to his policy came from local newspapers but also surprisingly from his own family: his brother Arthur vehemently opposed tariff reform, and his nephew John Sutton Nettlefold, treasurer of the Midland Liberal Unionist Association, refused to agree funds for this campaign. Chamberlain's response was to have him replaced by his own son, Neville.

Disenchantment with Balfour's leadership led him to bring down the government in December 1905. Liberal Unionists remained popular in Birmingham, with considerable successes in the January 1906 election, but this was out of line with the rest of the country. Everywhere else, the Liberals and the nascent Labour Party did well, and the Liberals gained a large majority, returning to government. In effect, the country had rejected tariff reform, and Chamberlain, although successful in Birmingham, was now out of government, never to return.

The 8th July 1906 saw a considerable demonstration of Birmingham's affection for Chamberlain, with extended celebrations of his seventieth birthday, coinciding with his thirtieth anniversary as an MP. These included factory closures for several days, extra trains to bring people into Birmingham, commemorative medals for schoolchildren, and fireworks in public parks, as well as a civic banquet and speeches. In a speech at Bingley Hall, Chamberlain reflected on his achievements and heaped praise on the 'Birmingham School' and its use of governing powers to promote social reform. He expounded that this approach could be applied to strengthening and developing the Empire, asserting that this would 'secure for the masses of the industrial population in this country constant employment at fair wages', and that 'England without an empire would be a fifth rate nation, existing in the sufferance of its more powerful neighbours', reported in the Birmingham Daily Post on 10th July 1906.[299] Chamberlain was escorted home by crowds holding torches.

Having enjoyed the adulation, Chamberlain and Mary travelled to 40, Princes Gate, his home opposite Hyde Park, close to the Royal Albert Hall, London. A few days after his birthday, he suffered a severe stroke in his bathroom, paralysing his right side, affecting his ability to speak, and removing his ability to write. In effect, this ended his political career, certainly as a visible and active politician. Although he gave instruction to his supporters, principally through Austen, he could not campaign personally any more, and his family kept him largely out of sight.

Chamberlain made his last sad visit to the Commons after being elected unopposed in the second general election of 1910, in December. A painful and upsetting scene, as he needed to be formally sworn in, he was carried into the chamber by Austen and a colleague, after the other MPs had left: 'For a few moments he sat, piteously but proudly motionless, whilst his eye slowly surveyed the empty benches and galleries, and then he indistinctly repeated the Oath after the Clerk. To sign the Roll was for him a physical impossibility, but Austen guided his hand sufficiently to make a shaky cross, and then after another poignant pause we carried him out again. As he passed the Chair the Speaker leaned over to touch his helpless hand, and the tragic ceremony was over.'[300]

Incredibly, judged by today's scrutiny of those seeking public office, he was re-elected for Birmingham West in 1910 (twice) and 1914, despite his disability. On this last occasion, he announced his intention to stand down at the next election, but he died from a heart attack, in Mary's arms, in London on 2nd July 1914, six days before his seventy-eighth birthday. Publicly, his death was somewhat overshadowed by the assassination of Archduke Franz Ferdinand at Sarajevo on 28th June, and the looming outbreak of the First World War. Prime Minister Herbert Asquith said in tribute in the House of Commons that: 'in that striking personality, vivid, masterful, resolute, tenacious, there were no blurred or nebulous outlines, there were no relaxed fibres, there were no moods of doubt and hesitation, there were no pauses of lethargy or fear.'[301]

---

299 Marsh, 'Chamberlain, Joseph [Joe] (1836-1914)', *Oxford Dictionary of National Biography*
300 Rhodes James, *The British Revolution: British Politics 1880-1939*, p.253
301 *Joseph Chamberlain*

In accordance with his lifelong resistance to honorific titles, and in line with his stated wishes, his family refused the offer of burial in Westminster Abbey, and he was buried after a simple funeral on 6th July in Key Hill Cemetery. This was in his Birmingham West constituency, a short distance from the Nettlefold and Chamberlain factory. He was laid to rest in a vault with his first two wives. The memorial stone is carved simply with the words: 'also of Joseph Chamberlain, born July 8th 1836; died July 2nd 1914.' Two years later, a memorial to Chamberlain was unveiled at Westminster Abbey.

In terms of legacy, nationally and internationally, it can be concluded that Chamberlain was on the wrong side of the three major issues dominating his time in government: he opposed Irish Home Rule, independence for the Boers, and supported protectionist trade tariffs. This is perhaps unfair, as he needs to be judged by the standards, challenges and political thought of the time, rather than with the dubious benefit of hindsight. He was clearly a highly effective, charismatic, principled and high achieving political force, responsible for creating and leading for many years a major school of political thought in Great Britain.

Locally, his legacy is immense. He was 'certainly Birmingham's greatest man'[302] and rightly seen as 'the father of modern Birmingham.' His achievements far exceed those of any other Brummie, either native or adopted, as he transformed the town physically through his 'Improvement Scheme'. He ensured effective provision of essential utilities by securing local control and management, and improved finances for the Corporation. In doing so, he reduced ill health and secured the basis for permanently reduced death rates among the town's residents. In education, he made this accessible to local children through improved elementary schools and established the first red brick university, now the fourth largest in the country. Through these actions, Chamberlain was instrumental in increasing the life chances of countless thousands of Birmingham's residents, and there are physical reminders of him and his work visible to Brummies every day as they go about the city.

The most prominent is the Joseph Chamberlain Memorial Clock Tower, built as part of the University of Birmingham, Edgbaston, which is the tallest free-standing clock tower in Europe. It is visible on the city skyline from many parts of Birmingham. The Chamberlain Square fountain, adjacent to the Town Hall and Council House, nicknamed 'Squirt Square', was built in his honour

---

302 Bird, *Portrait of Birmingham*, p.139

in 1880, when Chamberlain was fifty years old. It has been refurbished in the redevelopment of the Paradise area. Highbury Hall in Moor Green is a conference and wedding venue and at times open to the public. This has a blue plaque erected by Birmingham Civic Society.

The Chamberlain Clock was erected in 1903 to commemorate his visit to South Africa. Joseph Chamberlain Sixth Form College in Belgrave Road, Highgate, is named after him, reflecting his commitment to, and substantial reform of, education in the city. It opened on its current site in 2008.

The Midland Metro has a tram named 'Joseph Chamberlain', and the Two Towers Brewery, which operates The Gunmakers' Arms in Bath Street, produces a most enjoyable Chamberlain Pale Ale!

Joseph Chamberlain with trademark monocle and orchid buttonhole, 23rd January, 1909, from the George Grantham Bain Collection at the US Library of Congress

Joseph Chamberlain Memorial Clock Tower, known locally as 'Old Joe', at the Edgbaston campus, University of Birmingham

Blue plaque at Highbury Hall, 4, Yew Tree Road, Moseley, Birmingham, B13 8QG

Public health issues generated municipal action around housing, sanitation, water and gas to ensure people could be increasingly clean, dry and warm, thereby improving their health and life chances. However, provision for those with illnesses and disabling conditions remained poor and continued to rely on a combination of local authority provision (workhouses for the sick who could not afford cure or care), voluntary hospitals (dependent on charitable giving), and private health care (paid for directly, before the development of health insurance schemes). This highly variable and frankly, dangerously inadequate, set of arrangements remained in place until the creation of the National Health Service, on 5th July 1948. Although a political opponent, Chamberlain would surely have agreed with Aneurin Bevan's assertion that 'private charity can never be a substitute for organised justice.'[303]

Until then, for more than a hundred years, voluntary and charitable hospitals relied on local fundraising and the beneficence of the wealthy, to subsidise or fund substantially the provision of care and buildings, and the exceptional efforts and skills of a small number of innovators. Their contributions deserve recognition.

JOHN JAFFRAY

'The educational and health care philanthropist
who co-founded the Birmingham Post'

There were several prominent citizens who ensured improvements in health care in nineteenth century Birmingham. One of Chamberlain's contemporaries was Sir John Jaffray, a newspaper editor, who became a philanthropist and ardent supporter of improved hospital provision for all people.

John Jaffray was born on 11th October 1818, in Stirling, Scotland, to John Jaffray and Agnes, née Wilson. John Senior was a weaver and a spirit dealer, and a burgess (a magistrate or member of the local town council). John Junior was originally educated at a private school in Stirling and then at Glasgow High School.

John Jaffray's career in journalism began in Shrewsbury as a newspaper reporter, the paper being owned by a relative. He came to Birmingham in 1844, aged twenty-five, to work at the Birmingham Journal, a weekly newspaper owned by John Frederick Feeney. He had only £20, but threw himself heart and soul into developing the range and relevance of the Journal.

In 1850, on 12th February, John Jaffray married Anna Munton, from Bourne, Lincolnshire. They had three children: Annie (date of birth not recorded, died April 1941), William (born June 1852, died November, 1914), and John (born December 1853, died June 1906).

John Jaffray was recruited by Feeney as a literary reporter but demonstrated a greater range of skills and abilities. In a history of the Birmingham Post, he is described as extremely energetic and: 'he could do anything on the paper, from stoking the boiler to writing the leader', and 'in the early years of the struggle, writing and setting up in type his articles for the paper.'[304] Feeney must have been impressed with this young man, as he made him a partner in 1852. It is said that: 'Mr Jaffray's resolute independence, energy and rare business capacity

---

303 *Bevan's speech to the Manchester Labour rally 4 July 1948,* no date
304 Phillada Ballard, 'Jaffray, Sir John, first baronet (1818-1901)', *Oxford Dictionary of National Biography,* (Oxford: 2013)

contributed more than anything else to the ultimate triumph of the Birmingham Journal.'[305]

The Birmingham Journal was established by Tories in Birmingham in 1825, with William Hodgetts being the sole owner from 1827. Five years later, in the year of the Great Reform Act, 1832, the paper became a Liberal publication, owned by Joseph Parkes, William Redfern and Joshua Scholefield (who was elected as one of Birmingham's first two MPs). They appointed Robert Kellie Douglas as editor, and he is credited with drafting the Chartist National Petition in 1838. By 1844, however, sales had fallen from 2,500 to no more than 1,200 per week, and John Feeney bought the paper, setting out to maintain its moderate liberal reputation and expand its circulation.

Jaffray and Feeney increased the profits made considerably, due to their dedication and expertise, and through increased advertising revenues from the expansion of the railways in the 1840s. There was considerable change ahead for newspapers as well, as the abolition of stamp duty by the Stamp Act of 1855 encouraged more frequent, and cheaper, newspapers to be published. The Journal's cost was reduced from seven to four pence, considerably increasing circulation. Without the tax, papers were produced and sold for as little as a penny, and at that cost, people bought papers much more frequently. We are not the first generation to crave more immediate and up to date news!

Responding to this competition, and George Dawson's short-lived Birmingham Daily Press, Feeney and Jaffray established the Birmingham Daily Post on 4th December, 1857, with Feeney as the editor until 1862. This eventually became the Birmingham Post. A further daily paper was created in 1869, the Birmingham Daily Mail, and the weekly Birmingham Journal ceased publication as its circulation fell.

The Birmingham Daily Post remained at the centre of liberal and radical reform politics in the rapidly expanding town, supporting the election of Joseph Chamberlain to the Council in 1869. It supported his efforts at municipal reform over the following years, as well as publishing the views of radicals such as John Bright, Robert William Dale, and George Dawson.

Feeney died in 1869, and his son John took up the ownership of the newspapers with Jaffray. Their success continued, as the Birmingham Daily Post became the newspaper with the largest daily circulation in the Midlands by the 1870s.

Jaffray's involvement with the Birmingham Journal, the Birmingham Daily Post and the Birmingham Daily Mail was controversial at times, and he was not

305 *BMI The Priory Hospital,* no date

afraid to espouse unpopular causes. These included support for religious freedom in 1850, when attempts were made to restore Roman Catholicism as the leading religion, support for the Union side in the American Civil War (in contrast to most other newspapers), and in condemning the Birmingham anti-Catholic riots in 1867.

As a prominent citizen, John Jaffray had many interests. An effective businessman, he was founder of the Midland Wagon Company, chairman of Muntz's Metals, and the Birmingham Joint Stock Bank (taken over by Lloyds Bank in 1869). He had interests in northern England coal mines.

As well as commercial success, Jaffray was active in wider Birmingham life, particularly in education and health care. He was described by a friend as: 'a curious mixture of shrewd commercialism and kind-heartedness',[306] a combination seen in many philanthropists at the time.

His involvement with improving education began with membership of the Birmingham School Association in 1850, becoming treasurer of its successor, the National Education League, formed by Chamberlain in 1865. He was involved with the Birmingham and Midland Institute from its establishment in 1854, as well as president of the Blue Coat School, and a governor of King Edward VI School. As a trustee of the Public Picture Gallery Fund, he wanted to make paintings available to the public and included some he had purchased, by David Cox, the landscape painter, who lived in Greenfield Road, Harborne.

John Jaffray was involved in the establishment and running of the most important hospitals in Birmingham, including the Children's Hospital, the Women's Hospital and the Birmingham General Hospital. Remarkably, he personally paid for a convalescent hospital to be built and equipped. Originally called the Jaffray Suburban Hospital for Chronic Patients, it later became known simply as the Jaffray Hospital. Built at Gravelly Hill, Erdington, it was opened on 27th November 1885 by the Prince of Wales, later Edward VII. It occupied eight acres, providing fifty-six beds for recovering patients from the General Hospital to convalesce. It remained operational until 1991, and was demolished in 1995. Jaffray is noted, along with Chamberlain, as a subscriber in efforts to increase annual subscription funds to £71,000 for the Birmingham Royal Institute for the Blind, in 1897.

Unsurprisingly, given these credentials, John Jaffray was an ardent and active member of the Liberal Party, encouraging John Bright to stand for Parliament

---

306 Ballard, 'Jaffray, Sir John, first baronet (1818-1901)', *Oxford Dictionary of National Biography*

in 1857. He was active in the National Liberal Federation and treasurer of the Birmingham Liberal Association when it was founded in 1865. He stood for Parliament himself, at the 1873 East Staffordshire by-election, but was unsuccessful. He was appointed High Sheriff of Warwickshire in 1888 and was also Deputy Lieutenant of Warwickshire and Justice of the Peace.

He was made a baronet in 1892 for public services to Warwickshire (Birmingham being within the county at the time).

Sir John Jaffray lived at Park Grove, Bristol Road, Edgbaston, a classical-style villa, where he died on 4th January 1901, one of the wealthiest men in Birmingham. This later became the BMI Priory Hospital, and a blue plaque is attached to Stanley House, a Grade II listed building at the rear of the new hospital building, used as Consulting Suites, but previously a school. He had a country estate, The Skilts, in Mappleborough Green, Studley, Warwickshire.

Jaffray is remembered in the name of Jaffray Close, Erdington, and in the Jaffray Nursing Home and Resource Centre, built on the site of Jaffray Hospital. This is part of Jaffray Care, a registered charity dedicated to helping people with developmental disabilities achieve their full potential. As a progressive, kind and philanthropic supporter of those facing difficulties in life, this is a legacy of which Sir John Jaffray would have been rightly proud.

John Jaffray, cartoon by 'Spy' (L. Ward), 1890, reproduced in Vanity Fair

Blue plaque at Stanley House Consulting Suites, BMI Priory Hospital, Priory Road, Edgbaston, Birmingham, B5 7UG

Two Birmingham surgeons introduced innovations in surgical practice in the second half of the nineteenth century which would not only benefit the residents of Birmingham, but would also be adopted world-wide, offering relief to countless thousands of people as these techniques became standard medical practice. The first featured, Joseph Sampson Gamgee, was an inspirational clinical teacher and founder of the Birmingham Hospital Saturday Fund, the first health care insurance scheme available to working class people, giving them access to improved quality of treatment and care.

JOSEPH SAMPSON GAMGEE

'The eminent surgeon and pioneer of cleanliness in surgery, who
founded the Birmingham Hospital Saturday Fund, providing access
to health care for thousands of poor and working class people'

Joseph Sampson Gamgee was born on 17th April 1828 in Livorno, Italy, the son of Joseph Gamgee (born 1801, died 1894), a Scottish veterinary surgeon and pathologist, and Mary Ann West, daughter of a vet. Two of his siblings became eminent and distinguished veterinarians and medical doctors: his brother John became Professor of Anatomy and Physiology at Edinburgh's Dick Veterinary College, and Arthur qualified as a doctor, becoming Professor of Physiology at Owens College in Manchester, specialising in biochemistry.

Joseph Gamgee was educated in Florence, Italy, from 1829 and did not visit England until the age of fifteen. He moved permanently to London three years later, in 1847, to pursue a career as a veterinary surgeon, entering the Royal Veterinary College, and qualifying as a member aged twenty-one. He was invited to be a student at University College London by three professors and began to develop his interest in physiology and surgery.

Several years before Gamgee entered surgical training, the operating theatre at University College London had been the scene of the first use of ether to render a patient unconscious for surgery. Prior to that, surgical operations had been undertaken as a last resort, as the operation itself, perilous and performed without anaesthetic, was excruciatingly painful for the patient. It was believed that pus was a natural part of the healing process rather than evidence of sepsis, but operations frequently left the patient with a post-operative infection that killed them. The mortality rate in hospitals was up to five times that for patients receiving care at home, although this was available only to the wealthy.

As Lindsey Fitzharris describes: 'Public dissections were *theatrical* performances, a form of entertainment as popular as cockfighting or bearbaiting', so 'theatre' is an appropriate term. Jean Jacques Rousseau said: 'What a terrible sight an anatomy theatre is! Stinking corpses, livid running flesh, blood, repellent intestines, horrible skeletons, pestilential vapors [sic]!' The spectacle was enhanced by eminent but cavalier surgeons, like Robert Liston, who prided himself on fast operations above good outcomes. Good hygiene was yet to be understood as a means of reducing infection and mortality, and the depiction is nightmarish: 'The surgeon, wearing a blood-encrusted apron, rarely washed his hands or his instruments and carried with him into the theater [sic] the unmistakable smell of rotting flesh, which those in the profession cheerfully referred to as "good old hospital stink".'[307] Sawdust on the theatre floor soaked up copious amounts of blood lost by patients. To control pain, nitrous oxide, discovered in 1772 by Priestley, had been tried but was felt unreliable. Some surgeons had tried hypnosis, called 'Mesmerism' after its inventor Franz Anton Mesmer, but, unsurprisingly, this also failed.

On 21st December 1846, Robert Liston amputated the leg of Frederick Churchill, a thirty-six year old butler, while the patient was anaesthetised with ether. This was hailed as a great success and the conquest of pain. It would, perversely, lead to higher rates of post-operative death, as surgeons became more adventurous with radical interventions, secure in the knowledge that the patient was pain-free, at least during the operation itself. The profession had yet to address the cause of infections, or to identify any type of response to them. One of the enthralled audience members at this exhibition was Joseph Lister, who would develop effective methods of identifying and killing infection with antiseptic. Gamgee studied and lodged with Joseph Lister and they became friends, although they would disagree professionally on how best to prevent infection later in their careers.

Gamgee's early career was impressive, including visiting hospitals in continental Europe in 1849, befriending Louis Pasteur, and winning five gold medals, including the Liston Gold Medal for Surgery. He became a Member of the Royal College of Surgeons in 1854, and a Fellow of the Royal Society Edinburgh, in 1868.

Having worked as a house surgeon at London's University College, and then as surgeon to the British-Italian Legion, and first-class staff surgeon in the Royal Navy, he served as Superintendent of the Military Hospital in Malta during the Crimean War (1853 to 1856). His fluency in French, Italian, Spanish and German was greatly advantageous during these travels.

Gamgee left his post as Honorary Surgeon at the Royal Free Hospital in 1857, because he felt: 'the management of that hospital was not in accordance with the only principles consistent with due regard for the interests of mankind and of

---

307 Lindsey Fitzharris, *The Butchering Art: Joseph Lister's Quest to Transform the Grisly World of Victorian Medicine*, (London: 2017), pp.4-5

science.'[308] Coming to Birmingham, he lived at 18, Harborne Road, Edgbaston, as he took up the post of Honorary Surgeon at Queen's Hospital, in part, to work with the town's large Italian community. Gamgee's appointment was controversial, as his recommendation to the post by the five professors at the Medical School (which normally secured the appointment of their preferred candidate), was rejected by one vote by the lay members of the Governing Council of the Hospital and Medical School, in favour of J. F. West, a house surgeon at the hospital. This had been West's only post, in contrast to Gamgee's considerable experience and testimonials from distinguished superiors and colleagues at every stage of his career. The row became public, with comments in the British Medical Journal, local newspapers and even from the pulpit of St. Martin's in the Bull Ring, by the Rector, Reverend Dr Miller, chair of the Governing Council. To resolve the controversy, it was agreed that both Gamgee and West would be elected, with seniority being defined later (it was given to West four years later).

Gamgee married Marion Parker, daughter of an Edgbaston veterinary surgeon, in 1860. She helped him throughout his career with his writing. They had seven children, of whom four survived him. His son Leonard Parker Gamgee became Professor of Surgery at the University of Birmingham.

While at Queen's Hospital, Gamgee published articles and books, which expounded ten principles of surgical practice, all of which remain relevant to health care today. These included, reassuringly: 'be prepared for every emergency'; 'swiftness is good, but safety is better; the best evidence of skill is not in the rapidity of movements or sleight of hand, but in the recovery of the patient'; 'treat every case as if your reputation depends upon it' and 'after operation, work is only changed, not ended; postoperative watchfulness is indispensable.'[309]

He undertook fifty-four operations in this first year, including strangulated hernia, gallstones, fractures and wounds. In 1862 he carried out an amputation at the hip, a difficult procedure, with his brother Arthur assisting, and the patient recovered. This was written up in a report described as: 'carefully detailed and splendidly illustrated.'[310] In 1865, he performed his first ovariotomy (removal of Fallopian tube), which was then extremely risky. This operation would not generally be performed successfully until one of his successors at the Queen's Hospital, Mr Robert Lawson Tait, did so in the 1880s.

308 H.M. Kapadia, 'Sampson Gamgee: a great Birmingham surgeon', *Journal of the Royal Society of Medicine*, (London: 2002)

309 Ibid.

310 Ibid.

Gamgee was an innovator throughout his career, using his experiences abroad and at home to inform further development of his practice. After meeting an eminent Belgian surgeon in Florence, Baron Seutin, Gamgee developed a treatment for fractures, using 'starched apparatus and bandages' in 1853, this being the subject of his Liston prize essay. He introduced Plaster of Paris to England in 1854, in place of starched bandages. This light firm casing for the limb involved reduction of the fracture immediately and was ahead of its time, with excellent results. He is best known clinically for the development of the Gamgee Tissue, which was revolutionary in the treatment of wounds by providing dry, absorbent dressings left in place for over a week. This came from his reading of 'La chirurgie simplifiée' from 1842 by Matthias Mayor. The Gamgee Tissue was a layer of absorbent cotton wool between two layers of absorbent gauze, which could be medicated. It was an alternative to Lister's antiseptic carbolic spray, in common use at the time. This was widely used locally, so much so that 'gamgee' became a local Birmingham dialect term for 'cotton wool'. His ideas led to the first manufacture of absorbent sanitary towels by Robinson & Sons, of Chesterfield, Derbyshire. Remarkably to us, a further innovation was washing his hands before operating, and he is believed to be the first surgeon to do so in Birmingham!

Although 'Gamgee Tissue' remains in common usage (it can be bought on Amazon), his most lasting legacy is not to do with his surgical expertise. Gamgee believed that the charitably-provided hospital services should be accessible to those in greatest need. However, they were often used by people not in great need, limiting their availability to the poor. In 1868, at a meeting arranged with businessmen and working men in Birmingham, he proposed, and it was agreed, that working people be asked to make regular donations of small amounts that would add up to considerable sums to be invested in local hospitals. The Working Men's Fund for the Extension of the Queen's Hospital was established to provide an outpatient and accident department. By 1871, the considerable amount of £3,500 had been raised and the new block opened in 1873. This precursor of social health provision resulted in the establishment of the Birmingham Hospital Saturday Fund, so called as it was funded by people working overtime on 'Hospital Saturdays' and donating these earnings to the Fund. By 1876, these contributions to medical charities in the town amounted to £5,200, over ten times the level in 1867. Similar contributory schemes developed around the country, continuing until the NHS was created in 1948. To mark Gamgee's contribution, he was presented with an address from the residents of Birmingham, along with 400 guineas.

Well known and admired internationally, he was a foreign corresponding member of the Society of Surgeons in Paris (for a paper on amputation at the hip joint); an honorary member of the Massachusetts Medical Society; a foreign corresponding member of the Royal Medical Academy of Rome; and a member of the Medical Society of Christiania and St. Petersburgh.

Gamgee was regarded as 'a most eloquent and instructive teacher',[311] becoming Professor of Clinical Surgery at Queen's Hospital, with an excellent reputation locally and an extensive private practice.

Gamgee became secretary of the Birmingham Society for Aid to the Wounded during the Franco-Prussian War 1870-71, using his surgery as an ambulance depot. He took positions of responsibility in medical organisations, being president of the Birmingham and Midland Counties branch of the British Medical Association, as well as president of the Midland Medical Society and the Birmingham Medical Institute. He advocated representation of surgeons on the Royal College council, and for direct representation of surgeons on the General Medical Council. An active author, he wrote books, pamphlets and articles on the treatment of wounds and fractures, and reform of hospital and medical provision and care.

In 1881, a year after announcing his innovative Gamgee Tissue in The Lancet, he retired due to haematuria, a serious blood infection, and was appointed consulting surgeon to Queen's Hospital. Five years later, walking with his sons on a visit to Dartmouth, Devon, he fell and broke his right femur. Although recovering initially, he died from a haemorrhage, exacerbated by his history of Bright's disease (acute nephritis), at home at 22, Broad Street, on 18th September 1886. Aged fifty-eight, he was survived by his wife and his father, who lived to the age of ninety-four.

Gamgee's popularity in his adopted city was apparent, as thousands of people lined the streets for his funeral, with more than twenty carriages following the hearse. In his obituary in the British Medical Journal of 25th September 1886, an unnamed friend's testimonial described him as: 'a model, in every sense of the word', a loving and devoted family man, who made deep and long-lasting friendships. He had 'deep and true religious feeling', which intensified after his illness five years previously. 'His wonderful gifts of language, feminine delicacy of touch, and perfect tact, were such as fall to the lot of few men to possess.' As one who could not do things by half, the writer speculates, implausibly, that his death may have been: 'hastened considerably by the immense amount of brain and body work which he crowded into his useful life.'[312]

---

311 'Obituary', *British Medical Journal,* (London: 25th September 1886), p.604
312 Ibid., p.604

Gamgee is remembered as the first president of the Birmingham Medical Institute in their library named after him, having donated several hundred books during his year as president. Quirkily, it is said that J.R.R. Tolkien, who lived in Birmingham for several years, named his 'Lord of the Rings' character Samwise Gamgee after the inventor of the Gamgee Tissue.[313] His greatest legacy however must be the Birmingham Hospital Saturday Fund, which continues as a not for profit health insurer, covering 375,000 people, and which made a significant and tangible improvement to the range and quality of facilities and services available to not only Brummies, but by its example, in many parts of the country. Joseph Sampson Gamgee is remembered by a blue plaque erected by Birmingham Civic Society in 1993, on Birmingham Repertory Theatre, Broad Street, at the site of his home.

Joseph Sampson Gamgee photograph, date unknown

Blue plaque on outside of Birmingham Repertory Theatre, Broad Street, Birmingham, B1 2EP

Robert Lawson Tait, a Scot who moved to Birmingham aged twenty-five in 1870, developed several innovative techniques in the developing area of surgery for women, and was such a leading figure in this new specialty that he became known as 'the father of modern gynaecology.' He was the driving force behind the founding of the Birmingham and Midland Hospital for Women which opened in 1871 at Showell Green, Sparkhill, a year after his arrival in the town. Described as forceful and assertive, he was also disputatious, having a famous argument about

313 Kapadia, 'Sampson Gamgee: a great Birmingham surgeon', *Journal of the Royal Society of Medicine*

antiseptic techniques with Joseph Lister. Time has validated Tait's views, as his aseptic techniques are now used world-wide. His legacy in his chosen field is very considerable, although not well-known or celebrated in Birmingham.

ROBERT LAWSON TAIT
'The often controversial father of modern gynaecology and a driving force in the founding of Birmingham's Women's Hospital'

Robert Lawson Tait was born on 1st May, 1845 at 45, Frederick Street, Edinburgh, the son of a vintner and butler, Archibald Campbell Tait. His mother was Isabella Stewart Lawson (born 1812, died 1882). Having shown promise from the age of seven when he began attending George Heriot's school, he attended lectures at the University of Edinburgh in 1859 aged fourteen. He did not initially take a medical degree, but was apprenticed to an obstetrician, James Young Simpson. Tait qualified as a Licentiate of the Royal College of Surgeons and the Royal College of Physicians in Edinburgh in 1866, aged twenty-one. As an adult, he preferred to be known as Lawson Tait, rather than Robert.

Lawson Tait moved to Wakefield, to become the only resident House Surgeon at the twelve-bedded Clayton Hospital in 1866. This involved substantial outpatient work, home visits and surgery in the hospital. Having observed thirty operations to remove ovaries in Edinburgh, with every one resulting in the patient's death, it must have been daunting for him to perform his first ovariotomy procedure on 29th July 1868, especially as the operation was 'tantamount to murder.'[314] Sadly, this resulted in the twenty-six year old patient's death, from peritonitis. However, by 1872, he had undertaken nine such operations, with eight of them being successful (the patient who died did so after a month, from complications caused by cancer). He advocated undertaking ovariotomy earlier than others, arguing that recovery was swifter, with lower rates of morbidity and mortality of patients. Given this remarkably good survival rate, when the best practitioners had survival rates of around twenty-seven percent, Tait was noticed by the medical establishment for the first time.

Becoming a member of the Royal College of Surgeons in England and a Fellow of the Royal College of Surgeons in Edinburgh in 1870, Tait moved to Birmingham, aged twenty-five, to take over the practice of Dr Thomas Partridge. He remained for the rest of his surgical career. He lived at the corner of Burbury Street and Lozells Road, near today's Finch Road Primary Care Centre, Lozells.

---

314 D'A. Power, updated by Jane Eliot Sewell, 'Tait, (Robert) Lawson (1845-1899)', *Oxford Dictionary of National Biography*, (Oxford: 2004, updated 2013)

After a year of general practice, he established himself as a consulting surgeon in rooms in Waterloo Street. He immersed himself in the town's medical societies, contributing leading articles to the Birmingham Morning News, edited by George Dawson. He became lecturer in physiology at the Midland Institute from 1871 to 1879.

Tait's self-confident and assertive personality came to the fore in his advocacy of the still controversial theory of evolution propounded by Charles Darwin, and in his campaign for a specialist hospital devoted to 'the alleviation of diseases peculiar to women' in 1871, supported by influential figures, including Dawson and Joseph and Arthur Chamberlain. He faced considerable opposition, including from The Lancet. In addition, the British Medical Journal commented on his 'want of respect for age and authority remarkable even in Birmingham.'[315] It seems Tait decided to work in exactly the right environment of free thinking and innovation, well-known characteristics of Birmingham at the time. Despite opposition and denigration, Tait was successful, and the Birmingham and Midland Hospital for Women opened in 1871 at Showell Green, Sparkhill. Aged just twenty-six, Tait was one of the three chief surgeons. Working at the hospital enabled him to establish himself as a leading doctor, and develop a healthy private practice. In the same year, on 28th June, he married Sybil Anne Stewart, a solicitor's daughter from Wakefield, but they had no children.

Tait held strong and committed views, characterised in his boldness in surgical procedure and innovation, but also became embroiled in many debates and arguments. He established a nurse training programme to ensure his patients received excellent care alongside his pioneering surgical expertise, and advocated education and professional lives for women, both as nurses and doctors. He was ahead of his time in strongly opposing vivisection to test surgical procedures on animals ahead of their use on humans. He argued that vivisection was not justified on moral or religious grounds, and that it reflected the frivolous and careless attitude of the wealthy. It did not help treating diseases in humans, as techniques still had to be tried on people, however well or otherwise they worked on animals. This was contrary to many colleagues' views in the Royal College of Surgeons, and the British Association for the Advancement of Science. It probably did not help him in his wish to be elected as Fellow of the Royal Society, and it was Charles Darwin who informed him that he had been unsuccessful, despite Tait's courting of the eminent evolutionist's good opinion.

---

315 *Robert Lawson Tait,* no date

His famous dispute was with Joseph Lister, the proponent of antiseptic techniques in surgery. While he agreed with Lister that scrupulous cleanliness by surgeons was important, like Gamgee he eschewed the then current use of carbolic acid spray to achieve sterilisation in abdominal operations, as a 'strange phase of medical eccentricity.'[316] Instead, he advocated asepsis, ensuring that disease-causing micro-organisms were removed. He boiled his instruments, laundered his linen, washed his hands thoroughly with soap and water and completed operations quickly. He was thus able to achieve impressive results, equivalent to those achieved by surgeons employing antiseptic techniques, without any deleterious effects from the use of chemicals. He reported undertaking a hundred ovariotomies using aseptic techniques, with only three patient deaths. It is testament to him that these principles are the basis of aseptic practice throughout the world today.

Tait was not only innovative in preventing infection. Importantly, he introduced a number of new gynaecological surgical techniques at the Birmingham and Midland Hospital for Women. As well as being the first surgeon to prove that ovariotomy could be undertaken successfully, he performed a salpingo-oophorectomy, involving removing both the ovary and Fallopian tube, which became known as 'Tait's operation'. He undertook the first removal of a Fallopian tube to treat ectopic pregnancy in 1883. By 1888, he reported two deaths from forty-two operations, a significantly better survival rate for a condition previously virtually invariably fatal. This technique of salpingectomy has been adopted worldwide, saving thousands of women's lives. He is credited with the first oophorectomy (removal of an ovary to relieve pain), removal of infected tubes, surgical induction of menopause by removal of ovaries, draining of pelvic abscesses, and the first gall-bladder surgery (cholescystotomy). He undertook some of the first appendectomies, kidney and liver surgery, and introduced the flushing of the peritoneal cavity at the end of an operation. Tait invented surgical instruments to improve his practice, including a device for draining ovarian cysts.

In 1872, the British Medical Association awarded him the Hastings Gold Medal for his articles on diseases of the ovaries, and by the 1880s, Tait was one of the leading surgeons in the world. As a consequence, he was consultant surgeon to regional hospitals, in Southampton, Nottingham and West Bromwich. In 1887, he became the first Professor of Gynaecology at Queen's College and created the Birmingham School of Gynaecology. Nationally, he was the second president of the British Gynaecology Society and editor of the British Gynaecological Journal.

---

316 Moscucci, quoted by Power, updated by Sewell, 'Tait, (Robert) Lawson (1845-1899)', *Oxford Dictionary of National Biography*

Locally, Tait became Bailiff of Mason College in 1890, and supported the incorporation of Queen's College into this organisation in 1892, thereby preparing the way for the foundation of the University of Birmingham. One of the founding members of the Birmingham Medical Society, he was its honorary secretary, as well as president of the Birmingham Medical Institute from 1889 to 1893. He held appointments at the Birmingham Royal Society of Artists and Birmingham School of Design as professor of anatomy.

He was the author of papers and textbooks of gynaecological practice, publishing articles regularly in the Birmingham Medical Review. In 1884, he visited medical schools and hospitals in North America, and was awarded an honorary MD from New York University in 1886 and another from St. Louis College of Physicians and Surgeons in 1889. He visited clinics in Europe, notably France and Switzerland. Some of his works were translated into French and published in Paris. In 1890, his contribution to abdominal surgery was recognised by the award of the Cullen and Liston prize in Edinburgh.

Tait held strong, progressive views on medical issues and demonstrated this trait in other areas of his life. Non-conformist in religion, and a Radical Liberal politically, he initiated the formation of the Home Rule Association in 1886 in support of Chamberlain's position. He was not afraid to court controversy and outraged some female listeners at a Birmingham lecture during which he stated that female sterility was often caused by venereal disease.

He was active in civil society, elected a town councillor in 1866, representing Bordesley ward, and served as Chair of the Health Committee, and on the Asylums Committee. He stood as a Gladstonian Liberal for Birmingham Bordesley in the 1886 general election but secured only 18.9% of the vote, so was heavily defeated by Jesse Collings, the Liberal Unionist. Tait and his wife were members of the Birmingham Natural History Society (Tait was president in 1884-85) and the Birmingham Philosophical Society. He chaired the Birmingham Dramatic and Literary Club.

Tait worked at the Birmingham and Midland Hospital for Women for twenty-two years, from 1871, and after it moved to a converted farmhouse on Stratford Road, he bought the old premises in 1882 as a home and a clinic. He resigned from active clinical practice in 1893, due to a combination of declining health and legal problems, including a lawsuit brought by Dr Andrew Denholm. In 1892, a patient treated by Denholm with electrolysis died following an operation performed by Tait, and Tait blamed Denholm, who then sued Tait for libel. Although the case was dropped, Tait suffered adverse publicity as he had used Medical Defence

Union funds to meet his costs. Worse followed, as a former nurse, Caroline Burnell, claimed that Tait had got her drunk, sexually assaulted her, and fathered her child. The charges, including demands for financial support, were dropped, but the adverse publicity about these controversies were so damaging that many doctors stopped referring to Tait, and his income fell.

He developed sepsis in his hand from an infected surgical wound and then chronic nephritis, and retired to his St. Petrocks home, Llandudno, North Wales. He continued to attend medical meetings and was highly respected by many younger doctors. Dying in Llandudno on 13th June 1899, aged only fifty-four, from kidney failure, he was survived by his wife. His ashes were interred in Gogarth's cave, a burial site in the grounds of his home in Llandudno.

Robert Lawson Tait was a complex, frequently controversial, always compelling figure. Despite being 'offensive and invidious',[317] he was courageous, highly skilled, determined and driven, and is rightly remembered as the father of modern gynaecology. He is memorialised in The Lawson Tait Society, an undergraduate society, and the Lawson Tait Chair of Gynaecological Cancer at the Institute of Cancer and Genomic Sciences, both at the University of Birmingham Medical School. The only physical memorial to him is a blue plaque erected by Birmingham Civic Society in 1991, at Norton Tower in Civic Close.

Robert Lawson Tait, by unknown photographer, date unknown, from the collection of the National Library of Medicine, USA

Blue plaque on Norton Tower, Civic Close, Birmingham, B1 2NN

---

317 *Lawson Tait,* no date

Nineteenth century Birmingham, as described earlier, was a town open to new ideas, innovative ways of doing things, amenable to radical ideas and freedom of thinking. All these characteristics are demonstrated by the lives of many of those described so far. The passionate work of Joseph Sturge towards the abolition of slavery gave Birmingham a degree of prominence as a town opposed to racism. Similarly, religious tolerance has always been important in Birmingham, as a civilised and laudable response to respecting the validity of the views of migrants coming to live and work in the city. Although not widely known, it is therefore perhaps not surprising that Birmingham had its first black minister of religion before the nineteenth century ended, once more giving opportunity to someone who may have been shunned by less open-minded and welcoming towns or cities.

PETER THOMAS STANFORD
'Birmingham's first black minister'

Peter Thomas Stanford was born in 1860, although the precise date is unknown. Born to enslaved parents on a plantation in Hampton, Virginia, USA, he never knew his father, who was sold by the plantation owner before he was born, and sadly he was separated from his mother when he was four, when she was sold on to slave traders. The boy was only five years old when the American Civil War ended, and although he became free, he had no-one to care for him. The position of freed slaves remained extremely harsh, as W.E.B. Du Bois, a founder of the National Association for the Advancement of Colored People recorded: a freed black person: 'felt his poverty; without a cent, without a home, without land, tools, or savings, he had entered into competition with rich, landed, skilled neighbors [sic]. To be a poor man is hard, but to be a poor race in a land of dollars is the very bottom of hardships.'[318]

The child was fortunately taken in by Native Americans, fellow victims of persecution, and he learned their language, how to run, fish and shoot. He came to the attention of Samuel C. Armstrong, a brigadier general on the Union side in the Civil War, who led several units of African American soldiers. Armstrong founded and became the first principal of a school for African Americans. Over time, this became Hampton University in Virginia and now houses the African American museum which Armstrong founded, the oldest such museum in the USA.

The child was taken to Boston, and adopted from an orphanage by Perry Luther Stanford and his wife. A coal merchant, he put the now named Peter to

318 *Samuel C. Armstrong*, no date

work, for five years which Stanford later described as a time of 'ill treatment.'[319] He stayed with the Stanfords until he was twelve and then ran away, becoming a member of a New York street gang. In this circumstance, his life as a street urchin is described in the Biographical Sketch which forms a preface to Stanford's life story, 'From Bondage to Liberty'.

Curious by nature, Stanford attended meetings of the evangelists Dwight L. Moody and Ira D. Sankey, whose revivalist meetings featured Moody's powerful sermons, and Sankey's songs and hymns. Stanford converted to Christianity and came into contact with prominent Christians involved in the abolitionist cause, including Reverend Henry Ward Beecher, and his sister, Harriet Beecher Stowe, author of 'Uncle Tom's Cabin'. Published in 1852, this classic description of the conditions black people suffered in the South before the Civil War was widely read and influential. In 1872 Stanford met the Reverend Henry Highland Garnet, pastor of Shiloah Presbyterian Church. Garnet was an educator and orator, himself an African American, who had escaped slavery as a child in Maryland, and moved with his family to New York City. Garnet supported Stanford, helping him to find employment as a yard boy at Suffield Institute in Connecticut, which trained Baptist ministers. Stanford became a student at the Institute and then a minister at Mount Zion Baptist Church, in Hartford, Connecticut, on 26th September 1878, aged only eighteen. This was a missionary post, offering help to African Americans who had been slaves before the Civil War, or who simply needed support.

In 1882, Stanford moved again, this time to Canada, becoming pastor of a church in Hamilton, Ontario, before joining the African Baptist Association, in Amherstburg, Ontario. While there he was pastor of Horton Street Baptist Church, in London, Ontario, and editor of a religious newspaper, 'The Christian Defender'.

Stanford came to Great Britain in May 1883, to raise funds for his church in Canada, which was experiencing financial difficulties. After spending time in London, as an evangelist associated with 'The Christian Herald' newspaper, and living in Yorkshire for two years, he moved to Birmingham in June 1887. By mid-1888, he had become a member of the Victoria Street Baptist Chapel, Small Heath, and he settled in Birmingham for the next few years.

He was happy and popular, and comfortable with Birmingham people. He married an Englishwoman, Beatrice Mabel Stickley, from Smethwick, daughter of a shoemaker and a committed Christian, on 13th August 1888. In May 1889,

---

319 Paul Walker, 'Stanford, Peter Thomas (1860-1909)', *Oxford Dictionary of National Biography*, (Oxford: 2013)

he was asked to become minister of Hope Street Baptist Chapel, in Highgate, which today is Highgate Baptist Church. The letter from the Chapel, dated 8th May 1889, offering Stanford the post reflects the open-minded approach of its leaders, and an admirable attention to economy: 'You know our condition will not allow us to offer you a large salary, but we offer you our prayers, willing hearts, and hands. Remember, dear Brother, this call is from God, and He has promised to supply all our needs.'[320] With his acceptance, Stanford became the first black minister in Birmingham.

Stanford's time there was fulfilling and satisfying, but not without challenges. As a black man in a predominantly white city, he met with prejudice and abuse. This was balanced, and more than compensated for, by the attitude of many of the working people with whom he worked, and he became well-known by leading citizens of the growing city. The current minister at Highgate Baptist Church, Reverend Paul Walker, who has studied Stanford in detail, says in a film made by History West Midlands:

'To think that back in the 1890s, an African American ex-slave was the minister of a white working class church is quite moving and profound. He found a great deal of comfort in Birmingham because it had been the centre of anti-slavery, it was a place of industry, social and racial justice, and it was a progressive town. For someone like Stanford, who believed you could raise yourself up through hard work and education, the environment of Birmingham suited him entirely.'[321]

In 1889, Stanford published his life story, 'From Bondage to Liberty: Being the life story of the Rev P.T. Stanford who was once a slave! And is now the recognised pastor of an English Baptist Church', and continued his ministry in Birmingham, expanding it to include the Union Church in Priestley Road, Sparkbrook, in 1891. In tribute to 'the great benefactor of the Negro', the renowned anti-abolitionist William Wilberforce, the church was re-named 'Wilberforce Memorial Church'.

With its historical opposition to slavery and persecution, Birmingham became a focal point for campaigns against continuing injustices against former slaves in the US. Stanford was extremely interested in highlighting and preventing the high and growing number of lynchings taking place, especially in the previously Confederate, slave-owning, Southern states. At a public meeting held on 28th May 1894 at Wilberforce Memorial Church, entitled: 'Lynch Law and the Negro', a resolution was passed that: 'the rev. PETER STANFORD (England's Coloured Preacher) be deputed, in the interests of the philanthropic and Christian public of

320 Israel Olofinjana, *Black Baptists: their contributions to mission*, (13th March 2014)
321 *Peter Thomas Stanford: Remarkable life of freed slave who became a famous Baptist minister,* no date

England, to visit the States for the purpose of investigating these alleged outrages, and of there pleading with the prominent white Christians to induce them to exert their influence in preventing further reprisals, and in insisting on the enforcement of law and order.'[322] This was a decision actively supported by the most influential people in Birmingham. Those named include aldermen, ministers, lawyers and leaders of charitable organisations and many provided letters of support and encouragement. The meeting assured Stanford of 'their entire sympathy and support', and their 'implicit confidence' in his 'impartiality and good judgement.' The esteem in which Stanford was held can be seen from gifts given to him at this meeting, including: 'an illuminated address containing a photo of the chapel and public buildings of the city, costing $30; a farewell address; a number of volumes rebound; a fountain pen; a traveling [sic] reading lamp; a traveling [sic] dressing case, and a jug with Revs. John Wesley and Peter Stanford's pictures engraved thereon; a gold ring with Masons' emblems.'[323]

Stanford travelled to Boston, Massachusetts, in September 1895, and for two years observed the conditions for black people in the Southern states, and investigated the nature, stated reasons for, and the numbers of lynchings and injustices taking place. While in Boston, in August 1895, he founded the first congregational church in the city, St. Mark's Congregational Church, Roxbury, being its first pastor until 1897, when he moved to New York. Stanford lectured regularly, including to other, white, ministers on: 'What the influence of the ministry should be in literature,' and on 'Imaginary obstructions to true spiritual progress' during a service at the Day Street Congregational Church on 14th August 1898. This included an account of his extraordinary life.

Stanford's main preoccupation remained investigating the problems faced by black people, and his travels and endeavours resulted in a further book, published in 1897, 'The Tragedy of the Negro in America: a Condensed History of the Enslavement, Sufferings, Emancipation, Present Condition and Progress of the Negro Race in the United States of America'. This illustrated the broad sociological background to the treatment of black people, comparing the 'authorised tragedy of slavery' with the 'unauthorised tragedy' of injustices after emancipation. He attacked the false Christianity which justified slavery, allowing it to grow throughout the seventeenth and eighteenth centuries. This is contrasted with the beneficial attempts to alleviate the effects of slavery by Quakers and other

---

322 Peter T. Stanford, *From Bondage to Liberty: Being the life story of the Rev P.T. Stanford who was once a slave! And is now the recognised pastor of an English Baptist Church*, (Smethwick: 1889), p.xi
323 Ibid., p.x

religious movements, and the early abolition or restriction of slavery by Northern states. President Andrew Jackson is blamed for permitting racist laws in the Southern states, after the Civil War, and Stanford indicated that freed slaves suffered economic deprivation virtually equivalent to that they suffered as slaves. This echoes the effects of the 'indentured apprenticeship' schemes uncovered by Joseph Sturge in his report in 1834 and it is at least disappointing such conditions persisted over sixty years later. There is an entire chapter on lynchings, which were not appropriately punished by the legal system. Detailed statistics show the growth of these murders in the 1890s, with brutal accounts of individual lynchings. He highlights the work of campaigners for justice for black people, including Frederick Douglass, and sets out the growth of schools and universities in the South that serve to offer hope for them. Stanford writes: 'I have consulted the most reliable histories, and made personal inquiries with great care, and can conscientiously present the story as trustworthy….the Oppressors of the Negro have been looked at from every point of view in the hope of finding some excuse for their cruelty….I was born a slave, and lived for several years with the poorest of the poor, and can never forget my own poverty and sufferings; to help the down-trodden is a desire which never leaves me.'[324]

Peter Thomas Stanford
photograph before 1897

Blue plaque at Highgate Baptist Church, Conybere
Street, Highgate, Birmingham, B12 0YL

---

324 Peter T. Stanford, *The tragedy of the Negro in America A condensed history of the enslavement, sufferings, emancipation, present condition and progress of the negro race in the United States of America*, (Boston, Mass, USA: 1897)

Leaving New York, Stanford returned to North Cambridge, Massachusetts, and founded the Union Industrial and Stranger's Home for homeless women and children. Cambridge was the last place he lived, dying of kidney failure on 20th May 1909, aged only forty-nine, and he is buried in Cambridge Cemetery.

Peter Thomas Stanford was a very remarkable man, well ahead of his times in what he achieved as a black man in an overwhelmingly white man's world. He found an appropriate and supportive home in Birmingham, allowing him to fulfil his mission as a minister, before returning to the States to pursue his lifelong interest in ensuring those in similar situations had better opportunities from the outset of their lives, without the struggles he faced. He is remembered by Highgate Baptist Church, and in many non-conformist churches and movements throughout the world. A blue plaque, erected by Birmingham Civic Society in 2011 is on the exterior of Highgate Baptist Church, Conybere Street, Highgate.

9.

Birmingham in the first half of the twentieth century – Wars, Recovery and Public Service

As the twentieth century began, the British Empire remained the world's dominant military and political force, notwithstanding the damage to its prestige from the Boer War. Europe was dangerous, as nation states asserted their right to survive, or challengingly, to expand. These movements brought war to the continent twice in the first half of the century.

The 1901 census showed the population of Birmingham growing to 522,204, with 630,162 in the wider urban area. Birmingham was a prosperous and expanding city, as the town was granted city status in 1889. Although this 'long overdue decision'[325] did not make a material difference, it indicated to its residents, now citizens, that it was moving forward and developing. In 1890, J. Ralph, in 'Harper's Monthly Magazine', called it 'the best-governed city in the world',[326] reflecting the remarkable improvements made since the early 1870s.

Significant issues remained to be addressed, however. While Chapter 8 identified the Corporation's actions in improving sanitation and housing in the centre, deaths up to five years of age were stubbornly high at around 47.7% in 1884. Although survival had improved, massive challenges remained, as Dr Alfred Hill pointed out in his report in 1901, with the effect most acutely felt, as ever, by the poor. A fifth of deaths were from infectious diseases: smallpox, measles, scarlet fever, diphtheria, whooping-cough, fever and diarrhoea, with higher rates

325 Upton, *A History of Birmingham*, p.188
326 Quoted in Bird, *Portrait of Birmingham*, p.161

in crowded, poorer areas, notably in the centre. It is noticeable that these diseases have been virtually eradicated now, but were then rife in Birmingham.

Hill made the case for improvements, by: 'the building of houses for the labouring classes, the demolition of a house or two in or abutting on every congested court, the removal...of entire blocks of very old and worn-out property, the conversion of pan and ashpit privies [sic], the paving of courts, and the improvement of the domestic habits of the poor, through systematic visiting by...women health visitors.'[327] Hill confirmed that death rates from cancer and heart disease showed no distinguishable difference between individual areas, focussing the reasons for poor health and death on living conditions. Although comprehensive public health improvement programmes are now commonly accepted worldwide, in Birmingham it would take another forty years until they were fully and properly implemented.

The principal ironworking and metal bashing industries flourished, with Birmingham Small Arms in Small Heath producing guns and rifles to support the Empire's wars. Other significant industrial concerns in the early years of the century included GEC and Kynoch's in Witton, as well as Austin at Longbridge and Cadbury's at Bournville. Providing employment opportunities to hundreds of thousands, their workers moved out of central back to back courts to better environments in the suburbs.

Changes in transport infrastructure and routes made this possible and attractive. Since the Birmingham Improvement Act 1861, the Council had laid tracks and cables for tramways. The first privately-run trams ran from Monmouth Street (now Colmore Row) to Hockley in 1873. Initially horse-drawn, steam powered trams were introduced in 1884, but proved sometimes unpopular, one Moseley resident complaining they were: 'monstrously heavy, outrageously noisy... and most offensive to the sense of smell.'[328] Cables in the roads were replaced by electric overhead cables in 1900. Costing one penny per journey, these trams enabled quick easy transport to industrial and housing estates around the city's periphery. Private transport companies were taken into council ownership between 1904 and 1911, and 'motor buses' operated from 1913, with acquisition of the Midland Red Omnibus Company in 1914. These operated for years alongside trams, and by 1930, Birmingham had the largest fleet of trams in the world.

The impact of improved transport was dramatic, with, for example, Erdington's population increasing from 2,500 in 1881 to 32,500 in 1911, a thirteen-fold

327 Dr Alfred Hill, *Report on the Health of the City of Birmingham for the year 1901*, p.3
328 Upton, *A History of Birmingham*, p.189

increase in thirty years. Birmingham Council campaigned vigorously to expand its borders, often requiring a vote by ratepayers. Such changes were opposed by the county councils of targeted areas, including Warwickshire, Worcestershire and Staffordshire. The Corporation engaged in gerrymandering, offering improved infrastructure or lower rates in prospective suburbs. Harborne joined for a public library, Saltley and Balsall Heath gained libraries and swimming baths, and Quinton joined in 1909. Handsworth, Kings Norton and Yardley joined under The Greater Birmingham Act 1911. By natural and economic growth, and incorporating these villages, the city's population reached 840,202 in that year, increasing 61% in a decade.

The First World War brought further business expansion for Birmingham. The armaments and munitions produced were critical to the prosecution of the war. As Field Marshal John French said in 1915: 'The issue is a struggle between Krupps and Birmingham.'[329] Production by Birmingham's factories was astonishing. 50 million shells and 25 million cartridges were produced in three and a half years, along with hundreds of thousands of Mills grenades, invented in Birmingham. BSA made 10,000 Lewis guns every week, while Kynoch's delivered 300 tons of cordite. Industries established for other purposes became providers of vehicles and ordnance, with Austin making shells and armoured vehicles, as their workforce increased from 2,800 to 25,000, and Cadbury's produced food supplies to feed troops on the Western Front. Railway manufacturers built armoured waggons, trucks and aeroplanes.

As the men went off to fight, their places on production lines and in workshops were taken by 15,000 women, and on the trams, 450 boy scouts worked as bell-boys. Birmingham was the pilot area for food rationing in 1917, working so successfully that it was adopted nationwide.

150,000 Brummies volunteered to fight, 4,500 in the first week of recruitment alone. 12,400 never saw Birmingham again. Those enlisting made up 54% of the male population of Birmingham, and joined the 'Pals' battalions, groups of friends signing up and fighting together. They are remembered by a plaque at the Birmingham Museum and Art Gallery entrance on Great Charles Street. Highbury Hall, vacated by Mary Chamberlain after Joseph's death, was converted to a military hospital, along with the University of Birmingham Great Hall, and Rubery Hill provided care for shell-shocked soldiers.

---

329 Bird, *Portrait of Birmingham*, pp.161-2

Peace in November 1918 brought the troops home, amidst joyful celebrations and obvious relief. The close of hostilities brought a recession as the country had enormous debt as a consequence of war spending. The country's returning troops were famously promised 'homes fit for heroes' by Prime Minister Lloyd George, and the housing crisis that prompted this promise dominated the next stage of Birmingham's development. The Housing and Town Planning Act 1919 required councils to provide more houses, including council houses for the working class.

The first council house, in Alum Rock, opened in 1919 as part of the first wave of municipal house building. Some employers had built housing estates for workers, most famously Cadbury's Bournville Estate of 313 homes in 1900. Less well known is Austin Village, built to accommodate Herbert Austin's Longbridge workers, at Central Avenue in Northfield. Pre-fabricated bungalows, imported from Bay City, Michigan, USA, made from Canadian cedar wood, were rapidly erected in 1917 around a central reservation, the first dual carriageway in Birmingham. Two blue plaques, one for Austin Village and one for Herbert Austin himself, erected by the Austin Village Preservation Society in 2002, are fixed to a freestanding low brick wall on the central reservation. By 1939, one third of the population lived in council houses, with the proportion still in back to backs in city centre slums falling to less than a fifth.

Birmingham was moving ahead with a growing population, with ambition and vision. An excellent example of this confidence in the strength of municipal power was the plan to redevelop the centre of Birmingham, drafted by William Haywood, with a foreword by Neville Chamberlain, Alderman and Deputy Lord Mayor, in February 1918. Even with the country at war, attention in Birmingham turned to urban re-development, and the plan was published in a one hundred and one page document, 'The Development of Birmingham: An Essay'. To make this freely available, it was supported by twenty subscribers, including Neville, and nineteen prominent citizens, including Arthur Chamberlain, Neville's uncle, whose company Kynoch's printed it. Neville's 'Introduction' recommended that: 'a new plan of the old city should be put in hand at once.' Its ambitions included: 'such transit facilities to and from the City as are enjoyed by no other town in the Kingdom', and 'new and even startling suggestions for City development', with 'bold and original ideas' based on 'a higher conception of Civic dignity and Civic responsibility.'[330] This was intended to be an achievement in the tradition of his father's concept of the 'City State'.

---

330 William Haywood, *The Development of Birmingham: An Essay*, (London: 1918), pp.13-4

The scheme, grandiose and far-reaching, would involve major redevelopment, particularly the area bounded by Easy Row (at the top of Great Charles Street), Suffolk Street (now Queensway), Holliday Street, the lower part of Broad Street and a new road linking Broad Street to Cambridge Street, which joined Easy Row. The plan advocated a 'Town Place' to constitute: 'the centre from which the conduct of the city is mapped out and ordered....To the citizens it is an object of pride and affection to which they naturally gravitate, and for the stranger it is the chief measure of the condition and standing of the townspeople.'[331] With the Town Hall a key feature, the scheme would provide around an open space laid out as a formal garden between two parallel roads: 'The Cathedral; two Exhibition Halls, for the general purposes now served by the Curzon and Bingley Halls; a Natural History Museum; the War Museum and Memorial; sites...suitable for Musical, Literary or Collegiate purposes; a site...for Municipal use; an Opera House or Theatre,...; additions to Mason's College; a Library extension,...a Children's Library, a Commercial Library, etc.,...a Hall of Consulates, or Bank; a Post Office,...having a large central hall for the public; a Municipal Building; and a Hall for the exhibition of historical and modern machinery...a sort of town showroom of goods, for...the display of their output.' The garden area to be provided was: 'sufficiently spacious to give a proper setting to the buildings', with 'formally arranged trees,...fountains, lawns, seats, bandstands, shrubberies, and pedestals for statuary.'[332]

The Municipal Building would have been an arresting evocation of civic power in concrete, brick and glass. The 'Sky Scraper' [sic] of thirty-five floors: 'naturally marks the centre of the town's affairs, and is the building which claims pre-eminence in the civic scheme.' The tower would have a 'Hall of Marriages' and in front an equally imposing symbol of Birmingham, a thirty-five foot metal statue on a thirty-five foot pedestal: 'a central monument which is intended to symbolise the spirit of Birmingham, conceived as a metal worker.'[333] The location is now occupied by the Holiday Inn Express and Crowne Plaza hotels and Alpha Tower.

The plan provided for social and community activities, with echoes of Nettlefold's Garden Suburb Movement. It contained 'A People's Hall', and 'A Pleasure Grounds [sic] and Zoological Gardens', to be provided at Rotton Park Reservoir. Rather than the Tower Ballroom, recalled by generations of Brummies, the scheme proposed substantial buildings 'for public benefit', including an arena

---

331 Haywood, *The Development of Birmingham: An Essay*, p.84
332 Ibid., pp.85-8
333 Ibid., pp.89-91

for 'outdoor theatricals, or general sporting events', with 10,000 seats, a further 6,000 standing. The reservoir would host 'Water Polo, Boat racing, Regattas, Yachting, Swimming, Water Pageants and Fireworks', while the arena would hold 'cup ties and special matches', with a capacity of 30,000. A 'toy railway' would run around the lake. The Zoo would be comprehensive, with every species of animal, except pandas. The grand entrance would be at the junction of Rotton Park and Portland Roads.[334]

This massively ambitious plan represented an end to the 'aimless procedure of casual improvement.'[335] In the event, this scheme suffered a similar fate to the vaulting ambition of Joseph Chamberlain's Improvement Scheme, being completed only in part, due to cost. The war memorial, the Hall of Memory, was built, opening in 1925. Baskerville House, housing council offices, followed only in 1938.

Haywood is remembered by a blue plaque at The Wellington Specialist Real Ale Pub, Bennetts Hill, where he is memorialised as 'Architect & Urban Planner, Secretary of Birmingham Civic Society 1918-1947'. His architectural model of the Town Place is in Birmingham Museum and Art Gallery, and convenes the scheme's grandeur and beauty. So, sadly, the grand, even grandiose, vision for completely redeveloping the centre of Birmingham was never realised. But just imagine if it had been. Just imagine.

The city's boundaries expanded further even during the 1920s recession, taking in Perry Barr in 1928 and Castle Bromwich and Sheldon in 1931. The first trolley buses operated from 1922, and getting around the city was greatly eased in April 1926, with the introduction of the Outer Circle bus route. Using this, a Brummie could see all parts of the outer suburbs travelling its twenty-five mile length in just over two hours, and it remains a great way to get a sense of Birmingham's size and variety. The eleven mile Inner Circle Number 8 route began in 1928.

As the long recession abated, Birmingham prepared for war again. Re-armament meant industries changed production again to deliver guns, aircraft, vehicles and ordnance, and factories responded superbly. Rover produced parts for Hercules aircraft in Acocks Green and Solihull, Vickers delivered 11,000 Spitfires and 300 Lancaster bombers in Castle Bromwich, Austin produced 2,700 aircraft at Longbridge, and BSA's factories produced machine guns for Spitfires and Hurricanes, and more than half the country's small arms. Some 400,000 Brummies were involved, with women once more enlisted to secure continuation of these industries.

---

334 Haywood, *The Development of Birmingham: An Essay*, pp.41-6
335 Ibid., pp.99-100

Brummies' experience of war for the second time in twenty five years was very different. While there was little danger of injury for citizens in the first conflict, more sophisticated technology put Birmingham well within the range of Luftwaffe bombers. The first raid happened on the night of 8th August 1940, and there were a further seventy six until the last on 23rd April 1943. These terrifying raids killed 2,241 people, with 3,010 seriously injured and 3,682 slightly injured. 140,336 houses were damaged, 12,125 completely or substantially destroyed. 4,003 business premises and 2,365 factories, workshops and public buildings were bombed.

The experience of war seared itself into the memories of those living through these frightening times. My dad told the tale of 'the night Bulpitts went up'. Bulpitt & Sons manufactured brass ware originally, later producing 'Swan' brand kettles. Converted to war production, the factory at the top of Icknield Street, opposite Spring Hill Library, Ladywood, was targeted, and exploded spectacularly. Dad said that he and his friends, aged fourteen, dived into a 'back-entry', the passageway from the road into a back to back court, in Ingleby Street where he lived, to avoid the resulting fireball. My mom, aged twelve, was bombed out of her home in Prescott Street, a few streets away.

Parents were terrified for their children, my maternal grandparents ensuring Mom and her brother were evacuated to a safer location. Among 4,700 children evacuated by December 1940, she and my uncle were taken in by a family in Presteigne, mid-Wales. Mom hated this, as she was made to do the household chores, her resentment made more acute by the later realisation that families were paid by the government to take in these children.

After the Second World War, prosperity increased, the economy grew, and Birmingham returned to pre-war production, becoming a major centre of transport manufacturing, producing cars, bicycles, motorcycles, trains and buses. Tram production stopped, as the last tram, No. 616, ran from Steelhouse Lane to Short Heath and back on 4th July 1953, driven by Alderman James Crump, who, remarkably, as a tram driver had driven the first tram at the beginning of the century. There is a beautifully preserved tram in the Thinktank Science Museum at Millennium Point, Eastside. Cars became the dominant form of transport, and work on the Inner Ring Road began in March 1957. The first section opened in 1960 and was completed in January 1971, costing £33m.

Continued development by the Council has produced Brindley Place, including the International Convention Centre and National Indoor Arena. The pedestrianisation of Victoria Square in 1993 provided an Italianate experience, with fountains and public art, including 'the floozie in the jacuzzi', as she is affectionately known. Recent developments include the Central Library, Centenary Square, an upgraded Bull Ring Shopping Centre, redevelopment of New Street Station as Grand Central, the Paradise development around the Town Hall, and new electric tramways from Snow Hill to New Street Station, now extended up Broad Street to Five Ways.

All these have required civic power to achieve clearance of slums, which have been eradicated from the city today. Having seen Joseph's contribution, it is time to go back to see how Chamberlain's sons, Austen and Neville, responded to these challenges.

Politically, Birmingham remained a Liberal Unionist city and as Joseph declined and died in 1914, his sons, Austen and Neville, rose to prominence. Austen is now overlooked, as if he had not existed. In the first three decades of the new century, however, Austen Chamberlain was a major political figure.

AUSTEN CHAMBERLAIN

'Successful and influential in his time, the Nobel Peace Prize winner, remembered as "The nearly man, who just missed greatness"'

Joseph Austen Chamberlain, known as Austen, was, by all measures, an extremely successful politician, becoming leader of the Conservative Party, Chancellor of the Exchequer twice, Foreign Secretary, a knight of the realm and Nobel Peace Prize winner. Despite these remarkable achievements, he is seen as always having been in the shadow of his father, Joseph Chamberlain, that towering figure of radical politics. In any other context, Austen's career would be judged a success, but he is not well-regarded by historians, being described as a perpetual 'nearly man'. He is barely remembered at all in Birmingham, the city of his birth.

Joseph Austen Chamberlain was the second child of Joseph and Harriet Chamberlain, born in Birmingham on 16th October 1863. He was known as 'Austen' to avoid confusion with his father. The family lived at Giles House, 83, Harborne Road, Edgbaston. Sadly, his mother died from puerperal fever, a urinary tract infection, a few days after his birth, leaving his father distraught. The baby Austen and his sister Beatrice, born 1862, were cared for by Joseph's sister-in-law and wider family for the next five years, as he wrestled with his grief and then returned to businesses and later local and national politics. Joseph had high ambitions for his eldest son, saying he was 'born into a red despatch box.'[336]

---

336 D.J. Dutton, 'Chamberlain, Sir (Joseph) Austen (1863-1937)', *Oxford Dictionary of National Biography*, (Oxford: 2004, updated 2013)

In 1868, Joseph re-married, to Florence, his first wife's cousin, and there were four children over the next five years, Arthur Neville, born 1869, Ida in 1870, Hilda in 1871 and Ethel in 1873. Tragically, Florence also died in childbirth, and as Joseph spent some time abroad, Austen and his siblings were left in the care of Joseph's sisters, Mary and Clara. Austen was sent to a preparatory school near Brighton, an unhappy experience for him, and was further educated at a private school in Hampstead.

Austen attended Rugby School, aged nearly fifteen, in 1878, his father choosing this for him very deliberately. As eldest son, Austen was expected to succeed in the world of gentlemen. Although always a distinguished figure, Joseph was conscious of the prejudice and condescension he experienced as he moved from local to national politics, and he was determined that Austen would have the gentleman's education he needed to overcome this disadvantage. To secure this, 'Austen was set on a manicured path to Cambridge and Westminster.'[337]

Austen succeeded academically, loving his time at the school. It engendered a lifelong love of the institution as he developed, rising to be Head of House. In later life he returned frequently, becoming Chair of the School Governors. He went to Trinity College, Cambridge, again deliberately chosen, for the college's reputation for producing statesmen. He read history and involved himself in political debate, making his first political speech to the university's Political Society in 1884, and became Vice President of the Union.

By this time, Joseph Chamberlain had been an MP and a member of the Cabinet, as President of the Local Government Board. Austen was therefore well-received into society, including by the aristocracy and the intellectual elite. Beatrice Potter, who became famous as Beatrice Webb, a radical socialist thinker and activist, met Austen at the time she had formed something of a crush on his father. Recognising that Joseph, considerably older, would be likely to stifle her intellectual independence, Beatrice decided against encouraging Joseph's interest. On a visit to Highbury in 1884, she described Austen as: 'a big, fair-haired youth of handsome feature and an open countenance and sunny sympathetic temperament.'[338]

Having graduated, Austen completed his education in Europe. He lodged with a family in France from September 1885 to May 1886, attending the École des Sciences Politiques in Paris, and visited Germany in February 1887. His father's connections allowed him to spend time with leading politicians in these countries, including the German Chancellor, Otto von Bismarck.

---

337 Tim Bouverie, *Appeasing Hitler: Chamberlain, Churchill and the Road to War,* (London: 2020), p.122
338 Ward, *The Chamberlains: Joseph, Austen and Neville 1836-1940,* p.66

The next year, his father met, fell in love with, and married Mary Endicott, while he was in America, on behalf of the UK government, arbitrating a fisheries dispute between Canada and the USA. Mary was aged twenty-three, while Austen was twenty-five. This could have been a difficult relationship but they became friends, shared many interests and political views, and Mary later became a loving grandmother to Austen's children. They also, with the rest of the family, cared for Joseph after his stroke in 1906, and Mary and Austen worked particularly closely together until Joseph's death in 1914, concealing the extent of his disability, and continuing his work in the Liberal Unionist cause.

In 1891, Joseph involved Austen in a business decision intended to restore the family's finances. As he was no longer receiving a ministerial salary, Joseph was considering investing in growing sisal in the Bahamas. Sisal is an agave plant used to produce hemp, a fibre used in rope making and matting. He asked Austen and Neville to visit the Bahamas to assess the potential for profit and was persuaded by Austen's enthusiasm for the venture, estimating potential profits at thirty percent. It is difficult to understand how Austen made his judgement, having no experience in business. It is likely that he wanted to support improving his father's financial position and so Neville, his younger half-brother, was given the task of moving to Andros Island and making a success of this project. Eventually, after five years, the family wrote off the enormous £70,000 commitment they had made in this disastrous investment.

In Birmingham, Joseph secured Austen's adoption for the parliamentary seat of Hawick, in the Scottish Border Boroughs constituency, as the Liberal Unionist candidate in 1888. While waiting for a general election, Austen stood for Birmingham Council, for St. Thomas's ward, in November 1889. This time, his family connection worked against him, as Joseph had split from the Liberal Party, and their supporters took revenge on Austen by abstaining in large numbers. This was effective, as the winning candidate polled eleven more votes than Austen. Although disappointed, this was the only election that Austen ever lost! It did mean that he would not gain any experience in local politics before trying for the House of Commons. Service in local government was then, as now, seen as an indicator of suitability for national politics and government. As Bunce commented, local councils: 'confer incalculable benefit upon the country, by training the citizens who serve in them to take their places in the more conspicuous though scarcely severer labour of the administration of the State.'[339]

---

339 Bunce, *History of the Corporation of Birmingham: with a Sketch of the Earlier Government of the Town, vol.1*, p.356

In East Worcestershire, the constituency in which Highbury was located, the sitting MP, a fellow Liberal Unionist, embezzled trust funds and fled justice and the country, so a local by-election was called for 30th March 1892. At the time, the Tories and the Liberal Unionists had a national agreement not to field candidates against each other, ensuring a conservative-thinking candidate would be elected. This meant that candidates so adopted might be elected unopposed. Local Tories favoured their own candidate, Victor Milward, a needle manufacturer. Undeterred, Joseph secured the support of the national Tory leadership to overrule them in Austen's favour. Once again, Austen's father had been instrumental in procuring advantage for him, and he was duly elected, unopposed. Austen remained an MP until his death forty-five years later, the longest serving parliamentarian among the Chamberlains.

In an emotional family scene in the Commons, Austen took the oath, supported by Joseph and his uncle Richard, formerly Mayor of Birmingham, now MP for Islington. Recalling this in his 1935 autobiography, 'Down the Years', Austen commented: 'I remember the strong feeling stirred in me by the occasion made my hand tremble so violently that I could scarcely sign my name on the Roll.'[340]

In the general election that year, Austen was opposed by a Liberal candidate, Oscar Browning, a Cambridge historian. Austen received 5,111 votes, 67% of the vote, securing a majority of 2,594. Forty-seven Liberal Unionist MPs were returned and Austen was identified as a rising star, being appointed a junior whip, even though he had only recently entered Parliament. His maiden speech in April 1893 on the second reading of the government's Home Rule Bill was an impressive performance noticed by all, even the Prime Minister, William Gladstone, who called it: 'a speech which must have been dear and refreshing to a father's heart.'[341] Given the enmity between Gladstone and Chamberlain Senior, this was praise indeed.

Although a very frequent public speaker, Austen was not a natural orator, and reflected that: 'To this day I never rise to address it [the House of Commons] without trepidation and that uncomfortable feeling in the pit of the stomach which in our childhood we used to call "bath-pain" because we associated it with the first sudden plunge into cold water.'[342] Austen was in awe of those who commanded their audiences through oratory or charisma, as he was unable to do this, and devoted a chapter of his autobiography to 'How Great Speakers Prepare Their Speeches'.

340 Austen Chamberlain, *Down the Years, 7th edn.,* (London: 1937), p.69
341 Ward, *The Chamberlains: Joseph, Austen and Neville 1836-1940,* p.69
342 Ibid., p.69

Austen worked assiduously and supported his father in his campaigns for greater access to education, and in the divisive and visceral debate about Irish Home Rule. Austen also emulated his style and appearance, reinforcing the closeness of their political positions. In personal style, Austen always sported a monocle and orchid buttonhole, like his father, and was one of the last MPs to wear his top hat inside the Commons Chamber. This closeness to his father, in politics and appearance, left him susceptible to unfair criticism which has persisted. Although Rhodes James described Austen as: 'in many ways the most attractive of the Conservatives; certainly in most respects, he was the most attractive of all the Chamberlains', his old-fashioned values and behaviour led Rhodes James to conclude that: 'in spite of much *gravitas* and earnestness, there was always something faintly preposterous, if also rather touching, about the frock-coated, top-hatted, monocled, Austen.'[343]

The Liberal government fell in June 1895, following months of fractious arguments and difficult disagreements in Cabinet. Austen was returned, unopposed, as he would be in the 1900, 1902 and 1909 elections. As a Liberal Unionist-Liberal coalition remained in government for ten years, both Joseph and Austen were offered cabinet posts, Austen as Civil Lord of the Admiralty. A young man of thirty-two, he must have been exhilarated to have advanced so far so quickly. Once again, his success was soon overshadowed by his father, whose association with the Boer War in South Africa became the defining issue of the 1900 general election campaign, in which the Liberal leader, David Lloyd George, based his campaign on a promise to 'Go for Joe'.

In 1900, Austen was promoted to Financial Secretary to the Treasury, aged thirty-seven. With a change in Prime Minister to Arthur Balfour in 1902, Austen was promoted again, to the Cabinet post of Postmaster General, with an annual salary of £2,000, and he was made a Privy Councillor. Although his father's patronage benefitted him considerably, it meant that Austen had to support his father in his increasingly acrimonious arguments and splits from his coalition colleagues. This was difficult for Austen, who instinctively preferred conciliation and seeking agreement to antagonism. Balfour promoted him again, to Chancellor of the Exchequer, in October 1903, at the age of forty. This provided an increase in salary to £5,000 per year, but meant that Austen had to carefully negotiate his relationship with both his father and his Prime Minister, without unduly upsetting either. Some historians believe this was a clever move by Balfour, who knew he

343 Rhodes James, *The British Revolution: British Politics 1880-1939*, p.411

could trust Austen's integrity, but believed it might temper Joseph's more aggressive approach, as he would not wish to damage his son's career.

On the evening of his appointment, 4th January 1904, sitting in 11, Downing Street, Austen acknowledged this could be a two-edged sword: 'I do not think there are many fathers who have been and are to their sons all that you have been to me; and my prayer tonight is that the perfect confidence which I have enjoyed for so long may continue unimpaired by our separation, and that I may do something to help you in the great work which you have undertaken. It is at once a great encouragement and a great responsibility to be heir to so fine a tradition of private honour and public duty and I will do my best to be not unworthy of the name.'[344] This is illuminating. It shows Austen's love and respect for his father, and that even having reached one of the three great offices of state, he still perceived this, at least in part, as a fulfilment of his father's project, rather than his own career ambition. The hand of history, and family, laid heavily on Austen's shoulder.

As Chancellor, Austen was competent, delivering effective budgets in 1904 and 1905, as the country recovered financially from the cost of the Boer War. The argument about tariff reform continued to rage, forming the background to the January 1906 election. Austen won well again in East Worcestershire, with 10,129 votes, a majority of 4,366 over the Liberal candidate John Morgan. He was shocked, however, that the Conservative-Liberal Unionist coalition suffered a catastrophic defeat, and even Prime Minster Balfour lost his Manchester seat. The Chamberlain effect in Birmingham and the West Midlands had resulted in healthy majorities for supporters of tariff reform, but this was directly contrary to the rest of the country, and the doctrine of 'Imperial Preference' seemed to have been irrevocably defeated.

Out of office for the first time in eight years, Austen suffered ill-health, including sciatica, and was described by Neville as 'a chronic invalid' at the age of only forty-seven.[345] Travelling to Algiers to recover, Austen met the twenty-seven year old Ivy Muriel Dundas, daughter of Colonel Henry Dundas, and fell in love rapidly. Engaged in May 1906, they married at St. Margaret's in Westminster a few weeks later on 21st July, in a high society wedding. With Neville as best man, the wedding was opulent, the bride having eight bridesmaids, and a dress made by Mary Chamberlain's dressmaker. Unfortunately Joseph could not attend having suffered a stroke days earlier at his London home. The 12,000 guests included all senior politicians of the day, and presents were sent by the King and Queen.

---

344 Austen Chamberlain, *Politics from Inside: An Epistolary Chronicle 1906-1914*, (London: 1936), p.20
345 Ward, *The Chamberlains: Joseph, Austen and Neville 1836-1940*, p.73

Austen and Ivy had a very happy family life, living in London in the main, at 9, Egerton Terrace, off Brompton Road, and had three children, sons Joseph and Lawrence, and daughter Diane.

In the years of opposition, until his father's death in 1914, Austen shouldered the burden of representing his father's views locally, around the country, and in Parliament, even though his natural tendency was to be more conciliatory and less aggressive. Austen's natural conservatism led him to oppose the Suffragette Movement, telling a policeman: 'Drat the Women! I wish the magistrate would give the leaders a good heavy sentence.'[346] In March 1909 he wrote disparagingly: 'Lord! How I do dislike the suffragists *en masse*, though there are very charming women among *them*, if not among the screeching sisterhood of suffragettes; and how I hate their whole movement and all it means in politics and social life. The more I think of it, the more my whole soul revolts against it.'[347] Introducing his collection of letters from 1909, writing in 1936, Austen concedes he was wrong about votes for women: 'I fear that my views on Women's Suffrage as expressed at the time will anger some of my readers, but I have let them stand. I am bound to admit that, if the results of its adoption have not realised all its promoters' hopes, neither have they justified my fears.'[348] Although a typically graceful apology, these comments indicate that he failed to grasp the importance of such a significant social movement at the time and place him on the wrong side of history.

Austen was influential in debates at a Constitutional Conference in June 1910 to resolve the divisive issue of the Lords' behaviour in opposing financial policies proposed by the government, and was involved in the meetings over five months to resolve this. The conference failed to find a solution and Lloyd George was less than complimentary about Austen's contribution, indicating that he had: 'such a slow and commonplace mind that he didn't count.'[349]

When Balfour resigned as leader of the Conservative Party in November 1911, Austen was expected to replace him, but his reaction was reluctant, and full of personal regret that Balfour had resigned. Rather than grasp this golden opportunity, Austen was diffident and not prepared to battle for the leadership. Austen wrote of his ambitions and fears, in a letter to Mary, to be read to his father, on 27th October 1911: 'I suppose I did want to succeed if it fairly came my way, though, like anyone else who thought of what it meant, I was appalled by the difficulties of the position

---

346 Ward, *The Chamberlains: Joseph, Austen and Neville 1836-1940*, p.75
347 Chamberlain, *Politics from Inside: An Epistolary Chronicle 1906-1914*, p.169
348 Ibid., p.137
349 Ward, *The Chamberlains: Joseph, Austen and Neville 1836-1940*, p.77

and well aware of how many of the necessary qualities I lacked.'[350] Eager to avoid unpleasantness, Austen proposed to his leadership rival, Walter Long, that they both withdraw to allow Andrew Bonar Law, an outsider, to become leader. Bonar Law was consequently elected unopposed at the Carlton Club meeting on 13th November 1911. Joseph was less than impressed, as might be imagined.

This wish to be correct in all his dealings held him back on several occasions, as Leo Amery, a fellow Unionist MP in Birmingham, commented: 'he had an exaggerated fear of being regarded as pushful…or other than scrupulously correct and loyal in all his personal dealings,' which he described as a 'weakness.'[351]

Austen's father decided to step down from his constituency in January 1914, as his health deteriorated. This led to another dilemma for Austen, as he was asked to stand in Birmingham West. While attracted to the idea, taking into account 'our family's obligations to the City and its claims on me',[352] it meant standing down from his East Worcestershire seat which he had represented since 1892, for twenty-three years. The force of his father's influence is reflected again in his statement: 'I suppose I have done right. At any rate, with Father's strong feeling before me I could not do otherwise.'[353]

When Joseph died on 2nd July 1914, Austen had already been adopted by the Birmingham West constituency and represented it for the next twenty-three years. Although this might be thought to have strengthened his ties to Birmingham, in fact the reverse was the case. Mary sold Highbury and moved to London by the end of the year, leaving Neville to lead the Birmingham caucus, as the most prominent Chamberlain still in the city.

In August 1914, Austen was again re-elected unopposed, as he was in two further elections in 1918 and 1921, and returned to government during the war, as Secretary of State for India in Asquith's coalition government of May 1915. For the rest of his career, now freed from the shadow of his father, he focussed on European or international issues, rather than those local to Birmingham.

Once more, Austen resigned as a matter of honour on 12th July 1917, when 9,000 British and Indian troops surrendered during an ill-fated campaign to protect oil fields in the Persian Gulf, at the Siege of Kut, in Mesopotamia (modern Iraq). Having been widely praised for this act of principle, he returned to the War Cabinet as Minister without Portfolio in April 1918, despite the Daily Mail's

---

350 Ward, *The Chamberlains: Joseph, Austen and Neville 1836-1940*, p.79
351 Amery, quoted in Ibid., p.79
352 Chamberlain, *Politics from Inside: An Epistolary Chronicle 1906-1914*, p.602
353 Ibid., pp.602-3

description of him as: 'an ineffective mediocrity' and an 'amiable insignificance.'[354] As peace brought joy to the country, 1918 was a mixed year for Austen. While Neville was elected to Parliament for the first time, their sister Beatrice died in the Spanish influenza pandemic in November 1918.

On 10th January 1919, despite previous reservations, Prime Minister David Lloyd George appointed Austen as Chancellor of the Exchequer for the second time. Austen faced the problem of dealing with the costs of war and increased national debt, and although suffering ill health initially, enjoyed and flourished in the role. He had purchased Twitt's Ghyll, a seven bedroom country house in Mayfield, East Sussex, which gave him helpful diversion and relaxation. By his second budget, Austen experienced 'the pleasant feeling that men of all parties like and respect me.'[355] He succeeded in reducing the deficit from £1.69m in 1918/19 to achieving a surplus of £238m by 1920/21.

He was elected leader of the Unionist Party at the Carlton Club in March 1921, following Bonar Law's resignation due to ill health. Typically less than enthusiastic, Austen saw it as: 'an obvious duty but without any pleasure or any great expectations except trouble and hard duty.'[356] This proved correct, as he urged the continuation of the coalition with Lloyd George to his disenchanted parliamentary colleagues in October 1922. He lost the vote on his proposal heavily and had to resign, this decision also forcing Lloyd George's resignation and departure from government, to which he never returned.

Austen was out of government again, and this was made bitter for him when Neville was appointed Postmaster General by the new Prime Minister, the returning Bonar Law. His ungracious response engendered an angry riposte from Neville. Austen had to resile from his embittered stance, and agreed to support the government, so as not to prevent his half-brother's first experience of office at the age of fifty-three.

The extent of Austen's distance from Birmingham is completely encapsulated in his comment during the 1922 general election, describing his shock at the living conditions in his own constituency, stating: 'why anyone who lives in such slums should not be a Socialist, a Communist or a Red Revolutionary I am at a loss to say.'[357] In truth, Austen was an outsider, and willingly detached from local issues, and the infrequency of his visits were even criticised by Neville.

---

354 Ward, *The Chamberlains: Joseph, Austen and Neville 1836-1940*, p.80
355 Ibid., p.87
356 Ibid., p.87
357 Ibid., p.91

After the now Conservative and Unionist Party victory in October 1924, with a secure majority, Austen became Foreign Secretary and Deputy Leader of the House, but once more he was apprehensive, feeling 'no elation, but only a sobering sense of great difficulties in my path.'[358] However, he began to enjoy the role, dealing credibly with many difficult issues in the aftermath of the war. His preference for negotiation and conciliation over aggression and domination suited the circumstances at last, and he played the crucial role of chairing the Locarno Conference from 5th to 16th October in 1925. In a fine example of his attention to detail, he describes how he tried to secure a 'round table where there should be neither top nor bottom', and when this was not available, he obtained a square table that was set up 'with no sign to differentiate one place from the other.'[359]

These discussions led to a treaty that sought to resolve problems and tensions between France, Belgium and Germany about borders, and the latter's failure to pay reparations. Austen's driving principle was to ensure that Germany would not be encouraged or incentivised to become an aggressive power in the future, and he felt that: 'Peace rested, not on goodwill or assent, but solely on the incapacity of the vanquished to renew the struggle.'[360] The Treaty was welcomed as 'peace at last', and seen as restoring the state of world affairs prior to 1914. Austen encapsulated this by misquoting Bismarck, saying that the Polish corridor was something 'for which no British government ever will or ever can risk the bones of a British grenadier.'[361] Austen called the Locarno Treaty 'the safety-curtain of Europe', after this phrase appeared in 'The Daily Telegraph'.[362] The palpable relief nationally was evident in many dance halls and cinemas being named 'The Locarno', some of which still survive. Austen was given considerable praise for his role and accepted a knighthood, unlike his father, and Neville, who refused the honour in 1940. He was made a Freeman of Birmingham and London and offered the French Grand Cross of the Legion d'Honneur, but refused this. Austen's role was acknowledged worldwide when he was awarded the Nobel Peace Prize, as joint winner with Charles Dawes, the American banker and envoy to Locarno. This was the pinnacle of Austen's political career, but the high cost personally of being Foreign Secretary led him to sell his much-loved Twitt's Ghyll, in 1929. He and Ivy moved into a house in Rutland Gate, London.

358 Ward, *The Chamberlains: Joseph, Austen and Neville 1836-1940*, p.94
359 Chamberlain, *Down the Years*, p.174
360 Ibid., p.152
361 Dutton, 'Chamberlain, Sir (Joseph) Austen (1863-1937)', *Oxford Dictionary of National Biography*
362 Chamberlain, *Down the Years*, pp.162-71

The 1929 general election was traumatic, close to catastrophic, for Austen as he only narrowly retained his seat, beating the Labour candidate George Willey by a mere forty-three votes. Since the previous election, his majority had fallen by almost 35%. The Labour Party flourished, but Austen's explanation for his narrow victory was prosaic and ungracious: 'The old people still supported us, but the young were sullen and voted socialist solidly.'[363] The Labour leader Ramsay MacDonald remained Prime Minister leading a minority government.

In August, 1931, Austen returned to government as First Lord of the Admiralty, and thereby ironically completed his time in government in the same post which he held on first entering in 1895. Although capable, Austen felt his appointment was a demotion, as he had wanted to return to his favoured post of Foreign Secretary. Austen's tenure was very short, as he resigned once again on a matter of honour, on 17th September, taking responsibility for the Invergordon Mutiny. This would be the last time he would hold government office.

In the general election of October 1931, Austen defeated George Willey again, securing more than 68% of the vote, with a restored majority of 11,941. This reflected nationwide support for the National Government, which Ramsay MacDonald led, and Austen remained a backbencher over the next six years, serving on Commons Committees, and drafting the India Act of 1935. He served as the government's representative on the executive committee of the League of Nations Union, observing the rise of Hitler's Germany with trepidation and arguing against accommodating Nazi demands: 'There should be no running after Germany and no payment of blackmail this time.'[364] He was considerably influenced as a young man in Germany by lectures of the firebrand Treitschke. In a letter of 31st October 1887, Austen said he: 'has opened to me a new side of the German character – a narrow-minded, proud, intolerant Prussian chauvinism….If you continuously preach to the youth of a country that they stand on a higher step of the creation to all other nations, they are only too ready to believe it….It's very dangerous'. With Churchill and Baldwin, he was one of the few senior politicians to raise concerns about Hitler, outlining the extent of his fears in the Commons on 13th April, 1933: 'What is this new spirit of German nationalism? The worst of all-Prussian Imperialism, with an added savagery, a racial pride, an exclusiveness which cannot allow to any fellow-subject not of 'pure Nordic birth' equality of rights and citizenship within the nation to

---

363 Ward, *The Chamberlains: Joseph, Austen and Neville 1836-1940*, p.99
364 Ibid., p.102

which he belongs. Are you going to discuss revision [of the Treaty of Versailles] with a nation like that?'[365]

In November 1935, the Conservatives secured a large majority, with Stanley Baldwin, having taken over from MacDonald in June, remaining as Prime Minister. Austen was re-elected for the last time, with a majority of 7,371 over the persistent but continually unsuccessful George Willey. As the Conservatives again secured all twelve seats, Austen's view of local electors was markedly different this time: 'Bravo Birmingham. There's not another city like it.'[366]

Offered a post in government, Austen felt slighted by, and refused, Baldwin's offer of Minister of State, and was particularly upset by the Prime Minister's comment that he was too old, at seventy-two, to return to being Foreign Secretary. What was clear was that he was more and more removed from the centre of politics. One of Baldwin's supporters, Sir Henry 'Chips' Channon, called him, incorrectly as the re-armament of Germany later proved, 'ossified, tedious and hopelessly out of date.'[367]

A significant figure in public life, Austen had been Rector of Glasgow University and from 1935 to 1937 Chancellor of Reading University, and he remained Chair of Governors at Rugby. He chaired the London School of Tropical Medicine, created by his father, and the British Postgraduate Medical School. He received honorary degrees from Oxford, Cambridge, London, Birmingham, Glasgow, Toronto and Lyons. Austen produced three books: 'Down the Years' (1935), 'Politics from Inside: An Epistolary Chronicle, 1906-1914' (1936) based on his letters to Mary and Joseph, and 'Seen in Passing' (posthumously, November 1937), a collection of reminiscences of his foreign travels.

Austen wrote his autobiography 'Down the Years' to provide the family with income. This chronicled his time in high office in particular, and reinforces the view that this was the main preoccupation in his successful political career, rather than representing the interests of his constituents. The book is easy to ready, as Austen has a graceful, flowing style, and he demonstrates his erudition and political sensitivity throughout. It does however lack a narrative arc and is far from a coherent exposition of events in his life. In the Preface, Austen says it gives 'sidelights on history' and 'no more than random recollections of men and events, among which I have moved.'[368] There are very few biographical or career details, although some can be inferred.

---

365 Dutton, 'Chamberlain, Sir (Joseph) Austen (1863-1937)', *Oxford Dictionary of National Biography*
366 Ward, *The Chamberlains: Joseph, Austen and Neville 1836-1940*, p.103
367 Ibid., p.105
368 Chamberlain, *Down the Years*, p.5

His second book, 'Politics from Inside: An Epistolary Chronicle 1906-1914' is a collection of letters to Mary, by which Austen kept his father updated and engaged in predominantly national politics. In a tangible display of the mutual regard between Austen and his stepmother, the book includes a full page plate of Mary, and the dedication is to her: 'in love and gratitude for all she has been to me and mine.'[369]

Austen suffered a heart attack at home in Egerton Terrace on 16th March 1937 and died in his bathroom, aged seventy-three. Tributes included Lloyd George's ambivalent description of him as 'a man who strained the point of honour always against himself' and Churchill's view that Austen's 'life added lustre to the famous name he bore.'[370] Austen would surely have been more appreciative of this judgement, but less welcoming of Churchill's later jibe that Austen was someone: 'who always played the game and always lost it.' This niggardly comment has also been ascribed to Lord Birkenhead, so may not have been an original judgement on Churchill's part.[371] Unfortunately, Austen did not live to see Neville reach the ultimate pinnacle of British politics by becoming Prime Minister, just ten weeks later. His wife Ivy survived him, dying in 1941.

Appropriately, given where the majority of his politics took place, and where he favoured, Austen was buried in St. Marylebone Cemetery in East Finchley, London, rather than his native Birmingham.

There are differing perspectives on Austen's perceived failure to achieve the highest office in the land, with some taking the view that his early career was overshadowed by his father, and his later career by his half-brother Neville. He lacked Joseph's ruthlessness and self-serving self-confidence, although another interpretation is that this indicated a man with a well-developed sense of honourable behaviour. Although unusual, this is to be admired in a high-achieving politician. It is certainly kinder to conclude that, as fellow Birmingham MP, Leo Amery, stated: 'He just missed greatness and the highest position, but his was a fine life of honourable service.'[372] Stanley Baldwin's judgement was that Austen was: 'a great Parliamentarian who excelled in loyalty and integrity.'[373] These are appropriate epitaphs.

Despite his high offices, knighthood, political influence, and his achievements at Locarno securing the Nobel Peace Prize, there is remarkably only one memorial

369 Chamberlain, *Politics from Inside: An Epistolary Chronicle 1906-1914*, pp.5-11
370 Ward, *The Chamberlains: Joseph, Austen and Neville 1836-1940*, p.105
371 Rhodes James, *The British Revolution: British Politics 1880-1939*, p.411
372 Dutton, 'Chamberlain, Sir (Joseph) Austen (1863-1937)', *Oxford Dictionary of National Biography*
373 Ward, *The Chamberlains: Joseph, Austen and Neville 1836-1940*, p.105

to Austen in Birmingham, a blue plaque erected by Birmingham Civic Society at Giles House, 83, Harborne Road, Edgbaston, the site of his birth. Scant acknowledgement perhaps for his life of honourable service.

Portrait of the Rt. Hon. Sir Austen Chamberlain, by Philip de Laszlo, 1920

Blue plaque at Giles House, 83, Harborne Road, Edgbaston, Birmingham, B15 3HG

Although Austen Chamberlain is now largely forgotten by Birmingham, and the rest of the country, the same is unequivocally not the case with his half-brother, Neville. Neville Chamberlain has become a by-word for weakness and misjudgement, based on his policy of appeasement of Adolf Hitler in the mid to late 1930s. This is in many respects a harsh and unforgiving judgement, particularly when seen in the context of political thinking and military preparedness of the time.

NEVILLE CHAMBERLAIN
'The highest-achieving politician Birmingham has produced, and the most reviled'

For Arthur Neville Chamberlain, known as Neville, being the son of Joseph Chamberlain was difficult, as the lives and careers of both Neville and Austen demonstrate. Neville struggled to be the perfect son, with Austen for years the more favoured, expected to succeed at the political game so dear to Joseph. This may have been a reason for Neville's initial aversion to national politics, preferring to concentrate on his business career, and serving as a Birmingham councillor and alderman.

Neville came late to national politics, being fifty when elected an MP. Particularly as Minister of Health, he was a relatively liberal social reformer, having a notable impact on housing provision and standards, and the relationship between local and national government. His achievements have, however, been completely forgotten in the light of his mistaken policy, as Prime Minister, of appeasement of Adolf Hitler prior to the Second World War. Although this policy was widely supported at the time as the right approach to avoid a second European war, it was catastrophic, and consequently, Neville Chamberlain has been vilified as an austere, reserved and arrogant patrician, unfit for office, and guilty of a heinous miscalculation about Hitler that led directly to war. Although this chapter covers the period before the Second World War and Chamberlain's role, it will bring back into the light his earlier achievements to balance the darkest shade with glimmers of light.

Arthur Neville Chamberlain was born on 18th March 1869 to Joseph Chamberlain and his second wife, Florence, being the third child of Joseph and the first for Florence. Joseph's first wife, Harriet, died shortly after giving birth to Austen in 1863. The same fate befell Florence in 1875, giving birth to a stillborn son. As a five year old, this must have been terribly hard, and Neville did not have time to develop strong memories of her, apart from having been 'deeply conscious of her love.'[374] Neville had three further siblings, Ida, born 1870, Hilda, 1871 and Ethel, 1873. Much of Neville's personal and private thoughts about issues of the day are drawn from his correspondence with Ida and Hilda, to whom he was particularly close.

After Florence's death, the wider family cared for the children, and young Neville spent more time with family and godparents than with his father, often away on political business as he developed into a politician of national prominence. Neville was taught to shoot and fish by his godfathers, to hunt bugs in the grounds of Highbury with Ida, and he loved these hobbies throughout his life. He confirmed that his relationship with Joseph was formal, and he was afraid of him, and his 'piercing eyes that few could face with comfort',[375] including himself.

Aged seven, Neville went to boarding school near Southport in 1877, and to another preparatory school which he liked less well. Neville joined Austen at Rugby in 1882, thought to be appropriate to prepare them for their careers.

374 Peter Neville, *Neville Chamberlain – A Study in Failure?*, (London: 1992), p.7
375 Ibid., p.7

Unlike Austen, who loved Rugby, Neville hated it, and having left, never returned. He was bullied, as a shy and nervous pupil, and shyness marked his personality throughout his life, often taken as aloofness or arrogant reserve by contemporaries and commentators alike.

Neville did not participate in the school debating society until 1886, when he defended his father's position in a debate on Irish Home Rule. He studied modern subjects, as Rugby began to offer these as an alternative to the Classics. His Unitarian upbringing helped him to understand the virtue of hard work, and he learned to grasp details to understand a subject entirely to be effective in its use. This trait can be observed in all his activities, from cataloguing precisely his father's orchid collection in the Highbury glasshouses, to preparing complex legislation and steering it through the Commons. His love of flowers resulted in him becoming a member of the Royal Horticultural Society. Returning from Rugby, Highbury Hall became his home, and he lived there until he married in 1911, apart from five years running a family business in the Bahamas. The family home was busy and lively with political debate, with Austen and his sisters living there as well, and they were joined by Joseph's third wife, Mary, in 1888. Mary was only twenty-three and got on well with her step children, Neville then being nineteen.

Neville enrolled at Mason Science College in Edmund Street to study metallurgy and engineering, in preparation for his business career. Unlike Austen, he was not expected to enter politics, so a university education would have been a waste of money. His father, on comparing his two sons in 1902, said that while he thought Austen had a reasonable chance of leading a government, Neville was 'the really clever one', and if he became interested in politics, he would 'back him to be Prime Minister.'[376] Of course, neither Joseph nor Austen lived to see this prophetic statement realised. Studying at Mason Science College from 1887 to 1889, Neville overlapped with another student, Stanley Baldwin. It is not clear, however, if these two young men, destined to become political and personal friends, and both of whom would be Prime Minister, knew each other at the time.

After his studies, Neville was apprenticed to Howard Smiths, a firm of accountants, but this was short-lived, as Joseph decided to invest in a sisal plantation in the Bahamas, and Neville was required to make it successful. Both Joseph and Austen were engaged in politics and not drawing ministerial salaries. Joseph's sharp business sense eluded him on this occasion, as he was convinced to

---

376 Dilks, quoted by Andrew J. Crozier, 'Chamberlain, (Arthur) Neville (1869-1940)', *Oxford Dictionary of National Biography*, (Oxford: 2004, updated 2018)

invest in growing sisal, an agave plant used to produce hemp, a fibre used in rope making and matting. Austen and Neville visited the Bahamas in 1891 to assess the potential for a profitable enterprise and Joseph was persuaded to invest by their report, and particularly by Austen's enthusiastic support, although neither he nor Neville had had any direct business experience.

This decision had a major impact on Neville, as he moved to Andros Island, purchased the land, employed a workforce, built a plantation, and strived to make it profitable. This was a daunting prospect for any twenty-two year old, but Joseph brooked no argument, and invested £50,000 initially in establishing the Andros Fibre Company. Neville arrived in May 1891 and initially, made a success of it. Having 'secured the best site available in the Bahamas',[377] by 1893 more than 4,000 plants had been planted on 10,000 acres near the harbour at Mastic Point, increasing to more than 6,000 plants by 1895, and the plantation had 800 employees.

Although busy during the day, this proved a lonely life for Neville, as there were few Europeans nearby, and he took to the solitary pastime of studying the flora and fauna of the island. Joseph visited in October 1893 and was sufficiently encouraged by progress to invest a further £20,000. In 1896, a large fire destroyed one of the buildings storing hemp, and the venture was failing. Neville returned to England to consult with his disappointed father, and the decision to write off the £70,000 investment was made. Although selling equipment raised £1,000, the land could not be sold, so the financial impact was substantial. Joseph's reaction was that this 'was indeed… a catastrophe', and Neville said: 'I cannot blame myself too much for my want of judgement.'[378] This was made more acute by Austen's success as a parliamentarian. He was elected as MP for East Worcestershire in 1892 and became a junior whip and the Civil Lord of the Admiralty in Salisbury's administration in 1895. Neville creditably expressed great regret at the effect of his failure on all those working on the plantation, saying that the fact 'all my people will relapse into what they were is extremely distressing to me.'[379]

Aged twenty-eight, Neville needed to find a new occupation, and with the help of his uncle Arthur, then chairman at Kynoch's, a large armaments business in Birmingham, he became a director at Elliotts in Selly Oak. This company manufactured copper, brass and other metal products, putting Neville's knowledge to good use. Becoming chairman, he demonstrated the concern for making

---

377 Ward, *The Chamberlains: Joseph, Austen and Neville 1836-1940*, p.111
378 Ibid., p.112
379 Neville, *Neville Chamberlain – A Study in Failure?*, p.12

improvements in the lives of workers and ordinary people which became a feature of his later political career. He introduced a surgery at the factory, welfare supervisors and benefits for men injured in the war, unable to return to employment, and for their dependants. Long before national social insurance or the NHS, this was forward-thinking.

Uncle Arthur recommended that the family purchase another well-run, profitable business, Hoskins and Son, at their Neptune Works in Trinity Street, Bordesley. This company, which made berths for ships' cabins and later became a major supplier of beds to the NHS, was purchased using family money and a bank loan. Neville ran it successfully, recovering his self-belief and business confidence. With more than 200 employees, Neville introduced a pension scheme and a 5% productivity bonus, and was proud that his enlightened approach meant that the firm was not subject to industrial action as many companies were. Industrial action became prevalent, as workers gained an understanding of their collective bargaining potential, and trade unions flourished.

Although Neville was in charge, his father characteristically controlled his salary, at £500 per annum, rising to £600 in 1900, with occasional £250 bonuses. By 1910, Neville headed a very profitable concern, earning £5,000 a year, a considerable sum. The profits from Hoskins and Elliotts, to which Neville devoted one day a week, sustained the whole family, as political changes meant Joseph and Austen were at times out of government, and not earning salaries. Neville took control of the family finances, a redemptive action after his Bahamas experience.

Outside business, Neville was active in the community, bringing his assiduous, careful manner to all he did, including being a Sunday schoolteacher at the Church of the Messiah, like his father. He became a member of governing bodies, at Birmingham General Hospital and the University of Birmingham. As a hospital visitor, Neville surprised many by the diligence he applied to this role, seeing it as a duty rather than an occasional activity, as many others did. Neville became chair of the General Hospital's governing body, and treasurer of the Birmingham General Dispensary. He designed a scheme to relieve pressure on the hospital's outpatient services and demonstrated the grip of detail, assiduous research, and determination which stood him in good stead in his later political career. In great demand, he became a director of Birmingham Small Arms (BSA), and a board member for Birmingham's Botanical Gardens.

His involvement with politics was limited to being Secretary of the Birmingham Liberal Unionist Association (BLUA), the model used as the powerbase for Liberal Unionism locally, and later nationally. In business terms, Neville saw the advantage of his father's policy of 'Imperial Preference', tariff protection for goods produced locally, exported to the colonies on advantageous terms. He enthusiastically supported Austen's and Joseph's election campaigns during the 1900 and 1906 elections and his political involvement expanded after Joseph's stroke in 1910, as Neville represented him at many meetings, until 'Brummagem Joe' died in 1914.

In 1911, Neville decided to enter politics, although on a strictly local basis. He turned down the opportunity to stand for Parliament in South Birmingham. The seat was won by Leo Amery, who was an MP for thirty-four years and made a significant intervention in Neville's last days as Prime Minister in 1940. Giving evidence to a Commons Select Committee looking at expanding the boundaries of Birmingham, which resulted in the Greater Birmingham Act 1911, Neville became more prominent in the public sphere.

Birmingham had tripled in size and was established as 'the Second City of the Empire', with a population of 840,202. In November 1911, Neville was elected as councillor for All Saints ward, within the Birmingham West constituency of his father. His election platform argued for social reforms and improvement in living conditions, including provision of more open spaces and parks, as part of effective and thoughtful town planning. This approach was advocated by the Garden Suburb Movement, supported by his cousin John Sutton Nettlefold, and resulted in the creation of the Moor Pool Estate, Harborne in 1910. Neville argued for improved technical education, informed by his need for skilled labour as an employer, and for the extension of the canal system, crucial to moving raw materials and manufactured products around the city and country.

1911 saw significant change for Neville. A bachelor for many years, expecting to remain so, when aged forty-two, he met Anne De Vere Cole, in her late twenties, daughter of an army officer, William Utting Cole. They fell in love and married in January 1911 after a whirlwind romance. Annie, as she was known, was very different from Neville's buttoned-up personality, being warm, vivacious, and completely disorganised. They had a happy marriage, with two children, Dorothy, born 1911, and Frank, born 1913, for whom Neville made up games in their new home, Westbourne, in Westbourne Road, Harborne, next to the Botanical Gardens.

In local government, Neville was not immune from national politics, as his father's support for tariff reform generated an argument, and a never-resolved schism, with Nettlefold, who, with Neville's Uncle Arthur, was an advocate of free trade. Nettlefold's refusal to use BLUA funds for the tariff reform campaign led to his removal by Joseph from the post of BLUA treasurer, and the loss of his council seat for Harborne and Edgbaston. Neville replaced him as treasurer, and as chair of the Housing and Town Planning Committee, combined with the chairmanship of the Health Committee. This combination presaged many of the social reforms which Neville pursued in government when Minister of Health and Chancellor of the Exchequer.

Under his chairmanship, the Town Planning Committee saw the delivery in late 1913 of the first two town planning schemes in Britain. Neville believed that well-being was significantly impacted by the conditions of housing and this led to a number of innovations. These included identifying separate and distinct zones for industrial and residential areas, improving the environment, and moving sections of the population from inner city back to back courts to more spacious suburbs, with green spaces, parks, gardens and allotments. As quoted in the Birmingham Daily Post on 10th November 1915, as he became Lord Mayor, he saw the need to move: 'the working classes from their hideous and depressing surroundings to cleaner, brighter and more wholesome dwellings in the still uncontaminated country which lay within [the city's] boundaries.'[380]

An alderman since 1914, as Lord Mayor he was following eleven members of the wider family who held this prestigious and powerful position. The authority wielded by Lord Mayors of Birmingham was far wider and impactful than now, with control over transport, education, welfare and, since his father's mayoralty, water and gas utilities. A closer comparison would be to today's directly-elected Mayors in London, Greater Manchester and the West Midlands.

As Lord Mayor, Neville was hard-working, effective, and naturally supportive of the war effort, but keen to improve life wherever possible for Birmingham people. He established a Citizens' Society providing practical relief to families in distress, and a Civic Recreation League which organised morale-boosting activities. The Corporation purchased essential supplies in bulk, using its scale to achieve effective prices, and sold them to local people at cost. This was achieved alongside rationing of milk and coal, to ensure limited supplies were available for everyone, and convincing the Ministry of Munitions to underwrite the cost of extending the city's electricity supply.

The first air raid on the city in January 1916 prompted understandable widespread panic. Neville established an air defence system which was recommended to the Home Office for adoption elsewhere. The former family home Highbury was converted to a convalescent hospital, and Neville persuaded

---

380 Crozier, 'Chamberlain, (Arthur) Neville (1869-1940)', *Oxford Dictionary of National Biography*

the University of Birmingham to do the same with the Great Hall. The city offered considerable relief for refugees from Europe, especially Belgium.

Two outstanding successes are recorded for his mayoralty. The establishment of a first class orchestra in the city was prompted by the visit of the Manchester-based Halle Orchestra in 1916. The City of Birmingham Symphony Orchestra was set up in 1919, complete with a large concert hall, bringing classical music to everyone through low cost concerts, subsidised by the Corporation. Secondly, the creation of the Birmingham Municipal Savings Bank was a unique initiative. Neville wanted to encourage working people to save and support the war effort, by purchasing war bonds with regular savings deducted at source from workers' wages. The Bill for parliamentary approval engendered considerable opposition at this suggestion of deducting directly from wages. Resisted by national organisations, including Friendly Societies, banks and even the Treasury, the proposal looked likely to fail by May 1916. A proviso that workers could buy stamps or coupons instead enabled the law to pass in August 1916. Birmingham Corporation hosted the bank in its Water Department premises, as it was intended to close three months after the war ended. However, the enthusiastic take up of its guaranteed 3.5% return, underwritten by the Corporation, meant that within two years, there were 30,000 depositors and the bank became permanently established in July 1919 by Act of Parliament. Branches sprang up across Birmingham, and the bank's headquarters moved to Broad Street, opposite the Hall of Memory, where the foundation stone bearing Neville's name can still be seen, on the HSBC building. The bank existed until 1976, and was the only such organisation in the country.

As Lord Mayor, Neville was happy and productive, restoring further his confidence in his own ability, and delivering considerable benefit to ratepayers and the city's population. He was more closely the successor to his father's civic legacy than Austen. He wrote to Mary on his forty-seventh birthday: 'if the good things came to me rather later in life than they do to some, I am making up now for lost time.'[381] People locally agreed, as he was re-elected Lord Mayor in December 1916. This month, however, brought further significant, unexpected and unsought change for Neville, as his abilities and achievements had been noticed beyond Birmingham.

On 19th December 1916, days after his re-election, Neville attended a London conference on municipal borrowing and, when boarding his train home, he was given a message to go and see Austen, then Secretary of State for India at his office

---

381 Ward, *The Chamberlains: Joseph, Austen and Neville 1836-1940*, p.121

in The Strand. On arrival, Austen insisted that Neville go directly to meet David Lloyd George, the Prime Minister, at 10, Downing Street. Lloyd George talked with Neville for ten minutes, and then offered him the newly-created post of Director of National Service, requiring him to decide immediately, as the Prime Minister wanted to announce the appointment in the House of Commons. Neville felt obliged to accept, and Lloyd George told the Commons that evening that the government had 'been fortunate in inducing the Lord Mayor of Birmingham to accept the position',[382] but this was a decision that Neville, and Lloyd George himself, would regret.

The role was to achieve substantial voluntary recruitment of men and women for essential war work which did not require compulsory conscription. Neville's role was made difficult as he was not given a clear, detailed brief, even after three discussions with Lloyd George. Not being an MP or peer, he had to be represented by government ministers in the Commons or Lords, and his role and proposals were opposed by other ministers, including those for War and Labour, making delivery very difficult. Neville tried hard to make this work, having renounced his beloved mayoralty to do so, but it proved impossible and he resigned on 8th August 1917, upset at a further failure. By the date he resigned, after eight months' effort, only 3,000 volunteers had been placed.

As well as unadvisedly appointing Ernest Hiley, the former Town Clerk of Birmingham, as his senior aide, who did not understand how the civil service worked, his difficulties were further significantly compounded by the fact that the Prime Minister did not like him, and did not hide the fact, his opinion based ridiculously on the size of Neville's head! In conversation with Leo Amery, MP, Lloyd George said: 'When I saw that pin-head, I said to myself "He won't be any use".'[383] This enmity between them, fully shared by Neville, lasted a lifetime, and came up repeatedly in their numerous future contacts.

Returning to Birmingham and his businesses, Neville became involved again in local government, chairing the Citizens' Committee and becoming Deputy Lord Mayor in November 1917, but he was depressed and unconvinced that a political career was for him. On 17th December 1917, he wrote: 'my career is broken. How can a man of nearly 50, entering the House with this stigma upon him, hope to achieve anything?'[384] He turned down the opportunity, however, to become Lord Mayor again in 1919, as by then he had recovered his equanimity and self-belief enough to try to enter Parliament.

---

382 Neville, *Neville Chamberlain – A Study in Failure?*, p.18
383 Ibid., p.18
384 Crozier, 'Chamberlain, (Arthur) Neville (1869-1940)', *Oxford Dictionary of National Biography*

Increasingly involved in Liberal Unionist politics, he established a new central office in Edmund Street, and created junior, and women's, unionist associations. This was important, as the Representation of the People Act 1918 expanded the electoral franchise to women over thirty, with a property qualification, and women made up 43% of the electorate. In Birmingham, the electorate more than quadrupled from 95,000 in 1914 to 427,000 in 1918, of which 165,000 were women over thirty.

As the number of seats in Birmingham increased from seven to twelve, Neville was adopted by the Conservative and Unionist Party for the seat of Birmingham Ladywood. In the December 1918 general election, he won decisively, with a majority of nearly 6,000. His platform, designed to appeal to his predominantly working class electorate in the slums of Ladywood, included a minimum wage, reduced working hours and an expanded role for government in housing. He joined Austen in the Commons, as his half-brother became Chancellor of the Exchequer, and while pleased for him, Neville commented on tensions between them, on policy issues. In a letter to Hilda, Neville said: 'He thinks me wild and I think him unprogressive and prejudiced.'[385]

1918 was a difficult year, with the loss of his cousin Norman Chamberlain, who died in the trenches in France, and his half-sister Beatrice, who succumbed to the Spanish influenza epidemic.

In the Commons, in a well-received maiden speech, made without notes, on the Rent Restriction Bill, Neville focussed on housing reform. The Birmingham Post called it 'an admirable performance',[386] and the Attorney General included some of the points made into the Bill, preventing landlords from increasing rents unless they produced a certificate that the properties were fit for human habitation.

In Neville's early parliamentary career he advocated local authority control of housing development and gained a reputation as hard-working and dependable, demonstrating again his socially liberal tendencies by sponsoring a bill to improve the legal status of illegitimate children, uncharitably dubbed 'the Bastardy Bill'.

The mutual dislike between Lloyd George and Neville surfaced again in 1921, when the Prime Minister, a successful war leader, was made a Freeman of Birmingham. While Austen offered congratulations and a speech of compliments and support, Neville's response was bitter: 'to think that at this moment our pure-souled Prime Minister is receiving the freedom of Birmingham. I can scarce

---

385 Neville, *Neville Chamberlain – A Study in Failure?*, p.28
386 Quoted in Ibid., p.28

restrain a tear.'[387] When Lloyd George fell from power, Neville offered 'profound thanks to Providence for delivering us from the goat.'[388]

His opportunity to enter government came from the new Prime Minister, Andrew Bonar Law, with the post of Postmaster General in October 1922. This created tension with Austen, reacting very badly to his younger sibling being offered a Cabinet post, but, after Neville's threat to leave politics altogether if forced by Austen to refuse office, the latter recovered his composure and withdrew his objection. This reflects badly on Austen and well on Neville, who was prepared to forego the chance of office to keep the family peace.

Neville's career improved further when, in March 1923, he was appointed Minister of Health, a role which he came to enjoy as much as the mayoralty of Birmingham, as it combined his major political interests of housing and health. He moved quickly to ensure the Rent Restriction Act was passed by the summer of 1923.

Housing was a major issue for government after the First World War, from Lloyd George's election pledge in 1918 to build 'homes fit for heroes', through to the Great Depression. As Upton details, by 1918, there was a massive shortage of homes in Birmingham, some 600,000, and the city's 43,366 back to back houses housed 200,000 residents, but offered overcrowding, poor sanitation and high levels of preventable disease and death. The 1923 Housing Act, introduced by Neville, provided a further 438,000 houses nationally by 1929, providing subsidies for smaller properties, to give the working classes the opportunity to access good quality housing.

By the 1929 general election, policy changes, including Neville's, had resulted in almost one million new houses being built and fifty-eight slum clearances, an area of focus of which his father would have approved. As Neville explained in a speech on 12th May 1938, it was seeing his father's 'deep sympathy with the working classes and his intense desire to better their lot which inspired me with an ambition to do something in my turn to afford better help to the working people and better opportunities for the enjoyment of life.'[389]

The first council houses in Birmingham were built in Alum Rock in 1919. In 1930, the city opened its 30,000th new house in Kingstanding, with the 40,000th opening at Weoley Castle in 1933. The ceremony was performed by Neville, then Chancellor again, saying: 'Birmingham celebrates an achievement on the part of

---

387 Ward, *The Chamberlains: Joseph, Austen and Neville 1836-1940*, p.127
388 Ibid., p.128
389 Crozier, 'Chamberlain, (Arthur) Neville (1869-1940)', *Oxford Dictionary of National Biography*

the City Council which has no parallel in this or any other country.'[390] Spread across the city, by 1939, 50,000 had been built providing good quality housing to a third of the population, with the percentage of people living in slums falling from 27.6 to 18.8 percent between 1921 and 1939. By 1943, death rates in Birmingham achieved parity with the national average, at 12.1 deaths per 1,000, and continued to fall until it reached 10.9 per 1,000 in 1938. While medical advances, cleanliness, and better nutrition all played a part, the impact of the council house building programme is incontrovertibly clear.

Stanley Baldwin, MP for Bewdley, Worcestershire, became Prime Minister and appointed Neville as Chancellor of the Exchequer in August 1923. Their fourteen year partnership was based on their mutual regard and trust, although they were very different characters. Baldwin was personable and relaxed, good with people and in cultivating MPs, while Neville was hard working, dedicated to mastering his brief, and delivering complex legislative changes. Many colleagues felt him aloof and withdrawn, to the point of extreme arrogance. His private secretary at the Treasury commented on his 'fallibility in his judgement of persons' and 'a lack of sureness in appraising political situations',[391] a shrewd anticipation of the nature of Neville's relationship with Adolf Hitler fifteen years later.

Neville's career as Chancellor did not last long, not even long enough to present his first Budget, as Baldwin unexpectedly called a general election for December 1923. However, this was a major mistake by the Prime Minister, and brought electoral disaster to the Conservative and Unionist party, as they lost their majority, and a new minority government, the first led by a Labour politician, James Ramsay MacDonald, was formed. Neville became shadow spokesman on Health and Housing, the issues most dear to him and in October 1924, returned to being Minister of Health, which he considered his area of expertise: 'I ought to be a great Minister of Health, but am not likely to be more than a second-rate Chancellor.'[392] In his favourite ministerial role, Neville displayed his reforming tendencies, securing support for contributory old age pensions, another cause dear to his late father's heart.

In 1925, Neville introduced the Ratings and Valuations Bill. This complex legislation sought to make sense of complicated and divergent approaches to rating and valuation of property across the country, introducing new regional assessment areas, with a five year re-valuation process. Passed into law, Neville achieved

---

390 Bird, *Portrait of Birmingham*, p.163
391 Neville, *Neville Chamberlain – A Study in Failure?*, p.31
392 Ward, *The Chamberlains: Joseph, Austen and Neville 1836-1940*, p.134

this predominantly by mastering immense detail, and answering immediately objections made in the Commons.

Neville's debating style often provoked enmity from opponents, as he could be cruel and harsh in dismissing their objections. As he himself acknowledged when challenged by Baldwin: 'I always gave him the impression when I spoke to him in the H[ouse] of C[ommons] that I looked on the Labour Party as dirt. The fact is that intellectually, with a few exceptions, they are dirt.'[393] Austen wrote: 'Neville's manner freezes people…Everybody respects him, but he makes no friends.'[394]

In 1929, Neville promoted the Local Government Act, transferring the responsibility for health and running workhouses providing accommodation for the poorest in society to local authorities. It established block grants to local authorities to offset reductions in business and farming rates. The principles underlay the operation of local authorities and government to modern times, until the changes brought in by the 2010 coalition government. The Times newspaper called this: 'one of the outstanding legislative achievements of the twentieth century.' Dilks commented that Neville 'contributed more than any minister to the conception of national politics locally administered',[395] while Harold Wilson stated: 'The truth is that his reforms used national power to transfer real authority to ensure democratic local control.'[396] The highlight of an impressive legislative record, this session saw twenty-five bills presented by Neville, twenty-one of which became law.

Although disappointed by the loss of the 1929 general election, Neville stood for the first time in the Birmingham Edgbaston seat, and won with a huge majority of 14,760, securing 63.7% of the vote.

Neville joined Ramsay MacDonald's National Government as Minister for Health again and after an improved conservative performance in the October 1931 general election, Neville became Chancellor again, a post he would hold until becoming Prime Minister in 1937. Given rising unemployment, and the economy still in deep recession, the role of Chancellor was pivotal, challenging, and formidable. Neville attacked the issues in his usual manner, convinced as always that he was right.

In proposing the Abnormal Importation Bill in November 1931, Neville imposed a ten per cent duty on excessive imports, and a ten per cent tariff on all imports, except from the Dominions and other exceptions, including foodstuffs.

393 Ward, *The Chamberlains: Joseph, Austen and Neville 1836-1940*, p.135
394 Rhodes James, *The British Revolution: British Politics 1880-1939*, p.585
395 Neville, *Neville Chamberlain – A Study in Failure?*, pp.43-4
396 Harold Wilson, *A Prime Minister on Prime Ministers*, (London: 1977), p.220

This was the fulfilment of Joseph's dream of the 'Imperial Preference' policy. Neville was understandably highly emotional, and took his father's old and battered red despatch box to the Commons, last used when he resigned as Colonial Secretary in 1903. Neville described the day the Act passed, 4th February, 1932, as 'the great day of my life', as he fulfilled his father's greatest political ambition. With sisters Ida and Hilda in the gallery, and Austen in the chamber, at the end of Neville's speech, as the Birmingham Daily Post reported: 'there was an extraordinary demonstration of enthusiasm by members who rose in their places, waved order papers, and cheered and cheered again. Labour members alone remained seated.'[397] Austen, now a backbencher, came to the front bench to congratulate Neville and shook his hand as almost all around cheered.

Despite the approbation and praise, the next stage was an international conference to develop the implementation of the policy agreed in the Act, as it required the co-operation of the Colonies. To Neville's disappointment, they did not share his enthusiasm, as they looked to secure their own national interests ahead of those of Great Britain, as they did in Joseph's time. Neville therefore never achieved the Empire-wide customs union he, and especially his father, had promoted.

Several tough Budgets followed, described as austere, 'hair-shirt', and of 'puritanical severity.'[398] As Ward comments: 'the austerity of his message, together with his somewhat gloomy appearance and Victorian style of dress, would earn him sobriquets such as "the coroner" and even "the undertaker" from Birmingham.'[399] The Unemployment Act of 1934 established the Unemployed Assistance Board, Neville's attempt to neutralise the issue of unemployment assistance as a party political issue. The Board was essential to 'providing some interest in life for the large numbers of men never likely to get work',[400] and this marked movement towards welfare for the unemployed, a significant social development benefitting millions.

By 1934, the economic picture improved to the extent that he introduced his Budget with a literary allusion, telling the chamber: 'We have finished the story of Bleak House and could sit down to enjoy the first chapter of Great Expectations.'[401] Neville hoped that these successes by the National Government might help create

---

397 Quoted in Ward, *The Chamberlains: Joseph, Austen and Neville 1836-1940*, p.141
398 Ibid., p.141
399 Ibid., p.143
400 Crozier, 'Chamberlain, (Arthur) Neville (1869-1940)', *Oxford Dictionary of National Biography*
401 Neville, *Neville Chamberlain – A Study in Failure?*, p.62

a new national political party that would enable him 'to get rid of that odious title of Conservative which has kept so many from joining us in the past.'[402] He never considered himself a Conservative; rather he saw himself as a Liberal or Liberal Unionist, and was elected as such. Although described as a Conservative Prime Minister, he never stood in elections as a Conservative candidate.

In the 1935 general election, Neville won Birmingham Edgbaston again very comfortably, with 81.6% of the vote and as Chancellor pursued his economic strategy through to 1937, balancing trade, with low interest rates, reductions in tax and gradual restoration of wage levels in public service. In Neville's mind, he had to balance this issue with the need, since the early thirties, to spend more of the nation's income on re-building the nation's armed forces, in the face of the growing threat from Hitler, Mussolini, and the Stalinist USSR.

Neville became Prime Minister on 28th May 1937, after Baldwin became Earl of Bewdley and retired to Astley, Bewdley, following the Edward VIII abdication crisis. Neville was the obvious, overwhelmingly popular, choice as Leader within the Conservative Party, and was even proposed by Churchill. Neville had attained the pinnacle of political success, and despite not being the favoured son, had in fact outperformed Austen, and even his extremely ambitious father. Austen had died on 16th March 1937, just ten weeks earlier. This must have brought a strange combination of pride, satisfaction and regret that neither had lived to see this.

It has been pointed out that Neville had many failings as Prime Minister in the two years before the Second World War, and part of this was his lack of foreign affairs experience. As Bouverie indicates, Austen's comment of: 'Neville, you must remember you don't know anything about foreign affairs' was unfair, but has been used subsequently by many commentators and historians.[403] He was involved in the Lausanne Conference on war reparations in 1932, arguing for the cancellation of reparations, borne of his view that Germany was being too severely punished, too long after the end of the war, and this has often been portrayed as the beginning of the policy of appeasement of Hitler.

Neville's motivation was to achieve a diplomatic solution so that the funds used for re-armament could be applied to improve domestic problems and issues. The approach therefore was negotiation with Germany and Italy, while improving the strength of defensive forces, known as the 'double-line' approach, a straightforward twin-track policy. This is the policy of 'appeasement', which held that the country

---

402 Feiling, quoted in Crozier, 'Chamberlain, (Arthur) Neville (1869-1940)', *Oxford Dictionary of National Biography*

403 Bouverie, *Appeasing Hitler: Chamberlain, Churchill and the Road to War*, p.129

needed to buy time to complete re-armament, and that Hitler's demands could be met in part, avoiding a military conflagration.

Neville's conviction that his judgements were always right, and his lack of care for the sensitivities of others, can rightly be criticised. For example, he sent Lord Halifax, his own foreign policy adviser, to meet with Hitler in November 1937, rather than Anthony Eden, Foreign Secretary, who understandably resented this. Neville certainly ensured his Cabinet and advisers were of similar mind to him, and put in place to execute, not challenge or debate, his policy decisions. By March 1938, he had a 'congenial, subservient and mediocre Government which he personally dominated, usually ignored, and, as some thought, bullied.'[404]

It is interesting to note the subversion of the meaning of the term 'appeasement' as a direct result of the history of the period from 1933 to 1939 and Neville's policy. 'Appeasement' is now a term with negative connotations, meaning negotiating with an unreasonable adversary, in wilful ignorance that the adversary will not behave with good faith. Before the thirties, 'appeasement' meant to conciliate, to listen and work constructively to meet someone's grievances. The Oxford English Dictionary definition was: 'to pacify or placate (someone) by acceding to their demands; to assuage or satisfy (a demand or a feeling)'. In this definition, the atmosphere of the word is positive and could be thought the right thing to do. A similar corruption of meaning has happened with 'collaborator', originally someone with whom to work to achieve a mutually beneficial or shared goal, but now can be used to indicate 'a person who co-operates traitorously with an enemy; a defector'.

Neville is absolutely linked to appeasement as a failed policy, wrong-headed, and verging on the treasonous. Although never declared as a deliberate policy approach, it is crucial to note that in the 1930s, appeasement was seen as legitimate to pursue to avoid another European war. There was very limited criticism from Tory colleagues, apart from Churchill and his small group of supporters, and the Labour Party. In addition to this, the Chiefs of Staff of all branches of the armed forces continually advised Neville that they were not at sufficient strength to engage in armed conflict and repeatedly asked for more time to allow re-armament to complete.

Having said that, Neville's stance developed into preparedness to sacrifice small, weak countries in Europe to appease Hitler's demands for German-speaking people to be returned to the Reich, outside the boundaries set by the Treaty of

---

404 Rhodes James, *The British Revolution: British Politics 1880-1939*, p.587

Versailles, and this is impossible to defend. Great Britain stood aside as Germany occupied and annexed Austria, through the Anschluss, in March 1938, and trampled on Czechoslovakia's sovereignty, without the Czech President, Edvard Beneš, even being present at Munich in September 1938. Neville revealed his dismissive attitude when he reflected: 'How horrible, fantastic, incredible it is that we should be digging trenches and trying on gas-masks here because of a quarrel in a faraway country between people of whom we know nothing.'[405] This indifference was crass and insensitive, and is valid evidence that Neville would go to any length to avoid war, and this judgement is valid.

Although Neville is repeatedly portrayed as supportive of Hitler's aims, this is simply not true, and he had quite an aversion to Germans generally. He wrote that: 'the Germans who are bullies by nature are too conscious of their strength and our weakness and until we are as strong as they are, we shall always be kept in this chronic state of anxiety.'[406] He referred to Hitler himself as 'half mad' and capable of 'mad dog' acts.[407] Despite these misgivings about him, Neville felt that he could develop a personal relationship with Hitler and establish a bond of trust. He was completely and utterly wrong in this judgement, as evidenced by Neville's request for Hitler to sign the Anglo-German Naval Agreement, immediately after the Munich Conference. Hitler signed this in an attempt to 'please the old gentleman',[408] but clearly did not feel bound by it in any way. Given Hitler's recent repeated ignoring of international agreements, Neville's judgement in even asking for such an agreement is questionable, let alone believing that Hitler would stand by its terms.

On his return after Munich, Neville was feted as the returning hero who had secured peace at a time of almost certain war. In this atmosphere, it is perhaps not surprising that Neville felt that he had succeeded, and he declared: 'This is the second time in our history that there has come back from Germany to Downing Street peace with honour. I believe it is peace for our time.'[409]

This is the image and the words that have defined virtually everyone's memory of Neville Chamberlain. It is now forgotten that he retracted them the next week, that the Birmingham Daily Gazette called Neville a hero, stating: 'Birmingham is proud that the peace of Europe when all but lost had been saved by a cool-brained

---

405 Rhodes James, *The British Revolution: British Politics 1880-1939*, p.597
406 Neville, *Neville Chamberlain – A Study in Failure?*, p.92
407 Ibid., p.70
408 Ibid., p.99
409 Rhodes James, *The British Revolution: British Politics 1880-1939*, p.599

and determined Birmingham man.'[410] It is now irrelevant that the Commons voted 344 to 144 to support the Munich Agreement and that subsequently, when visiting Paris and Rome, Neville received rapturous welcomes from people relieved that war had been averted. What really mattered, as events would prove, was that Hitler had not been appeased, only delayed slightly.

After the invasion of Poland forced Neville to declare war on Germany on 3rd September 1939, Neville broadcast to the nation, stating: 'Everything I have worked for, everything that I have hoped for, everything I have believed in during my public life, has crashed into ruins….You can imagine what a bitter blow it is to me that all my long struggle to win peace has failed. Yet I believe that there is nothing more or anything different that I could have done…'[411] This is not the judgement of history, and it is clear that there were opportunities for other actions to be put in place.

Neville Chamberlain remained as Prime Minister for several months, until the Commons debated the disastrous Norway campaign, led poorly by Churchill, which failed completely to make any impact on the German invasion. In the debate, Neville's Liberal Unionist Birmingham colleague, Leo Amery, quoted Oliver Cromwell's chastisement of Parliament three hundred years earlier: 'You have sat here for too long for any good you have been doing. Depart, I say, and let us have done with you. In the name of God, go!'[412] Although he won the vote, there were so many votes against or abstentions, that Neville went to King George VI on 10th May 1940 and resigned.

Neville was retained as Lord President of the Council by the new Prime Minister, Winston Churchill, and Neville himself thought that Churchill had behaved with 'the most unimpeachable loyalty' towards him.[413]

Ill health developed very quickly, and Neville had surgical treatment for bowel cancer before returning to the Commons on 17th September, to a rapturous reception from Conservative MPs, and attending his final Cabinet meeting the next day. Now ailing rapidly, Neville went to Highfield Park, Sussex, his Aunt Lilian's home, and resigned from Cabinet on 27th September. Churchill offered Neville a knighthood, which, like his father, he declined. He apparently remained convinced that his approach had been right until the very end. His fall from grace and adulation clearly troubled him, as he wrote to Baldwin: 'Few men can have

410 Quoted in Ward, *The Chamberlains: Joseph, Austen and Neville 1836-1940*, p.158
411 Ward, *The Chamberlains: Joseph, Austen and Neville 1836-1940*, p.161
412 Wilson, *A Prime Minister on Prime Ministers*, p.235
413 Ward, *The Chamberlains: Joseph, Austen and Neville 1836-1940*, p.164

known such a tremendous reverse in so short a time'[414] and 'I doubt I shall ever visit Brum again.'[415] He was right on both counts.

Neville Chamberlain died on 9th November 1940, aged seventy-one. His ashes were interred in Westminster Abbey on 14th November, next to another former Prime Minister, Andrew Bonar Law. Two days earlier, Churchill offered fulsome praise for Neville in the Commons: 'Whatever else history may or may not say about these terrible, tremendous years, we can be sure that Neville Chamberlain acted with perfect sincerity according to his lights and strove to the utmost of his capacity and authority, which were powerful, to save the world from the awful, devastating struggle in which we are now engaged. This alone will stand him in good stead as far as what is called the verdict of history is concerned.'[416]

Clearly this has not been the case, as Churchill himself ensured by his depiction of Neville in his history of the Second World War. He said: 'Poor Neville, he will come badly out of history. I know, for I shall write the history',[417] and he did. He writes that Neville displayed: 'a narrow, sharp-edged efficiency within the limits of the policy in which he believed. Both as Chancellor..., and as Prime Minister, he kept the tightest and most rigid control upon military expenditure....His all-pervading hope was to go down in history as the great Peace-maker; and for this he was prepared to strive continually in the teeth of facts, and face great risks for himself and his country. Unhappily he ran into tides the force of which he could not measure, and met hurricanes from which he did not flinch, but with which he could not cope.'[418] Churchill proclaimed this a 'sad tale of wrong judgements formed by well-meaning and capable people',[419] and when Chamberlain gave the Polish guarantee: 'Here was decision at last, taken at the worst possible moment and on the least satisfactory ground, which must surely lead to the slaughter of tens of millions of people.'[420] Churchill places full responsibility for delaying the military conflict with Hitler on Neville. This disingenuous assessment cleverly damns Neville, while by implication highlighting his own strength of character and purpose.

---

414 Ward, *The Chamberlains: Joseph, Austen and Neville 1836-1940*, p.165

415 Neville, *Neville Chamberlain – A Study in Failure?*, p.117

416 Wilson, *A Prime Minister on Prime Ministers*, p.238

417 Ward, *The Chamberlains: Joseph, Austen and Neville 1836-1940*, p.107

418 Winston S. Churchill, *The Second World War, Volume I: The Gathering Storm*, (London: 1948), pp.172-3

419 Ibid., pp.270-1

420 Ibid., pp.271-2

The second major influence in how Neville is remembered was the publication while he was still Prime Minister, on 5th July 1940, of 'Guilty Men', by 'Cato', a pseudonym for three journalists, Frank Owen, Peter Howard and Michael Foot. This angrily indicted fifteen politicians, particularly Stanley Baldwin, Ramsay MacDonald and of course Neville Chamberlain, as culpable of bringing Britain to the brink of disaster. This relatively short, highly readable book is excoriating about the failings of government, in what Foot describes in the 1997 Preface as 'the shameful Chamberlain era.'[421] Described as a 'blistering polemic' in the Penguin edition introduction,[422] it details forensically the egregious failings leading to the British Expeditionary Force's near destruction at Dunkirk in June 1940, then fresh in readers' minds. The book, in Foot's words, 'sold like a pornographic classic',[423] selling 50,000 copies in days and 200,000 by the end of 1940. It succeeds by clearly, logically and unequivocally describing facts and especially actions, or failures to act. It had an immediate and lasting effect, and Neville in particular has remained guilty in the public's memory ever since.

Public consciousness and memory seems incapable of remembering more than a single defining legacy of our leaders, so Margaret Thatcher is defined by the Poll Tax debacle, Tony Blair by the Iraq War, Nick Clegg by reneging on his promise to abolish tuition fees, and David Cameron by calling the 2016 referendum on EU membership. Defining Neville by appeasement enacts Shakespeare's dictum that: 'The evil that men do lives after them; the good is oft interred with their bones.'[424]

Historians argue both sides of this case, and it will never be resolved to everyone's satisfaction. Wilson's judgement is clear and succinct: 'It was not only that he was totally inadequate: many are and some get by. What was tragic was that he was totally opinionated, totally certain he was right.'[425] The most recent study of appeasement reflects on Neville's honourable nature, concluding: 'Chamberlain's motivation was never in doubt. His efforts were considerable and determined. But his policy critically misunderstood the nature of the man with whom he was treating and neglected those contingencies which might have contained him or defeated him more quickly. It was, in every sense, a tragedy.'[426]

---

421 'Cato' (Michael Foot, Peter Howard, Frank Owen), *Guilty Men*, (London: 2010), p.vi
422 Ibid., p.xi
423 Ibid., p.vi
424 William Shakespeare, *Julius Caesar*, Act III, Scene ii
425 Wilson, *A Prime Minister on Prime Ministers*, p.215
426 Bouverie, *Appeasing Hitler: Chamberlain, Churchill and the Road to War*, p.421

Unfortunately for Neville, and indeed for us, he did not live long enough either to defend his actions, or to write his own record of history. As we know, it is the winners who write the history.

While Neville was undoubtedly and palpably wrong in his judgement of Hitler, it is important that his social reforming achievements are recognised and weighed in the balance against this very substantial failure. He achieved considerable political success, both in Birmingham and in national government, marked by a number of social reforms, especially in housing, and many legislative changes that resonate in how we live now. As Wilson wrote: 'Chamberlain must go down in history as one of the greatest social reformers in the sphere of housing and local government of his own or any other age.'[427] He quotes Harold Macmillan's judgement that Neville 'proved himself as one of the great reformers – not in words or promises, but in deeds and performance. Those who today only think of Neville Chamberlain in connection with Munich and the tragic years of his premiership, should not, in justice, forget this splendid period of solid achievement.'[428]

These achievements are usually overlooked in the rush to severe judgement. For example, although acknowledging legislative success as Minister of Health,

Neville Chamberlain, oil painting by Sir William Orpen, © Parliamentary Art Collection, WOA 6771 www.parliament.uk/art

Blue plaque at the site of Westbourne (now Edgbaston High School for Girls), in Westbourne Road, Harborne, Birmingham, B15 3TS.

427 Wilson, *A Prime Minister on Prime Ministers*, p.220
428 Ibid., p.220

Bouverie gives only twelve lines to Neville's civic work in Birmingham, as councillor and Mayor, omitting completely the establishment of the CBSO.[429] It seems unreasonable that such tangible successes are ignored, and that there are very few reminders of Neville Chamberlain, the only memorials being a single blue plaque, erected by Birmingham Civic Society at the site of Westbourne, Harborne, and the foundation stone of the Birmingham Municipal Savings Bank in Broad Street. The local church at Heckfield, Hampshire, close to Highfield Park, has a simple plaque which implores: 'Write of me as one that loves his fellow-men.' His actions demonstrated the truth of this. There is an argument for a more substantial memorial to the only Brummie to attain the highest office in the land.

The provision of high quality, low cost housing in Birmingham to meet the needs of the population was one of Neville's political achievements, now overlooked. Another member of the extended Chamberlain family made a substantial contribution to housing provision in the city. This was John Sutton Nettlefold, responsible for the creation of social housing in Harborne, and the father of town planning.

JOHN SUTTON NETTLEFOLD
'The innovative creator of the Moor Pool Estate
and the father of town planning in Britain'

John Sutton Nettlefold was born into a wealthy, politically influential family, and became 'the most important guardian of the Chamberlain tradition',[430] of municipal dynamism, through his service on Birmingham City Council, as head of the Housing Committee. He ensured that legal powers were available to support town planning across the country and is best remembered for his innovative development of the Moor Pool Estate in Harborne.

John Sutton Nettlefold was born in Highbury, London, on 2nd May 1866, to Edward John Nettlefold (born 1826, died 1878), and his wife Frances, née Whyman (born 1835, died 1907). Edward was a screw manufacturer, the business having been established by his own father, also called John Sutton Nettlefold (born 1792, died 1866), with factories in London and at Baskerville Place, Broad Street. The first John Sutton Nettlefold married Martha Chamberlain (born 1794, died 1866), her nephew being Joseph Chamberlain.

---

429 Bouverie, *Appeasing Hitler: Chamberlain, Churchill and the Road to War,* p.124
430 Briggs, quoted in Michael F. James, 'John Sutton Nettlefold, Liberalism and the Early Town Planning Movement', *Journal of Liberal History, vol. 75,* (2012), p.32

In 1854, John Sutton Nettlefold Senior and Joseph's father jointly invested in a new American technique of producing woodscrews and established a factory in Smethwick, named Nettlefold and Chamberlain, that would later become Guest, Keen and Nettlefold (GKN). This would be managed by Edward, his brother Joseph Henry Nettlefold, and Joseph Chamberlain.

John Sutton Nettlefold, the grandson, named in memory of his grandfather who had died three weeks before his birth, was the fourth son and was brought up in the Unitarian faith, attending the non-conformist boarding school at Amersham Hall, Caversham. When his father died in 1878, Nettlefold, aged twelve, came to Birmingham, and, on completing his education, joined the family business, then called Nettlefold & Co., in Broad Street. He managed the company's steelworks at Newport, Monmouthshire for a period, before becoming managing director of Kynoch Limited, in Witton, Birmingham, a munitions, wire and nail manufacturer. This later became Imperial Chemical Industries (ICI), and then Imperial Metal Industries (IMI). Nettlefold's other business interests included being chairman of a forging and stamping company, Thomas Smith's Stampings Ltd, in Aston and Coventry, and a director of Henry Hope and Sons Ltd, in Smethwick, a manufacturer of metal framed buildings, including horticultural buildings, roofing, gearing and ironmongery. They supplied steel and metal windows, including the bronze windows in the Houses of Parliament, installed from 1845 to 1857.

Nettlefold married Margaret Chamberlain (born 1871, died 1949), the eldest daughter of Arthur Chamberlain and Joseph Chamberlain's niece. They married on 14th September 1891, at the Unitarian Church of the Messiah. They had eight children: Evelyn, Annie, John Kenrick, Beatrice, Lois and Valerie survived into adulthood. Sadly Louisa and Robert died in childhood.

With his business ventures being successful, Nettlefold became active in municipal politics, and was elected unopposed on 28th November 1898, as councillor for the Edgbaston-Harborne ward, representing the Liberal Unionists. He was re-elected for Edgbaston-Harborne ward, again unopposed, in November 1900, such was the domination of Liberal Unionism in the city. In November 1903, he defeated an Independent Labour candidate, then stood in further elections as an independent himself, being elected twice more, in November 1906 and November 1909. Nettlefold had not changed his political views, but as treasurer of the Birmingham Liberal Union Association, he had fallen out with his uncle, Joseph Chamberlain, on the issue of use of the BLUA's funds for Joseph's Tariff Reform programme. Joseph's remedy to this vexatious opposition was to replace Nettlefold with his son, Neville.

In 1901, he became the first Chairman of the Housing Committee, created to develop and implement housing policy for the city. The separation of housing from the previous Estates and Health Committee meant there could be a clear and distinctive focus on the formidable problem of overcrowded slum housing, and Nettlefold was keen to exploit these possibilities. He remained Chairman of this committee until leaving his role as a councillor in 1911.

In the second half of the nineteenth century, the population in England had grown dramatically. As Upton indicates, the population almost doubled from 9.2m in 1801 to 17.9m in 1851, and doubled again by 1901, to 36.1m. Of more concern to cities like Birmingham was that, within this large and rapid growth, the proportion living in towns and cities grew from 26% of the total population in 1801 to 72% by 1891. In Birmingham, the population increased from 60,882 in 1801 to 522,204 in 1901. This increase of more than 750% included the effect of extending the city boundaries, but nonetheless, this was a dramatic influx of people, bringing overcrowding in sub-standard accommodation, and concerns over sanitation and high levels of mortality. All these issues demanded action from the city's councillors.

Nettlefold wanted to improve housing conditions for the poor while ensuring that private landlords took seriously their responsibility for maintaining properties to a habitable standard. Landlords often allowed properties to become dilapidated and unfit for human habitation, in expectation of significant compensation from the Council as part of slum clearance schemes. This involved additional cost for ratepayers which Nettlefold wanted to avoid, as would providing houses built by the Council. Favouring holding private landlords to account and encouraging private house building, his view was that: 'municipal housing amounted to charity on the rates.'[431]

From 1902 to 1907, he led the Housing Committee in forcing landlords to repair and maintain 4,000 properties, making them habitable, and encouraging new building by private builders, thereby replacing unfit homes on a one by one basis, at little direct cost to the public purse. While successful, this approach was limited in terms of scale and he became interested in the concepts developing around planning of towns by local authorities, combining the benefits of free enterprise with co-ordinated municipal control. Over three years, he set out his views in the books 'Slum Reform and Town Planning' (1906), followed by 'A Housing Policy' (1907) and 'Practical Housing' (1908).

---

431 James, 'John Sutton Nettlefold, Liberalism and the Early Town Planning Movement', *Journal of Liberal History*, vol. 75, p.33

His own living circumstances were enjoyable and attractive, to say the least. The Nettlefold family lived in Beechenhurst House, 10, Serpentine Road, Selly Oak. In 1903, Joseph Lancaster Bell, a Birmingham architect, was commissioned to build Winterbourne House, in Edgbaston Park Road, in the architectural style of the Arts and Crafts movement. This delightful home included a beautiful garden, developed by Margaret, and they lived there until 1919. The house is now part of the University of Birmingham, and it and the gardens are open to the public. The house contains displays of family furniture, photographs, children's games and mementoes in the upstairs rooms, as well as the lovely and peaceful garden and the tea room, which provide an oasis of peace and quiet in the midst of a busy city.

In August 1905, having become a member of the Garden City Association (founded in 1899) and having studied the German model of town planning, he took colleagues to Germany to see how these concepts were put into practice. They visited Berlin, Cologne, Dusseldorf, Frankfurt, Mannheim, Stuttgart and Ulm, and presented a report on the visit to the Council on 3rd July 1906. James describes this as: 'a document of seminal importance, locally and nationally.'[432] The approach set out involved developing areas on the outskirts of cities, to provide low-density housing amidst community amenities and green spaces, to offer attractive and affordable suburbs in which to live, with good links to the city centre. Through new powers, all undeveloped land within the city could be acquired for development of such estates. These areas would offer light and fresh air to all residents, moving away from back to back houses. This was predicated on the importance of the home, as Nettlefold stated that: 'the home of the individual is the most important factor in the prosperity of the nation, and the strength of the Empire. We can, if we will, arrange wholesome surroundings for every Birmingham adult, and, even more important, give every Birmingham child light and fresh air which is so essential to its healthy development.'[433]

Extension of this thinking into championing the provision of children's playgrounds as a responsibility of local authorities was based on a model from Chicago, and Nettlefold chaired a group dedicated to pursuing these aims, called the Birmingham Playgrounds, Open Space and Playing Fields Society.

By October 1906, he developed this thinking into what he called 'intelligent town planning'. This involved the local council buying land which would then be leased to private builders, on the agreement that they built houses for rent,

---

432 James, 'John Sutton Nettlefold, Liberalism and the Early Town Planning Movement', *Journal of Liberal History*, p.34
433 Ibid., p.34

with front and back gardens, and provided civic amenities, such as community halls, playgrounds, shops, allotments and green spaces. This approach required new legal powers to acquire considerable tracts of land so that whole areas could be redeveloped. In 1907, he put these ideas into practice through developing the Moor Pool Estate in Harborne. Fifty-four acres of land were acquired, and the Harborne Tenants' Association was formed, which continues today.

On 5th November 2010, one hundred years after opening, the Birmingham Civic Society erected a plaque at The Circle on the Moor Pool Estate, which states: 'the estate provided affordable housing in a garden city setting. Local tenants contributed to the planning, financing and management of the estate, and received a dividend from rental income. This co-partnership venture created homes with gardens, allotments, shops, a club building and sports facilities to provide a healthy and spacious community, different from the unplanned, uniform and overcrowded housing estates, which were common in British towns.' 500 houses were built, with an average of 9.25 houses per acre, and this still provides a popular and attractive living environment. As chair of the new Harborne Society, which also continues today, Nettlefold secured re-election to the Council in 1907, but as an independent, given his differences with Liberal Unionists.

Based on this innovative model, Nettlefold became chairman of the planning committee of the Association of Municipal Corporations. In August 1907, he took the case for legislative changes, to give local authorities the powers to control the use and disposal of land for housing within their boundaries, to the Liberal Prime Minister, Sir Henry Campbell-Bannerman. In December 1909, the Housing and Town Planning Act was passed, creating procedures for local authorities to use, but this was more restrictive and complicated than Nettlefold had hoped, and was therefore not used as widely by other cities and towns as it could have been.

Nonetheless, Nettlefold continued his involvement in town planning issues, as chair of the Council's committee for extending Birmingham's boundaries. By 1909, the Local Government Board, set up by government to oversee such changes, supported the proposal, and in May 1911, the Greater Birmingham Act was passed. From November, Birmingham became the second largest city in England, in terms of both land area and population, now 850,000, as it included the former villages of Aston Manor, Erdington, Handsworth, Kings Norton, Northfield and Yardley, extending in all directions from the centre.

Nettlefold was active in other areas and organisations, being a Justice of the Peace for Worcestershire, a magistrate in Birmingham, honorary secretary and chairman of the Women's Hospital, and honorary treasurer of a charity school in Graham Street.

Despite his success in the life of the city, Nettlefold became embittered, believing the 1909 Housing and Town Planning Act to be unnecessarily restraining and restrictive. He set out his very strong opposition in a further book, 'Practical Town Planning' in 1914, described as a 'tirade.'[434] He was by this time creating opposition from the strength of his views, with the Birmingham Daily Post reporting, on 2nd November 1911, his failure to be elected to the new ward of Harborne and Quinton, coming last out of five candidates, and described as 'a party to himself', who had offended friends and colleagues.[435]

In 1919, Nettlefold and his family moved to the Manor House in Bampton, Oxfordshire, and he died on 3rd November 1930, at Barnwood House, in Barnwood, Gloucestershire, a privately run mental hospital. He was sixty-four and was survived by Margaret. As well as the plaque at the Moor Pool Estate, John Sutton Nettlefold is remembered by a blue plaque, also erected by Birmingham Civic Society in 2010, at Winterbourne House and Garden, in Edgbaston Park Road, Edgbaston. The plaque is to the right of the main entrance.

John Sutton Nettlefold by unknown photographer, c.1886-1896, from Winterbourne House and Garden, University of Birmingham

Blue plaque at Winterbourne House and Garden, University of Birmingham, 58, Edgbaston Park Road, Edgbaston, Birmingham, B15 2RT

434 Cherry, quoted in Michael F. James, 'Nettlefold, John Sutton (1866-1930)', *Oxford Dictionary of National Biography*, (Oxford: 2011, updated 2013)

435 Birmingham Daily Post, 2nd November 1911, quoted in James, 'Nettlefold, John Sutton (1866-1930)', *Oxford Dictionary of National Biography*

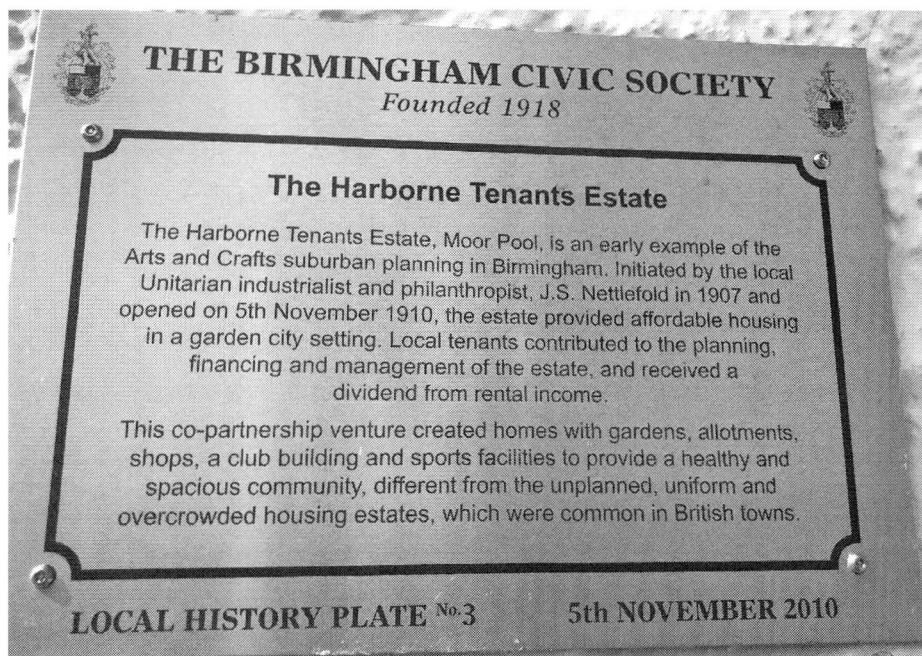

History Plate No. 3 at 26, The Circle, Moor Pool Estate, Harborne, Birmingham, B17 9DY

The provision of health care remained disjointed and partial until the creation of the NHS in July 1948. Before then, individuals could still make a major difference to everyone's life chances, as we shall see through the lives of four Birmingham doctors.

Whether born in Birmingham or 'adopting' the city, their dedication and expertise in developing new services, or discovering new diagnostic and treatment techniques, have delivered life-saving care to millions of people in Great Britain and throughout the world. They were pioneers whose work and legacies were incorporated into how the NHS operated.

HARRY GILBERT BARLING

*'The accomplished surgeon who planned and opened the expanded
General Hospital and ran the Birmingham Hospital Saturday Fund
and the Birmingham Civic Society'*

Harry Gilbert Barling was born at Blythe Court, on 30th April 1855, in Newnham on Severn, Gloucestershire. The sixth child of William Barling, a farmer and veterinary surgeon and his wife, Eliza, née Sharpe, Harry had four brothers and a sister. After his early education at boarding school in Weston, near Bath, he was apprenticed to a Manchester chemist. Although not supported by his employer in his apprenticeship, and used mainly as an errand-boy, he qualified as a chemist, passing the matriculation examination of the University of London.

He entered St. Bartholomew's Hospital, London in 1874, aged nineteen, and, as his family could not support him financially, worked part-time to fund his studies. He coached younger students, including a Birmingham surgeon's son. He was admitted to the Royal College of Surgeons in 1879. At St. Bartholomew's, Barling was an excellent student, winning scholarships (in anatomy and physiology, and the Brackenbury scholarship in surgery), and was awarded the Kirkes gold medal in clinical medicine. He graduated M.B. Lond. in 1879, and using his contact in Birmingham, was appointed resident pathologist at Birmingham General Hospital.

In 1881, Barling became a resident surgical officer. He was made a Fellow of the Royal College of Surgeons, and served on its Council from 1904 to 1912. In 1883, he was awarded his B.S. degree from St. Bartholomew's and Birmingham. His career progressed and he was promoted steadily at Birmingham General, holding successive posts of assistant surgeon, from 1885, and full surgeon from 1891.

He married Katharine Jaffray on 21st October 1885, daughter of an Edgbaston bank manager, and they lived at Blythe Court, Norfolk Road, Edgbaston. They had two daughters, and Katharine died in 1920, after which Barling moved to 6, Manor Road, Edgbaston, and lived there for the rest of his life.

Barling's career is notable for the many surgical and administrative posts he held. An extremely able and versatile individual, he contributed many articles and papers to clinical journals. The clinical areas covered by these reflect his broad interests as a general surgeon. He was committed to improving clinical care and services in the General Hospital, and when assistant surgeon, developed a hospital rebuilding scheme, with the new General Hospital based on this, opening in 1897. He developed a deep and abiding love and respect for Birmingham itself, as his later achievements proved.

He became chief surgeon in Birmingham, and was appointed, on retirement from active clinical practice, as Consulting Surgeon in 1915, and later, from 1924 to 1927, as President of the Hospital Board.

As with many clinicians, the outbreak of the First World War meant that Barling, aged fifty-nine, joined the Royal Army Medical Corps, being called up in August 1914, having been a member of the territorial reserve since 1908. He served as Consulting Surgeon to the Southern Command, and was then sent to the Western Front in October 1916, staying there until August 1917. He was made a Commander of the Order of the Bath (CB) for his service in 1917, and then a Commander of the Order of the British Empire (CBE) in 1919. Further recognition came on 10th September 1919, when he was made a Baronet by King George V.

Barling always demonstrated considerable commitment to medical teaching, and was Demonstrator of Anatomy at Queen's College in 1885, before becoming a professor, initially in pathology (from 1886) and then in surgery (from 1893), at the Birmingham Medical School. He was Dean of the Faculty of Medicine from 1904 before being appointed as Vice Chancellor of the University of Birmingham from 1913 and he played an instrumental role in the development of the University, as Pro-Chancellor from 1927 to 1932 (as the post of Vice Chancellor was then named). He founded research departments for mental illness and for cancer and demonstrated excellent business sense, expanding staff and facilities considerably while steering the university to high levels of income, with no debt.

He participated widely in medical circles, representing the University of Birmingham on the General Medical Council from 1917 to 1927, and had a long association with the British Medical Association (BMA), having joined in 1880 and served for two years on the Parliamentary Bill Committee. In 1890, the BMA met in Birmingham and Barling was honorary secretary of the Surgery Section. By 1901, he was Vice-President of this Section when the BMA met in Cheltenham. From 1904, he was Chairman of the Central Division and President of the Birmingham Branch in 1911. He delivered the surgical address, on the management of malignant disease, at the BMA London meeting in 1910.

His involvement in the life of Birmingham was equally wide-ranging, demonstrating his commitment to people being able to access the health care they needed. He was involved in discussions to merge the Queen's Hospital with the General, to form the Birmingham United Hospital, the genesis of today's Queen Elizabeth Hospital. He chaired a committee which established the Hospitals Centre Scheme, an ambitious project to build a new hospital teaching centre and medical school adjacent to the University of Birmingham. Although his active involvement ended through ill health in 1926, he saw these facilities open before his death. He was recognised for his broad, longstanding contributions to surgery, medical teaching, and health services development by an honorary Doctorate of Laws (LLD) awarded by the University in 1937.

He was Chairman of the Birmingham Hospital Saturday Fund for many years and in 1923, he helped to establish, and became the first Chairman of, the British Empire Cancer Campaign. This organisation is now known as Cancer Research UK. His pride in all things Birmingham was evident in the huge contribution he made to the Birmingham Civic Society (BCS), as Vice President and Chairman of its Council, from its creation in 1918, until his death. In 1936, in recognition of this, and his substantial public service in Birmingham, he was awarded the BCS Gold Medal, one of a small number of recipients.

Though retired from clinical practice and administrative work, he supported and guided the BCS for many years, chairing his final meeting of its Executive Council on 19th March 1940. He died from heart failure on 27th April 1940, three days before his eighty-fifth birthday, in his garden at 6, Manor Road, Edgbaston. His funeral was held on 1st May 1940, at the nearby St. Augustine's Church, where he was a churchwarden, and it was attended by the Lord Mayor as a mark of the esteem in which he was held.

His obituary in the British Medical Journal (BMJ), dated 4th May 1940, recorded that governors at the Birmingham United Hospital regarded him as: 'an inspiring teacher, a great administrator and a devoted servant of the hospital.' It notes that the Prime Minister, Neville Chamberlain, Barling's MP, wrote to the governing body 'declaring [his] admiration for Sir Gilbert Barling's long record of public service in Birmingham.' The BMJ summarises his contribution in the address given when Barling retired from professional practice and administration, at the unveiling of a portrait in his honour which hung in the General Hospital's Board Room. This 'placed on record Mr. Barling's exceptional abilities as a surgeon and the invaluable work he had done in the conception, planning and equipment of the hospital and in the promotion of it as a medical, surgical, and nursing school.'[436]

Photograph of Sir Harry Gilbert Barling, unknown date, by Lafayette Ltd and from Wellcome Images

Blue plaque at 6, Manor Road, Edgbaston, Birmingham, B16 9ND

436 'Obituary', *British Medical Journal*, 4th May 1940, p.748

There is another portrait of Barling in his Pro-Chancellor's robes, which hangs in the Great Hall of the University of Birmingham. The Medical School has a Barling Chair of Surgery in his honour.

Harry Gilbert Barling is remembered through the organisations with which he was associated and those he led with such distinction for many years, in the fields of medicine, administration and in the provision of services to those less fortunate. The church to which he belonged and supported for many years erected a funerary hatchment in his memory in 2018. This comprises his coat of arms and includes his motto: 'Je Sers, Je Servirai', which translates, appropriately, as 'I serve, I will serve.' How very apt.

JOHN HALL-EDWARDS

'The dedicated soldier and doctor who pioneered the
use of X-rays in Great Britain, to the benefit of many,
but at great personal cost to himself'

Major Dr John Hall-Edwards was a pioneer in radiography and its application to improve diagnosis and treatment in health care. He was dedicated in his medical and military careers, and determined to improve care and outcomes, unaware initially of the disastrous impact it would have on him personally. Even when this became clear to him, as he contracted the cancer that would, after thirty years, kill him, he continued to work and contribute to civil society and public health improvement.

John Francis Hall-Edwards was born on 19th December 1858 in Moseley Road, Kings Norton, the son of Dr John Edwards. His father was a druggist who qualified medically and became a Member of the Royal College of Surgeons, practising in Sparkbrook. John Senior married Fanny Dixon, née Hall. For the first forty years of his life, John Junior was known as John Edwards, like his father.

After attending King Edward VI Grammar School, Hall-Edwards was apprenticed to Professor Richard Hill Norris, Professor of Physiology at the Medical School at Queen's College. He was Assistant Demonstrator in practical histology from 1880 to 1882, graduating in 1885, achieving the Licentiate of the Royal College of Surgeons in Edinburgh, and began working as a general practitioner in Woodstock Road, Moseley. Hall-Edwards was an active member of the Midland Photographic Club, its president from 1891 to 1893, and gave an address to the London Camera Club in 1895, when he became a Member of the Royal Photographic Society. Elected Honorary Fellow on 3rd July 1911, he won many prizes for his photography throughout his life.

Hall-Edwards married Constance Marie di Pazzi Clutton Blair Salt (born 1866), daughter of a Birmingham art dealer, on 14th February 1893, at Aston Registry Office. They had one daughter, Violet Primrose Bell, who was adopted.

Professor Hill Norris invented the first dry plate used in photography, and influenced Hall-Edwards, who combined his interest in photography with his medical knowledge. Initially he used photography through microscopes, and in experiments in the application of electricity in surgical procedures. Wilhelm Roentgen discovered 'a new form of ray', X-rays, on 8th November 1895.[437] On 11th January 1896, Hall-Edwards became the first UK physician to use X-rays for clinical purposes in radiographing an associate's hand, revealing a sterilised needle under the skin. On 14th February, he took the first X-ray picture used to direct a surgical operation. His other 'firsts' included a demonstration of X-rays on Hodge Hill Common on 4th March 1896, and X-raying a human spine.

X-rays could be used for many purposes and he pursued their application in health care, from his private practice in Newhall Street. Having sold his general practice, he undertook X-rays for Birmingham hospitals, helping to treat lupus, ringworm and other skin diseases. He pursued uses of radiography in other fields, including industry, such as detecting flaws in metals. An image from an 1897 advertisement for the Non-Collapsible Tyre Company, in Ryland Street, Birmingham, shows an X-ray of a tyre with various sharp objects inserted without it deflating. The image's authenticity is attested by Hall-Edwards's signature.

At the turn of the century, he began using his hyphenated surname. Hall-Edwards's reputation as a leading exponent of this new technology led to his appointment as the first Surgeon Radiographer (as the specialty of Radiology did not yet exist) at Birmingham General Hospital. This included leading X-ray departments in other hospitals (Royal Orthopaedic and Spinal Hospital, Birmingham Dental Hospital, Birmingham and Midland Eye Hospital), and being Consulting Radiographer to the Guest Hospital, Dudley. Throughout his career, he regularly submitted articles on radiation, and later cancer, to medical journals and publications.

Medical practitioners were required to support the British Empire's wars, and in February 1900, Hall-Edwards joined the 1st Volunteer Warwickshire Regiment, becoming the first military surgeon radiographer during the Boer War (1899 to 1902). He was based in Deelfontein and Pretoria, South Africa

---

437 J. Patuzzi, S. Lee, M. Crean, A. Thomas, and U. Busch, (Eds.), *The Story of Radiology*, European Society of Radiology, Vol. 2, (Vienna: 2013), p.8

for fourteen months. X-ray equipment was provided in all military hospitals for the first time, and the Imperial Yeomanry Hospital in Deelfontein, where Hall-Edwards was Chief Radiologist from March 1900, was the largest in South Africa, staffed by thirty doctors, sixty nurses and capable of treating 1,100 patients. Water, electricity and sewage services were installed, as well as a steam laundry, X-ray department, and operating theatre. Hall-Edwards needed to improvise to ensure a reliable source of power for the X-ray machines. Having unsuccessfully tried bicycle-generated power, and re-charging accumulators in Cape Town or Kimberley, he acquired a second-hand oil engine to provide the electric power required. This enabled him to X-ray 280 patients, often involving multiple images per patient, during his stay. He wrote commentaries on the war to the Birmingham Daily Post, including descriptions of the treatment of horses during the conflict. As recognition of his service, he was awarded the Queen's Medal, with four clasps.

Returning to Birmingham, he resumed his previous position. As well as running his practice in Newhall Street, he edited the journal 'The Archives of Roentgen Rays' from 1904 to 1905 and was elected first president of the British Electro-Therapeutic Society in 1906. His dedicated pursuit of developing further uses of radiation had an extremely unfortunate personal consequence for Hall-Edwards. Through considerable exposure to radiation in experimentation and research, and in treating patients, in 1896 he contracted cancer in his hands, then called X-ray dermatitis.

In a lecture to the British Medical Association in 1904, he explained his condition, as a means of calling for appropriate protection for practitioners, and continued this campaign for the rest of his life. The cancer was extremely debilitating and painful, as he explained in a remarkably frank letter to the British Medical Journal on 19th September 1906. Describing the fifty to sixty warts on the back of each hand, 'despite all methods of protection', he stated: 'I have not experienced a moment's freedom from pain for more than two years, and at times the pain is so severe that I am rendered absolutely incapable of work, either mental or otherwise. In the cold weather I am unable to dress myself, and the pain experienced cannot be expressed in words.'

Relating how drugs and lotions failed to give anything but minimal relief from his symptoms, his medical training comes to the fore, as he dispassionately explains that the 'excruciating, ever-present pain' seems to be from irritation of cutaneous nerves, and is 'neuralgic in character.' He states that he has 'given up all hope' of finding relief, and ends by asking for suggestions from readers, and pleading for 'all those engaged in x-ray work to protect themselves before it is too late.'[438]

By 1908, his pain had become so considerable and the disease had progressed so far that, despite his use of opium to alleviate his suffering, his left arm was amputated to the elbow, along with four fingers on his right hand at a later date, leaving only his thumb. His left hand has been retained by the University of Birmingham Chamberlain Museum of Pathology to assist in the teaching of medical students on the effects of unprotected radiation. To help with his disability, local colleagues raised funds, and he was granted an annual civil service pension, by King Edward VII, of £120 in 1908.

Despite this disability, Hall-Edwards continued to work, and was elected a Fellow of the Royal Society of Edinburgh in 1911. When the First World War broke out, he joined the Royal Army Medical Corps working as a medical examiner at the Birmingham recruitment station, and appearing on platforms at public meetings to recruit troops and raise funds for the war effort. He was promoted to Major and assigned the post of Senior Medical Officer at the Military Command Depot, Sutton Coldfield. As Surgeon Radiographer, he took charge of the X-ray departments at the First Southern General Hospital, including Hollymoor, Monyhull and Rubery Military Hospitals.

He continued his private practice, combined with his appointment at the General Hospital, and designed steel gauntlets and lead aprons to protect practitioners. Cambridge University conferred the Diploma of Radiological Medicine in 1920, and two years later, Hall-Edwards became the first doctor in civilian life to be awarded the Carnegie Hero Fund Trust UK medallion, including an annuity of £100. This fund, established in Scotland in 1866, continues, with the objective to: 'recognise civilian heroism and give financial assistance, where necessary, to people who have been injured or to the dependants of people who have been killed in attempting to save another human life in peaceful pursuits.'[439]

After the war, he was elected, as a Unionist, to Birmingham City Council, representing the Rotton Park ward from December 1920 to 1925, and was re-elected in 1922. He served on the Public Health, Museum and Art Galleries, and Public Libraries Committees, and on the Midland Institute Committee, reflecting all his interests. In 1924, he published an article in The Hospital and Health Review titled 'The Problem of Cancer: A Plea for Immediate Action'. This

438 John Hall-Edwards, 'Treatment of Chronic X-Ray Dermatitis', *British Medical Journal*, 19th September 1906, p.806

439 *Andrew Carnegie Hero Fund Trust*, no date

entreated the medical profession to support a comprehensive public education and information campaign on the causes and early symptoms of cancer. Inconceivably today, many doctors then argued that such information campaigns would promote general alarm among the public, and eschewed the benefits of seeking early treatment of symptoms, as advocated by Hall-Edwards. As he stated: 'Cancer is largely a disease of ignorance, and the only cure for ignorance is the provision of trustworthy information.' He asserted forcefully that: 'Public apathy with regard to cancer is largely due to the fact that in the early stages of the disease there is frequently little or no pain. This apathy can only be combated by the public being urged to seek medical advice when – in certain forms of the disease – premonitory symptoms present themselves, and drawing attention to the fact that by certain precautions the inception of the disease can be prevented.'[440] This call to provide protection and seek early treatment has considerable resonance today. In 1926, he published 'Cancer: its control and prevention', reiterating the need to offer medical professionals protection against the damaging effects of X-rays.

Despite his disabilities, Hall-Edwards was described as 'thoroughly companionable',[441] throughout his life and pursued many hobbies zestfully. These included, incredibly, landscape painting, using his remaining right thumb and an artificial finger. He maintained his interest in photography, and nineteen lantern slides produced by him are in Birmingham City Archives. He doubted the infamous Cottingley 'fairy photographs', held to be real by many prominent people, including Sir Arthur Conan Doyle, but which proved to be fake.

His wife died in 1923, and he was then cared for by his housekeeper and nurse at home. Having been an active contributor for over twenty-five years, the British Medical Association elected him an honorary member, one of only twelve people to have been given this prestigious honour. He died of his cancer, described as 'X-ray dermatitis 24 years and chronic nephritis 2 years' on his death certificate, on 15th August 1926, aged sixty-seven, at his home at 112, Gough Road, Edgbaston. Following a memorial service at St. Philip's Cathedral, he was cremated at Perry Barr Crematorium. He was survived by his daughter, Violet Primrose.

He is remembered by the inclusion of his name on the Monument to the X-ray and Radium Martyrs of All Nations. This listed 169 people when unveiled on 4th April 1936 in Hamburg, Germany, and now lists 359. Locally, in November 2016, to mark the 120th anniversary of the first demonstration of X-rays in Birmingham,

440 John Hall-Edwards, 'The Problem of Cancer: A Plea for Immediate Action', *The Hospital and Health Review*, October 1924, p.301
441 Birmingham City Council, *Major John Hall-Edwards*, archived 28th September 2012

Hippodrome Creative commissioned a new innovative digital/dance film for World Radiography Day and the International Day of Radiology. This can be seen on YouTube.

In the summer of 2017, Hall-Edwards inspired 'X-ray Ed', one of 100 bear sculptures in Birmingham and surrounding areas, as part of The Big Sleuth public art trail in aid of the Birmingham Children's Hospital Charity, which raised £250,000. X-ray Ed, a sun bear, stood 1.65m high and weighed twenty kilograms. Given his disposition, it is tempting to believe that Hall-Edwards would have been amused and gratified to see the bear's bone structure shown as in an X-ray, as well as its stomach contents (bees,

Portrait of Major Dr John Hall-Edwards, by Arthur Trevethin Nowell, date unknown, showing his damaged hand. Reproduced by kind permission of Art Ware Fine Art, http://www.artwarefineart.com/

honey, figs, nuts and small lizards, of course). A blue plaque was erected by Birmingham Civic Society in 1987, at Birmingham Children's Hospital, on the wall facing Steelhouse Lane to the right of the main entrance.

Advertisement for Midland Tyre Non Collapsible Tyre Company Ltd, 1897. Reproduced by kind permission of Princeton University Art Museum, New Jersey, USA

Blue plaque at Birmingham Children's Hospital, Steelhouse Lane, Birmingham, B4 6SE

Hall-Edwards' acute suffering and terrible experience prompted effective protection for patients and staff involved in radiography to be put in place for the first time. Truly, a remarkable man, pioneer, and humanitarian. The motto of the Andrew Carnegie Hero Fund Trust seems apposite: 'The false heroes of barbarous man are those who can only boast of the destruction of their fellows. The true heroes of civilisation are those alone who save or greatly serve them.'[442] John Hall-Edwards deserves to be remembered as a true hero of civilisation, and of Birmingham.

NAUGHTON DUNN
'The Scottish surgeon who developed revolutionary orthopaedic operations, particularly on the foot, and helped to establish this field as a separate specialty, as well as being an inspirational clinical teacher'

Naughton Dunn was born at 5, Queen's Road, Aberdeen on 22nd November 1884, the youngest of eight, five daughters and three sons. His father was a successful businessman, owning shoe and boot shops throughout Scotland who married his assistant, Jessie MacNaughton, a crofter's daughter from Milton Eonan, Glenlyon, west of Perth.

Naughton Dunn was christened Peter MacNaughton Dunn, but at school aged five, he gave his name as Naughton Dunn, to avoid being associated with the fairies in the recently published 'Peter Pan' by J.M. Barrie. He did not appear to aspire to academic excellence and his sister Meg said that 'he didn't tire himself out on matters that didn't interest him', taking this as a 'sign of intelligence.'[443] After preparatory school, he attended the city's grammar school.

His father died in 1900, and two elder brothers joined the family business. Dunn entered the University of Aberdeen, achieving a Master of Arts degree. He joined the Scottish Horse, the battalion having returned from the Boer War. He 'unexpectedly' decided to train as a doctor, and graduated in Medicine in 1909 aged twenty-five. His first post, senior house surgeon, was at Scarborough Hospital, Yorkshire and he was 'conscientious, hard-working' and with 'an original mind.'[444]

---

442 *Andrew Carnegie Hero Fund Trust*

443 Peter M. Dunn, (1986), 'Naughton Dunn, Orthopaedic Surgeon, His Life and Times, 1884-1939', transcript of the first Naughton Dunn Memorial Lecture to the British Orthopaedic Association, Southampton, 17th April 1986, p.1

444 Ibid., p.2

He became known to Sir Robert Jones, an eminent Orthopaedic Surgeon, at the Royal Southern Hospital, Liverpool, through the latter's visits to Scarborough. In 1910, Dunn became House Surgeon to Sir Robert, moving to Liverpool. He visited Baschurch Hospital, Shropshire with Sir Robert, who was appointed as first surgeon there in 1904. From 1910 to 1913, Dunn developed his interest in Orthopaedics and in addition to his hospital post, he worked as private assistant to Sir Robert in his famous Nelson Street practice in Liverpool, and as Assistant Demonstrator of Anatomy at the University of Liverpool. His working relationship with Sir Robert became a professional and personal friendship that lasted the rest of his mentor's life. In 1912, Dunn published his first papers in the British Medical Journal, on spasmodic club-foot and flat feet. He was ship's surgeon on RMS Southwark, to work his passage from Liverpool to Quebec, allowing him to visit orthopaedic surgery schools in North America.

In October 1913, at the age of twenty-nine, Dunn was recommended by Sir Robert to the Birmingham Cripples' Union and was appointed their surgeon, based at The Woodlands, Northfield (given by the chocolate manufacturer and philanthropist, Richard Cadbury, to the Crippled Children's Union in 1907). He established consulting rooms at his home, 3, Calthorpe Road, Edgbaston. He was unsuccessful in his application to be a part-time radiologist at the Queen's Hospital.

When war broke out in 1914, Dunn's career was interrupted, as his orthopaedic skills were obviously required to treat injured soldiers. Enlisting in June 1915, he served in the Royal Army Medical Corps in the eastern Mediterranean. His brother Bertie had joined up, and fought and died at Arras in 1917 with the Gordon Highlanders. Dunn was appointed Medical Officer to the Mediterranean Expeditionary Force, on Lemnos in the Aegean Sea, and survived Gallipoli, but contracted severe hepatitis and typhoid, and he was sent home.

Sir (now Colonel) Robert Jones was promoted to Brigadier and appointed as head of the Military Orthopaedic Department, and he enlisted Dunn in March 1916 to develop an orthopaedic centre, providing preventive and corrective surgery, at Shepherd's Bush Military Orthopaedic Hospital (now Hammersmith Hospital), London. Dunn published several papers on trauma surgery. At the end of 1917, Sir Robert transferred Dunn to Birmingham to take charge of a military orthopaedic centre, covering all military hospital care in the area.

From January 1918, Dunn was based at the 800-bedded Highbury Hospital (previously Highbury Hall), until he was demobbed in March 1920. At this hospital, and at Hollymoor Hospital (the second Birmingham War Hospital, a specialist orthopaedic hospital) in Rubery, and at the Uffculme Centre in Kings

Heath, Dunn developed an approach to rehabilitation of wounded soldiers through occupational therapy. This involved personalised programmes of care for those disabled permanently, or temporarily, by gunshot or shrapnel wounds to limbs. In 1919, he published details of an operation (the triple arthrodesis) for stabilisation of the paralysed foot, which is still known by his name. On 3rd September 1918, he married Ethel Jackson, a theatre and plaster room Voluntary Aid Detachment (VAD) nurse at Highbury Hospital. Ethel was twenty-one and daughter of a councillor and businessman in Birmingham. They had four children, Jean (born 1921), Stella (born 1923), Beryl and Peter. The family moved from Henley-in-Arden to Metchley Abbey in 1925. All the children were involved in health care: Jean was a doctor, Stella a nurse, Beryl a physiotherapist (for the Royal Ballet), and Peter became a perinatal paediatrician.

In peacetime, Dunn continued at the Birmingham Cripples' Union and held an appointment at Oswestry Hospital that became the Robert Jones and Agnes Hunt Orthopaedic Hospital, as well as resuming working at Baschurch Surgical Home. He became the senior Surgeon in Oswestry after Sir Robert's retirement. He set up and supported the Warwickshire Orthopaedic Hospital, St. Gerrard's, Coleshill, and helped a friend establish the orthopaedic department at St. Thomas's Hospital, London. As his consulting practice grew, he became a medical leader, attracting the attention of young doctors and teaching, in his post of Lecturer in Orthopaedic Surgery, University of Birmingham, from 1926.

In Birmingham, he worked assiduously to improve coherent orthopaedic provision, leading to the merger of several organisations, including the Crippled Children's Union and the Royal Orthopaedic and Spinal Hospital at The Woodlands. In 1925, King George V approved the name of 'The Royal Cripples' Hospital'. Within the NHS from 1948, it was re-named the Royal Orthopaedic Hospital, the name it retains. He held honorary appointments at several organisations, including Corbett Hospital, Stourbridge, Hartshill Cripples' Hospital, Stoke-on-Trent, Birmingham Education Authority, Derbyshire County Council, and the Ministry of Pensions in the Midlands.

One of the leading orthopaedic surgeons in the country, Dunn was a founding member of the British Orthopaedic Association (BOA) in 1917 and sat for several years on its executive committee. He was President of the Orthopaedic Section of the Royal Society of Medicine in 1928, his presidential address being on 'The Surgery of Muscle and Tendon in Relation to Infantile Paralysis'. He actively corresponded with foreign orthopaedic associations, in the US, France and Australia. He received honorary membership of the American Orthopaedic Association in Chicago in 1934.

He was particularly pleased by the award of an honorary Doctorate of Laws to him by his alma mater, the University of Aberdeen, in 1937. He became President of the BOA in 1938 until his untimely death in 1939.

His obituary in the British Medical Journal (BMJ) noted that: 'During the years which followed the last [First World] war he maintained a steady output of contributions to surgical literature on practical and clinical aspects of orthopaedic surgery.'[445] Known internationally for work on the operative treatment of paralytic deformities of the foot, he developed a method for fusing paralysed feet which was used throughout the world. He worked very hard, as an operating list of 1932 at the Shropshire Orthopaedic Hospital attests, with sixteen operations.

Described as being: 'inherently sound, sane and thoughtful, and characterised by an underlying care for the patient', he was a 'singularly attractive personality', with his 'white hair, rugged countenance and twinkling smile' making him stand out in meetings.[446]

He died at the early age of fifty-four after 'a distressing illness', on 18th November 1939, in Dolgelly (Dolgellau), Snowdonia, North Wales. His ashes were scattered around three Scots Pines at the family home in Milton Eonan, Glenlyon.

Photograph of Naughton Dunn, date unknown. Reproduced by kind permission of the Royal Orthopaedic Hospital, Northfield, Birmingham, B31 2AP

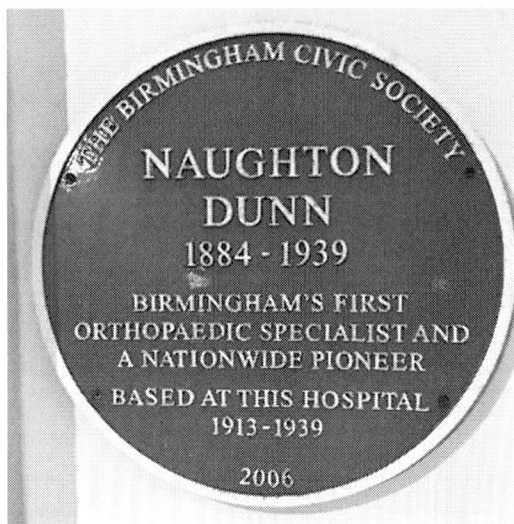

Blue plaque at Royal Orthopaedic Hospital, The Woodlands, Bristol Road South, Northfield, Birmingham, B31 2AP

445 'Obituary', *British Medical Journal*, 2nd December 1939
446 Ibid.

He is remembered for the quality of his teaching to younger colleagues, and his enduring support for them, earning him the affectionate nickname of 'N.D'. Dame Agnes Hunt wrote his BMJ obituary that: 'perhaps the greatest work he did for crippled humanity was by passing on Robert Jones's teaching to younger orthopaedic surgeons, training them in the work he loved so well.'[447]

Naughton Dunn is remembered by the annual Naughton Dunn Memorial Lecture, given at meetings of the British Orthopaedic Association, and by the Naughton Dunn Club, a regional orthopaedic surgical trainees' meeting held twice a year, including a Best Paper prize for research. The first Naughton Dunn Memorial Lecture was given in Southampton on 17th April 1986 by his son Peter, and constituted a biographical account of his father's life and times. A blue plaque was erected by Birmingham Civic Society in 2006, to the right of the entrance to the Management Offices, Royal Orthopaedic Hospital, The Woodlands, Northfield.

HILDA LLOYD

'The creator of the Obstetric Flying Squads in Birmingham,
and the first female President of any Royal Medical College'

Hilda Nora Shufflebotham was born on 11th August 1891 at 170, Moseley Road, Balsall Heath, to a middle class family. Her father, John, was a master grocer and owned several shops in the area. Her mother was Emma Amelia Jenkins. The younger of two daughters, Hilda attended King Edward VI High School for Girls, Edgbaston, as a foundation scholar from 1902 to 1910. Attending the University of Birmingham, she graduated in 1914 with a BSc degree in Pure Science, before studying Medicine, qualifying MB, ChB in 1916.

The First World War broke down societal barriers and afforded many women opportunities they might not otherwise have been able to access. At the time, 40% of medical students were women. Hilda undertook house officer posts in London and was awarded the Membership and Licentiate of the Royal College of Physicians in 1918, before returning to Birmingham as a resident in Obstetrics and Gynaecology at Birmingham Maternity Hospital, and at the Birmingham and Midland Hospital for Women. She became a Fellow of the Royal College of Surgeons in 1920 and was later appointed as a Consultant at these hospitals.

On 27th December 1930, Hilda married Bertram Arthur Lloyd, a pathologist who became Professor of Forensic Medicine at the University of Birmingham in

---

447 'Obituary', *British Medical Journal,* 2nd December 1939

1932, and they were extremely happy. They had no children, and sadly Bertram died in 1948 after a long illness. Hilda's own career had progressed, as she became a lecturer at the University in 1934, a Fellow of the Royal College of Obstetricians and Gynaecologists (RCOG) in 1936, and a professor in 1944. As medical education became more specialty-specific, Lloyd was appointed to the Chair of Obstetrics and Gynaecology in 1946, one of the most eminent doctors in her field.

Lloyd was interested in issues faced by poor women in the city, and took direct action to reduce the impact of poverty on pregnant women, including treating the effects of sexually transmitted diseases and illegal abortions. This led her to establish 'flying squads' in Birmingham in 1936. These were initially established in Lanarkshire and Newcastle-upon-Tyne, and were beginning to be developed in several areas. Lloyd gave a detailed proposal in a note entitled 'Emergency Obstetric Service (Flying Squad)'. This articulated the need for flying squads to be differently structured according to the needs of each area, and to be adequately staffed, equipped and resourced. They were to be used when moving the pregnant woman to hospital might result in greater harm or death, compared to treating her at home. Treatment included: 'not only obstetric aid, but also means of resuscitation…by means of blood transfusion.' In cities like Birmingham, it would often be better for the patient to be stabilised by the Flying Squad and transferred to hospital for the remainder of her care. However, it was the case that the Flying Squad 'must be prepared to meet the emergency to the full in the patient's home.'[448] Statistics showed this approach saved many lives.

Lloyd outlined how the Flying Squad operated, detailing the equipment involved: one holdall containing blankets and hot water bottles, three leather bags with all necessary equipment, two sterile drums holding instruments, two insulated boxes with blood supplies and an oxygen cylinder. These were transported by ambulance, with one dedicated vehicle always ready to respond. There were two sets of equipment available so that two emergencies could be answered simultaneously. The staffing of the service was set out. The Obstetrician, from the hospital on call rota, received the emergency call from the patient's doctor, community midwives, ambulance personnel or the police. He or she assembled the team to go to the patient, within a target arrival time of thirty minutes. They were required to ensure the general maintenance of the equipment, and had to be skilled in resuscitation as well as obstetrics. The other members of the team were a nurse, from a rota of staff midwives on call 24/7, who ensured the

---

448 Hilda Lloyd, 'Emergency Obstetric Service (Flying Squad)', (1936), p.1

equipment was in order after returning from the call out, ready for the next one, and a medical student, to provide practical help and assistance. Providing blood transfusions outside hospital was new, owing to recent advances, and constituted an essential component in the success of the Flying Squad: 'for without it obstetric skill would be considerably hampered.' This was particularly important when treating haemorrhages after illegal back street or self-induced abortions, which were common, as the Abortion Act was not passed until 1968. Lloyd was more than a theoretical pioneer, undertaking the first shift as the Flying Squad began operating. In a human touch, Lloyd indicated that: 'we always include a tin of biscuits for the personnel as frequently their attendance is required for long periods.'[449]

Lloyd was active in health care planning in Birmingham, serving on committees for blood transfusion, cancer, radiotherapy, and planning, as well as on the hospital governing body. Regionally, she served on the NHS Maternity Committee and the Royal College of Nursing Advisory Board. She was the first president of The Birmingham and Midland Obstetrical and Gynaecological Society, founded in March 1949.

Having served as council member and examiner, she was elected the first female President of the RCOG in 1949, and became the first ever female President of a Royal Medical College. Her stature and performance in the role was such that she was re-elected unanimously twice. Lloyd was successful in developing a new journal, and leading successful opposition to the separation of obstetrics and gynaecology into two distinct specialties in 1952. She achieved the creation of Midwifery Committees in every NHS region to co-ordinate, standardise, and develop services. Through her efforts, she ensured that the RCOG was represented on the General Medical Council, serving as the first representative.

Lloyd felt passionately that women should be enabled to pursue their careers, including after having children. To help women pursue medicine in general, and obstetrics and gynaecology in particular, she set up the Women's Visiting Gynaecological Club in 1936, with only female members of the RCOG able to join. She was vice president of the Family Planning Association, and was influential in establishing the National Confidential Enquiry into Maternal Deaths, an innovative approach to data collection, which still allows analysis of problems, leading to much safer obstetric and gynaecological care.

In 1949, Lloyd married Baron Theodore Rose, a Birmingham colleague, who also graduated there in 1916. She was made a Dame of the British Empire in 1951

---

449 Lloyd, 'Emergency Obstetric Service (Flying Squad)', p.1

for her pioneering work and medical leadership. Dame Hilda and her husband retired from active practice in 1954, and moved to Kilvert Country, Radnorshire. She continued to be active, lecturing to the Medical Women's Federation on domiciliary midwifery, and on the need for contraceptive advice to women postnatally. She was awarded honorary Doctorates of Law by the Universities of Leeds and Birmingham in 1958, and advised the Medico-Legal Society, through their medical manpower committee. Following Rose's death in 1978, Dame Hilda moved nearer to Birmingham, living at Broome House, Clent, Worcestershire, and attended university and hospital social occasions until shortly before her death. Dame Hilda died there on 18th July 1982, aged ninety, following a stroke. She left legacies to the Medical Women's Federation, the NSPCC and the RSPCA.

Her obituary in the British Medical Journal commented that: 'her cheerful, friendly, and kind nature ideally complemented her professional skills' and that 'she was a magnificent woman of whom the University of Birmingham and its associated hospitals are justly proud.'[450] While not prolific in publishing clinical papers, her real, effective, and long-lasting legacy is her indefatigable commitment to improving care for women and babies, and her astonishing persistence and resilience in challenging established norms and customs surrounding clinical care and medical leadership.

Dame Hilda is remembered in the Dame Hilda Lloyd Congress Medal, awarded at the RCOG World Congress, her portrait by Anthony Devas, which hangs at the RCOG, London, the bust of her by Sir Jacob Epstein in the University of Birmingham

Blue plaques at Birmingham Women's Hospital, Queen Elizabeth Medical Centre, Mindelsohn Way, Edgbaston, Birmingham, B15 2TG and at the University of Birmingham Medical School, Vincent Drive, Edgbaston, Birmingham, B15 2TJ

450 'Obituary', *British Medical Journal, vol. 285,* 7th August 1982, p.449

Portrait of Hilda Lloyd by Anthony Devas, 1951. Reproduced from: Royal College of Obstetricians and Gynaecologists. RCOGM/P0031 the image of Dame Hilda Lloyd. London: RCOG; 1951, with the permission of the Royal College of Obstetricians and Gynaecologists

Medical School, and in the professorial chair in her name, the Dame Hilda Lloyd Professor of Fetal Medicine at the Institute of Metabolism and Systems Research at the University. There is a building named after her at City Hospital. Two blue plaques attest to her clinical practice and pioneering establishment of new methods of care for women in difficulty: one was erected by Birmingham Civic Society in 1985, at Birmingham Women's Hospital, Queen Elizabeth Medical Centre, to the right of the main entrance; the second commemorates the 'Flying Squads', erected by the University of Birmingham at the Medical School, to the right of the main entrance. These are appropriate memorials to a ground-breaking woman who improved and saved many thousands of women's lives, by her actions, example and teaching.

Bibliography

Books and Authored Articles

Allen, Peter. (no date) 'The Extraordinary Natural History Books of Samuel Galton Jnr.' Available at https://historywm.com/file/historywm/the-extraordinary-natural-history-books-of-samuel-galton-jnr-1.pdf (Accessed: 26 June 2019)

Almond, J.K. (2004, updated 2010), 'Attwood, Charles (1791-1875)', *Dictionary of National Biography*, Oxford: Oxford University Press, 23 September, updated 23 September. Available at https://doi.org/10.1093/ref:odnb/52577 (Accessed: 19 February 2019)

Aronson, Jeffrey K. (2004) 'Withering, William (1741-1799), physician and botanist', *Dictionary of National Biography*, Oxford: Oxford University Press, 23 September. Available at https://doi.org/10.1093/ref:odnb/29805 (Accessed: 24 January 2019)

Ballard, Phillada. (2013), 'Jaffray, Sir John, first baronet (1818-1901)', *Dictionary of National Biography*, Oxford: Oxford University Press, 3 October. Available at https://doi.org/10.1093/ref:odnb/104637 (Accessed: 8 February 2019)

Ballard, Phillada. (2013), 'Ryland, Louisa Anne (1814-1889)', *Dictionary of National Biography*, Oxford: Oxford University Press, 3 October. Available at https://doi.org/10.1093/ref:odnb/103438 (Accessed: 1 March 2019)

Behagg, Clive. (2004, updated 2009), 'Attwood, Thomas (1783-1856)', *Dictionary of National Biography*, Oxford: Oxford University Press, 23 September, updated 8 October. Available at https://doi.org/10.1093/ref:odnb/878 (Accessed: 19 February 2019)

Bettany, G.T. (revised by Wallis, Patrick), (2004, updated 2012), 'Cox, William Sands (1802-1875)', *Dictionary of National Biography*, Oxford: Oxford University Press, 23 September, updated 5 January. Available at https://doi.org/10.1093/ref:odnb/6532 (Accessed: 11 January 2019)

Bettany, G.T., (updated by Loudon, Jean), (2004, updated 2010), 'Gamgee, Joseph Sampson (1828-1886)', *Dictionary of National Biography*, Oxford: Oxford University Press, 23 September, updated 23 September. Available at https://doi.org/10.1093/ref:odnb/10326 (Accessed: 20 January 2019)

Bird, Vivian. (1974), *Portrait of Birmingham*, 2nd edn., London: Robert Hale & Company

Bird, Vivian. (no date), *The Priestley Riots, 1791, and The Lunar Society*, Birmingham: Birmingham and Midland Institute

Boase, G.C. (updated by Hopkins, Eric), (2004, updated 2013), 'Mason, Sir Josiah (1795-1881)', *Dictionary of National Biography*, Oxford: Oxford University Press, 23 September, updated 3 October. Available at https://doi.org/10.1093/ref:odnb/18286 (Accessed: 19 September 2019)

Bode, Harold. (1980), *James Brindley: An illustrated life of James Brindley, 1716-1772*, 2nd edn., Aylesbury, Buckinghamshire: Shire Publications Ltd., Lifelines 14.

Boissoneault, Lorraine. (2018), 'How British Gun Manufacturers Changed the Industrial World Lock, Stock and Barrel', 18 May. Available at https://southasia.stanford.edu/news/how-british-gun-manufacturers-changed-industrial-world-lock-stock-and-barrel-lorraine (Accessed: 26 June 2019)

Bouverie, Tim. (2020), *Appeasing Hitler: Chamberlain, Churchill and the Road to War,* London: Vintage

Briggs, Asa. (1952), *History of Birmingham, vol.2, Borough and City 1865-1938*, London: Oxford University Press

Buckley, Jemma, *Peter Thomas Stanford – the slave who became an inspiration to Birmingham,* 20 January 2014. Available at www.birminghammail.co.uk/news/midlands-news/peter – thomas-sandford – -slave-6528507 (Accessed: 25 February 2019)

Bunce, John Thackray. (1878), *History of the Corporation of Birmingham: with a Sketch of the Earlier Government of the Town...*, Birmingham: Cornish Brothers (vol. 1)

Bunce, John Thackray. (1882), *Josiah Mason: A Biography*, Birmingham

Bunce, John Thackray. (1885), *History of the Corporation of Birmingham: with a Sketch of the Earlier Government of the Town...*, Birmingham: Cornish Brothers (vol. 2)

Burnaby, Fred. (1876), *A Ride to Khiva: Travels and Adventures in Central Asia*, London: Cassell, Petter and Galpin

'Cato' (Foot, Michael, Howard, Peter, Owen, Frank). (2010), *Guilty Men*, London: Faber and Faber Ltd

Chamberlain, Austen. (1936), *Politics from Inside: An Epistolary Chronicle 1906-1914,* London: Cassell and Company Limited

Chamberlain, Austen. (1937), *Down the Years*, 7th edn., London: Cassell and Company Limited

Chancellor, V.E. (2004, updated 2007), 'Lloyd [*née* Shufflebotham], Dame Hilda Nora, (1891-1982)', *Dictionary of National Biography*, Oxford: Oxford University Press, 23 September, updated 24 May. Available at https://doi.org/10.1093/ref:odnb/61394 (Accessed: 1 February 2019)

Chinn, Carl (Ed). (2003), *Birmingham: Bibliography of a City*, Birmingham: University of Birmingham Press

Churchill, Winston S. (1948), *The Second World War, Volume I: The Gathering Storm*, London: Cassell and Company Limited

Crozier, Andrew J. (2004, updated 2018), 'Chamberlain, (Arthur) Neville (1869-1940)', *Dictionary of National Biography*, Oxford: Oxford University Press, 23 September, updated 14 November. Available at https://doi.org/10.1093/ref:odnb/32347 (Accessed: 29 August 2019)

Daniell, David. (2004), 'Rogers, John (*c.* 1500-1555)', *Dictionary of National Biography,* Oxford: Oxford University Press, 23 September. Available at https://doi.org/10.1093/ref:odnb/23980 (Accessed: 22 February 2019)

Dargue, William. (2012), Duddeston, 19 October. Available at https://billdargue.jimdo.com/placenames-gazetteer-a-to-y/places-d/duddeston/ (Accessed: 26 June 2019)

Davis, John. (2004, updated 2008), 'Webb [*née* Potter], (Martha) Beatrice, (1858-1943)', *Dictionary of National Biography*, Oxford: Oxford University Press, 23 September, updated 24 May. Available at https://doi.org/10.1093/ref:odnb/36799 (Accessed: 15 October 2019)

Dent, Robert K. (1880), *Old and New Birmingham: A History of the Town and its People,* Birmingham: Houghton and Hammond

Dick, Malcolm (Ed). (2005), *Joseph Priestley and Birmingham*, Studley, Warwickshire: Brewin Books

Dunn, Peter M. (1986), 'Naughton Dunn, Orthopaedic Surgeon, His Life and Times, 1884-1939', transcript of the first Naughton Dunn Memorial Lecture to the British Orthopaedic Association, Southampton, 17 April

Dunphy, Angus. (2001), *Cradley (South) 1901: Worcestershire Sheet 4.12*, Consett, County Durham: Alan Godfrey Maps

Dutton, D.J. (2004, updated 2013), 'Chamberlain, Sir (Joseph) Austen (1863-1937)', *Dictionary of National Biography*, Oxford: Oxford University Press, 23 September, updated 3 October. Available at https://doi.org/10.1093/ref:odnb/32351 (Accessed: 15 October 2019)

Fairclough, K.R. (2004), 'Brindley, James (1716-1772)', *Dictionary of National Biography*, Oxford: Oxford University Press, vol. 7

Fitzharris, Lindsey. (2017), *The Butchering Art: Joseph Lister's Quest to Transform the Grisly World of Victorian Medicine*, London: Allen Lane

Gamgee, Joseph Sampson. (1858), *Treatment of Contracted Knee-Joints*, British Medical Journal, 10 April, vol.1 (67), p.299. Available at https://www.ncbi.nlm.nih.gov/pmc/articles/PMC2251110/ (Accessed: 20 January 2019)

Gilbert, T.R., Boothroyd, J.B. (1951), *The Lloyds of Lloyds Bank*, Supplement to *The Dark Horse* (Lloyds Bank Staff Magazine), June.

Gill, Conrad. (1952), *History of Birmingham, vol.1, Manor and Borough to 1865*, London: Oxford University Press

Goodwin, George. (2016), *Benjamin Franklin in London*, London: Weidenfeld & Nicholson

Hall, Catherine. (2008), 'Anti-Slavery Society (act. 1823-1833)', *Dictionary of National Biography*, Oxford: Oxford University Press, 24 May. Available at https://doi.org/10.1093/ref:odnb/96359 (Accessed: 12 February 2019)

Hall-Edwards, J. (1906), 'Treatment of Chronic X-Ray Dermatitis', *British Medical Journal*, 19 September 1906

Hall-Edwards, J. (1924), 'The Problem of Cancer: A Plea for Immediate Action', *The Hospital and Health Review*, October

Hall-Edwards, J. (1926), *Cancer: its control and prevention (education will lower the death rate)*, Birmingham: Cornish Brothers Ltd

Hamilton, Polly. (2004, updated 2013), 'Taylor, John (1710/11-1775)', *Dictionary of National Biography*, Oxford: Oxford University Press, 23 September, updated 3 October. Available at https://doi.org/10.1093/ref:odnb/50560 (Accessed: 28 February 2019)

Haywood, William. (1918), *The Development of Birmingham: An Essay*, London: FB&c Ltd

Hill, Alfred. (1902), *Report on the Health of the City of Birmingham for the Year 1901*, Birmingham: Birmingham City Council. Available at https://archive.org/details/b28928416/page/4/mode/2up (Accessed: 29 June 2020)

Howe, A.C. (2008), 'Anti-Corn Law League (act. 1839-1846)', *Dictionary of National Biography*, Oxford: Oxford University Press, 24 May. Available at https://doi.org/10.1093/ref:odnb/42282 (Accessed: 12 February 2019)

Hutton, William. (1783), *An History of Birmingham*, 2nd edn., Wakefield, West Yorkshire: EP Publishing

Hutton, William. (1816), *The Life of William Hutton*, with introduction Chinn, Carl (1998), Studley, Warwickshire: Brewin Books

Hutton, William. (1819), *An History of Birmingham, continued to the present day by Catherine Hutton*, 4th edn., London: J. Nichols and Son

Innes, Arthur D. (1912), *A History of the British Nation: from the earliest times to the present day,* London: T.C. & E.C. Jack

James, Michael F. (2011, updated 2013), 'Nettlefold, John Sutton (1866-1930)', *Dictionary of National Biography,* Oxford: Oxford University Press, 19 May, updated 3 October. Available at https://doi.org/10.1093/ref:odnb/101218 (Accessed: 2 April 2019)

James, Michael F. (2012), 'John Sutton Nettlefold, Liberalism and the Early Town Planning Movement', *Journal of Liberal History,* vol 75, Summer, pp.30-37. Available at https://liberalhistory.org.uk/wp-content/uploads/2014/10/75_James_Nettlefold_Liberalism_and_Town_Planning.pdf (Accessed: 4 June 2020)

Jephcott, W.E. (1945), 'James Keir, Hill Top's Most Famous Man', 2 March. Available at https://www.westbromwichhistory.com/wp-content/uploads/2018/07/OWB-101-James-Keir-WEJ.docx (Accessed: 14 June 2019)

Jones, Brian. (1995), *Josiah Mason 1795-1881: Birmingham's Benevolent Benefactor,* Studley: Brewin Books

Kapadia, H.M. (2002), 'Sampson Gamgee: a great Birmingham surgeon', *Journal of the Royal Society of Medicine,* 1 February, 95 (2), pp.96-100.

Keers, R.Y. (1980), 'Two forgotten pioneers: James Carson and George Bodington', *Thorax,* July; 35(7): pp.483-489. Available at https://www.ncbi.nlm.nih.gov/pmc/articles/PMC471318/ (Accessed: 27 January 2019)

Lane, Joan. (2004, updated 2013), 'Ash, John (bap. 1722, d. 1798), physician', *Dictionary of National Biography,* Oxford: Oxford University Press, 23 September, updated 3 October. Available at https://doi.org/10.1093/ref:odnb/736 (Accessed: 4 March 2019)

Langford, John A. (1868), *A Century of Birmingham Life: or, A Chronicle of Local Events, From 1741 to 1841,* vol. 1, Birmingham: E.C. Osborne

Langford, John A. (1868), *A Century of Birmingham Life: or, A Chronicle of Local Events, From 1741 to 1841,* vol. 2, Birmingham: E.C. Osborne

Lea, Roger. (2013), *George Bodington: Pioneer Physician Treating TB and Mental Illness.* Available at www.boddington-family.org.uk (Accessed 27 January 2019)

Lea, Roger. (2016), 'Lunacy 2 Maney [412]', 29 April. Available at www.sclhrg.org.uk (Accessed 27 January 2019)

Lee, Elizabeth (revised by Reynolds, K.D.). (2004, updated 2013), 'Schimmelpenninck [née Galton], Mary Anne (1778-1856), author', *Dictionary of National Biography,* Oxford: Oxford University Press, 23 September, updated 3 October. Available at https://doi.org/10.1093/ref:odnb/24809 (Accessed: 26 June 2019)

Lee, M.R. (2005), 'William Withering (1741-1799), a biographical sketch of a Birmingham Lunatic', *JLL Bulletin: Commentaries on the history of treatment evaluation.* Available at https://www.jameslindlibrary.org/articles/william-withering-1741-1799-a-biographical-sketch-of-a-birmingham-lunatic/ (Accessed: 24 January 2019)

Lloyd, Hilda. (1936), 'Emergency Obstetric Service (Flying Squad)'. Available at https://www.rcog.org.uk/globalassets/documents/guidelines/library-services/heritage/rcog_a4_7_5_obs_flying_squad.pdf (Accessed: 1 February 2019)

Lloyd, Samuel. (1907), *The Lloyds of Birmingham,* Birmingham: Cornish Brothers, Limited. Available at https://archive.org/stream/lloydsofbirmingh00lloyuoft/lloydsofbirmingh00lloyuoft_djvu.txt (Accessed: 28 February 2019)

Macklin, Graham. (2006), *Chamberlain,* London, Haus Publishing

Marsh, Peter T. (1994), *Joseph Chamberlain: Entrepreneur in Politics,* London: Yale University Press

Marsh, Peter T. (2004, updated 2013), 'Chamberlain, Joseph [Joe] (1836-1914)', *Dictionary of National Biography*, Oxford: Oxford University Press, 23 September, updated 3 October. Available at https://doi.org/10.1093/ref:odnb/32350 (Accessed: 2 August 2019)

McConnell, Anita. (2005), 'Avery, Thomas (1813-1894)', *Dictionary of National Biography*, Oxford: Oxford University Press, 26 May. Available at https://doi.org/10.1093/ref:odnb/46576 (Accessed: 23 June 2020)

McEvoy, John G. (2020), 'Joseph Priestley: English Clergyman and Scientist', *Encyclopaedia Britannica*, Encyclopaedia Britannica, inc., 9 March. Available at www.britannica.com/biography/Joseph-Priestley (Accessed: 10 May 2020)

Mosley, James. (2004, updated 2013), 'Baskerville, John (1706-1775)', *Dictionary of National Biography*, Oxford: Oxford University Press, 23 September, updated 3 October. Available at https://doi.org/10.1093/ref:odnb/1624 (Accessed: 14 April 2019)

Mould, Richard F. (2014), 'Military Radiology Before & During the First World War 1896-1918', *The Invisible Light, The Journal of The British Society for the History of Radiology*, The British Society for the History of Radiology, October, No.39

Musgrove, Arthur. (1926), *The History of Lench's Trust, Birmingham 1525-1925*, Birmingham: The Midland Educational Company Limited

Neville, Peter. (1992), *Neville Chamberlain – A Study in Failure?*, London: Hodder and Stoughton

Newholme, H.P. (1944), *Report of the Medical Officer of Health for the year 1943*, Birmingham: City of Birmingham. Available at: https://archive.org/details/b28928829/page/6/mode/2up (Accessed: 30 June 2020)

Olofinjana, Israel, 13 March 2014, *Black Baptists: their contributions to mission.* Available at www.baptist.org.uk/Articles/390375/Black_Baptists_Their.aspx (Accessed: 25 February 2019)

Parsons, L.G., updated by Reznick, Jeffrey S. (2004), 'Barling, Sir (Harry) Gilbert, baronet (1855-1940)', *Dictionary of National Biography*, Oxford: Oxford University Press, 23 September. Available at https://doi.org/10.1093/ref:odnb/30593 (Accessed: 4 February 2019)

Patuzzi, J., Lee, S., Crean, M., Thomas, A., and Busch, U. (Eds), (2013), *The Story of Radiology*, European Society of Radiology, Vienna, Vol.2

Power, D'A., (updated by Sewell, Jane Eliot). (2004, updated 2013), 'Tait, (Robert) Lawson (1845-1899)', *Dictionary of National Biography*, Oxford: Oxford University Press, 23 September, updated 3 October. Available at https://doi.org/10.1093/ref:odnb/26919 (Accessed: 24 March 2019)

Price, Jacob M. (2004), 'Lloyd, Sampson (1699-1779)', *Dictionary of National Biography*, Oxford: Oxford University Press, 23 September. Available at https://doi.org/10.1093/ref:odnb/37682 (Accessed: 28 February 2019)

Reinarz, Jonathan. (2013), 'Hall-Edwards, John Francis, (1858-1926)', *Dictionary of National Biography*, Oxford: Oxford University Press, 3 October. Available at https://doi.org/10.1093/ref:odnb/104431 (Accessed: 29 January 2019)

Rhodes James, Robert. (1978), *The British Revolution: British Politics 1880-1939*, London: Methuen & Co. Ltd

Schofield, Robert E. (2004, 2013), 'Priestley, Joseph (1733-1804), theologian and natural philosopher', *Dictionary of National Biography*, Oxford: Oxford University Press, 23 September, 3 October. Available at https://doi.org/10.1093/ref:odnb/22788 (Accessed: 5 April 2019)

Schranz, Kristen M. (no date), 'James Keir – A Renaissance Man of the Industrial Revolution'. Available at https://historywm.com/file/historywm/james-kier-a-renaissance-man-of-the-industrial-revolution.pdf (Accessed: 14 June 2019)

Shill, Ray. (2013), *Birmingham Canals*, Stroud, Gloucestershire: The History Press

Simkin, John. (1997, updated 2020), 'Thomas Attwood', September, updated January. Available at https://spartacus-educational.com/CHattwood.htm (Accessed: 22 May 2020)

Skipp, Victor. (1996), *The Making of Victorian Birmingham*, Studley, Warwickshire: Brewin Books

Skipp, Victor. (1997), *A History of Greater Birmingham – down to 1830*, 2nd edn., Studley, Warwickshire: Brewin Books

Smith, Barbara M.D. (2004, updated 2013), 'Keir, James (1735-1820), chemist and industrialist', *Dictionary of National Biography*, Oxford: Oxford University Press, 23 September, updated 3 October. Available at https://doi.org/10.1093/ref:odnb/15259 (Accessed: 14 June 2019)

Stanford, Peter T. (1889), *From Bondage to Liberty: Being the life story of the Rev P.T. Stanford who was once a slave! And is now the recognised pastor of an English Baptist Church*, Smethwick.

Stanford, Peter T. (1897), *The tragedy of the Negro in America. A condensed history of the enslavement, sufferings, emancipation, present condition and progress of the negro race in the United States of America,* Boston, Mass, USA. Available at http://worldcat.org/identities/lccn-n88646720/ (Accessed: 25 February 2019)

Timmins, Samuel. (1866), *The Resources, Products, and Industrial History of Birmingham and the Midland Hardware District*, London: Robert Hardwicke

Tyrell, Alex. (2004a, updated 2009), 'Sturge, Joseph (1793-1859)', *Dictionary of National Biography*, Oxford: Oxford University Press, 23 September, updated 21 May. Available at https://doi.org/10.1093/ref:odnb/26746 (Accessed: 12 February 2019)

Tyrell, Alex. (2004b), 'Sturge [née Dickinson], Hannah (1816-1896)', *Dictionary of National Biography*, Oxford: Oxford University Press, 23 September. Available at https://doi.org/10.1093/ref:odnb/55214 (Accessed: 12 February 2019)

Tyrell, Alex. (2004c, updated 2009), 'Sturge, Sophia (1795-1845)', *Dictionary of National Biography*, Oxford: Oxford University Press, 23 September, updated 21 May. Available at https://doi.org/10.1093/ref:odnb/56584 (Accessed: 12 February 2019)

Uglow, Jenny. (2002), *The Lunar Men: The Friends Who Made the Future*, London: Faber and Faber

Upton, Chris. (2005), *Living Back-to-Back*, Chichester: Phillimore & Co.

Upton, Chris. (2011), *A History of Birmingham*, Stroud, Gloucestershire: Phillimore & Co.

Walker, Paul. (2013), 'Stanford, Peter Thomas (1860-1909)', *Dictionary of National Biography*, Oxford: Oxford University Press, 3 October. Available at https://doi.org/10.1093/ref:odnb/104527 (Accessed: 25 February 2019)

Ward, Roger. (2015), *The Chamberlains: Joseph, Austen and Neville 1836-1940*, Stroud, Gloucestershire: Fonthill Media

Whates, H.R.G. (1957), *The Birmingham Post, 1857-1957: A Centenary Retrospect,* Birmingham: The Birmingham Post and Mail

Wilcox-Lee, Naomi. (2017), 'Dame Hilda Lloyd And The Birmingham Flying Squads', 17 August. Available at https://sheroesofhistory.wordpress.com/2017/08/ (Accessed: 1 February 2019)

Wilson, Harold. (1977), *A Prime Minister on Prime Ministers*, London: Book Club Associates

Withering, W. (1785), *An Account of the Foxglove and some of its medical uses: with practical remarks on Dropsy, and other diseases,* London: C.G.J. and J. Robinson

Websites

A brief history, no date. Available at https://www.birmingham.ac.uk/university/about/history/index.aspx (Accessed: 2 August 2019)

A Portrait of Samuel Galton jnr, no date. Available at https://www.revolutionaryplayers.org.uk/a-portrait-of-samuel-galton-jnr/ (Accessed: 26 June 2019)

About Us, 2020. Available at https://www.bhsf.co.uk/about/ (Accessed: 12 May 2020)

Andrew Carnegie Hero Fund Trust, no date. Available at https://www.carnegiehero.org.uk/ (Accessed: 29 January 2019)

Ashted, no date. Available at https://en.wikipedia.org/wiki/Ashted (Accessed: 4 March 2019)

Aston Parish Church: St Peter & St Paul, Birmingham – Monuments, no date. Available at http://www.speel.me.uk/sculptplaces/bhamaston.htm (Accessed: 22 February 2019)

Aston University bids farewell to X-ray Ed, 20 September 2017. Available at https://www2.aston.ac.uk/news/releases/2017/september/aston-university-bids-farewell-to-x-ray-ed (Accessed: 29 January 2019)

Austen Chamberlain, no date. Available at https://en.wikipedia.org/wiki/Austen_Chamberlain (Accessed: 15 October 2019)

Autherley Junction, no date. Available at https://en.wikipedia.org/wiki/Autherley_Junction (Accessed: 1 May 2020)

Birmingham Hippodrome to Mark 120th Anniversary of the first medical X-Ray, 3 November 2016. Available at https://www.birminghamhippodrome.com/birmingham-hippodrome-mark-120th-anniversary-first-medical-x-ray/ (Accessed: 29 January 2019)

Birmingham Political Union, no date. Available at https://www.parliament.uk/about/living-heritage/transformingsociety/electionsvoting/chartists/case-study/the-right-to-vote/thomas-attwood-and-the-birmingham-political-union/birmingham-political-union/ (Accessed: 19 February 2019)

Bevan's speech to the Manchester Labour rally 4 July 1948, no date. Available at https://www.sochealth.co.uk/national-health-service/the-sma-and-the-foundation-of-the-national-health-service-dr-leslie-hilliard-1980/aneurin-bevan-and-the-foundation-of-the-nhs/bevans-speech-to-the-manchester-labour-rally-4-july-1948/ (Accessed: 2 August 2019)

BMI The Priory Hospital, no date. Available at https://www.bmihealthcare.co.uk/hospitals/bmi-the-priory-hospital (Accessed: 8 February 2019)

Carl Chinn: Heartbreak led to Louisa Anne Ryland's gift to Birmingham, 9 March 2013. Available at www.birminghammail.co.uk/news/nostalgia/carl-chinn-heartbreak-led-louisa-1730012 (Accessed: 1 March 2019)

Carl Chinn: Louisa's generous parkland gift was fit for a queen, 25 May 2013. Available at www.birminghammail.co.uk/news/nostalgia/carl-chinn-louisas-generous-parkland-4006428 (Accessed: 1 March 2019)

Dame Hilda Lloyd (1891-1982), 2020. Available at https://www.rcog.org.uk/en/guidelines-research-services/library-services/archives-and-heritage/archives/parliament-week-15-21-november-2013/dame-hilda-lloyd-1891-1982 (Accessed: 1 February 2019)

Days of May, no date. Available at https://en.wikipedia.org/wiki/Days_of_May (Accessed: 19 February 2019)

Edmund Burke, no date. Available at https://en.wikipedia.org/wiki/Edmund_Burke (Accessed: 5 April 2019)

Essex Street Chapel, no date. Available at https://en.wikipedia.org/wiki/Essex_Street_Chapel (Accessed: 5 April 2019)

Faith & Disunity: Samuel Galton and the Quakers, 22 March 2018. Available at https://centralenglandquakers.org.uk/2018/03/22/from-the-archives-faith-disunity/ (Accessed: 26 June 2019)

Frederick Burnaby, no date. Available at https://en.wikipedia.org/wiki/Frederick_Burnaby (Accessed: 2 August 2019)

Gilbert Barling, no date. Available at https://en.wikipedia.org/wiki/Gilbert_Barling (Accessed: 4 February 2019)

Great Barr Colony (St Margaret's Hospital), no date. Available at https://opacity.us/site77_great_barr_colony_st_margarets_hospital.htm (Accessed: 26 June 2019)

Great Barr Hall, 1 July 1986. Available at https://historicengland.org.uk/listing/the-list/list-entry/1001202 (Accessed: 26 June 2019)

Henry Hope & Sons Ltd, no date. Available at https://en.wikipedia.org/wiki/Henry_Hope_%26_Sons_Ltd (Accessed: 2 April 2019)

Heritage, no date. Available at http://www.bullring.org/heritage/ (Accessed: 1 May 2020)

History of BMEC, no date. Available at http://bmec.swbh.nhs.uk/about-us/history-of-bmec/ (Accessed: 18 June 2020)

History of Cannon Hill Park, no date. Available at www.birmingham.gov.uk/info/20089/parks/1680/cannon_hill_park/4 (Accessed: 1 March 2019)

History of the University of Birmingham Medical School, 1825-2001, 2020. Available at https://www.birmingham.ac.uk/university/colleges/mds/about/history.aspx (Accessed: 1 February 2019)

James Brindley, no date. Available at https://en.wikipedia.org/wiki/James_Brindley (Accessed: 31 January 2020)

James Keir, no date. Available at https://en.wikipedia.org/wiki/James_Keir (Accessed: 14 June 2019)

James Keir, no date. Available at https://www.lunarsociety.org.uk/lunar-men/james-keir/ (Accessed: 14 June 2019)

James Keir: Member of the Birmingham Lunar Society, no date. Available at https://www.westbromwichhistory.com/people-places/james-keir/ (Accessed: 14 June 2019)

John Ash (physician), no date. Available at https://en.wikipedia.org/wiki/John_Ash_(physician) (Accessed: 4 March 2019)

John Baskerville, no date. Available at https://en.wikipedia.org/wiki/John_Baskerville (Accessed: 14 April 2019)

John Brooke (1755-1802), no date. Available at https://en.wikipedia.org/wiki/John_Brooke_(1755%E2%80%931802) (Accessed: 4 March 2019)

John Hall-Edwards, no date. Available at https://en.wikipedia.org/wiki/John_Hall-Edwards (Accessed: 29 January 2019)

John Jaffray, no date. Available at https://en.wikipedia.org/wiki/John_Jaffray (Accessed: 8 February 2019)

John Rogers (Bible editor and martyr), no date. Available at www.en.wikipedia.org/wiki/John_Rogers_(Bible_editor_and_martyr) (Accessed: 22 February 2019)

John Rogers, 1st of Many Martyrs, 3 May 2010. Available at www.christianity.com/church/church-history/timeline/1501-1600/john-rogers-1st-of-many-martyrs-11629985.html (Accessed: 22 February 2019)

John Sutton Nettlefold (social reformer), no date. Available at https://en.wikipedia.org/wiki/John_Sutton_Nettlefold_(social_reformer) (Accessed: 2 April 2019)

John Sutton Nettlefold, no date. Available at Wikipedia – https://en.wikipedia.org/wiki/John_Sutton_Nettlefold (Accessed: 2 April 2019)

Joseph Chamberlain, no date. Available at https://en.wikipedia.org/wiki/Joseph_Chamberlain (Accessed: 2 August 2019)

Joseph Priestley, no date. Available at www.en.wikipedia.org/wiki/Joseph_Priestley (Accessed: 5 April 2019)

Joseph Sturge 1793-1859, no date. Available at http://www.quakersintheworld.org/quakers-in-action/285/Joseph-Sturge (Accessed: 12 February 2019)

Joseph Sturge, no date. Available at https://en.wikipedia.org/wiki/Joseph_Sturge (Accessed: 12 February 2019)

Josiah Mason, no date. Available at https://en.wikipedia.org/wiki/Josiah_Mason (Accessed: 19 September 2019)

Kynoch, no date. Available at https://en.wikipedia.org/wiki/Kynoch (Accessed: 2 April 2019)

Lawson Tait, no date. Available at https://en.wikipedia.org/wiki/Lawson_Tait (Accessed: 24 March 2019)

Letter from Samuel Galton, jnr to the Friends of the Monthly Meeting in Birmingham, no date. Available at https://www.revolutionaryplayers.org.uk/letter-from-samuel-galton-jnr-to-the-friends-of-the-monthly-meeting-in-birmingham/ (Accessed: 26 June 2019)

Louisa Anne Ryland Mystery, 14 April 2007. Available at https://birminghamhistory.co.uk/forum/index.php?threads/louisa-ann-ryland-mystery.6416/ (Accessed: 1 March 2019)

Louisa Anne Ryland, 1814-1889, 31 December 2000. Available at www.ancestry.ca/boards/surnames.ryland/105/mb.ashx (Accessed: 1 March 2019)

Louisa Anne Ryland: Heiress and Philanthropist, 12 September 2014. Available at http://www.barfordheritage.org.uk/content/people/louisa-ryland-2 (Accessed: 1 March 2019)

Louisa Ryland, no date. Available at https://en.wikipedia.org/wiki/Louisa_Ryland (Accessed: 1 March 2019)

Major John Hall-Edwards, archived 28 September 2012. Available at https://web.archive.org/web/20120928204852/http:/www.birmingham.gov.uk/xray (Accessed: 29 January 2019)

Mason College, no date. Available at https://www.birmingham.ac.uk/university/about/history/mason.aspx (Accessed: 19 September 2019)

Municipal Corporations Act 1835, no date. Available at https://en.wikipedia.org/wiki/Municipal_Corporations_Act_1835 (Accessed: 19 February 2019)

Naughton Dunn Club, no date. Available at https://www.bon.ac.uk/naughton-dunn-club/ (Accessed: 23 January 2019)

Nettlefold, John Sutton, 2013. Available at http://mimsy.bham.ac.uk/detail.php?type=related&kv=11002153&t=people (Accessed: 2 April 2019)

Neville Chamberlain, no date. Available at https://en.wikipedia.org/wiki/Neville_Chamberlain (Accessed: 29 August 2019)

Oswestry Surgeons and Physicians, August 2011. Available at https://www.rjah.nhs.uk/RJAHNHS/files/6c/6cac9cc2-51b2-46a6-a7b3-49226221069e.pdf (Accessed: 23 January 2019)

Our History, no date. Available at https://www.bcu.ac.uk/art/about-us/our-history (Accessed: 1 March 2019)

Our History, no date. Available at https://www.lenchs-trust.co.uk/our-history-2 (Accessed: 12 November 2019)

Our History, no date. Available at https://www.roh.nhs.uk/recruitment/our-history (Accessed: 23 January 2019)

Our History & Our Future, no date. Available at www.jaffraycare.com/who-we-are/our-history-our-future/ (Accessed: 8 February 2019)

Our Story: The Building, no date. Available at http://www.birminghamcathedral.com/building/ (Accessed: 1 May 2020)

Parishes: Studley, no date. Available at www.british-history.ac.uk/vch/warks/vol3/pp175-187 (Accessed: 8 February 2019)

Peter Thomas Stanford: Remarkable life of freed slave who became a famous Baptist minister, no date. History West Midlands film available at www.historywm.com/films/peter-thomas-stanford-remarkable-life-of-freed-slave-who-became-a-famous-baptist-minister (Accessed: 25 February 2019)

Puddling (civil engineering), no date. Available at https://en.wikipedia.org/wiki/Puddling_(civil_engineering) (Accessed: 31 January 2020)

Reform and the Birmingham connection, no date. Available at https://www.parliament.uk/about/living-heritage/transformingsociety/electionsvoting/chartists/case-study/the-right-to-vote/thomas-attwood-and-the-birmingham-political-union/reform-and-the-birmingham-connection/ (Accessed: 19 February 2019)

Robert Barclay Allardice, no date. Available at https://en.wikipedia.org/wiki/Robert_Barclay_Allardice (Accessed: 26 June 2019)

Robert Lawson Tait, no date. Available at http://www.whonamedit.com/doctor.cfm/3623.html (Accessed: 24 March 2019)

Robert Rawlinson, no date. Available at https://en.wikipedia.org/wiki/Robert_Rawlinson (Accessed: 22 June 2020)

Sampson Gamgee, no date. Available at https://en.wikipedia.org/wiki/Sampson_Gamgee (Accessed: 20 January 2019)

Sampson Lloyd, no date. Available at https://en.wikipedia.org/wiki/Sampson_Lloyd (Accessed: 28 February 2019)

Samuel C. Armstrong, no date. Available at www.en.wikipedia.org/wiki/Samuel_C._Armstrong (Accessed: 25 February 2019)

Samuel Galton from 1785, no date. Available at http://greatbarrhall.b43.co.uk/galton.html (Accessed: 26 June 2019)

Samuel Galton Jr., no date. Available at https://en.wikipedia.org/wiki/Samuel_Galton_Jr. (Accessed: 26 June 2019)

Sir John Jaffray, 1st. Bt., no date. Available at http://thepeerage.com/p30796.htm#i307952 (Accessed: 8 February 2019)

Sir Robert Peel Statue, October 2019. Available at http://www.historywebsite.co.uk/listed/princealbert.htm (Accessed: 1 June 2020)

SJMT: people at heart, no date. Available at https://www.sjmt.org.uk/ (Accessed: 19 September 2019)

Society of Dilettanti, no date. Available at https://en.wikipedia.org/wiki/Society_of_Dilettanti (Accessed: 4 March 2019)

Taylors and Lloyds Records, no date. Available at https://archiveshub.jisc.ac.uk/search/archives/16003939-5f21-3395-8252-249d49da245e (Accessed: 28 February 2019)

Thomas Attwood (economist), no date. Available at https://en.wikipedia.org/wiki/Thomas_Attwood_(economist) (Accessed: 19 February 2019)

Thomas Attwood 1783-1856, no date. Available at http://www.chartistancestors.co.uk/thomas-attwood-1783-1856/ (Accessed: 19 February 2019)

Thomas Attwood, no date. Available at https://www.historyofparliamentonline.org/schools/content/biography/ks3-political-reform-mps-thomas-attwood (Accessed: 19 February 2019)

Thomas Avery, no date. Available at https://en.wikipedia.org/wiki/Thomas_Avery (Accessed: 23 June 2020)

Thomas Smith's Stamping Works, no date. Available at https://www.gracesguide.co.uk/Thomas_Smith%27s_Stamping_Works (Accessed: 2 April 2019)

University of Birmingham, no date. Available at https://en.wikipedia.org/wiki/University_of_Birmingham (Accessed: 2 August 2019)

Warley Abbey, Warley Woods Park, Bearwood, Smethwick, no date. Available at http://blackcountryhistory.org/collections/getrecord/GB146_PHS_92/ (Accessed: 26 June 2019)

311

William Sands Cox, no date. Available at https://en.wikipedia.org/wiki/William_Sands_Cox (Accessed: 11 January 2019)

William Withering, no date. Available at https://en.wikipedia.org/wiki/William_Withering (Accessed: 24 January 2019)

Wolverhampton's Listed Buildings, Prince Albert's Statue, Queen Square, no date. Available at http://www.historywebsite.co.uk/listed/princealbert.htm (Accessed: 1 June 2020)

Newspaper and Unauthored Articles

(1882), 'Obituary', *British Medical Journal,* 11 March, p.362 (Accessed 27 January 2019)

(1886), 'Obituary', *British Medical Journal,* 25 September, p.604 (Accessed 27 January 2019)

(1926), 'Obituary', *British Medical Journal,* 21 August, p.363

(1939), 'Obituary', *British Medical Journal,* 2 December, pp.1121-2

(1940), 'Obituary', *British Medical Journal,* 4 May, p.748 (Accessed: 4 February 2019)

(1956), 'Birmingham Revives Two "Ghosts": Sir Arthur Conan Doyle: Dr. Bodington', *Birmingham Daily Post,* 16 April, p.19 (Accessed 27 January 2019)

(1963), *Birmingham Daily Post,* 2 April, p.15

(1982), 'Obituary', *British Medical Journal,* 7 August, vol. 285, p.449

(2010, 2013), 'George Fowler Boddington', *Plarr's Lives of the Fellows,* The Royal College of Surgeons, 25 March, 7 August. (Accessed 27 January 2019)

(9th edn., 2011), 'Chamberlain, (Arthur) Neville 1869-1940, English statesman', *Chambers Biographical Dictionary,* London: Chambers Harrap Publishing Ltd

(9th edn., 2011), 'Chamberlain, Joseph 1836-1914, English politician', *Chambers Biographical Dictionary,* London: Chambers Harrap Publishing Ltd

(9th edn., 2011), 'Chamberlain, Sir (Joseph) Austen 1863-1937, English politician and Nobel Prize winner', *Chambers Biographical Dictionary,* London: Chambers Harrap Publishing Ltd

(2011), 'Dame Hilda Lloyd (1891-1982)', *Blue Plaque Guide,* Birmingham: University of Birmingham Research and Cultural Collections. Available at https://www.birmingham.ac.uk/Documents/culture/BookletfinalPDF.pdf

(2013), 'Dame Hilda Lloyd (Born Hilda Nora Shufflebotham)', *The Moseley Society Local History Group Newsletter,* April. Available at https://moseley-society.org.uk/wp-content/uploads/2015/02/Moseley-History-News-April-2013.pdf (Accessed: 1 February 2019)

(2014), *Who Was Who,* 7th edn., London: A & C Black, vol. 1 (1897-1915)

Index

References for images are shown in *italics*
Names of Forgotten Brummies and page numbers of their life stories are shown in **bold**